M000312925

IT Manager's Handbook

Third Edition

IT Manager's Handbook
Getting your new job done

Third Edition

Bill Holtsnider

Brian D. Jaffe

AMSTERDAM • BOSTON • HEIDELBERG • LONDON
NEW YORK • OXFORD • PARIS • SAN DIEGO
SAN FRANCISCO • SINGAPORE • SYDNEY • TOKYO

ELSEVIER

Morgan Kaufmann is an imprint of Elsevier

Acquiring Editor: Andrea Dierna
Development Editor: Robyn Day
Project Manager: Jessica Vaughan
Designer: Joanne Blank

Morgan Kaufmann is an imprint of Elsevier
225 Wyman Street, Waltham, MA 02451, USA

Notices

Knowledge and best practice in this field are constantly changing. As new research and experience broaden our understanding, changes in research methods or professional practices, may become necessary. Practitioners and researchers must always rely on their own experience and knowledge in evaluating and using any information or methods described herein. In using such information or methods they should be mindful of their own safety and the safety of others, including parties for whom they have a professional responsibility.

To the fullest extent of the law, neither the Publisher nor the authors, contributors, or editors, assume any liability for any injury and/or damage to persons or property as a matter of products liability, negligence or otherwise, or from any use or operation of any methods, products, instructions, or ideas contained in the material herein.

Library of Congress Cataloging-in-Publication Data
Holtsnider, Bill, 1956-
    It manager's handbook : getting your new job done / Bill Holtsnider, Brian D. Jaffe. – 3rd ed.
        p. cm.
    Summary: "This book provides a practical reference that you will return to again and again in an ever-changing corporate environment where the demands on IT continue to increase. Make your first 100 days really count with the fundamental principles and core concepts critical to your success as a new IT Manager outlined in this valuable resource. The book also discusses how to work with your customers, manage your budget, develop an overall IT strategy and demonstrate the value of IT to the company"– Provided by publisher.
    ISBN 978-0-12-415949-5 (pbk.)
    1. Industrial management–Data processing. 2. Management information systems. I. Jaffe, Brian D. II. Title.
    HD30.2.H657 2012
    004.068–dc23

                                                                                            2011044174

British Library Cataloguing-in-Publication Data
A catalogue record for this book is available from the British Library.

ISBN: 978-0-12-415949-5

Printed in the United States of America
12 13 14 15 16   10 9 8 7 6 5 4 3 2 1

For information on all MK publications visit our website at www.mkp.com

For M & D
—B.H.

For Jenine
—B.D.J.

About the Authors

Bill Holtsnider is an experienced writer, educator, and software professional with more than 27 years of experience working in the computer industry. His IT expertise includes working in such diverse areas as stock portfolio management, identity management, Web analytics, and software development. He is the author of six books and a wide range of technical and marketing documentation.

Brian D. Jaffe is an IT professional who has worked for several Fortune 500 companies including Bristol-Myers Squibb, Time Warner, Philip Morris, and The Interpublic Group of Companies. Currently he is Senior Vice President for Global IT at McCann Worldgroup in New York City, one of the country's leading advertising agencies. His articles have appeared in *Computerworld*, *InfoWorld*, *eWeek*, and *The New York Times*, and he is the editor of *Thanksgiving Tales: True Stories of the Holiday in America*.

Brief Table of Contents

About the Authors   vii
Key Changes for This Edition   xxi
Preface   xxiii

CHAPTER 1 The Role of an IT Manager   1

CHAPTER 2 Managing Your IT Team   31

CHAPTER 3 Staffing Your IT Team   65

CHAPTER 4 Project Management   103

CHAPTER 5 Software, Operating Systems, and Enterprise Applications   135

CHAPTER 6 Managing the Money   161

CHAPTER 7 Getting Started with the Technical Environment   189

CHAPTER 8 Security and Compliance   205

CHAPTER 9 Disaster Recovery   247

CHAPTER 10 Working with Users   263

CHAPTER 11 Connectivity: Social Media, Handhelds, and More   287

Glossary   305
Index   317

Contents

About the Authors vii
Brief Table of Contents ix
Key Changes for This Edition... xxi
Preface xxiii

CHAPTER 1   The Role of an IT Manager.. 1

    1.1 Just What Does an IT Manager Do?.. 2
         Why All That Change and Flexibility Is Good.. 2
         Why All That Change and Flexibility Is Bad 2
    1.2 Managers in General.. 3
         Definition of a Manager 3
         Styles of Management 3
         Pros and Cons of Being a Manager: Reasons to Become a Manager, and
         Reasons Not to Become One.. 5
         The Hidden Work of Management... 6
         Resentment toward Management 7
         Babysitting versus Managing 7
         Politics.. 7
         Managing in Four Directions.. 7
    1.3 The Strategic Value of the IT Department 8
         Application Development versus Technical Operations........................... 9
         IT Department Goals 10
         The Value of IT Managers 10
    1.4 Developing an IT Strategy 10
         Determine Who Your Team Members Are... 11
         Determine How Important Technology Is to Your Organization 11
         Determine Who Your Customers Are and What Their Needs Are........... 12
         Keep Your Department Central to the Company's Operations............... 12
    1.5 Leadership versus Management 13
    1.6 Starting Your New Job 14
         The First Day 14
         Meeting the Staff 14
         A Few Ideas for What to Say to Break the Ice....................................... 15
         Some Don'ts.. 15
         One-on-One Meetings... 15
         What to Say to Those Who Wanted Your Job and Didn't Get It 16
         Establish a Relationship with Your Manager and Your Peers 17
         Learning the Landscape: Key Users and Key Applications 18

1.7 The First 100 Days 20

No Organization Is Perfect 20

Quietly Advertising What You Bring to the Table 21

Projects in Progress and Projects on the Horizon 22

Is the Status Quo Good Enough? 23

People to Meet and Know 24

Quick Introductory Meetings 24

Human Resource Issues 25

Budgeting 26

Making Those First Decisions 26

1.8 Two IT Departments—What Happens If Your Company Merges
with Another? 27

CHAPTER 2   Managing Your IT Team **31**

2.1 Keeping Employees Focused 32

Establish Priorities 32

Communicate with Your Team 32

Company Mission, Vision, and Values 34

Be as Clear as Possible about Your Real Priorities 35

Avoid Burnout in Your Employees 35

Make Your Employees Aware of the Dangers of Burnout 36

Deal with the Situation 36

Managing Remote Workers (or Teleworkers) 37

2.2 Employee Training 39

Cost 39

Need 39

Scheduling Demands 40

Employee Morale 40

How Do You Know When Your Employees Need Training? 40

Certification 41

What If the Employee Takes a Training Class and Then Uses His New-Found
Skills to Find Another Job? 41

Nontechnical Training 42

Maximizing the Value of Training 42

2.3 Employee Performance 43

Performance Reviews 43

Key Areas of Evaluation 44

Specific Evaluation Statements 47

Guidelines for Reviews 48

Negative Reviews 49

Have Employees Review Themselves 50

360 Reviews 51

How to Conduct the Actual Review Discussion 52
Development Plans and Goals 52
Salary Review 53
Disciplinary Problems and Terminations 54
2.4 Generational Issues at Work 57
Managing across Generations 58

CHAPTER 3 Staffing Your IT Team **65**
3.1 Why IT Managers Need to Deal with Hiring People 65
Human Resources Department's Role 66
Justifying a Hire 67
Start with Internal and External Referrals 68
Internal versus External Hires 68
Should You Hire a Full-Time Employee or a Consultant? 70
3.2 Write a Position Description 74
Position Descriptions versus Contracts 75
General Requirements 75
Advertising Options 77
3.3 Recruiters 79
Finding the Right Recruiter 81
3.4 Selecting Candidates 83
Reviewing Résumés 83
Telephone Screening 84
At What Level Should I Interview? 84
Narrowing Down the List 84
General Interview Guidelines 86
Prepare a List of Questions 87
Who Else Should Interview a Candidate? 88
Key Concepts for a Good Technical Interview 89
Rank Criteria 93
The Value of Certification 94
Education 95
Checking References 97
Common Hiring Mistakes 98
Offering the Correct Salary for an IT Position 99

CHAPTER 4 Project Management **103**
4.1 Projects and Project Management: A Quick Overview 104
Different Kinds of Projects 104
The Value of Project Management 104
Five Key Phases to a Project 104
Do You Have to Be a Certified Project Manager to Run a Project? 105

The Project Management Institute (PMI) 105

A Project Management Office 106

4.2 Phase One: Scope the Project 106

Clearly Define the Project's Objective and Scope to Avoid Scope Creep 106

Department versus Company Objectives 107

Get Proper Sponsorship for the Project 107

Identify the Stakeholders 108

Identify the Constraints, Interdependencies, and Risks 109

The Project Charter 110

Get Historical Perspective 110

4.3 Phase Two: Develop a Project Plan 111

Three Critical Components to Any Project 111

Write the Project Plan with the Closeout Report in Mind 112

Time Estimates 112

Resources Required: Employees (Internal and External to IT) 113

Money 114

Roles and Responsibilities 115

Multiple Projects 115

4.4 Phase Three: Launch the Project 116

Range of Launch Options 116

Stage a Kick-Off Meeting 116

4.5 Phase Four: Track the Project's Progress 117

Microsoft Project 117

Other Project Management Tools 118

Gantt Charts and Time Lines 118

PERT Charts and Critical Paths 118

Project Milestones 119

Updates to Management and the Team 120

4.6 Phase Five: Close Out the Project 121

Writing a Closeout Report 121

4.7 Decision-Making Techniques 122

Four Types of Decision-Making Methods 122

4.8 What to Do If/When the Project Gets Off Track 123

Some Issues out of Your Control 124

When a Project Gets behind Schedule 124

Your Project Is Costing More Than Expected 125

4.9 Useful Project Management Techniques 126

Project Teams 126

Create a War Room 126

Formalized Project Frameworks 127

Participate in the Project Yourself 127
Offer Project Perks 127
Give Your Project a Code Name.. 127
Productive Project Meetings.. 128
4.10 Funding Projects 130
Estimating Costs: Go High.. 130
Projects Always Cost More Than Estimated 131
Exactly Who Is Going to Pay for It? 131
Justifying the Costs.. 132
4.11 Multiple Projects: How to Juggle Them Well 132
You Will Have Multiple Projects.. 132
4.12 Dealing with Non-IT Departments on a Project 133
Motivating Employees outside of Your Department 133
Who Is in Charge?... 133

CHAPTER 5 Software, Operating Systems, and Enterprise Applications 135
5.1 Types of Software.. 135
5.2 Operating Systems 137
Windows 137
Mac.. 137
Unix Variants and Linux 138
Choosing an Operating System 138
Multiple Operating Systems 139
5.3 Open Source... 141
Definition 141
Cost 142
5.4 Managing Software 142
Total Cost of Ownership (TCO)... 142
Software Management Techniques 142
Software Licensing 144
Licensing Issues.. 145
5.5 Cloud Computing.. 148
The Many Flavors of Cloud Computing 148
Private versus Public Cloud.. 149
Considerations When Moving to the Cloud....................................... 150
5.6 Enterprise Applications.. 152
E-mail... 152
Managing E-mail 153
Unified Messaging 155
Directory Services.. 156

5.7 Enterprise Resource Planning (ERP) 157

The Value of ERP Software 157

General ERP Implementation Issues 157

Costs of Implementing ERP 158

Major Changes Required 158

It Isn't Only IT's Decision 158

Disadvantages to ERP 159

CHAPTER 6   Managing the Money 161

6.1 The Budgeting Process 161

Possible Budget Items 162

Chargebacks—Who Really Pays? 164

Reviewers for Your Budget 164

Estimating (and Overestimating) Your Numbers 165

Getting Approval and Defending Your Budget 165

During the Year: Tracking and Revising Your Budget 166

6.2 The Difference between Capital Expenditures and Operating
Expense Items 167

Capital Expenditure Details 167

Check with Your Company's Policies 168

Gray Areas 168

6.3 Lease versus Buy: Which One Is Better? 168

Leasing 169

Who Makes This Decision? 170

6.4 Other Budgeting Factors to Consider 170

Growth of Your Department's Workload 170

Technological Change 171

Staff 171

Software Maintenance 171

Hardware Maintenance 172

6.5 Managing Vendors 173

Establish a Relationship 173

Help Your Vendors 174

Request for Proposals 174

Get Multiple Bids 175

Set Up a Trial 175

Reviewing Contracts with Vendors 175

Evaluating Alternatives 176

Set Up a Matrix 177

6.6 Managing the Money during Difficult Times 179

Managing Costs 179
Leverage IT for Increased Business Value 180
Demonstrating Leadership 181
6.7 Outsourcing and Offshoring 182
Offshore Outsourcing Overview 182
Which Functions to Outsource 184
Does Outsourcing Make Sense? 184

CHAPTER 7 **Getting Started with the Technical Environment** **189**
7.1 The Technical Environment 189
What Do We Have Here? 189
Define Your Scope 190
The Elements 190
Tools for Tracking the Technical Environment 194
The Value of Good Infrastructure Documentation 195
What You May Find 196
7.2 Understanding the User Environment 196
7.3 TCO and Asset Management: What Are They? 196
Total Cost of Ownership 197
Asset Management 198
7.4 Standards 199
Issues That Users Care About 199
Issues That IT Cares About 200
Standards for IT 201
7.5 Technology Refreshing 201

CHAPTER 8 **Security and Compliance** **205**
8.1 How We Got Here 206
Get Perspective 206
Computer Security Themes 207
8.2 Managing Security 209
Action 1: Evaluate Your Environment's Needs, Exposures, and Defenses 209
Action 2: Get Upper Level Management Buy-In 212
Action 3: Mitigate the Risks 212
Action 4: Work with Users to Make Everyone More Secure 213
Action 5: Remember That Security Is an Ongoing Process 214
8.3 Security Solutions and Technologies 214
Tracking and Controlling Access 214
Authentication 219
Security Defenses 220
Security Incident Response 223

8.4 Types of Threats 224

Malware.. 224

Phishing and Social Engineering... 225

8.5 Compliance and IT 226

Overview 226

Victims of Non-Compliance.. 227

8.6 The Rules 227

Sarbanes–Oxley... 227

Health Insurance Portability and Accountability Act (HIPAA) 228

Basel II 229

SB-1386.. 230

Massachusetts Data Protection Law 230

Fair and Accurate Credit Transactions Act (FACTA)................................. 231

Gramm–Leach–Bliley 231

U.S. Securities.. 232

Patriot Act 232

Dodd–Frank Act... 233

Office of Foreign Assets Control (OFAC) 233

CLERP-9 (Australia) 233

Personal Information Protection and Electronic Documents Act (PIPEDA) 233

Privacy and Electronic Communications Directive (European Union)................. 234

Data Protection Directive (European Union) 234

8.7 How to Comply with the Rules.. 234

Document the Policies 235

Identify Control Mechanisms 236

Educate Employees.. 236

Maintain Evidence 236

8.8 Hidden Benefits of Compliance 237

The Hidden Benefit of Documentation 237

The Hidden Benefit of Control Mechanisms 237

The Hidden Benefit of Educating Your Employees 237

Hidden Benefits of Maintaining Evidence 238

8.9 Methodologies and Frameworks.. 238

IT Governance 238

Committee of Sponsoring Organizations (COSO)....................................... 239

Control Objectives for Information and Related Technology (COBIT) 239

IT Infrastructure Library (ITIL) 240

Capability Maturity Model Integration (CMMI) 240

International Organization for Standards (ISO 9000)................................... 240

Six Sigma... 241

8.10 It's Not Just Regulatory Compliance 242

Electronic Discovery.. 242

Information and Records Retention 242

Working with Auditors... 242

Disaster Recovery and Business Continuity 243

Definition of Policies and Procedures... 243

Outsourcing 244

CHAPTER 9 Disaster Recovery **247**

9.1 Defining the Scope 248

Key Questions... 248

Recovery Time and Recover Point Objectives 249

Disaster Recovery Committee 249

Application Assessment.. 250

The Value of Your Data 252

9.2 Creating a Disaster Recovery Plan.. 253

Communication Plan... 253

Documentation 254

Real Estate and IT Facilities 254

Off-Site Storage of Data.. 256

Hardware Availability... 257

Regular Updating and Testing.. 257

After the Disaster... 259

Regional and Catastrophic Disasters... 259

The ACT Model.. 259

9.3 A Word about Incident Response, Business Continuity,
and Disaster Recovery 260

9.4 The Hidden Benefits of Good Disaster Recovery Planning............... 261

CHAPTER 10 Working with Users **263**

10.1 Relationships with Users 263

Who Are Your Users? 264

Find Out Who Your Department Thinks Its Users Are............... 264

Find Out Who Your Boss Thinks Your Users Are...................... 265

Meet the Users 265

Being Available and Reachable 266

Sharing Information.. 266

Collecting Information.. 267

Proactive Solutions 268

Being Flexible.. 270

User Training 270

10.2 The Consumerization of IT 271

How to Deal with Consumerization 272

Support Issues Associated with Consumerization and Handheld Devices 272

Bring Your Own (BYO) Policies 273

10.3 When Your Users Are Part of a Mobile Work Force 274

Techniques for Supporting Your Mobile Users 274

10.4 The Help Desk 275

Typical Help Desk Activities 276

Procedures 276

Access 277

Self-Service 277

Tools 278

User Surveys 280

Measuring the Help Desk Workload 281

Staffing 281

10.5 Service Level Agreements 283

Positive Values of SLAs 283

Ask for Help from Your Staff 283

Writing Good SLAs 284

CHAPTER 11 **Connectivity: Social Media, Handhelds, and More** **287**

11.1 Get in Front of the Curve 288

The Blurry Line between Company-Owned and Personally-Owned Equipment
(BYO Policies) 288

The New Technologies of Connectedness 289

Benefits and Challenges of Connectivity 290

Dealing with a Lot More Empowered Users 292

Wisdom of Crowds 293

11.2 The Power of All These Connections 293

How Companies Use the Web 293

How Companies Use Intranets 294

How Companies Use Social Media and Mobile Devices 295

Mobile Device Operating Systems, Apps, and Hardware 296

Handheld Hardware 297

11.3 How Does This Affect You as IT Manager? 298

Lead, Encourage, and Experiment 298

It's Not the Tools, But How They Are Used 299

Remember Your Goals 301

What Is "Focused" and What Is "Distracted"? 301

Glossary **305**
Index **317**

Key Changes for This Edition

Technology has the shelf life of a banana.
Scott McNealy

IT ain't what it used to be. When we starting writing the first edition of this book, large hard drives were measured in megabytes, the "World Wide Web" was just getting started, and everyone's phone was tied to copper wires. If you wanted to locate a piece of information, you looked it up in a book. And technology was the exclusive purview of IT.

Thirteen years later, portable terabyte drives are sold as consumer items. The Web is beyond pervasive. Phones are—well, making calls is now just an incidental feature of what they can do. Paper books are outsold by ebooks. And terms like "IP addresses," "Wi-Fi," and "Bluetooth" are no longer the jargon of just tech-heads.

MAJOR CHANGE: PRINCIPLES AND CORE CONCEPTS

For these reasons, we have decided to make the third edition of this book about the *principles and core concepts* of the new IT Manager's job. There are lots of recently-minted IT Managers and they still need to learn important things like how to hire (**Chapter 3, Staffing Your IT Team** on **page 65**), how to manage a project (**Chapter 4, Project Management** on **page 103**), and how to deal with users (**Chapter 10, Working with Users** on **page 263**).

IT Managers may also need to learn about converting their network to IPv6, or how to optimize a SQL database, but they will go to other sources for that information, like the Web, or training. Or they will go to books dedicated to very specific subjects, not to a general book like this one. The *fundamental concepts* of management do not change, although technical details do—which is why we have decided not to include the technical material from the first two editions.

ANOTHER MAJOR CHANGE: CONNECTIVITY

Another major change is the addition of **Chapter 11, Connectivity: Social Media, Handhelds, and More** on **page 287**. This is the fastest growing area in IT, and in addition to new hardware and software considerations, it also means *new ways of thinking* about IT in general.

Back in the old days (just a few years ago!) *scalability* was the issue, not mobility. Now most data needs to be accessed almost all the time from almost anywhere. As a consequence, discussions about the mobile workforce are interspersed throughout the book. For many users, if it cannot be done from a handheld device (e.g., phone or tablet), it's not worth doing.

Regardless of the correctness of that sentiment, that is clearly the direction organizations of all sizes are heading. And, as a new IT Manager, you should be embracing this trend. Rather than being caught flat-footed when someone asks you about accessing sales data from a tablet device, you should be prepared with an answer. They might not like the answer you give them, but you'll be much better served if you have a meaningful response ready.

Lastly, we've expanded the material on cloud computing to reflect the growing shift in the industry to move functions (e.g., server, storage, applications) to service providers and reduce the investment in on-premise infrastructure.

We know our readers' time is valuable, so we've continued to make the book easy to use with an expanded glossary, index, and lists of sources. We've received positive feedback on the elements such as the chapter-to-chapter references, a robust bibliography and index, sidebars, bulleted lists, and pro/con tables. This edition includes enhancements of these elements as well as new examples and updates of old ones.

"IT ain't what it used to be," as we said at the beginning of this section. This book is not a simple rehash of previous material—we have striven to make the most up-to-date book about the complex challenges *today's* new IT Manager faces. We hope we have succeeded.

Preface

I'm a great believer in luck, and I find the harder I work the more I have of it.
Thomas Jefferson

Many technical professionals are eager to join the ranks of management. But as the saying goes, "Be careful what you wish for." This book introduces you to the many key concepts you will face as a new Information Technology (IT) Manager. It also provides you with suggested methods for dealing with many of the large issues that arise, including specific recommendations for actions as well as places to look for further help.

We have seen many technical professionals—database administrators, programmers, desktop technicians, server engineers—suddenly thrust into positions of management in their IT departments. Not only were they given no formal training or clear idea of what the position entailed, they were also expected to know a great deal about a lot of different things. As senior IT professionals ourselves, we have seen this situation repeated many times. We set out to write a book that would help new IT Managers navigate the choppy seas of management. This book aims to help you with all those responsibilities that are suddenly thrust upon you, that you suddenly acquire, or that you suddenly realize need to be addressed. We don't spend much time talking about the theory of IT management. We spend most of the book describing what you need to worry about when you need to deal with a real-world situation, such as creating a budget or writing a job description.

We wrote the book for *new* IT Managers and *future* IT Managers. Much of the material in this book will be familiar to experienced IT Managers. But for many individuals, recent changes in the computer industry have brought a radical change in responsibilities with little or no help to go with it. This book is written to help you identify, deal with, and (if necessary) tell you where to look for further assistance on many of the key issues that are suddenly facing you as a new IT Manager. We also recognize that one of the more difficult career steps in the field of Information Technology is moving up from technician to manager. For those hoping to make this leap, this book can be useful in letting you know what awaits you on the other side. By learning more about an IT Manager's job, you will know what skill sets to focus on so that you can demonstrate to your company that you're prepared and ready to be a manager.

THE STRUCTURE OF THIS BOOK

We worked hard to write a book that we, as busy IT professionals, would use ourselves. We have structured the material in easy-to-read, easy-to-grab chunks. We don't have any free time and we assume you don't either. The book is designed to be scanned for critical information; it includes many cross references with page numbers, because one topic often leads to another and because readers want to make the jump right away. If you are reading this as an ebook, you can click on the links and be sent there directly. You'll also find that the book is replete with bulleted lists that are easy to scan through to find information. We hope you find the structure and format useful and helpful. The book also references real-world events that are related to IT, as well as numerous industry studies and surveys to help put a number of topics into perspective. Finally, the further references section provides many, many books, articles, and websites that you can explore for a deeper dive into the topics we explore.

CHAPTER-BY-CHAPTER SUMMARIES

Chapter		Summary	
1	The Role of an IT Manager	This chapter helps a wide range of technical professionals, some of whom have been suddenly thrust into a managerial role, understand the role of an IT Manager, why it's so important, and how integral it is to the company. It also discusses two additional key topics: the difference between leadership and management, and what happens if your company merges with another.	
2	Managing Your IT Team	It's tempting to think of hardware and software as an IT Manager's most critical IT resources, but actually the people who run, support, and manage the technologies are the most important resources you have. This chapter discusses how to keep your employees focused and trained, as well as generational issues at work that you might face. It also covers the employee evaluation process in great detail.	
3	Staffing Your IT Team	Hiring, and all of its aspects, is one of the important managerial responsibilities. This chapter talks about the issues and challenges you'll face and offers some concrete ideas for solving them.	
4	Project Management	As an IT Manager you'll go from one project to another; some are miniscule and others seem too big to be measured. Your success at being able to manage projects of all sizes and all degrees of complexity is a critical factor in being successful at your role. Based on the principles of classic project management, this chapter talks about topics as critical as "Five Key Phases to a Project," "What to Do If/When the Project Gets Off Track," and "Dealing with Non-IT Departments on a Project."	
5	Software, Operating Systems, and Enterprise Applications	These days, managing software is a much more diverse and complex job than it used to be. (Not that it was ever easy.) This chapter discusses the main classifications of software. It also talks about operating systems, open source, cloud computing, and enterprise applications.	
6	Managing the Money	It's likely that the IT department has one of the largest budgets in the company. This chapter helps you get a foundation in managing a budget, spending, leasing versus buying, etc. It also offers guidance on how to make the most of your vendor relationships so that it's beneficial to both parties. Finally, both outsourcing and offshoring are discussed in detail.	

Continued

Chapter		Summary
7	Getting Started with the Technical Environment	IT environments, as you probably know by now, are very complex. This chapter gives you guidance on how to get an understanding of what is in yours, and how it operates and connects to other environments. The technical environment, users, standards, technology refreshing, and the very important topic of TCO are all covered.
8	Security and Compliance	Security is a 24/7/365 concern that should be an integral part of every decision you make in IT. Regulations and legislations are increasingly having a major impact on how IT departments operate. This chapter presents detailed information on compliance issues as well as information about different methodologies being adopted by various organizations to help ensure compliance.
9	Disaster Recovery	With so many, and so much, depending on IT, your company may not be able to tolerate much downtime if disaster strikes. This chapter describes how to define the scope of the problem, how to create a disaster recovery plan, as well as the "The Hidden Benefits of Good Disaster Recovery Planning."
10	Working with Users	The support that you provide to your end users—regardless of where they may be—can be the most vital service you offer and the one that is the greatest influence on how you and the IT department are perceived by the rest of the company. This chapter discusses the complexities of dealing with users on another continent, and users down the hall from you using their own personal devices (tablets, smart phones, etc.) on your network. Managing the Help Desk and writing useful SLAs are also discussed.
11	Connectivity: Social Media, Handhelds, and More	This chapter discusses the challenges of the new hyper-connected workplace. What are the positives and negatives of these connections and how do they directly affect you as the IT Manager?

NOTE ON URLS AND WEB RESOURCES

State-of-the-art information is critical to IT Managers and IT professionals of all kinds. Many of the sources for this book are websites. And, as every web user understands, web content changes quickly. We have included web addresses whenever we can, knowing full well that websites change, material gets deleted or added, and links that worked when we wrote the book may not necessarily work when you read it. Regardless, we thought it best to give you a reference where we found worthwhile information. You can use that information as a starting point for your search for information.

Acknowledgments

Trying to condense the topic of IT management into one book isn't an easy task. It required a delicate touch to balance technical and nontechnical issues properly, as well as to determine which topics to focus on in each area. A large portion of the ideas presented here represent what we've learned from others. Accordingly, we must give credit to those who taught us (often unknowingly) throughout the course of our careers in corporate IT—colleagues, co-workers, those we have reported to, and those who have reported to us. We are indebted to, and grateful for, these accidental mentors.

Portions of this material appeared in previous editions of the *IT Manager's Handbook*. We would like to thank the following individuals who helped review those proposals and manuscripts and gave guidance: Frank Calabrese, Bruce Caldwell, James Chilton, Tom Conarty, Dan Deakin, Jonathan Ganz, Stan Gibson, Karen Godshalk, Rob Hawkins, Karen Hitchcock, Curtis Johnsey, Mark Jones, Brian McMann, Robert Rubin, James Snyder, Norma Sutcliffe, Matt Tavis, Philip Tolley, Curt Wennekamp, Nick Wilde, Janet Wilson.

We would also like to thank the people at Morgan Kaufmann: Rachel Roumeliotis, Andrea Dierna, Robyn Day, and Jessica Vaughan. They took the concept for this book and ran with it, and we are greatly indebted to their efforts. Diane Cerra, Greg Chalson, Karyn Johnson, Jennifer Mann, Heather Scherer, Asma Stephan, and Heather Tighe were involved with the earlier editions of the series.

Most importantly, we are tremendously indebted to our family and friends for their support and understanding while this book was being written. It's motivating to know that as the final edits are being made and this self-imposed exile ends, they are anxious and eager to forget about those declined invitations, missed dinners, and non-existent weekends. In particular:

Bill would like to thank The Five; as always, they know everything I do is for them.

Brian would like to thank Jenine—his girlfriend during the writing of the second edition, his fiancé during the writing of the business edition, and his wife for the third edition—whom he loves and depends on, and with whom he looks forward to the future, for her patience, love, and encouragement.

Bill Holtsnider
Denver, CO
bholtsnider@gmail.com

Brian D. Jaffe
New York, NY
brian@red55.com

The Role of an IT Manager

The manager is the dynamic, life-giving element in every business.
Peter Drucker

CHAPTER TABLE OF CONTENTS

1.1 Just What Does an IT Manager Do?...2
1.2 Managers in General 3
1.3 The Strategic Value of the IT Department..8
1.4 Developing an IT Strategy 10
1.5 Leadership versus Management 13
1.6 Starting Your New Job 14
1.7 The First 100 Days 20
1.8 Two IT Departments—What Happens if Your Company Merges with Another?.......27
1.9 Further References 28

Common issues and questions about IT Managers include:

- What does an IT Manager actually *do*?
- Did you recently receive a promotion into that job with no prior training?
- Are you glad you got the job?
- Do you eventually want to become one?

Before we help you answer those questions, we discuss the definition and the pros and cons of being a manager. Clearly management as a career path is well suited for some people, but not for everyone. Is it right for you?

IT Managers need to wear a lot of hats. Different parts of the organization will have different expectations of this position, and you'll have to address them all. Finance expects you to manage costs. Sales and Marketing will want to see IT help generate revenue. The auditors are looking over your shoulder. Your staff is looking for guidance, career development, and a work-life balance. The executive traveling to Dubai wants to know if his cell phone will work there, and how to use the hotel's Wi-Fi. And the administrative assistant down the hall just wants her printer to stop smudging. This chapter examines the varied roles and responsibilities of an IT Manager.

1.1 JUST WHAT DOES AN IT MANAGER DO?

IT Managers now have many responsibilities (data centers, staff management, telecommunications, servers, applications, workstations, websites, mobile access and devices, user support, regulatory compliance, vendor management, disaster recovery, etc.) and work with all the departments (accounting, human resources, marketing, sales, distribution, facilities, legal, etc.) within a company or organization.

This is both the good and the bad news. At some companies, an IT Manager can have direct influence on the strategic direction of the company, suggesting and helping implement web initiatives, for example. In other companies, an IT Manager is really only a technician, software developer, or network engineer. And to complicate things even further, those definitions change quickly over time. Yesterday's network engineer might become today's website consultant.

Why All That Change and Flexibility Is Good

The position of IT Manager can be very challenging. It is extremely varied in scope, allows you to come in contact with a large portion of your company, provides you with opportunities to directly affect the overall direction of your organization, and is very valuable professional experience to acquire. In addition, you get to increase your range of experience; you are forced to (and *get to*) keep up with the latest changes in technology (so your skill set will always be in demand) and your network of contacts gets large.

As important as all that is, there is an added bonus: In recent years, IT has taken on a strategic value in the roles companies play in the new economy. Information Technology is now a critical component of many companies and the U.S. economy. In the 2010–2011 Occupational Outlook Handbook released by the U.S. Department of Labor's Bureau of Labor Statistics, "computer and mathematical science occupations . . . are expected to grow more than twice as fast as the average for all occupations in the economy . . . driven by the continuing need for businesses, government agencies, and other organizations to adopt and utilize the latest technologies."

And for IT Managers, the report says, "faster than average employment growth is expected . . . [and] job prospects should be excellent." Specifically the report projects employment of computer and information systems managers to grow 17 percent over the 2008–2018 decade, which is faster than the average for all occupations. New uses for "technology in the workplace will continue to drive demand for workers, fueling the need for more managers." Not only is your job interesting and rewarding, it is also very important and increasingly in demand. Dependence on technology is only growing, and issues such as security, revenue generation, improved productivity, and compliance are making IT more visible throughout the organization. What more could you ask for?

Why All That Change and Flexibility Is Bad

However, being an IT Manager is a difficult, often thankless, task. Like many service jobs, if you do it superbly, most people do not notice. Mess up and they scream. In addition, responsibilities of the job differ radically from company to company. Some companies actually have many IT Managers and several layers of management. At others (although this number is shrinking) an IT Manager is a part-time role someone fills while doing their "real" job.

In addition, the role of an IT Manager can often vary widely within the same organization, depending on who is making the decisions at the time. The "Western Region Sales Manager" knows what his role is—get more sales as soon as possible in a specific area—and that is not going to vary much from company to company. An IT Manager, however, can mean many things to many people, and the job changes as technology and needs advance and evolve.

Addressing all these needs and people can mean that time for "extras" such as sleep and meals have to be sacrificed. As a manager, everyone else's crises become yours. People (your users, your management, your staff, etc.) demand quick resolutions to problems and look to you to fix them. In this book, we discuss in detail the positive and negative elements of the key components of being an IT Manager. If a process is littered with political landmines (budgeting, for example), we'll warn you about it; if a process has hidden perks (being an unofficial project manager for a project can put you in contact with many different people at many different layers of the organization), we'll tell you that, too. But before you decide if you should be an *IT* Manager, read the next section to determine if you want to be a *manager* at all.

1.2 MANAGERS IN GENERAL

Before you decide whether you want to become an IT Manager, you should decide whether you want to become a manager at all. One method of evaluating a potential career is to read books or take introductory classes about how to do it; sometimes, reading a book about a subject will make you realize you do *not* want to pursue that particular career (see Table 1.1).

Like most topics in this book, we present you with both the positive and the negative aspects of being a manager. We share our experiences and those of other managers we know; managers with over 100 years of combined experience contributed ideas to the following section.

Of course, the comments in this section are extremely subjective. Both positive and negative comments about such a broad topic ("management") are bound to be generalizations that can easily be counter-argued. So take each comment, idea, and suggestion as something to be considered, evaluated, and adapted; perhaps it applies to your experience and perhaps not.

Definition of a Manager

Management has been defined as "assembling the resources to achieve a mutually agreed upon objective" (G. Puziak, 2005) or as "getting things done through other people" (AMA President, 1980). A more mundane dictionary definition is the "authoritative control over the affairs of others." All three views are commonly held beliefs.

Note the radical difference between the definitions: the first two have a sense of collaboration ("mutually agreed upon" and "through"), whereas the last one defines management as "control." As always, flexibility is the key.

Styles of Management

These definitions reflect the two typical management structures American companies now employ:

- Command and Control
- Collaboration

These styles have many different names: "authoritarian" and "participative," or "military" and "worker responsibility."

Few companies, or individuals, are either purely one type or another, of course, but most are *generally* one kind or another. To succeed as a manager, it's best if you determine which type of management your company embraces. Also, determine which type of manager you want to become. Regardless of your answer, being flexible and adaptable will be a critical factor. While one type of style may work well in one situation, a different set of circumstances could call for an entirely different approach.

Command and Control

Based on classic military structure, this style was popular for much of American corporate history. You direct your employees and your boss directs you. In its extreme, this style doesn't allow for disagreement or input from subordinates. It emphasizes clear commands, and rewards those that follow these commands virtually without question.

This style has lost popularity and is most familiar to the older generations (see the section **"Generational Issues at Work"** in **Chapter 2, Managing Your IT Team**, on **page 57**). While some environments still operate under this style, many corporations are revisiting their commitment to such a rigid method of management. While execution of tasks under command and control systems is often faster and costs less, it also often leads to poor decisions and less-than-ideal results, and ends up costing more over the long term. In addition, employees under this system are often unhappy because they exercise little control in their jobs. It is also hard to know what value is lost in an environment where collaboration and teamwork are absent and discouraged.

Collaboration

This style of management has been growing in popularity and use for the past few decades. In a collaborative environment, all levels of the corporate organization are actively involved in the execution of business. It doesn't necessarily mean dock workers make decisions on plant relocations (although assembly-line workers are now much more involved in decisions that affect them than they ever have been). But it does mean that many workers who are affected or who can contribute to decisions are now asked to be involved—regardless of where they stand in the company hierarchy.

The goals of collaboration are better and more cost-effective decisions because the people affected by those decisions are involved in making them, with a very significant added benefit of increased personal satisfaction for workers. The negatives are summarized by that old adage "paralysis by analysis." When this happens, too many people involved in a decision don't make the decision and it bogs down.

Within the collaboration mode, there are also two extremes: managers who micromanage—they are involved in every decision and consult as many people as possible on even the smallest of issues—and managers who are so distant they provide no guidance or feedback to their team and ignore even the most pressing of issues.

In some companies, the collaborative culture has been fully embraced at the highest levels of the organization. Andy Grove, former CEO of Intel; Michael Bloomberg, Mayor of New York City; and Mark Zuckerberg, cofounder and CEO of Facebook chose to work at desks in open environments, as opposed to the traditional executive perk of having their own executive office.

What Kind of Manager Will You Be?

It's hard to predict, but study the two types of management styles discussed above. Which kind have you experienced as a staff member? Which kind did you like? What kind of style is common in your company? "Management style shock" is not uncommon; a manager comes from another company and, bringing her management toolbox with her, quickly discovers that her "style" and that of the new company radically conflict. She is used to a collaborative approach and this company has no patience for discussion; her bosses dictate what she should do and they expect her to do the same. Or, she starts commanding her staff around and they, used to group meetings to make important decisions, are shocked.

In a survey about senior management terminations released in 2009 by the Korn/Ferry Institute , it was found that a leading reason for termination "is difficulty with relationships in the organization, much more frequently cited than purely performance-related issues." Furthermore, the report stated "that 50 percent of performance at the CEO level is determined not by one's experience or technical abilities but by leadership characteristics. Leadership characteristics encompass areas such as personal and interpersonal skills, being organizationally savvy and [having] integrity" (source: www .kornferryinstitute.com/files/pdf1/KFceo_whtppr_jan30.pdf). Of course, this book isn't about succeeding as a CEO, but there is certainly a lesson here that individuals from all parts of the organization can appreciate and learn from.

Pros and Cons of Being a Manager: Reasons to Become a Manager, and Reasons Not to Become One

Table 1.1 Pros and Cons of Being a Manager

PRO	CON
May have more control over your life. You can delegate to others instead of being a resource of one. Of course, you will probably also have a manager above you.	May have less control over your life (since the problems of others now become your problems).
Typically make more money than those in nonmanagement roles, although this, too, is changing. There are technical tracks in many companies that are almost as lucrative as management, but not every company has this option.	Typically, but not always, a manager has more responsibility than a non-manager. There is more credit if things go right and a bigger price to pay if things go wrong.
Do work on a larger scale. A simplistic example might be: one non-management worker may generate $1000 a day in revenue for the company, but a manager may manage six such workers, generating $6000 daily for the company.	Management looks and sounds a lot easier than it is. Often, managers are seen attending endless meetings or just having casual conversations all the time—not doing "real work." In fact, they often carry a great deal of responsibility and have to make difficult decisions routinely.
Have greater potential to "make a difference."	Numerous headaches come with managing people: meeting your project's budget and schedule projections, dealing with challenging employees, and administrative annoyances. ("Those 200 new PCs arrived, where do we store them until we're ready to work on them?")

Continued

Table 1.1 Pros and Cons of Being a Manager—Cont'd	
PRO	**CON**
You get the *credit* for all the good work that your team does on your watch . . . whether it happened because of you, your staff, or by random chance.	You get the *blame* for all the bad stuff that happens on your watch. . .whether it happened because of you, your staff, or by random chance.
Get the opportunity to develop non-IT skills, working with other departments, vendors, partners, etc.	There are tough decisions to make: budget cuts, employee performance, having to choose between Jenine and Peter for the promotion, etc.
Have the opportunity to determine strategy and to set direction for both a department and the company as a whole.	
Acquire the ability to add more value to a department and a company.	
Have the opportunity to develop, coach, and mentor other people.	

The Hidden Work of Management

One challenging aspect of management is that the actual work done is often less apparent and less tangible than the work being done by subordinates.

Management Is Sometimes Hard to See

There are, of course, examples of useless and lazy managers. You may even be a victim of one. But management is not, in and of itself, easy. Nor are all of its components visible. A worker may see a manager spend several hours a day in meetings: "That guy just spends his days in meetings, and doesn't do any 'real' work." But the truth is probably quite different: The manager may be attending those meetings with fellow managers and performing some of the tasks discussed in this book: reviewing resources, discussing personnel matters, proposing or defending a budget, setting objectives and strategies, fighting with Human Resources (HR) and Finance about planned layoffs, or planning a system overhaul. In that scenario, a hard-working manager and a slouch look exactly the same to an outside observer.

Good and Bad Management Often Look Alike—For a While

In addition, because great—or even good—management is often hard to see, the effects of good management are sometimes clear only in retrospect. Consequently, bad management and good management can look the same until the outcomes are seen. A manager that has a critical meeting with a subordinate that gets that subordinate back on track looks, to the outside observer, exactly like a manager having an intense conversation with a coworker about weekend party plans. That worker's new attitude may take weeks, or months, to show itself concretely. A key decision not to pursue opening a new plant overseas happens in meeting rooms far from the general employee population; it may cost hundreds of jobs in the short term, but save thousands in the long term. Those results will show up in the financial results years after the decision was made.

Resentment toward Management

If you become a manager, you can assume there may be some resentment toward you in that role. This resentment could be because others in the department had hoped that they would get the job or some may think that you're not qualified. There are also challenges when you are promoted and now have to manage a group of people that used to be your peers. There can be a tendency for tension between non-managerial staff and managers: The role of one is to direct, steer, or manage the other. Most of the time, that relationship works well and each person knows her own role and understands the other's role to some degree. Occasionally, however, that tension needs time and attention by both sides before it disappears.

The key to dealing with this problem is to communicate. Talk with your staff. Build a relationship with *each* member of your team. Let each person know you recognize their talents and their contributions.

Babysitting versus Managing

There is a portion of any manager's job that is "just babysitting." People are unpredictable, but you can predict they aren't always going to act in ways that will help you and your department. Sometimes their actions will cause you a great deal of stress; anyone who has had to lay off employees will attest to the pain of delivering a pink slip. Some of your staff will do exactly as you request, which may mean they sit idle until you request something. Others are so eager to do more that you have to hold them back. Other times employees will drive you crazy with items so mundane you'll scarcely believe you are talking about the issue. Many managers know of the enormous "turf wars" that erupt over inches of desk size, who gets the larger monitor, or who is allowed to go to which training classes. Hence the name "babysitting."

Politics

Unlike non-managerial workers, many managers spend a large amount of time dealing with the political elements of the company. While some people dislike any form of politics at work, many others thrive on it. "Politics at work" can mean anything from jockeying for a larger role in an upcoming project to turf wars about who manages which department.

Some politics is necessary: the network support team needs someone to run it, and either a new person has to be hired (see **Chapter 3, Staffing Your IT Team** on **page 65**) or a current employee needs to be appointed. Since people are only human, some subjective considerations will eventually come into play. Does John in Accounting have the right personality for the job? If Mary is given that promotion, will she eventually merge the department with her old one? If Tom is hired, will he want to bring along his friend Chris that he always seems to have working for him?

Managing in Four Directions

Chapter 2, Managing Your IT Team on **page 31**, is dedicated to the issues of managing your staff. However, it is important to note that most managers have to manage in four directions (see Figure 1.1). Although managing your team is probably the most vital of these four and will consume a good portion of your time and energy, you cannot ignore the other three.

- **Managing up:** This includes your boss and other company management.
- **Managing your peers:** Your peers include people at the same level as you within the organization. This can be other managers in the IT department, as well as managers in other departments.

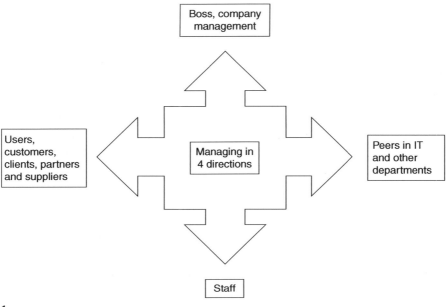

FIGURE 1.1

Managing in four directions.

- **Managing your users/customers/clients:** These are the people to whom you deliver your services. They could be users calling your Help Desk, customers using the company website, employees accessing e-mail or file-servers, or partners you exchange data with.
- **Managing your staff:** These are the individuals (employees, consultants, even vendor representatives) in the organization that report into you.

In all four of these directions, you're dealing with similar issues: setting expectations, developing relationships, aligning goals and strategies, demonstrating leadership as well as management, and so on. However, each of them has a different twist, too. For example, you set expectations differently when you manage up than when you are managing your staff. In the former, you're helping set a frame of reference for your management as to what they should expect, from you, from technology, and from your team. You are also outlining what you'll need from them (support, resources, etc.). When you set expectations for your staff, you are defining objectives for them, and holding them accountable. Similarly, aligning goals is something you would do in all four directions, but you would do them with a different approach and at different levels with each direction.

1.3 THE STRATEGIC VALUE OF THE IT DEPARTMENT

IT has become one of the most critical functions in the economy of the new century. As corporations have embraced the efficiencies and excitement of the new digital economy, IT and IT professionals have grown dramatically in value. IT is no longer "just" a department, no longer an isolated island like the MIS departments of old corporations where requests for data would flow in and emerge, weeks or months later, in some long, unreadable report. Many companies now make IT an integral part of their company, of their mission statements, and of their spending. Your role is more critical than ever before.

THE CEO'S ROLE IN IT

First, the CEO must be sure to regard information technology as a strategic resource to help the business get more out of its people. Second, the CEO must learn enough about technology to be able to ask good, hard questions of the CIO and be able to tell whether good answers are coming back. Third, the CEO needs to bring the CIO into management's deliberations and strategizing. It's impossible to align IT strategy with business strategy if the CIO is out of the business loop.

—*Bill Gates*
Business @ the Speed of Thought

Application Development versus Technical Operations

Most IT organizations have two primary functional areas: Applications Development and Technical Operations.

Application Development

Companies often see the real value of IT as only the applications that serve the company's core business. Applications are what allow one business to become innovative, more efficient, and more productive and set itself apart from its competitors. Careers within applications development include analysts, programmers, database administrators, interface designers, and testers, among others.

Many people within IT like working in application development because it allows them to learn how the business operates. As a result, it may often provide opportunities for increased involvement with people in other departments outside of IT. However, many programmers find the job is too isolating because their daily interactions may only be with the program logic displayed on their screen and the keyboard; they don't like being only "keyboard jockeys." Of course, other programmers welcome the isolation and embrace the opportunity to work in relative seclusion.

Technical Operations

The technical support function is the oft-forgotten area of IT. The Technical Operations organization is responsible for making sure that the computers are up and operating as they should. Their jobs go well beyond the computer hardware and include the network (routers, switches, telecommunication facilities, etc.), data center, operations, security, backups, operating systems, and so on. The Help Desk may be the most visible portion of the Technical Operations group. Within the industry, this infrastructure side of IT is often referred to as the "plumbing." Like most important and underappreciated jobs, when Operations is doing their job well you don't even know they exist. But if something goes wrong, their visibility within the organization suddenly skyrockets.

However, those working in Operations may find the time demands stressful. Some system maintenance can be done only during weekends and evenings when users won't be affected. Similarly, it will be the Operations staff that is roused by a mid-REM-sleep phone call when the system crashes in the middle of the night. (For a discussion of methods of preventing burnout, see **Chapter 2, Managing Your IT Team** on **page 31.**)

IT Department Goals

One of your objectives as an involved and caring manager is to make sure that your department's goals are in line with those of your organization. It doesn't matter if you're an IT Manager for a small non-profit or a midlevel manager for a Fortune 500 company, you need to discover what the organization's goals are and make them your own.

If you work for a corporate organization, your IT goals may be measured in the same terms as the business areas that you support—reduce per-unit costs of the division's products and increase the capacity and throughput of the business and manufacturing processes, for example. Your tactics must clearly satisfy these goals. If you work in a nonprofit or educational organization, your goals—and the way you are measured—will be different. Your boss should be clear about communicating those goals to you—they shouldn't be a secret.

The Value of IT Managers

IT is a complex, misunderstood part of many of today's organizations. Executives now know how to use Word, Excel, e-mail, their smart phones, and how to mine the Web for information, but some have little or no understanding of the deeper, more complex issues involved in IT. They imagine IT to be a powerful but multifaceted world where rewards can be magically great and risks are frighteningly terrible. These executives and their corporations need professionals to both explain and execute in this world. This is where you come in.

You can leverage your technical knowledge, experience, and interests with your company's direct profit and loss requirements. *Together*, you and your company can provide a powerful business combination. *Alone*, your individual skills and passions can wither into arcane interests, and your business expertise can build models relevant to an economic world decades in the past.

- Will your technical expertise and recommendations occasionally clash with the company's needs and vision? Absolutely.
- Will your ideas about technical directions sometimes be in direct opposition to others' perceptions of "market forces"? Absolutely.
- Will you "win some and lose some"? Absolutely.

The purpose of this book, however, is to help you succeed—and to help your company succeed. We want you, your IT department, *and* your company to work together as successfully as possible.

1.4 DEVELOPING AN IT STRATEGY

The cosmic question "Why are we here?" applies to corporate departments as well. It is entirely possible that many, if not all, of your staff don't have the full understanding of how the IT department serves the entire organization. When it comes to their job, they may understand what's critical for *today*. But, although today is important, it's also vital to know about tomorrow and beyond. If they're only looking at the trees, you have to be the one to let them know about the forest. The strategy should include feedback from your employees and should be cleared by your boss, but you should drive its formulation.

Without an IT strategy, you won't be able to align your long-term goals with your short-term responsibilities. You need to have these items decided and written down so that when your boss tells you to do X, your employee needs Y, and the other manager down the hall that helped you last week needs Z, you have a clear idea of which task should be addressed in which order.

Some companies have huge IT departments, with layers and layers of managers. Organizations of this size have formal IT strategies and sub-strategies. However, many smaller companies don't have formal IT departments with managers, budgets, and expectations. Wherever you are on the size and formal structure spectrum, you should have a strategy. And you should write it down. Your strategy should include the following:

- Who are your team members and what can they do?
- Why or how is technology important to your organization?
- What are your assets?
- Who are your customers?
- What are your customers' needs?
- How do you plan to satisfy these needs?

Although this all sounds simple, it's definitely not. Your customers may not even know what their IT needs are, for example. However, the very act of getting this in writing can be of great value. For more information on both the visible and the hidden benefits of documentation, see **Chapter 8, Security and Compliance** on **page 205**.

Determine Who Your Team Members Are

This also seems like a simple task—just list the people in your department. In fact, though, your team members may or may not be all the people on your staff. You may have someone on your staff who has part-time responsibilities to another department. This person is on your team, but you can't count on having his or her time when you need it.

Alternatively, there may be people from other departments who aren't on your payroll and report to some other branch of the organizational chart, but could be very useful to your department. They might call you when they hear about certain problems on the system, for example, or help you when someone in your department is out sick. They may have intimate knowledge of the business applications and could be in a better position than your team to do testing, understand the impact of changes, and how the application is used. These people aren't in your budget and aren't in your department, but they are on your team. See **Chapter 4, Project Management** on **page 103** for a discussion of how to work with, recruit, and "manage" people who are not directly under your supervision.

In addition to determining who the team members are, find out their skill sets and backgrounds. You may know a team member as a cable installer but he may have rudimentary .NET skills that the Applications Development team could use. She may be a sales manager who has some project management experience that could help you coordinate new phone system rollout.

Determine How Important Technology Is to Your Organization

The technology in use can vary tremendously from organization to organization. Originally, in a law firm, technology was used simply for word processing or for tracking client billings. Additionally, it could be used to scan and archive documents so that every single piece of paper related to a case is online where it can be indexed, cross-referenced, and immediately retrieved. But now, law firms are increasingly involved in technology through e-discovery, digital forensics, and lawsuits related to use of technology. In a retail organization, technology can be used for all the traditional back office activities (billing, purchasing, etc.) but probably serves its most vital function by helping the store managers know what products are generating the most sales and profits and which should be dropped from inventory. The store might also use it for space planning so that the shelves are stocked in a way that maximizes space usage, as well as sales and profitability. Customer lists and purchase history can be used to create customized marketing campaigns and increase sales.

Determine Who Your Customers Are and What Their Needs Are

Whether your customers are other employees, suppliers, consumers, or other businesses, they are the ones you need to serve. Find out who your customers are. Figure out what their needs are. Then spend your time addressing those needs. Issues to consider include the following:

- **Your customers are not necessarily *retail* customers (although they could be).** More likely, your customers are other internal departments in the company and your boss. Different jobs have different customers, and there are departments (such as Sales and Marketing) who should spend all day figuring out what their external customers need. IT, however, commonly serves other departments *within* the company, such as sales, marketing, accounting, and management.
- **Figure out what your customers' needs are.** Are they products or services? Data and information? Reduced costs? Mobile services? Improved efficiency or productivity?
- **Ask your customers directly about their needs.** Set up meetings with representatives from different departments, ask questions, note the answers, and change the way you're doing business to reflect your customer needs and concerns.

Keep Your Department Central to the Company's Operations

Make sure the strategy mentioned in the previous section is carefully aligned with the goals of the entire organization. This is critical. If the needs of your immediate boss are out of alignment with what the entire company is doing, you have a serious problem. (See the section **"Company Mission, Vision, and Values"** in **Chapter 2, Managing Your IT Team,** on **page 34** about the company's mission.)

Let the rest of the organization know what you're doing in IT. To many of the other department managers, IT may not mean much more than "the people at the Help Desk who can reset passwords." Periodically, have a meeting with the other department heads. Let them know what you're doing in IT, what you've accomplished, and what you plan to do. With a little luck, light bulbs will start going off. They may see uses for the technology that you hadn't thought of. Get some good discussion going and you may learn a way to deliver a lot more value by modifying your plans slightly. See the section **"Sharing Information"** in **Chapter 10, Working with Users,** on **page 266.**

The reality is that in today's corporate world, IT departments are by default in the middle of action. Everyone is aware of the values that computerization can bring to an enterprise. Wineries, toy shops, bookstores, and sandwich places now have sophisticated computerized inventory systems, customer service mechanisms, online ordering components, and pay by mobile phone capabilities. Information technology is everywhere. (For a more detailed discussion of this complex issue, see the section **"Consumerization of IT"** in **Chapter 10, Working with Users** on **page 271** and **Chapter 11, Connectivity: Social Media, Handhelds, and More** on **page 287.**)

1.5 LEADERSHIP VERSUS MANAGEMENT

Before you became a manager, the word "management" was probably the focus of your career path. Now that you're a manager, "leadership" should be in your sights.

If you do a search on "leadership vs. management" you'll find lots of definitions and examples. However, the common theme is that a manager is generally focused on daily operations and meeting deadlines and budgets, whereas a leader is more of a visionary and strategic planner, someone who can transform an organization, who inspires and motivates. From another perspective, managers are focused on the *short term*, whereas leaders are focused on the *long term*. Table 1.2 describes the differences between leadership and management, and has been highly regarded as the definitive comparison for years

Of course, leadership and management are not mutually exclusive. Managers frequently have to show leadership in their roles, and leaders must have some management skills to ensure that their visions are realized. While there is an incredible volume of resources to help people become leaders, there are those for whom leadership comes naturally. Even at an early age some people show great capacity for leadership. Think about your own childhood: In all likelihood one of your friends (possibly even you) was the one the others followed (sometimes into trouble) and looked to—perhaps to decide how to spend a free day, resolve a dispute, or find the way out of a jam.

Table 1.2 Comparing Leadership and Management

	Management	Leadership
Creating an agenda	Planning and budgeting—establishing detailed steps and timetables for achieving needed results and then allocating the resources necessary to make that happen	Establishing direction—developing a vision of the future, often the distant future, and strategies for producing the changes needed to achieve that vision
Developing a network for achieving the goals	Organizing and staffing—establishing some structure for accomplishing plan requirements, staffing that structure with individuals, delegating responsibility and authority for carrying out the plan, providing policies and procedures to help guide people, and creating methods or systems to monitor implementation	Aligning people—communicating the direction by words and deeds to all those whose cooperation may be needed so as to influence the creation of teams and coalitions that understand the vision and strategies, and accept their validity
Execution	Controlling and problem solving—monitoring results vs. plan in some detail, identifying deviations, and then planning and organizing to solve these problems	Motivating and inspiring—energizing people to overcome major political, bureaucratic, and resource barriers to change by satisfying very basic, but often unfulfilled, human needs
Outcomes	Produces a degree of predictability and order and has the potential of consistently producing key results expected by various stakeholders (e.g., for customers—always being on time; for stockholders—being on budget)	Produces change, often to a dramatic degree, and has the potential of producing extremely useful change (e.g., new products that customers want, new approaches to labor relations that help make a firm more competitive)

Source: *Kotter, John P., A Force for Change, Free Press, 1990.*

1.6 STARTING YOUR NEW JOB

Taking on new responsibility is always a little scary, but if your company promotes you to a manager's role, you can take comfort in the familiar surroundings. You know the staff, you know the organization, you know the technical environment, and you know how things operate. Nonetheless, you have new sets of responsibilities, new expectations, and your relationships with others will change.

Changing companies *and* changing jobs, though, is a whole different animal. It immerses you in unfamiliar surroundings. Aside from the people who interviewed you, the only familiar things may be the technology products being used (and even some of those may not be too familiar).

As you first get settled, your boss will be looking for signs to confirm to him that he promoted or hired the right person. And you'll be trying to determine if you made the right decision in your career path. Whether your new job is at a new company or not, it's vital to start things properly.

The First Day

Even if you went through an extensive interview process, you probably spent less than eight hours talking with people at your new company, and most of that time was spent for them to learn about *you*. There was only a limited opportunity for you to learn about *them*. You're hoping that your gut instinct about the company and its people have led you to the right choice. Your boss is hoping that the person he met on the interview, and to whom he extended the offer, is the same person who shows up for work.

Don't be nervous. The first day in a new position isn't all that different from the first day at a new school and trying to figure out the lay of the land. (Remember the tension of those days?) You've got every reason to be nervous, but keep it to yourself. You want to demonstrate confidence. In fact, in a manner not too different from the interview, you want to show a combination of confidence (but not cockiness), and experience (but not a know-it-all attitude), enthusiasm (but not giddiness). And, a little humility in showing that you don't know everything, and welcoming help from others can go a long way. In short, it's a good idea to try and maintain your interview persona, perhaps relaxed just a notch, when you first start a new job. And remember, you won't be the only one who is a little nervous. Your staff is probably just as uneasy about getting a new boss.

Meeting the Staff

Unless you were told otherwise, it's probably safe to assume that your staff is like many other IT staffs with a healthy cross-section of technically brilliant people, socially challenged people, hard-working people, under-performers, and various combinations in between. To make things more complicated, your boss (demonstrating his professionalism) didn't give you his thoughts on individuals because he thought you should form your own opinions . . . and he's right.

Unless it was made clear to you at the outset that your staff is a serious problem, you can probably assume that you have not been hired just to "kick some butts," although you may determine later that some kicking is called for. Most likely you were hired to demonstrate leadership, professional maturity, management, and to provide direction.

On that first day, you'll be introduced to everyone, and in short order you'll forget their names, their faces, what they do, and where they sit. That's okay, that's normal. Hopefully, you were provided with the department's organizational chart; it can be a handy map to help you become familiar with your new surroundings.

If your new role is a promotion at your company, you'll be starting off with your own ideas about the staff. There may be some colleagues who you always thought were underappreciated and those that you thought should've been let go years ago. However, instead of having those thoughts as a mere coworker, you'll now be in a position of authority to act on those thoughts. Also, you may find that you look at the world differently (and it looks at you differently)—through the lens of management.

Those first days will give you a chance to talk to your staff, perhaps as a group. They'll be judging what you say and how you say it.

A Few Ideas for What to Say to Break the Ice

Whether these are people you've worked with for years or you're just meeting them for the first time, here are a few things you might bring up in that first meeting:

- A little bit about your background (last company and position you held, areas of IT you've worked in, different industries you've worked in)
- Some recent projects the group has completed (hopefully, if you've changed companies, you got this information from your new boss)
- Upcoming projects and challenges facing the group (again, information your new boss provided)
- What goals you have, and what areas are important to you (e.g., customer service, reliability of systems, documentation, etc.)
- Why you're excited to be part of this company, and your new role
- "My door is always open" (although don't say this if it isn't true)

Use these as a way to let them get a sense of who you are and what type of manager they can expect.

Some Don'ts

As much as you want to get those first days off to a good start, you also want to avoid doing anything that leaves a bad taste in anyone's mouth:

- Don't talk too much about yourself and your accomplishments. You're not trying to impress them, just give them a sense of who you are.
- Don't try to make them afraid of you or to make them love you. You want their respect.
- Don't say things you're not reasonably certain you can do. For example, don't say you want to get everyone trained and then discover that you have virtually no training budget.

Be careful, but don't stress too much over this. You only have to look at the news to see that everyone from celebrities, business executives, and politicians has had their share of gaffes and putting their foot in their mouth.

One-on-One Meetings

More important than the small talk when you get started, however, is having one-on-one meetings with your staff. Even if you have a very large organization that has several layers below you, you should try to meet everyone on your staff. You'll benefit from hearing everyone's perspective, and they'll be pleased that you took the time and effort to talk to them. In many cases, the act of simply having a chat can be of more value than anything specific that's discussed.

Even if they are people you've worked with for years, a chat like this is very worthwhile. It'll be the first time you will have a discussion with them as the new boss. It will help set the tone of the relationship going forward and can be a strong foundation for it.

Of course, some of those one-on-ones may prove to be challenging. Your direct reports are probably seasoned enough to have a "conversation." However, those from the lower ranks may be uncomfortable, scared, or just not great at holding a business conversation with the big boss (especially one they just met). Then again, some may really bend your ear.

If warranted, especially if you have a large team, you may want to meet some of the lower level staff in small groups. This may dilute the pressure that some of the quieter ones may feel.

Some Topics to Get the Conversational Ball Rolling
- How long have you been working here?
- Where were you before?
- What do you like best/least?
- What projects are you currently on, and what's your involvement?
- What are the best and worst things about the department/company?
- What's your function? Have you always been doing that?
- What areas, projects, or type of work would you like to get involved with?
- What do you think of the department?
- What needs to get done?
- Is there anything you'd like to ask me or tell me?
- What are your concerns?
- What are the areas that you think need improving?
- Do you have any ideas for those improvements?
- Do you have any advice for me?

The last question may elicit some surprise that you asked for advice, and you may be surprised by some of the things that you hear. But it will probably buy you some goodwill as it's an indirect way of saying that you don't have all the answers and that you are eager for other people's input and help. Since no one is going to expect you to remember everything, it's okay to take notes during these conversations. Not only will the notes help you later when you're trying to remember who said what, but it shows the staff that you care enough about what they say to write it down.

Remember to treat everyone with respect and professionalism.

What to Say to Those Who Wanted Your Job and Didn't Get It

It's almost certain that someone on your staff (maybe even a peer) wanted your job—some may have even actively campaigned for it. For those who didn't get the job, they may not have really wanted it (and just applied as an opportunity to gain some visibility and face time with decision makers) and may even feel relieved they didn't get it. For others, though, the emotions may still be strong.

Unfortunately, you may not learn until later who wanted your job, why they were denied the opportunity, and, most important, what (and how) they were told about why they didn't get it. In a worst-case scenario, they only learned that they didn't get it when they heard you were showing up to take that spot.

If you do know who applied for your job, you probably are better off not mentioning it to them directly. They may feel like you're rubbing salt in the wound. Also, even if you try to be sensitive, they may resent the sympathetic posture from the person who took the job they wanted—you certainly don't want to appear condescending or patronizing.

The emotions from these individuals can be a combination of resentment, depression, disappointment, and indifference. The best thing you can do is to treat everyone equally with respect and professionalism. Over time, they'll come to terms with their disappointment and focus on their jobs. If they don't, that will be a signal that it's time for a heart-to-heart conversation with them. This conversation doesn't need to be any different from any conversation a manager may need to have with an employee demonstrating performance or outlook problems, which are discussed in the section **"Disciplinary Problems and Terminations"** in **Chapter 2, Managing Your IT Team,** on **page 54**.

There is also a chance, hopefully very small, that one of the individuals may be so bitter that they are actually working *against* you. The smart person, although disappointed, should realize that their best approach is to align themselves with you so that they become your indispensable right-hand person. Invariably, anyone who tries to sabotage their new manager will end up losing in a number of ways:

- Squandering the opportunity to look good to the new manager
- Losing the confidence and trust of the new manager
- Showing that they aren't a team player

In some cases, one of these individuals may have been unofficially filling your role while the position was vacant. It might be a very good move for you to allow them to continue doing some of the tasks that they had taken on—running some meetings, leading some projects, etc. If you let them know that you respect and value what they do, that you want to work with them, and that you're not going to take things away from them just because you're the new big boss, you'll be sending a very strong message about the type of person you are.

How you deal with individuals and individual circumstances is often a tough judgment call. But exercising judgment is pretty much what your job is about. How you deal with people who applied for the job you have now might be one of your first big challenges, and one of your first big opportunities, as a new manager.

Establish a Relationship with Your Manager and Your Peers

There are two key factors that can ensure a successful relationship with your new boss:

- Knowing what she expects from you
- Earning her trust that those expectations will be met

Both take time, and you can expect occasional missed signals or miscommunications along the way. Things to look out for include:

- Does she prefer e-mail, telephone, or in-person communications?
- What are her priorities: projects, technologies, certain applications or specific user groups?
- Does she prefer constant updates on details or just periodic status reports on the big picture?
- Does she like to get right down to business or does she enjoy a little casual conversation?
- What did she like most (and least) about the last person in your role?
- Is she more impressed with form or function?

- Is she focused on process or metrics?
- Is she involved with her staff, the mood of the department, etc.?
- Is she focused on building an empire and her own status and growth or is she just focused on doing the best job possible?
- Are her decisions based on raw data, judgment calls, or input from her staff?
- Is she a consensus builder?
- Is she more focused on strategy or operations?
- Does she make quick decisions and judgments or does she like to form opinions over a period of time?
- Does she have a very formalized project management methodology or does she prefer the "let's just get it done" approach?
- What is her own boss like? What is her relationship with her management—do you know what they expect of her?

Keep in mind that while you're figuring out how to deal with a new manager, your new staff is doing exactly the same thing with you. This frame of mind can help you keep some perspective about the dynamics of the situation.

Remember, your new manager wants you to succeed. When you succeed, it makes her life easier by having a winner working for her. Also, it makes her look good that she hired a good manager. You have a built-in ally.

In a similar vein, your peers (your fellow managers) also want you to succeed. They might have been frustrated that your team hasn't had much direction and leadership without a manager, and might have atrophied while there was a vacancy. They may also be a little bit more forthcoming about the weaknesses they see in your team's members and operations. They can also give you some insight into the culture of the department, your boss, the company, hot-button projects, and issues.

Just like you need to do with your boss, you'll want to build relationships with your peers, demonstrate that they can count on you, and that you're eager for their guidance and input as you get settled. You don't have to take all their guidance and input at face value, but there can be great value in listening to it.

Learning the Landscape: Key Users and Key Applications

If your new role is in a new company, there's a lot you don't know about your new environment, and the sooner you start closing the gap, the better off you'll be. Even if you're at the same company, you have to look at these issues with a new perspective.

The first thing you may want to know is who your key users are and what the key applications and systems are. Depending on the industry you're in, the answers could differ considerably. If you're working for a law firm, the key applications may be the document management system and the system for recording billable hours. In a manufacturing plant, the key applications probably revolve around the supply chain.

You also want to learn some basic information about the environment, some of which may have come out when you were interviewed.

- How many locations does the company have?
- How many users are there at each location?

- How large is the technical environment (e.g., number of servers, amount of storage, number of applications, size of the network)?
- What are the company's policies towards personal e-mail, cell phones, tablets, etc.?
- What are the key applications?
- Is it staffed 24/7? If not, how is after-hours support handled?
- Is IT distributed or centralized?
- What are the compliance requirements?
- Historically, where have the major problem spots been?
- Who are the key vendors and partners?
- Is there any documentation about policies and procedures and current projects?
- What are the high-level technology standards (messaging, development tools, database, storage, hardware, operating systems, etc.)?

Find the Key Meetings

Invariably, IT is involved in numerous regularly scheduled meetings—weekly, biweekly, monthly, etc. Some may strictly be for ITers, some may be with the users or other department heads, and some may be situations where IT is simply an invited guest.

Start asking around about these meetings and joining in. It sounds strange to ask around for meetings to attend (many people prefer to go to as few meetings as they can), but many meetings are critical. You'll find that some you'll want to attend regularly, some occasionally, and some not at all. Some you'll be invited to and some you'll have to wangle your way in. Meetings are also an excellent way to increase your visibility. A well thought-out and insightful question or comment, as opposed to just asking if there can be sandwiches at the next meeting, can speak volumes about you.

If meeting minutes and agendas are available (a worthwhile idea that is often overlooked), it can help you determine which meetings you need to be involved in.

Be Realistic about Timetables for Fixing Problems

Chances are that you'll notice problems more than you'll notice things that are going well. That's okay, it's just human nature. The important thing is to not feel overwhelmed by the problems. No one is expecting you to fix the world in your first week, or even your first month.

When starting a new job, it's very tempting to refer to the way things were done at your last job, especially if you're proposing it as some sort of example for your new company. Coworkers will quickly get tired of hearing it, and they'll invariably think "if your last job was so great, why did you leave?" You can propose the same ideas, but be careful about referring to your old job too often.

SOME FIRST-DAY-AT-WORK WAR STORIES

The following are true stories from various employees' first days on the job:

The Employee Got Surprised

- "A senior level technical director joined our company and had four direct reports and 10 more indirects. He assumed his job was to manage his team. However, the culture of our company was such that every engineer was expected to write code, including the CTO on occasion. It was a huge source of tension in the company and eventually the CTO asked the new director to leave. It never occurred to him to ask in the interview if he needed to code, since he had not done that in years."

Continued

SOME FIRST-DAY-AT-WORK WAR STORIES—Cont'd

- "A senior-level, reports-to-the-CEO type took a job after a series of interviews at the swanky downtown office. When he showed up for the work the first day, he was informed his office was located down the street at one of the manufacturing plants. The job went downhill from there."
- "Shortly after starting a new job I learned that my predecessor had quit after six weeks. Had I known that, I might not have taken the job to begin with. I kept wondering what he had uncovered in those first few weeks that made him decide to leave so abruptly. But I was there for six years."
- "I reported for work on Monday morning and the manager who had hired me had been fired between the time I last spoke with him and when I started work! Fortunately, my new boss turned out to be a great guy, and everything worked out, but I was very surprised that first day."

The Company Got Surprised

- "Back when ITers ruled the day, an engineer left her job and joined our company because the distance between her house and our company was exactly the distance she wanted to ride a bike every day. She had several other offers, but our 'roundtrip' distance fit the bill."
- "We made an offer to an engineer and he accepted. We then sent him the employee agreement to sign and he refused the job. He did a lot of coding on the side and was concerned that the employee agreement was worded in such a way that the company might be able to lay claim to his work in the future. (We tried to convince him otherwise but he didn't want to take the chance.)"

Everyone Came Out Ahead

- "A very good friend of mine took a job with a company because they said they would help finance his green card. And they did: they paid thousands of dollars and many man hours getting it done. In return, he stayed with them for 15 years and was a very loyal employee."

—Michele Robinson (and others)
Account Manager, 14 years

As you can see, sometimes things go as planned, or go better or worse than planned—it's to be expected.

1.7 THE FIRST 100 DAYS
No Organization Is Perfect

In the first few weeks (and perhaps months) on the job, you'll start to learn about things that might seem a little unusual. There could be strange reporting relationships (inside and outside of IT), odd standards, inconsistencies in centralized/decentralized policies, unusual job descriptions, people with titles that don't match their jobs (like the programmer with 20+ years of service with a manager's title, yet who doesn't manage anyone), overlaps of some areas, gaps in others, some things are overly complicated while others are overly simplified, and some divisions are wholly owned while some are only partially owned.

People who have worked there for a while will probably admit that certain things don't make complete sense. If you've worked there for a while, you may already be aware of some of these and their backgrounds. Certain corporate peculiarities may have a long and embedded history. Other situations may be the result of an errant decision made by an executive who won't admit the mistake, and as soon as he leaves, it'll be put back to "normal." Other conditions may warrant changing, but the hurdles (effort, time, political, cost) aren't necessarily worth it right now. But take note of these situations so that you don't lose sight of them and can begin developing a plan.

There probably are reasons for everything that seems odd or strange. They may not be very good reasons, but those are the reasons nonetheless. The important thing is to show flexibility and adaptability. If these are the way things are, then you simply have to work within that framework (at least at the start). You won't be judged for what you inherited, but you will be judged by how you deal with it.

The oddities you want to focus on are the ones in your department, the ones you have control over. But don't feel you need to correct everything your first week, or first month. They've probably been that way for years, and things will survive a little longer as you investigate why they're that way, and the risk and impact of changing things.

Quietly Advertising What You Bring to the Table

It's never a good idea to try and impress people right away—showing up on the job with a know-it-all attitude and boasting about what you've done before and what you'll do next. Let your results and actions speak for you. Still, there are subtle things you can do when you first get started to give people the sense that the company hired the right person. Professional courtesies and maturity can go a long way.

- Speak the language of your company and its users, and not of IT (i.e., talk in business terms, not technical jargon)
- Maintain a positive attitude
- Maintain open and effective communications
- Show up to appointments and meetings on time
- Treat everyone with professionalism and respect
- Recognize the difference between moving mountains and molehills
- Ask insightful questions (and be sure to *listen* to the responses)
- Try to convey a sense of perspective about time, which issues need to be addressed now and which can wait to be looked into later
- Return e-mail and voice-mail messages promptly
- Write professional and succinct e-mails and memos
- Take notes during meetings
- Follow through on your promises and commitments
- Deal with assigned tasks quickly and effectively

Do Some Preliminary Research before You Start

You can also show that you've done your homework. During the interview process you've probably learned some things about the IT department: which vendors they use, which project they're working on, which projects are coming up, etc. Doing some research on those things (as well as the new company itself) can be worthwhile. Check out vendor websites and trade journals. You'll never know when you might have the opportunity to subtly drop a nugget of information into a conversation that will let people know that you have some knowledge to share.

Bring a Fresh Perspective

In addition to your skills and experience, you bring something to the job that no one else at your new company can—the objectivity that comes with a fresh set of eyes. Take advantage of that. Of course, you don't want to use it to question the wisdom and reason of *everything* at your new job, but you may see things in a way others haven't before. There may be very good reasons, which a newcomer would have no idea about, for things being the way they are, but learning about them will give you a better understanding of the environment.

Be on the lookout for areas and activities that seem to be ignored or overlooked because no one wants to do them. Those are great opportunities to volunteer and show what you can do, especially if they are in an area you excel at or enjoy. For example, if cost/benefit analysis needs to be done, volunteering to do it is a great way to force yourself to become immersed in the topic. Similarly, if you're a wiz at Microsoft Project, and everyone else hates doing project plans, your expertise will be appreciated, you'll become fully versed on the project, and it's a great opportunity for you to begin to take on the project's management (which is probably what you were hired to do anyway).

The first few months on a new job are often known as the "honeymoon period." In the corporate world, this could be a period of less political maneuvering and less-demanding/more-forgiving colleagues. Usually, people will give you greater latitude during the start of your new job. The honeymoon period is a result of others (1) wanting to make sure you get off to a good start, (2) not holding you accountable things for you just inherited, and (3) recognizing that new people bring new ideas that often prove worthwhile. You may be able to take advantage of this to introduce your fresh perspective, and to gain some leverage for implementing change.

Ask and Listen

Don't forget that you can earn a lot of respect by asking good questions, and that asking insightful questions usually comes from effective listening. By asking the right questions, you can show that you're astute, that you've got the right perspective on things, and that you have some sort of understanding of the topic at hand.

The challenge is in knowing which questions are the right ones to ask. Asking how much the company reimburses for meals in a discussion about an important team trip to a remote site shows your priorities aren't right. Questioning the value of user-acceptance testing on a project shows you're not really interested in quality and like to take shortcuts whenever you can. However, asking about a back-out plan if a proposed change fails shows that you consider all contingencies. Asking about security, especially in today's environment, and about performance are always safe bets.

Projects in Progress and Projects on the Horizon

Projects will probably be a big part of your life (which is why we dedicated all of **Chapter 4** to **Project Management** on **page 103**). Every job has projects mixed in with all the day-to-day activities. Some projects are so small it's barely worth calling them projects, whereas others are so large that they often are several sizeable sub-projects rolled into one.

One of your first priorities in your new role should be to learn about existing projects and those coming up in the very near future. You should be asking everyone you meet (staff, boss, peers, department heads, etc.) about their particular projects. There's a good chance that in one way or another, you'll be involved in them soon.

Projects exist for a variety of reasons, and most of all because they are important to someone. Maybe they're important to you or your boss, maybe they're important to the CEO. Either way, by learning about the project activity, you get a sense of where the priorities are for individuals as well as the department and company.

Some of these projects may fall squarely on your shoulders, and you may find that you're the (unofficial) Project Manager. Some of your staff may be leading projects, and your involvement can vary depending on how well you determine they're being run. Other projects may just have you as a team member, perhaps playing a very large role or perhaps a very small role.

Whether you're forced to take ownership of a project, or simply sit in on some meetings, projects are an excellent way to quickly become knowledgeable about what's going on, meet others in the organization, be involved, and allow others to see why you were hired.

Is the Status Quo Good Enough?

Just because there aren't any complaints doesn't mean that things are "good enough." The lack of complaints may simply mean that people have grown tired of complaining and have just given up. You and your department should always strive to be better. Of course, "better" may have different meanings:

- Better Service Level Agreements (SLAs)
- Faster transactions
- Greater regulatory compliance
- More thorough documentation
- Higher system availability
- Better reliability
- Improved morale
- Fewer errors
- Processes with fewer steps
- Better communication with the user community

You certainly weren't chosen for this role to make things worse, and they probably wouldn't have selected you if all they needed was someone to keep things as they are. It's important to remember that making things better is often an *iterative* process, where a few changes now are followed by additional changes down the road, each contributing a little bit toward overall improvement.

For example, there are a number of things you can do to increase the up time of a database:

- Keep the database software up to date with vendor patches and fixes
- Run periodic recommended database maintenance procedures
- Stay abreast of suggestions and guidelines from the vendors (hardware, database, OS) on best practices
- Ensure that the database server doesn't have other applications running on it, which can increase the chances of crashes
- Keep the server's operating system up to date with vendor patches and fixes

Each of these steps can improve the reliability of the database to various degrees. Taken together, they may significantly improve the uptime statistics.

You may find that a similar approach works best in improving the overall performance of your department. Although there may be a small number of things that can be changed to have a big impact, your focus should also be on the continual process of small improvements that chip away at problem areas. From your perspective as a manager, it's sometimes very difficult to see changes on a day-to-day or week-to-week basis. You frequently have to look back over a period of months, or sometimes a year, and ask "remember when we used to . . . ?"

People to Meet and Know

At this point you're busy developing relationships with your staff, your peers, and your boss, but it doesn't end there. There are many people you should establish relationships with. It's a good idea to start collecting names and setting up introductory meetings with key people you'll be working with. Your boss, your peers, and even your staff can offer some names. If you were promoted into your new role without changing companies, you may already know many of these names. You may even have relationships with many of them, but you now need to forge those relationships from the perspective of the IT Manager.

Some areas you'll want to be sure to connect with include:

- **Key user areas:** Find out which areas are most dependent on IT and the services IT provides. Meet with those department heads, learn how they use IT, when they have their busiest periods, etc. Examples may include marketing and sales, accounting, HR, and manufacturing departments.
- **Senior executives:** It's always a good idea to have a strong relationship with upper management. Learn which ones are big proponents of IT and which have the worst experiences with IT. In addition to building a good rapport with executives, you should do the same with their assistants.
- **Human resources:** As described later in the section (**"Human Resource Issues"** on **page 25**), you'll probably quickly discover many HR issues. Find out who in HR you can work with to review different situations.
- **Finance and accounting:** IT often has one of the largest departmental budgets. You'll want to have someone to partner with in accounting to help you deal with budgeting issues, chargebacks, forecasting, tracking spending, etc. IT budgeting is discussed in depth in **Chapter 6, Managing the Money** on **page 161**.
- **Procurement:** IT has a large budget because it buys a lot of expensive hardware, software, and services, and all that buying generally goes through a formal procurement process. In some organizations, IT purchases go through the company's general Procurement group. In other organizations, IT purchases may be done directly by the IT team. If the former, you'll want to form a strong relationship with the Procurement group to make sure your orders are handled quickly and accurately. If the latter, find out how your own procurement process operates.
- **Legal:** With that large budget and all that purchasing come a lot of paperwork and contracts with an awful lot of legalese. Whether it's a maintenance contract or a volume agreement with a vendor, you'll be working with the company's Legal department to wade through it all.
- **Audit:** In all likelihood, especially if yours is a publicly traded company or if you work in a heavily regulated industry (e.g., finance, health care), you'll be doing a lot of work with your internal audit team, sometimes referred to as the Risk Management group. This is a result of the ever-increasing scrutiny and demand for integrity in the IT professional in recent times. **Chapter 8, Security and Compliance** on **page 205** details some of the topics that may have you working very closely with your Audit team.

Quick Introductory Meetings

Introductory meetings can be as short as 10 minutes or as long as an hour (usually it's dependent on how much either of you enjoys talking). You can start off by saying up front that you don't have a particular agenda and that you're simply in the process of meeting key people in the company to establish relationships. Ideally, it's best if you can go into these meetings with some background; for example, perhaps recent experiences (either good or bad) that this individual or department has had with IT or upcoming projects you know you'll be working on together.

More than likely, the people you meet with will ask you about your background, how you like your new role so far, and similar questions. They'll probably be reasonably honest, but polite, about their opinions of IT. As you meet with all the different people, you may begin to see a pattern emerge that tells you what kind of reputation your department has in the organization. This information can prove to be very valuable in figuring out where the strong and weak spots are.

Human Resource Issues

In short order, you'll start to learn about the HR problems that you'll be facing. Some you may have known about, others you may sense by intuition, but in all likelihood most of them will be brought directly to you, perhaps by your staff, the HR department, your boss and peers, and maybe even from the user community. **Chapter 2, Managing Your IT Team** on **page 31**, has further discussion about this subject.

Some of your staff will be delighted to bring their pet issues to you, in hopes that a new manager will finally take care of things. Some things to be on the lookout for are:

- Staff who are unhappy with their job, title, or salary
- Those who are unhappy with their cubicle or office
- Employees who think they are being treated unfairly compared to others
- Issues of racial or sexual discrimination
- Staff who think some of their coworkers aren't pulling their weight
- Individuals who feel their contributions aren't being recognized
- Employees who feel that they should be much further along in their career given their experience, education, certifications, etc.
- Coworkers who simply can't get along

As you become aware of these issues, it's important that you listen objectively and effectively. Repeating what someone has said in your own words works well since it shows them that you heard what they said. Ask questions about the situation and take good notes about what you're being told.

Soon, Later, and Tomorrow: When Should You Address Issues

Some issues may not require much follow-up aside from continued observation. For example, if an employee says he didn't get the rating he deserved on his last review, there's not much you can do about that as a new manager. However, you can promise the employee that you will judge everyone fairly and objectively when you do performance reviews.

Other issues may require some follow-up. For example, if an employee says that he should have an office instead of cubicle, you can check with HR to see what the policy is. Maybe the employee is in a position that doesn't merit an office, and you can explain the company policy. Perhaps they do merit an office, but there may not be one available right now. You can promise that offices will go to eligible employees, in order of seniority, when the space is available.

Some issues will require a longer term effort to deal with. If there are complaints about inequities in titles and salaries, for example, you may find that you agree with the people raising the issue. But correcting things of this nature will take time, careful planning, and perhaps some organizational upheaval.

Regardless of What Happens, Let Them Know You've Heard Them

The important things to remember as HR issues come your way are that each person deserves to know that they have your attention and that they each deserve a response. It may not always be a response that they like, but they each deserve one. You certainly don't want to earn a reputation in your first weeks that you ignore things. You can promise the team that if they bring you an issue, you will get them an answer, but they need to know that sometimes getting that answer may take time, and sometimes that answer may be no.

Budgeting

One of the less exciting and less interesting parts of your job, but important enough to get its own chapter (see **Chapter 6, Managing the Money,** on **page 161**), is IT budgeting. Few departments will spend more money than IT, and it's important that you become knowledgeable about your department budget. Since you aren't likely to be held entirely responsible for a budget you didn't create, you don't have to start sweating over it right off—you'll probably be given some leeway.

The easiest way to get started is to get a copy of your department's current budget. Then you'll want to ask Accounting for a report that indicates how much money your department is actually spending. By glancing at these reports you can quickly see which categories are the largest portions of the IT budget (and perhaps require the most scrutiny) and see where the biggest differences are between the actual spending history and what was budgeted. Make sure Accounting knows that you want to get *all* the budget reports for your department.

In general, you won't be expected to explain every dollar. However, you will want to learn about those items that have the biggest impact on IT budgets and items with significant changes from year to year.

As you learn about the budget you inherited, you should be thinking about next year's budget—the one you'll be responsible for preparing, presenting, defending, and adhering to. As is typical, each year's budget is compared to the previous year's. It's important that you make note of which items might go up so that you can explain them.

Making Those First Decisions

There's a saying that "20 percent of life is what happens to you and that 80 percent is how you deal with it." Another way to look at it is that your success is not much more than the cumulative results of the decisions you make.

Some decisions may be easy: "Can I leave a little early today?" Others could be more difficult: "Accounting is working on closing the books and won't allow any downtime, but we need to take their database off line to run a maintenance routine to prevent it from getting corrupted."

Anytime you make a decision, you want to make sure that it's based on sound reasoning that you can later defend if necessary. You may get faulted for making a bad decision, but if it's based on reasoned thinking, you can hold your head up with pride.

The first thing you need to do is make sure that you fully understand what the problem is, what the implications are, and the impact of the various alternatives. Those who bring the problem to you may provide some options, and you may have some of your own. You may want to run the issue by other people on your team to see if they have a different perspective.

Depending on what's involved, you may want to alert key people outside of IT, either to make them aware of the situation (such as the users) or to involve them in the resolution (such as the head of Accounting in the example given earlier).

Sometimes, the decision-making process is easier if you think about having to explain/defend the worst-case scenarios for each alternative—if it should happen. For example:

- Your database server crashed and it's taken seven hours to restore. To be certain that the restored database is 100 percent functional, you should run an integrity check utility, but that will take another three hours. Do you run the integrity check and sentence the users to another three hours of downtime or just hope for the best and bring the database online as soon as it's restored?
- If you don't run the integrity check, you risk the database being down for an additional 10 hours (seven hours to restore again and three hours to run the integrity check you decided against the first time). If you do run the integrity check, you have to explain why you decided against bringing it online as soon as possible.
- Many people might be willing to take the risk by rolling the dice and not running the integrity check, especially if they have reason to believe it may prove to be unnecessary. However, many of those people will also change their mind when asked if they are ready to explain their decision to senior management if they end up being wrong.

You want to appear confident and calm as you approach key decisions. These traits are important because they are contagious. If others see you keeping your cool, they'll probably do the same.

1.8 TWO IT DEPARTMENTS—WHAT HAPPENS IF YOUR COMPANY MERGES WITH ANOTHER?

Mergers and acquisitions are pretty common events in the business sector. They come in all shapes and sizes from mutually agreed upon merger plans to hostile takeover scenarios.

Any sort of organization merger or acquisition can have an enormous impact on the IT department, and you as its manager. Until it is complete, there are two IT teams—each with its own processes, standards, vendors, technologies, and culture.

With luck, your company has included you in the high-level planning for the merger. This lets you, as the IT Manager, learn about the other company's IT department. You'll then be able to report to your management and advise them as to what type of effort might be involved to join two teams, systems, and environments into one.

From an IT perspective, there are generally three ways to go about merging another company's IT environment. The path you choose may depend on your company's management style (e.g., centralized vs. decentralized), available resources, economic and market conditions, timetables, regulatory issues, and so on.

1. **Brute force.** This amounts to rebuilding everything at one company that isn't compatible with the other. This approach usually results in a shock to the system of the acquired company and its IT department. It's pretty painful, but is often the fastest way of getting the two companies integrated and operating as one. Usually, the first technology addressed is e-mail, followed by business applications, user support, operations, OS and database platforms, and networks. This process also

includes evaluating procedures and vendors. The brute-force approach won't be successful unless the appropriate authority and mandate from senior management are in place to see it through, along with the necessary budget and staffing resources. Expect a bumpy ride, culture clashes, and some staff turnover.

2. **Leave them alone.** The opposite extreme would be to just leave the other company as is. Your company may have a culture of decentralization or divisional autonomy that supports this kind of posture, or perhaps your company bought this other organization because they are lean, fast-paced, and profitable and may not want to tamper with that success. In fact, your management may hope that the parent becomes more like the adopted child, and not vice versa. In a case like this you may not need to do much more than add the acquired company's addresses into your e-mail system and establish some basic connectivity. Regardless, make sure you contact the other company's IT Manager to establish and maintain a relationship. Share with her information about resources your organization may have (e.g., staff expertise, volume purchase agreements) that she may want to take advantage of. The more you share with her, the more she's likely to share with you.

3. **Phased integration.** This is the obvious compromise path. In a case like this, you work with the IT Manager of the other company to set future milestone project manager targets, each of which brings you closer to full integration. Depending on the circumstances of the two companies, they may set common (and integrated) goals, but take different paths to get there.

No matter what the situation, it's vital to remember that what may have been the right choices for one of the companies in the past may not be the right choices for the unified organization. Equally important is that just because the acquired company is in the subordinate position doesn't mean they have nothing to offer—each can learn from the other. An emotional attachment to a technology or product limits your perspective and can backfire. At times like this, those who can demonstrate an ability to adapt to change will be the most successful.

1.9 Further References

Websites

careerplanning.about.com/cs/firstjob/a/new_job.htm (first-day tips from about.com).

www.amanet.org/index.htm (American Management Association).

www.asktheheadhunter.com/hastartjob.htm (tips from a headhunter about starting a job on the right foot).

www.bls.gov/oco (Occupational Outlook Handbook, Bureau of Labor Statistics, U.S. Department of Labor).

www.kornferryinstitute.com/files/pdf1/KFceo_whtppr_jan30.pdf (survey about senior management terminations).

www.managementhelp.org (library of resources for managers).

www.networkworld.com/news/2010/061010-job-growth-salaries.html (article on IT job growth).

www.techamerica.org (IT industry association).

Books and Articles

Bradt, G.B., Check, J.A., Pedraza, J.E., 2009. The New Leader's 100-Day Action Plan: How to Take Charge, Build Your Team, and Get Immediate Results. Wiley.

Daft, R.L., 2011. Management. South-Western College Pub.

Grimme, D., Grimme, S., 2008. The New Manager's Tool Kit: 21 Things You Need to Know to Hit the Ground Running. AMACOM.

Kotter, J.P., 1990. A Force for Change. Free Press.

Labadie, R., 2007. Hi! I'm Your New Manager! You're New—They're Not! So What Happens Now? AuthorHouse.

Murray, A., 2010. The Wall Street Journal Essential Guide to Management: Lasting Lessons from the Best Leadership Minds of Our Time. Harper Books.

Pettibone, T., 2009. The first 100 Days on the Job. Baseline Magazine March.

Pratt, M.K., 2008. IT Careers: 5 Tips for Charting Your 100 Day Plan. Computerworld October 28.

Tynan, K., 2010. Survive Your Promotion! The 90 Day Success Plan for New Managers. Personal Focus Press.

Weinstein, M., 2011. Mixing Business and IT. CIO Insight Magazine May/June.

Winters, G.C., 2010. What Your Boss Never Told You: The Quick Start Guide for New Managers. CreateSpace.

Zenger, J., 2010. The Complete New Manager. McGraw-Hill.

Managing Your IT Team

The best executive is one who has sense enough to pick good people to do what he wants them to do, and self-restraint enough to keep from meddling with them while they do it.

Teddy Roosevelt

CHAPTER TABLE OF CONTENTS

2.1 **Keeping Employees Focused** 32
2.2 **Employee Training**..39
2.3 **Employee Performance** 43
2.4 **Generational Issues at Work** 57
2.5 **Further References** 62

Even with the advanced functionality available in today's hardware and software, the human factor is still the biggest influence on how effectively technology is used in your environment. The members of your IT team are the ones who will select, implement, configure, monitor, and manage the technology in your corporation. The technologies in place are only as good as the people using them—that applies to both the end-users and the IT team.

The technology products in your environment behave in a fairly predictable manner, but people oftentimes don't. Managing a staff is an art, not a science.

The importance of managing a team can't be emphasized enough:

- Become a great manager and you've found a career path and skill that will serve you well for the rest of your life—both in and out of the workplace.
- Fail to manage well and you may find that your potential growth with the organization is limited at best.
- Become good at it, and it becomes your most valuable skill, and your staff and department become a critical component and vital asset of the organization.
- Without good staff management skills, you'll see your department's goals and objectives become an uphill battle, and you and your team's value to the organization will be questioned.

2.1 KEEPING EMPLOYEES FOCUSED

IT Managers must set clear priorities, explain the company and department mission, and communicate often with their team. Throughout this book, specific techniques are detailed to provide you with methods to accomplish these goals.

Establish Priorities

One of the most important, but often unnoticed, functions of a manager is to set priorities; these can include actions such as allocating staffing and funding to various projects, provisioning of technical resources (such as hardware), setting of deadlines, and so on. Employees who spend months working on a project often wonder what exactly it is that their manager does. In truth, the manager is doing one of the most important parts of his job by deciding *which* projects get worked on, *when* they need to start and finish, and *what* resources are assigned to them. A manager's real worth is in his ability to set goals and objectives, set priorities, make decisions, and manage and motivate the team to achieve them.

Setting goals and priorities means managing your staff and your team so that their work reflects, as close as possible, your own priorities. Those priorities should, in turn, reflect those of the organization. (See the section **"Company Mission, Vision, and Values"** on **page 34** in this chapter about the company's mission, as well as in **Chapter 1**, **The Role of an IT Manager**, the section **"Developing an IT Strategy"** on **page 10**.) A manager's merit is found in his staff's work. Of course, your decisions and priorities may be totally off-base or they may be 100 percent on target. But if you fail to manage your staff well, the quality of your priorities will not matter: Your goals and objectives will never be achieved anyway.

Communicate with Your Team

First and foremost, communicate your vision for the department to your staff. They should understand both where you want the department to go and the plans you have for getting there. Both are important. You don't want to be the manager who makes the trains run on time, but doesn't know what to put in the freight cars. Similarly, you don't want to be the manager who talks on and on about the wonders of train travel but never gets the tracks put down.

The communication of your goals and priorities to your team is vital. The way you communicate with them will vary with a project's scope. A two-year project to implement an Enterprise Resource Planning (ERP) application will require different communication than managing a weekend effort to upgrade the company's database servers.

The following guidelines can be used when communicating with your team.

Make Sure the Team Understands the Overall Objective and Goals

Explain it in practical terms; for example: "implementing a new accounts payable system will eliminate all manual processes and hard-copy documents, thereby reducing turnaround time to 24 hours, and ensuring that no unauthorized payments are made."

Explain How You Envision Achieving the Goal

You don't have to offer too much detail, especially on a large project, but you should have some thoughts, visions, and ideas you can articulate as a type of road map. "Our first milestone is the end of February; by then we should have a prototype system for the users to look at. By mid-year we should have finalized all the details. We're looking to plan for parallel testing in the fourth quarter, with the final cut-over set for December 31st."

Encourage Questions and Input from Your Staff

There are several reasons why you should do this:

- Asking for your staff's input (and taking it seriously) will make your team feel like they are involved and a part of the decision-making process; they will work better and harder on a process they feel a part of and understand.
- They are a lot closer to the work than you are—they'll be the first to recognize an opportunity, a potential landmine, or a dead end.
- The group will usually have important insights to share.

If the goal or plan is especially challenging, or perhaps it deviates somewhat from the company norm, you'll have to be that much more motivating and enthusiastic when you communicate with the team.

Ask questions of the team to ensure that they have an appropriate understanding of the project. For example:

- How do you think we should start?
- Where do you see danger zones and areas of risk?
- What are the key milestones?
- What kinds of resources do you think we will need?
- Who else in the company do you think might help?

Listen Carefully

Listening is more than just hearing the words. Notice the staff's comments, tone, and body language. Use these as clues to determine if your team is buying in and is behind you. This can be more of a challenge with team members who are remote. With remote team members, consider drawing them out more than you usually do to ensure you feel confident about their thinking. And consider using available tools besides e-mail and phone calls (instant messaging, web-cams and video-conferencing, social networking tools, web-conferencing) for greater interaction, and to help build a stronger relationship with them. Make sure everyone feels free to air any doubts or concerns. One technique is to go around the table at the end of each meeting and to ask each member to express any concerns they have and then address them accordingly. Another is to encourage the staff to call, send e-mails, or meet with you privately (before or after the meeting) if they feel intimidated by speaking in front of a group.

Make sure you provide some guidance to your team as to when they should bring something to your attention. Some managers prefer hearing about every detail, some want to hear only items at higher levels, and others want to know only when there are big problems or exceptions.

Meet Regularly

Meeting frequencies might vary depending on the work at hand. Weekly and monthly meetings are common. During critical project times, it isn't uncommon to have daily meetings. You can have too many meetings or too few—it depends on the project. Try to establish a rhythm that people can work with; if you establish a meeting time of every Friday morning, the team will work throughout the week with that in mind.

Meetings don't have to always be project-oriented. Regular department meetings, as well as individual meetings, with your direct reports can help foster a culture of open communication and sharing of information.

Agile Meetings

Agile is a software development methodology. Different "flavors" of Agile have daily meetings, often called "stand-ups" or "scrums," as critical components of their methodology. The primary idea is to radically increase communication but in much briefer formats; they are called "stand-ups" for a reason—people tend to ramble less when they have to stand up the entire meeting.

Project Meetings

Project meetings are a separate type of meeting that have both additional benefits and potential problems. For a fuller discussion of project management, see **Chapter 4, Project Management** on **page 103**. Also in that chapter see the section **"Productive Project Meetings"** on **page 128** for specific ideas on improving the quality of your project meetings.

Company Mission, Vision, and Values

Another method of keeping your employees focused is to clearly outline the company's mission, vision, and values. These terms can be confusing or off-putting to technical personnel, but they have an important role to play in the success of your organization. Devote a little time to understanding and following them and you will be rewarded many times over. All of these can provide helpful guidance and criteria when making operational and strategic decisions.

- A **mission statement** explains the fundamental purpose of the company or organization. It concentrates on the objectives for the present, who the customer is, and what the critical processes are. Starbuck's mission statement includes the phrase: "Apply the highest standards of excellence to the purchasing, roasting and fresh delivery of our coffee."
- A **vision statement** takes the mission statement to the next level by outlining what the organization wants to be. The vision statement focuses on the future and serves as a source of inspiration for employees. Starbuck's vision statement includes the phrase: "To establish Starbucks as the most recognized and respected brand in the world."
- **Company values:** Some companies place their highest value on customer service, or integrity and honesty. Some may have shareholder return (which is often a euphemism for profitability) as a priority. Many companies' value statements include references to being "green," or giving back to the community, etc. Starbucks' site includes the phrase "[being] dedicated to serving ethically sourced coffee, caring for the environment and giving back to the communities where we do business."

Defining and articulating the company's mission, vision, and values shouldn't be your responsibility as an IT Manager; someone else should be doing that for you (and the rest of the company). But once your company has a mission statement, communicate it to your staff. Make it clear how the company's mission, vision, and values will impact your group's projects, assignments, priorities, and contributions. Also, explain how your team's efforts will support the company's mission, vision, and values.

Company values are a means you should use to keep your employees on the right track. If your company hasn't made its values clear, ask your management to do so. Again, defining and communicating company values aren't your job; you can participate if a company-wide committee is formed, but you should not have to come up with these on your own. "Company values" are defined by the entire company and can be useful guides in determining employee behavior. They typically include statements such as "taking care of our people: The key to our success is treating people well. We do this by encouraging associates to speak up and take risks, by recognizing and rewarding good performance and by leading and developing people so they may grow" (corporate.homedepot.com).

In addition to communicating the company's mission, goals, and values to your team, it's also vital that you share with them *the goals and values of the IT department*, objectives that should reflect both the company's mission and your own goals and values. Coming up with the goals and values of the IT department is something you should do collaboratively with your team. Solicit their ideas and let them review and comment on drafts. You may want to even have the team take the first cut at putting these together by asking for volunteers for a small committee to develop them for your review.

Be as Clear as Possible about Your Real Priorities

It takes more than just stating that something is a priority for everyone on a team to realize that it is a priority. If coding a specific interface is a critical task for a larger project, you have to say so, but also remember that your actions can dilute your words. If you rarely ask about the status of the interface, or only one person is assigned to work on it part-time, even though you say it is a priority, you'll be sending mixed signals. You can demonstrate the task's importance by focusing on it during meetings, reallocating additional resources to it, sacrificing lesser priorities for it, and so on.

Avoid Burnout in Your Employees

With IT so critical to today's organizations, the demands on the staff can be enormous. Glassy-eyed programmers, cases of Red Bull, sleeping bags under desks, and 3 AM pizza deliveries have become routine. And, these demands have only increased in recent years as economic downturns have placed increased workloads on shrinking resources. IT demands are heavy because:

- Virtually every aspect of an organization is dependent on IT and its services.
- In the digital world we now live in, the workplace is 24/7/365 and the demands are nonstop. The technology allows people to work 24 hours a day, from anywhere in the world, on devices that slip into a pocket.
- The lure of a complex technical challenge often excites people to work 20 hours a day. (In the early days of developing the Macintosh, Steve Jobs handed out T-shirts that read: "Working 90 hours a week and loving it.")
- IT staff is needed during working hours to ensure that systems are running as they should and responding to problems. However, the staff is also needed during off hours because that's often the only time that certain work (e.g., maintenance, upgrades) can be done.
- Unlike the days of assembly-line labor, the work of IT isn't measured in products produced per unit of time so there are no clear external indicators of when the work is "complete." ("The IT job is one where you get an 'F' if you fail but only a 'C' if you succeed—this stuff is supposed to work, right?" Bill Gates, *Business @ the Speed of Thought*.)
- Highly energized and motivated employees may not even realize the condition they are getting themselves into. While it may be tempting to push your staff, or allow them to push themselves to the limit, it's important to remember that you won't get much work out of them once they've hit that wall.

- The new, streamlined corporate world demands even more of IT departments, while simultaneously either keeping staff at current levels or even cutting back. The challenges have stretched many IT departments to the breaking point.

Make Your Employees Aware of the Dangers of Burnout

Often people most susceptible to burnout are the ones unaware of the problem. They work like dogs for two years and then they crash. Keep your eye out for employees who seem to be burning out. Fatigue and difficulty concentrating are obvious symptoms. Also look for changes in employees' behaviors and attitudes. If a normally enthusiastic employee suddenly seems apathetic, it could be a tell-tale sign. Of course, there are other explanations for these symptoms as well. You may not notice these yourself; other members of the team may see them before you do, but they should be on the lookout for the signs and should feel comfortable alerting you.

Outline the Prices Employees Can Pay

When making them aware of the problem, outline the various possible costs of burnout:

- Deterioration of health
- Errors on the job
- Relationships with coworkers suffer
- Problems at home with family and relationships
- Loss of job

The short-term gains for working weekends for six months in a row don't outweigh the long-term losses of any of the ones just listed.

Deal with the Situation

As the manager, you need to be more aware of the problem of burnout and take steps to monitor and avoid it:

- Be very clear about your performance and productivity expectations regarding your employees. Define simple measures and metrics and communicate them clearly and often. Get realistic commitments from your employees regarding timelines and deliverables. Also, make sure they feel safe in telling you when your expectations are too demanding or unrealistic.
- Be very conscious of the levels of effort all of your team members are putting out. And don't think in absolute numbers. A 10-hour day may not seem like a big deal to you, but it can be an enormous commitment for a single parent or a person just coming off working three demanding projects.
- Spread the effort around. The amount of IT work is endless—as a manager, you have a responsibility to your company and your employees to carefully allocate work across the board. Certainly people have different work outputs, just as they have different working and communication styles. Your job is to consider the team as a whole, each person as an important part of that whole, and get the jobs done within that context.
- Make changes in personnel to reflect the needs of the jobs your team must perform. Need more people? Ask for them, and do so with concrete, numerical evidence of why you need them. Is one person on the verge of burning out because the company has overworked her? Shift that person's responsibilities. Is one person over his head in his job? Look for other places within

the department that this person can contribute more effectively. (Care needs to be taken when doing this, because the employee may not understand.) In general, the IT world isn't for the fainthearted.

- Be aware of how much different people can give. Some employees can only deliver 40 hours' worth of work in a week, even if they are at their desk 60 hours. Others can easily double their efforts, for short times, in response to specific needs. Often, running at top speed isn't the best way to get there. Be sensitive to what motivates your employees, as well as their needs and limitations. Be aware that people can only be pushed, or even push themselves, so far. Recognize when they can be pushed further and when you have to insist they take a break. Do this well and you'll be rewarded with a far more productive and motivated team.

Managing Remote Workers (or Teleworkers)

Technology has ushered in a global economy and the ability for employees to get their work done from anywhere in the world. In the past, working remotely may have meant working at home because a blizzard closed the roads or to take care of sick child. Today, teleworking may mean working from home full-time, certain days a week, or working in a different office from your boss and peers. Teleworking is used by employees, outsourcing companies, and contracts and consultants. These workers may be as far as around the world, or as close as around the block.

The trend for teleworking is growing because it provides a number of benefits:

- Improved work/life balance for employees
- Cost savings for employee (e.g., commute) and employer (real estate)
- Reduced environmental impact
- Considered a perk for (some) employees so it is easier to attract and retain talent
- Ability to recruit from a geographically wider talent pool
- Increased productivity

TELEWORK FINDINGS

A survey by WorldatWork released in 2011 reported that U.S. employers offer four types of telework, and many offer more than one kind of telework program at a time:

- Ad hoc telework (e.g., to meet a repair person, care for a sick child) (83%)
- Telework on a regular monthly basis (at least one day per month, but not full time) (58%)
- Telework on a regular weekly basis (at least one day per week, but not full time) (57%)
- Full-time telework (every regularly scheduled workday) (37%).

"Telework on a regular or full-time basis might be even more common if not for certain obstacles getting in the way of telework for many," said Alison Avalos, research manager for WorldatWork. "Nearly four in every 10 surveyed organizations say that resistance from top management or the lack of jobs conducive to these arrangements are keeping them from offering all types of telework programs."
Other results:

- Full-time telework is more commonly offered by large corporations (20,000 employees or more).
- Telework locations vary, but "home" is most frequent. Nearly 70 percent of organizations that offer at least one type of telework say employees routinely work from home.
- Telework programs often are featured in recruitment. Organizations with telework programs are more likely to feature those programs when attracting talent, indicating that organizations use these programs to distinguish themselves as an employer of choice.

Source: *www.worldatwork.org/waw/adimComment?id=48318*

The key thing to remember about teleworkers (also known as remote workers, mobile workforce, work-from-home staff, etc.) is that it is more challenging to develop and maintain effective relationships with them because you won't have the very important in-person, face-to-face interaction with them. That's not to say that you can't have an effective relationship with them, it just means that you have to work differently at it to do so.

Some guidelines to help you with managing teleworkers:

- Work with other departments (HR, Legal, etc.) to develop clear and consistent policies about teleworking. This can include what the company will do or provide, what is expected of the employee, what expenses will be reimbursed, etc.
- Make sure you understand—and convey this to your team—that there are a wide range of telecommuting options. Some employees need or want only one day a week (some companies offer four 10-hour days as an alternative solution to this issue) and some companies are fine with only occasional in-office days (as the rise in "hot-desking"—the practice of taking any desk that is available that day—demonstrates).
- Ensure that the employee has access to the appropriate tools to do the job (hardware, software, connectivity, etc.).
- Make sure that you and your team have access to tools to facilitate collaboration and communication with remote workers. This can include instant messaging (with voice and audio), webcams, web conferencing, video conferencing, etc.
- Consider telephony solutions (like call forwarding, VPN phones, soft phones) so that your remote workers can be reached just by dialing their extension, and not having to look up their home phone number.
- Make the effort to regularly talk (not just e-mail or IM) with your teleworkers. A regularly recurring appointment for status updates is ideal, in addition to the ad hoc chats.
- To help the teleworker feel that he's part of the team, be diligent about sharing information with him, at least as much as you ask for information. This can even include what other team members are working on, even if completely unrelated to the teleworker's projects.
- Include non-work topics (e.g., family, weekend activities, etc.) in your discussions with the teleworkers to help make up for the loss of small talk that helps develop relationships with people you see in person.
- Encourage, and directly ask for, feedback, advice, and suggestions from teleworkers. In fact, the number one pet peeve about teleworking, as reported in a 2011 report from Microsoft, was "cannot speak face-to-face" (source www.microsoft.com/presspass/download/features/2011/05-18Remote.pptx).
- Be prompt in responding to a teleworker's queries, just as you would for the employee who poked his head into your office to ask you something.
- At meetings, use a speaker phone to ensure that the teleworker feels that he's part of the group discussion, make sure he has copies of all documents in advance, and actively include him in the discussion by specifically asking him for feedback and comments.

While it's important to develop the skills and habits to effectively manage teleworkers, you, as an IT manager, need to be particularly knowledgeable about the subject since any sort of teleworking program at your company will rely on you, your department, and the technology solutions you bring to the table to help make it a success. And, don't forget, it's entirely possible that *you* could be the remote worker. If your boss is in another location, she may be relying on these very techniques in managing you!

2.2 EMPLOYEE TRAINING

Training is always an issue for managers. Although they know that it's a perk that employees often enjoy and it improves employees' skills, they are also concerned about the cost, the employee being away from his full-time responsibilities, and the fear that the employee will use the newly acquired skill to seek another job elsewhere. However, a few days or a week at a training class can serve as a respite for a hard-working employee as well as increase his skill set and usefulness to the organization. Some companies provide tuition reimbursement toward a degree.

Because learning new skills is such a critical part of working in IT, providing training is an important part of managing an IT staff. There are so many IT classes offered that it wouldn't be difficult to have someone spend more time at training classes (and trade shows) than they do at work. As a manager you have to balance a few items when doling out training:

- Cost
- Need
- Employee morale
- Scheduling demands

Cost

There are two issues associated with the cost of employee training:

- The cost of the training itself
- The cost of having the employee away from her full-time responsibilities

Often, the second issue far outweighs the first. The expenses for an employee to attend a training class vary greatly. Some classes are offered either locally or online, and may only be three hours in length. However, many training options include cross-country travel, which requires hotel, rental car, and travel expenses that can inflate the cost of the class by a factor of two or more.

Despite those variances, the real cost issue is often the expense of having an employee away from work for a period of time. Can you spare this individual for an entire week? Sometimes several people are sent to training together. Can you spare all of them? Sometimes contractors can fill in for staff members who are at training; in this case the costs are fairly easily measured. But other times, some of your other employees or people from other departments need to fill in; the "cost" of these solutions, while not always visible, is often much higher than a week in a hotel.

When thinking about the cost of training, it is important to remember that it is generally less expensive to train an existing employee than it is to recruit a replacement. In other words, training can be a relatively inexpensive tool to retain an employee and a more cost-effective way of improving the team's skills (as opposed to going out and recruiting for those skills).

Need

What is the short- and long-term value of this kind of training for an employee? Often the needs are well defined: Joe needs a Database Administrator class because he will be helping out Maria. But other times, the issue gets cloudy: Mark wants to take a class on programming for mobile and tablet devices, but that isn't his exact responsibility right now and it isn't clear that the company is going to be creating apps for those markets anyway.

"Need" may appear to be the clear deciding factor, but often the value of taking a training class is unclear. If that is the case, you should use some of the other criteria listed in this section to help you decide whether or not to agree to have an employee take a training class.

Scheduling Demands

This is probably the most difficult issue to deal with. Many of your own staff will find the issue difficult, rightly recognizing that a week away from the office means a week of catching up when they get back. Who will cover for them? If they are overburdened right now (as many IT people are), how are they ever going to make up for a lost week's worth of work? The answer is pretty simple: Evaluate the short-term costs versus the long-term gains. See the previously mentioned three items; if the direct costs aren't overwhelming, if the employee (and your department) needs the training, and if their morale will be improved, go for it—and have them go for it.

Remember that the traditional five-day instructor-led classes are just one option. Making use of shorter (and more content-targeted) classes, as well as online instruction (either interactive, or view-only) have proven to be very popular, effective, and cost efficient.

Employee Morale

Many employees view training as a reward. It provides them with concrete, resume-enhancing skills, sometimes lets them "get out of the house" by traveling to a warm spot in midwinter, and often allows them to interact with professionals with the same interests and questions.

In addition, sending a staff member to a trade show or training course can be an excellent way to motivate employees. Both you and your employees need to aggressively monitor your skill sets to make sure they are current and useful.

Also be aware that sending one person to training can occasionally cause a second person to feel resentment. One of the challenges any manager faces is how to juggle multiple responsibilities, such as how to manage multiple people. Make sure you spread the "wealth" around so that feelings like these have no basis in fact.

How Do You Know When Your Employees Need Training?

There are three principal ways to identify when an employee needs training.

1. **They tell you.** IT people are deluged by training class offers and by situations where they are aware of their technical shortcomings in one area or another. Asking the boss for a class or two is a common request. (Asking for a weeklong class on a cruise ship in the Bahamas is less common, but not unheard of.) You should consider an employee's request for training as a positive indication that they are interested in learning and doing more for the company. (It could also be an indication that they like being out of the office or are looking to beef up their resume.) In addition, look at your employee's goals. Are they asking for the training to meet the performance goals and development plan you both set together?

2. **Your customers tell you.** The IT department's customers can be one of a variety of groups: they can certainly be outside customers, but they can also be (sometimes exclusively) internal customers. In either case, if you solicit feedback from your customers about what their IT needs are, you may hear about specific technical services that your department can't provide without either (1) getting more training for current employees or (2) hiring someone else to do the job.

3. **You find out on your own because you are a *proactive* manager.** Learn to address training needs before they become problems. If you do this, you'll save yourself tremendous time, money, and effort over the long term. You'll anticipate your department's needs for Ruby on Rails developers and start running the ads months in advance, knowing that particular talent is hard to find. You'll budget for a new Help Desk support analyst in advance, before the seasonal sales cycle kicks in and all the calls come in. And you'll send your people for training in Windows network administration, for example, *before* the project to upgrade starts.

Certification

Most IT Managers don't have the luxury of sending people to training just for the sake of training. As such, few IT departments are willing to sponsor their employees for training that leads to vendor or technology certification. This is simply because managers know that some of the classes in a certification program these days are fillers—they are of little or no use to a specific employee's job responsibilities. Of course, there are exceptions. Some managers may use certification, or training in general, as a way of rewarding highly valued employees or for those employees whose responsibilities are very specialized. Also, while sending an employee to the requisite classes doesn't guarantee certification, the employee still has to pass the exam. (Note that some companies won't pay the exam fee if the employee doesn't pass, which creates a nice incentive for the employee to work hard to pass it on the first try.)

Different certifications have come in and out of fashion over the years. At the start, in the early 1990s everyone wanted to be a CNE (Certified Novell Engineer). Years later, network certification became the most popular, such as Cisco's CCNE. Beyond that, security and project management became the "it" certificates to have (CISSP and PMP). The value of certification is discussed in more detail in **Chapter 3, Staffing Your IT Team** on **page 65**.

What If the Employee Takes a Training Class and Then Uses His New-Found Skills to Find Another Job?

Be Honest about This Problem

One effective technique is simply to address the issue with the employee beforehand, while you are still making a decision about whether they should go to training. As is often the case in business situations, bringing the topic out in the open can go a long way toward easing everyone's fears. Just discussing the issue doesn't create any legal arrangement, of course, but it should let both sides know where the other stands. As a manager, you can openly express your concern about the possibility that the employee will "take the training and run." You hope the employee will reply that the job is much bigger than one skill set, they like the environment, they would work here for free they like it so much, and so on. But if they don't, if they hedge or are evasive, or blurt out a series of negative statements, you've probably got a problem that a training class isn't going to solve.

Employee Agreements

Some companies have a policy that says an employee has to sign an agreement to reimburse the cost of training if she resigns within X months of taking a class. Of course, many employers and employees are hesitant about even making such an agreement because it creates somewhat of a non-trusting, non-supportive relationship. Before asking your employees to agree to something like this, make sure you discuss the issue with your HR department—there is probably an existing policy about it.

Because the IT world is so fluid, this situation works the other way, too. Employees can spend months on certification programs for a company and then the company changes direction. For example, one IT Manager had his entire Oracle database certification paid for but the company decided (at the last minute) to stay with Microsoft SQL. He eventually left to go to an Oracle shop.

Nontechnical Training

When considering IT training, you generally think about technical training. It's important to remember that some of your staff may also benefit tremendously from nontechnical training as a way of expanding their horizons, such as the following:

- Time management (for those who have trouble staying organized)
- Business writing (for those who have to prepare memos and reports)
- Presentation skills (for those who have to give presentations to groups)
- Interpersonal skills (for those who need help with communications or conflict management)
- Supervisory skills (for those who have a staff to manage)
- Project management (for those responsible for keeping projects on track)
- Leadership skills (for enhancing management skills)

Nontechnical training can have tremendous value. Employees may not appreciate it as much as technical training, but *you* will value it. You can tell an employee that you're sending him to a nontechnical training class because you have hopes to move him up in the organization and he needs to increase his skill set, or you might tell him that his deficiencies in these areas are holding him and/or his team back.

Your HR department can be the best source for nontechnical training information. Training options are now more flexible and more accessible than ever before; in addition to the explosion of night and part-time schools, companies that provide on-site training, online courses, and the myriad of different media-based educational options make getting trained much more convenient.

Maximizing the Value of Training

If you send employees for training, it's because you see the need. It's then up to you as their manager to make sure that they're putting these skills to use. You should review the course curriculum to get a feel for what the employees should be able to do after completing the class. If an employee isn't using the skills learned in a class, it could be because the selection of that particular class was a poor one or that you haven't challenged them to use their newly acquired skills. In addition, consider the following training ideas.

- Have the employee who went to training give an informal training session to the rest of the team. You can then see how much the employee learned and give your entire team some of the benefits of the training.

- Have the employee formally train employees who didn't attend the training; if the employee goes to the initial training with that goal in mind, it can add value to their experience as well as save the company money.
- Consider on-site training where the content can be more contextually specific to your organization and your configuration, and more employees can attend.

You want to be sure that your employees are aware that you have expectations for the money you spend on their training and that you see it as an investment in them and the team.

2.3 EMPLOYEE PERFORMANCE

While employees are your biggest asset, they can sometimes become a large liability, too. As discussed earlier, one of your key roles as a manager is to keep employees focused on their tasks, objectives, and priorities. However, in addition to this, you're also responsible for employee performance reviews, dealing with disciplinary problems, and terminations.

Performance Reviews

Performance reviews are probably the single most important discussion you'll have with members of your staff. Although performance reviews are traditionally a once-a-year event, some companies are now doing them twice a year. Regardless of the frequency, a professionally done review should be approached the same was as your taxes: Do the work in small bits all year and you will be ready when the big moment arrives—eliminating any chance of surprises for you and the employee at what is discussed. The end result should be the formalization of 12 months of regular discussion, feedback, analysis, and evaluation. This should be your overall goal as a manager when working with the reviews of your employees. The annual review process gives you a chance to document the employee's accomplishments, dedication, commitment, challenges, and opportunities for improvement.

Performance reviews are often used to resolve two other important employment issues: rewarding good performing employees and addressing poor performing employees.

Poorly written evaluations make both of these tasks even more difficult and the costs of failing at this are high:

- Mishandled terminations can (and often do, these days) end in lawsuits.
- Mishandled reviews of good performers often lead to their changing jobs to get what they should have received from you.
- Poorly done reviews can leave an employee feeling demoralized, worried about her job, and discouraged, when what you had really intended to do was offer some motivation, encouragement, and constructive criticism.
- Ineffective reviews of poor performers may lead them to think that all is fine, and they can just "stay the course."

Many companies have evaluation forms that have been developed by the HR department. Some forms are generic, whereas others are designed to reflect the company's mission, values, and goals. There are also many offerings of applications that allow you to put the whole process online. Other companies have no forms and leave it up to each manager or simply rely on a memo-style format. However, a form generally won't help you since a useful evaluation should really consist of descriptive narratives, specifics, examples, and commentary—not merely checked boxes.

No Surprises!

Neither you nor your employee should be shocked when review time comes around. For example, you should not suddenly discover that the employee finds your project assignments to be lacking in clarity, and they should not suddenly discover you strongly resent the hours they spend on Twitter and Facebook. In both cases, the problematic behavior can't be corrected if the person isn't aware it is a problem. Any negative comments that you include in the review should be items that you've discussed with the employee multiple times in the course of the year. If they are a superstar employee, you should've acknowledged their work and achievements throughout the year; and they should know that, in general, the review is going to be a very positive experience. If the employee is struggling, they should be aware of that before the formal evaluation because of conversations you've had with them. In either case, a little work on your part throughout the year will richly reward you when it is time to do reviews. The last thing you want to hear from your employee during the review process is "this is the first I'm hearing of that" or "I wish you had told me sooner so I could've worked on correcting it." You can even consider doing informal reviews once or twice during the year.

Key Areas of Evaluation

Some of the areas that you want to consider when reviewing an employee's performance include:

- Quality of work
- Flexibility
- Creativity in solving problems
- Communication skills
- Innovation
- Going above and beyond the requirements of the job
- Coordination, interaction, and collaboration with others (particularly those they don't have direct authority over)
- Accountability
- Ability to complete assignments in a timely manner
- Ethics and compliance
- Ability to pick up new skills on their own
- Ability to work with and enhance the work of other staff members
- Ability to manage short- and long-term projects

Quality of Work

Is this person providing excellent, just mediocre, or subpar work? Not every staff member will give you spectacular performance. But your needs as a manager may be such that this person fulfills certain other critical functions: they may be a team member who keeps others enthusiastic about the project, sets a good example for keeping focused, or has a deep knowledge of company operations and history and provides long-term perspective to decisions.

Flexibility

Most roles have job descriptions, some job descriptions are even written down(!), but almost no job description adequately anticipates the real-world demands of the position. (See the section **"Position Descriptions"** in **Chapter 3, Staffing Your IT Team** on **page 74**). It's important for every employee to understand the real goals of the department and how he can help achieve those goals. Changing market conditions, changing project demands and priorities, and changing technical capacities all require employees to be flexible about their tasks. Has this employee adapted well to the fluid requirements of the job?

Creativity in Solving Problems

Along with flexibility about their job descriptions, good employees are often resourceful and creative in solving problems. Five new employees started Monday, but only four laptops were delivered; a creative employee might find one in the test lab to tide them over. The rush order for two new servers needs a manager's signature, but she called in sick today; a creative employee will find a manager from another department or the manager's boss to get the order started.

Communication Skills

Can this person communicate well? Are their e-mails clear and easy-to-read, or are they rambling and take 10 minutes to read and are still difficult to understand? Are they personable? Do they make eye contact? Do they speak well in meetings, do they make personal attacks, or do they say nothing at all? Technical people are often not great communicators because their jobs often don't require tremendous amounts of interaction. But there is a base level of information exchange that every job requires and a base level of interactive behavior that every organization requires. If a person works in a group, there are certain standards that must be met. And in the new agile, just-in-time corporate world we work in, communication is more important than ever. There is a much greater sense of urgency now and employees who are at the forefront of the work—as IT workers often are—find themselves having to be much more communicative than ever. Note this in the employee's review; often technical people do have a more difficult time communicating, and if they do a good job at this, that should be noticed and recognized by their manager.

Innovation

Today's technology can be used in many different ways. And when multiple technologies are combined, the possibilities for new ideas grow exponentially. Innovation is the ability to think outside the box, and is an attribute for finding new ways of doing things or doing new things. This could be anything related to simplifying processes, reducing errors, or finding additional uses for existing tools.

Going Above and Beyond Requirements of the Job

Many employees view their work as nothing more than a job, a day's work for a day's pay, and have almost an adversarial stance about doing anything more. Can you fault someone for doing only what they are supposed to do? However, for those who view their work as more of a career than a job and seek to be promoted and moved up, going above and beyond the job requirements is one of the best ways to achieve those goals. This can include helping out coworkers, putting in extra time, volunteering to do the more challenging tasks, working on items that no one else seems to want to do, and so on.

Coordination, Interaction, and Collaboration with Others (Particularly Those They Don't Have Direct Authority Over)

"Plays well with others" is another way to describe this attribute. It simply means that they work well with others—their peers on the team, as well as customers, clients, users, among others. This could apply to situations where a large team is formed for a particular project or routine activities, as well as the case of individual contributors that have to interact with others only periodically. It also means gaining the respect of those you work with. To do all this well requires a numbers of skills and traits: interpersonal style, influencing, leadership, communication/listening, trust, adaptability, compromise, and relationship building.

Accountability

Managers look for accountability in their employees primarily because it makes the manager's job easier. A manager prefers knowing that when an employee is assigned a task, it will be done, and the manager won't have to do regular checks to ensure that work is progressing. (See the next item on completing assignments on time.) Accountability also means that employees will recognize what their own responsibilities are and will not sit around waiting for the manager to tell them what to do. If your staff isn't accountable, you end up as a micromanager. However, it's up to the manager to make their employees feel accountable through follow-up, project assignments, stated goals and objectives, and a clear statement of the job requirements, as well as the impact to others when things don't go as planned.

Ability to Complete Assignments in a Timely Manner

Timely performance is critical in all environments. Gone are the days when deadlines were approximations and missing them had few consequences. "Just in time" no longer refers to an inventory technique; it now is often used to describe how entire departments and companies act in response to market conditions.

Be clear about your expectations for timely performance and let your staff know you'll be using that as a criterion for evaluation. Let them know that you are being evaluated on that basis as well. Installing the new phone system by Monday instead of Friday may be suddenly required, but create an environment where people feel comfortable suggesting coming in on Saturday (or at least discussing if it is necessary).

Ethics and Compliance

Over the past few years, society in general, and companies in particular, have placed increased emphasis on "doing the right thing." This involves everything from following laws (e.g., Sarbanes–Oxley, discrimination, harassment) to practicing common-sense integrity (not padding time sheets, not accepting large gifts from vendors, respecting confidentiality, professionalism, etc.). As a result, many companies have moved to fully integrate this tenet into every part of their existence—from the company mission to the employee code of conduct, as well as the performance review. This is an ideal situation where leading by example can have a huge impact. If employees see you taking a tablet device for personal use, they can easily begin to think that personal use of company resources is perfectly fine.

Ability to Pick Up New Skills on Their Own

The IT world changes so quickly that it's an employee's fundamental responsibility to help herself, her department, and her company stay current. Every department has the programmer still resting on his legacy coding skills—encourage your staff not to become that person. Some of the best and brightest are those who can pick up new skills on their own either through experimental trial and error, learning things on their own time, or by picking up a reference book, such as this one. See the section **"Employee Training"** on **page 39** earlier in this chapter for details on the issue of training.

Ability to Work with and Enhance the Work of Other Staff Members

You may have a Windows administrator with superlative technical skills but zero people skills. Let him know that your IT department is a team, not a random collection of individuals, and that everyone is expected to interact professionally with each other. He doesn't have to go to the team picnics, but snarling or swearing at anyone else who touches the system isn't acceptable either. These employees often don't realize the impact their behavior has on others or how IT Managers see it as a limitation on the individual's career growth.

Many a manager has had to say, "You don't have to *like* all your fellow IT department members, but you have to treat them with professionalism, respect, and work with them in a collaborative manner." This is a common problem with technical people, and one way of solving the issue is to inform them that their behavior in this area is part of their review.

Ability to Manage Short- and Long-Term Projects

Every employee in IT is given projects, some long and complex, some short and simple. Inform your staff that their ability to handle projects is an element you will be evaluating when it comes to review time. Many employees might not think in project-related terms; they think their task is to get the new laptops installed in the Sales department in the next two weeks and not see how it relates to the bigger goal of a new sales-force automation system implementation. Of course, that is a project, a set task with a specific goal, resources, and a timeline. For some levels and tasks, as long as they finish the projects on time and under budget, it isn't important for them to think in project management terms. But those who do see the bigger picture and take the long view will probably have brighter futures. (See **Chapter 4** on **Project Management** on **page 103** for further details on projects and project management.)

Specific Evaluation Statements

The words used in performance reviews can have a great deal of impact, or no impact at all. You want to be sure that you are clear and that each statement has meaning and value to the employee. Avoid ambiguity and use examples and facts to back up your assessments. See Table 2.1 for some samples.

Useful Metrics

If the individual being reviewed has a position that is operational in nature, you should include quantitative metrics in the review:

- Network uptime
- Systems response time
- Call resolution/response time
- Project delivery time (and budget)
- Number of incidents (or calls) addressed per hour (or day)
- System reliability

When thinking about metrics, think about the goals for that employee and their job. How would you determine or measure if they are meeting those goals? When goals can be measured, and are measured, it is easier for you and the employee to be aware of how well things are going.

Guidelines for Reviews

Don't forget: both you and the members of your IT staff are salaried professionals. Act as such, and treat them that way. Your respect will be rewarded.

Table 2.1 Sample Evaluation Comments

Statement type	Example	Comment	
Almost useless	"Mark is a fine worker with a good attitude; he works hard and has done a good job for the company."	While it may be true, this statement tells Mark nothing concrete about his past performance and gives him nothing to focus on for the future. Nor is the company served by this kind of statement. How valuable an employee is Mark, and how can it help Mark grow?	
Positive	"Martha was exemplary in her efforts to complete her implementation of the new healthcare plan project on time. In addition to working over several weekends, she also enlisted the help of two departments to meet the October 1 deadline."	This is a very useful comment for Martha; she knows her efforts were noticed and the company knows they have a committed employee.	
Negative	"Mary Jane showed no interest in expanding her professional skill set; she turned down several offers for training classes in new programming languages and she refused to move to a new project that would have required her to learn new procedures."	Mary Jane knows exactly what she did wrong and, if she chooses, how she can change her behavior to act differently in the future.	

Be Objective

It's important to remember that a performance review is the company's formal assessment of the employee's performance. Be as objective as possible. Remember reviews of your own performance—often the most contentious items are the subjective ones. With this in mind, your performance review should be full of examples and specifics to back up your assessment. Providing quantifiable accomplishments, specific examples, and measurable goals helps you remain objective.

Also, remember that others may read this review in the future. Other people in the company, for example, may read this review when thinking about transferring the employee into their department or the person may leave and may later reapply at your company. Be sure that your comments accurately reflect the employee's performance.

Carefully Record Details

The more specifics you can provide, the more valuable the review will be for the employee. And the more specifics you can provide now, the more meaningful it will be in the future. It's hard to recall the incidents you need when you're looking back on the past 12 months. Review your own status reports to help jog your memory. And, during the year, jot quick notes to yourself on scraps of paper that you toss into the employee's file, or write an e-mail to yourself that you can refer to later. Although this sounds like a great idea in theory, it is in fact something many good managers do on a regular basis. Details matter, and memories fade. Record them as they happen and both you and the recipient of your work—for this is real work that managers have to do—will be better for it.

When reviewing these notes, take the long view. Try and look over the course of the entire year and remember that you probably wrote those notes when something was going particularly well, or particularly poorly. Perhaps those comments are right on target or perhaps they represent an emotional high or low.

As you prepare the review, you can also ask the employee for her own list of accomplishments (and areas they think they can improve upon) over the past 12 months. (See the section later in this chapter **"Have Employees Review Themselves"** on **page 20**.) These notes can also help jog your memory and help you understand what the employee considers her greatest achievement. Additionally, it helps you see what the employee thinks were their important contributions. Getting her input can help you avoid embarrassment by failing to mention something that was important to her. Remember, employees take reviews very seriously, especially if they are less than stellar. The review becomes an important part of the employee's official records so you want to do your best to make sure it's comprehensive and accurate.

Negative Reviews

Performance reviews that are mostly or entirely negative are difficult for both the reviewer and the reviewed.

There are four important points to keep in mind if you are in this situation:

- Be as specific as possible, both about the problem area and ways to correct.
- Negative reviews should not be a surprise to anyone.
- Keep HR informed.
- Be professional.

Be Specific

Not only will the session(s) probably be very emotional, but the end result can be more positive when you can be very specific about what happened. This detail should include not only past performance but current events; be clear and detailed in your notes about what conversations took place and what each party said. If the employee failed to meet goals, identify what those goals were and where the employee came up short. Stick to the facts and be objective. Be sure the review also covers what steps the employee needs to take to address the problem.

It Should Not Be a Surprise

Follow the guidelines outlined in this chapter; constantly communicate with your staff and record both accomplishments and disappointments throughout the year. In some cases a written warning is called for. If you do all this, both you and the employee should be aware of the gap between goals and performance.

Keep HR Informed

Make sure to keep your HR department informed. HR can make sure that you're following procedures and policies, and can bring in other resources (e.g., Legal) if the situation warrants. Plus, HR has lots of experience in these situations and will offer guidance and assistance in the best ways to approach the situation. If your company doesn't have an HR department, find an appropriate third party to keep informed of (or sit in on) the situation—your own boss is a logical choice. If you keep someone else involved and aware of the situation, you will always have a third party to check back with later in the process (if required).

Be Professional

Take extra care to make sure that what you write comes off in a highly professional manner. Resist the urge to list failures. Instead, cite circumstances where the employee "fell short of expectations" or "needs development" to identify areas where the employee needs to focus his efforts. In some situations, an employee may not be aware of his own weakness; for example, his contributions and involvement at staff meetings are more like speeches instead of discussions. If this is the case, consider it a coaching opportunity for you and a development area for him.

The task of preparing for and conducting performance reviews really shouldn't be emotional, but in some cases it will be stressful and time-consuming.

EXAMPLE OF WHEN YOU MIGHT NEED TO GIVE A NEGATIVE REVIEW

Susie did a mediocre job, but more problematic was the fact that she was very difficult to deal with. As a result, most people avoided working with her. To make matters worse, she was used to getting very positive reviews.

When reviewing someone like this, you might want to ask them what they want out of the job. Do they want to move to the next level (e.g., from analyst to engineer), which would mean a raise along with the promotion? If they answer "yes," then you can proceed to list all the things they need to do in their current position that they aren't doing and then list the things that they need to do to get to the next level. For example, you could say: "You completed this first project, which is great, but the second one wasn't completed on time. Why not?"

After the explanation is given, you can say that you understand, and in the future, they need to report sooner or more effectively about what is going right or wrong. Then, you can add, for example, after they've completed all these tasks (as in the case of Susie), she would need to mentor someone else or be the lead on a project. It may be that both you and she know this isn't likely to happen. If that's the case, and she's unable or unwilling to say that, you have given her the motivation to either step up to the task or (honestly) find other work, because the next review will be much more explicit about this new task.

There is more discussion later in this chapter in the section **"Disciplinary Problems and Terminations" on page 54**.

Have Employees Review Themselves

Many companies have adopted the formal policy of having employees, in addition to their managers, review themselves. The employee uses the same form as the manager and evaluates her performance over the specified period of time. Naturally, self-assessment reviews (just like resumes) can contain some elements of (how shall we put it?) "skill inflation." Nonetheless, the exercise is a very valuable one for both the employee and the manager. The employee gets a chance to express her views and concerns and to talk about what she thought her strengths and weaknesses were. Identifying the gaps between the manager's assessment and the employee's self-assessment can help in figuring out development opportunities and identify where problems are.

360 Reviews

In a 360-degree review an employee receives feedback not only from his direct supervisor, but from other individuals he has worked with as well, which include peers and subordinates (see Table 2.2). An employee may work on a project run by another department manager, for example; in that case, the other manager can have direct input into the employee's review. Or an employee may work much more with two staff members and may only occasionally see their direct manager. (Some employees have management in other states or even other countries.) In these cases, 360 reviews allow the individuals who most directly work with the person to provide input on their performance. If your company is using them, or thinking of using them, be prepared for more feedback—both good and bad—at review time.

Table 2.2 Pros and Cons of 360 Reviews

Pro	Con
360 reviews provide opportunities for people traditionally not asked for their opinions to express them; customers, for example, often have to be proactive about providing feedback to suppliers.	They generally involve a lot more data. Also, the feedback from multiple people may be inconsistent, which makes it difficult to identify pluses and minuses and figure out a development plan.
The quality of review for some workers improves tremendously because the people best suited to evaluate an individual are now involved in the process.	People who haven't done performance reviews before are suddenly providing detailed review data; you may or may not want information on Ken's workplace cleanliness, for example.

A newer trend is to use 360 assessments not as formal review components, but as feedback mechanisms throughout the year. In other words, you or the employee may ask the manager from another department for feedback on your staff member once the project ends, store that feedback away, and use it during the review, or solicit input from project team members at the end of the project and use that data later. But when review time comes around, you don't need to poll five coworkers of the employee or customers that person has talked to; you already have that data. You do a performance review as you normally would using data you collected throughout the year.

A 360 review can be done in a few different ways:

- In some cases, a third party contacts the reviewers to collect their feedback and then strips out identifying information to keep the feedback anonymous. An online tool is often used for this.
- In a less formalized process, the employee can simply meet with her peers and subordinates.
- In some cases, particularly if a tool is used, a report of various charts and metrics is produced to help the employee identify highs and lows.
- After completing the 360 review, the employee is often asked to complete some sort of summary report to identify what strengths and weaknesses were identified in the 360 review, as well as an action plan to address those areas (e.g., correct weaknesses and further benefit from strengths).

If the 360 review is conducted anonymously, there is a greater chance of more candid feedback; obviously the more honest the better. However, if the review is not anonymous, it gives the employee the opportunity to further discuss the feedback with the reviewers, perhaps to clarify a point or even to say "the next time you see me do that, please point it out to me because I wasn't aware I do that." One of the great benefits of a 360 is that it gives the employee the chance to see herself as others see her. Very often, this leads to some surprises (both good and bad).

How to Conduct the Actual Review Discussion

When it's time to meet with the employee to go over the performance review, remember that it's a discussion—make this an interactive time, not a linear one. Do not simply read the review to him. Some managers give the employee time to read the review in advance of the review meeting so that the employee has time to digest it and can then discuss it intelligently and unemotionally. Remember though, as a manager, to discuss it with conviction. This is your assessment of his performance.

You should be willing to make changes for two reasons: factual error (e.g., a project was completed on time, when you said it wasn't, or forgetting to include key items in their list of accomplishments) or language nuances (e.g., the employee may feel that some of the words you used are particularly harsh). If you need to have this discussion with an employee who normally works remotely, the first choice would be to see if you can arrange for a face-to-face discussion. If not, review the material in this chapter on **"Managing Remote Workers"** on **page 37,** as well as the section **"Interviewing Candidates over the Web"** in **Chapter 3, Staffing Your IT Team** on **page 91,** for guidance on meeting and interacting with people you aren't in the same room with.

Respect Privacy

If you work in an open environment, make sure you reserve a conference room or an office for some privacy. You will both want the comfort of knowing the conversation isn't being overheard, regardless of whether everything is positive or not.

Tone of the Discussion

You need to be clear in your discussion with the employee. Depending on the employee's performance, your tone may need to include hints of motivation, hard-heartedness, appreciation, disappointment, optimism, and support. At the end of the review, there shouldn't be any doubt in the employee's mind as to what you think of his performance, where he has excelled, where he needs to improve, and steps he needs to take to do so.

In certain cases, you might want to have specific follow-up meetings with an employee at regular intervals after the formal performance reviews. If necessary, you may want to consider additional interim informal reviews at certain, pre-specified times. ("Let's meet again every three months to review progress and make sure you and I are on the same page about this issue.")

Make sure that you aren't distracted or interrupted. The review is very important to the employee, and they should feel it's very important to you as well. You should be sure to set aside enough time for the discussion.

Development Plans and Goals

While the annual review is the culmination of a year's worth of interaction and discussion with an employee, it's also the perfect time to start looking forward to the next 12 months to set the employee's goals and define a development plan.

The development plan includes those activities designed to increase the employee's skills and contributions. These can be technical skills or other professional development competencies, such as presentation or leadership skills. The development plan can include a variety of activities:

- Formal training (classes, trade shows, books, etc.)
- Project assignments that include exposure to new areas and opportunities to develop and practice new skills
- Working with a colleague either as a mentor (to develop coaching skills) or as a protégé

The goals represent the accomplishments you expect from the employee in the coming year. These can include:

- Specific project completions and deliverables
- Improvements in operational efficiencies
- Addressing weaknesses identified in the performance review
- Skills development—both technical and nontechnical

The goals and the development plan should be developed collaboratively by both you and the employee. You can even ask the employee to take the first cut at them and then review them with you. Both of these should be documented and discussed during the year to review progress and to see if they need to be updated to reflect changes in priorities or circumstances. A popular acronym to help set goals is SMART:

- **S—Specific:** Goals that are too generalized are less likely to be achieved than goals that are specific. Plus, being specific eliminates any ambiguity. For example, instead of "refresh older hardware" you could use "replace all servers that are more than five years old."
- **M—Measurable:** The more a goal can be quantified and measured, the easier it is to determine whether it is achieved. You may have a goal for improving user interface design, but if you don't have a way of measuring the effectiveness of the design (such as a survey), there's no way to know if the goal has been achieved.
- **A—Attainable/Achievable:** When a goal is attainable, it is doable, it is within the realm of possibility because others have done it before, and the resources exist for achieving the goal.
- **R—Realistic:** A goal is realistic because the resources needed to achieve it are available and can be assigned to this goal.
- **T—Timely:** Set a deadline for the goal so that it is not a continuous "work in progress" with no end in sight.

Salary Review

The salary review is often associated with the performance review. Some companies like to do them at the same time, whereas others intentionally like to treat them as separate events and schedule them at different times of the year. In general, when it comes to salary reviews, you as a manager will be told that the increase in your salary budget will be a certain percentage. In short, that means if you want to give one person a little more, you have to give someone else a little less.

Oftentimes, HR will give you some guidelines about increases based on the performance review ratings. For example, top performers should get an increase within a certain percentage range, average performers get another range, and poor performers get less or nothing. The guidelines from HR may also factor in where someone is on the pay scale. For example, if a programmer is already very well paid for their job, their increase may be scaled back some. In many cases, between the HR guidelines and the overall budget you were given, you may find that you have very little wiggle room for your own discretion—you may be tweaking increases by just a few tenths of a percentage point. You may end up spending a few hours with a spreadsheet trying to maximize the budget you've been given and come up with a reasonable increase for each employee. The process for bonuses can be just as involved.

If an employee is disappointed in their increase, it sometimes helps to explain the process so that they understand you just aren't deciding the increase amounts on a whim and that they see there's a structure and policy behind the decisions.

Be careful if an employee talks about another employee's salary. Your response should be direct and along the lines of: "anything related to Mark is confidential and has no bearing on you and is not something I will discuss with you. However, I'm happy to talk about your job, your goals and accomplishments, your salary, and my evaluation of your performance, as well as the overall salary review process."

Disciplinary Problems and Terminations

At some point in your career you're going to have to have some difficult conversations with a team member or make some difficult decisions. There can be a variety of reasons that lead up to these, including:

- A poor hiring decision
- Performance problems or skills deficiency
- Employee not fitting in with the organization's or team's culture
- Personal life impacting work life
- Economic conditions impacting the company

All managers hate having these types of conversations with employees. They are difficult and they generally make both you and the employee very uncomfortable. However, there are some basic guidelines to help ensure that the discussions are effective and to correct a problem before it gets too severe.

Disciplinary Problems

Employee problems come in all shapes and sizes, everything from problems with quality of work to punctuality, from bad attitudes and not following procedures to spending too much time on Facebook. More extreme situations can include things such as violence, theft, harassment, ethics violations, substance abuse, and racism. In some cases, a company may have a clearly stated zero-tolerance policy, and once the company believes there is sufficient evidence to confirm that an incident happened, the employee is immediately terminated—no coaching, no warning, no probationary period.

Although each situation has to be approached uniquely, depending on the circumstances and the individuals involved, there are general guidelines to follow.

First, when something is brought to your attention, you have to make the decision on how to handle it. In some of the more extreme cases, it is very clear that you must involve others immediately, such as HR, Security, Legal, and possibly even law enforcement. In the less extreme, and more traditional, employee problem situations, you have greater latitude as to how to handle them. How do you decide? Your HR rep can be a great source of guidance, as well as company policies. As a general rule, if you're unsure, speak to HR. Also, consider how it might reflect on you if you're made aware of a problem and decided to wait before informing others. In the case of an employee who takes too long a lunch, that's probably not much of a problem. However, it's a very different story if you don't do anything if someone tells you that one of your employees used racial epithets.

In extreme cases, such as situations where violence is involved, HR may step in entirely and take over the handling of the situation. In other cases, HR may work closely with you or just give you some guidance. For the less extreme cases, you may be handling it all on your own until you feel it is necessary to escalate to HR.

Outside of the extreme examples mentioned earlier, you should look at these situations as an opportunity to grow, learn, and, most rewarding of all, coach an employee to get him on the right track.

A less extreme example of an employee problem might be his excessive surfing of the Web during the workday. His performance is suffering and the rest of his team resents having to "carry" him. This is a problem you can—and should—address as a manager without involving others.

As is always the case, communication is the key from the outset. Also, you want to approach the situation in a measured manner. You should always be careful to have the facts correct, not just rely on some rumors you heard in the break room. Depending on the situation, you may want to give it some time to see if there's a pattern of this behavior or if it's just a one-off occurrence. In the case of the employee taking too long a lunch, for example, it makes sense to see how often this occurs. (You also don't want to be the manager who gets a reputation for calling someone on the carpet the first time they are 10 minutes late.)

When it's clear there's a problem, you need to discuss it with the employee. You need to explain to the employee what has occurred, why it is wrong, and the impact it's having on others and the department. Then you must make it clear what sort of change in behavior you are expecting to see and that you expect to see that change immediately. For more specific issues, such as delivering reports with errors, the corrective steps are pretty clear. In other cases, such as weak technical skills, you as the manager may have to be involved in arranging for training or partnering the employee with a more experienced team member. Still in other cases, such as poor attitude or disorganization, you may have to be even more involved to help coach the employee to see the problem, its impact, and how to address changing the pattern of behavior. Sometimes, the employee isn't even aware of the issue and as soon as it is brought up, it is resolved. At this point, you don't have to formalize anything in the employee's file, but do make notes for yourself about the discussion.

As you continue to monitor and observe the employee, make sure to keep the communication lines open. If you see that things are changing for the better, give some immediate and direct positive feedback. If things are not changing, point that out as well. While each situation varies, if you have two heart-to-heart conversations with an employee and the behavior doesn't improve enough or fast enough, it's time to have a discussion with HR. At this point, it may be appropriate to give the employee a formal written warning. A written warning generally recounts the problems, the discussions you've had, the problem's impact, and the behavior changes you expect to see. It will probably also make reference to the fact that failure to address the problem will lead to further disciplinary action, up to and including termination. HR usually has a standard template or format for these and will often have the Legal department review the document.

Delivery of a written warning usually comes in a meeting with yourself, HR, and the employee, where the situation is reviewed and the employee is given the warning memo. Very often, a written warning is the kick-in-the-pants necessary to get an employee on track. Other times, the employee may just "shut down" entirely and you can see that things are not likely to improve. The number and timing of the discussions and warnings will vary from organization to organization, on policy, and on the specific circumstances.

If the situation continues, the next steps are usually a final written warning and then termination.

Layoffs and Terminations

If an employee has been a performance problem and you've taken the appropriate progressive disciplinary actions outlined earlier regarding discussions and warnings and the employee has still not improved, it is time to terminate the employee. In all likelihood, by this point, the employee may not be terribly surprised. Whether you, HR, or both inform the employee, the phrase "you're fired" is usually not used. More common ways of saying it include "we are terminating your employment," "today is your last day," and "we're letting you go." While no termination is a good one, and more than one manager has lost considerable sleep over it, if you handled the disciplinary process properly, you should take some comfort in the fact that you did everything you could and gave this employee every opportunity to address the problem. It then fell to you to take the next step, and if you didn't it would now appear to your boss that you're not performing *your* job.

More difficult than terminations related to disciplinary problems are the layoffs related to economic conditions. In these situations, you may be directed that you have to cut a certain number of employees and it becomes your job (either alone or in discussion with peers, HR, or your manager) to decide who. These can be the most gut-wrenching decisions you'll have to make as a manager because you are severely impacting people's lives. You need to focus on thinking objectively:

- If the company is shutting down some projects and initiatives, who are the people in your organization on those projects?
- Which employees show the greatest capacity (technical skill sets, attitude, and work ethic) to take on additional work if the department size is reduced?
- Are there already any weak performers or disciplinary problems on the team?

These are difficult and challenging situations. Not only are the layoffs difficult enough, but morale will suffer, and it's entirely possible some of the remaining people will resign soon after because they are afraid that they "may be next."

Regardless of the situation, the discussion should be done in private, and enough time should be provided for an employee who becomes emotional and need to regain their composure. Sometimes HR will review some paperwork (e.g., regarding benefits, unemployment insurance) or tell them that they'll be receiving a packet in the mail in a few days. Depending on the policy and the circumstances, an employee may be escorted out of the building immediately.

HR will probably offer some guidance, but it's usually a good idea to speak to your team in these situations, particularly in the case of layoffs. Gather the team together, explain what happened, the difficult economic conditions, and so on. Allow them to ask questions. Give them time to be upset by the situation. Explain to them that things will be tougher now, with a reduced work force, and that you'll be relying on them more than ever. If possible, try to bring some closure to the situation by saying that these are all the layoffs that were planned.

In the case of a termination related to disciplinary problems, you should not reveal too much about the circumstances, but it's usually appropriate to inform the team that Francine is no longer with the company. It sure beats people spreading rumors about why Francine is no longer around.

The termination package available to employees who are let go is usually dictated by company policy and sometimes law (e.g., continuation of medical benefits). Some companies may offer things such as outplacement services, company-paid benefits, or perhaps even use of an office and phone for a while. Severance pay is often defined by some sort of formula that HR can provide. However, there is usually some latitude depending on the circumstances. The employee who was terminated for punching a coworker may not get any severance pay; on the other hand, the severance policy may be made more generous when there is a round of layoffs, as opposed to performance issues.

ALTERNATIVES TO COMPANY-WIDE LAYOFFS

None of the alternatives proposed here are perfect, but they can often be more efficient, more profitable (in the long run), more humane, and often better received than the layoff options discussed earlier. As global economic conditions worsened starting in 2008 and 2009, organizations experimented with all kinds of different methods to save money and cut employee costs:

- Cut everyone's hours a small amount instead of cutting certain employees' entire jobs. This option has benefits and drawbacks but it is widely practiced in some industries.
- Cut everyone's pay a small amount instead of cutting certain employees' entire jobs. As just described, often individuals would prefer to take a small pay cut rather than have their coworkers lose their entire jobs.
- Offer packages to employees who are willing to leave the company.
- Radically scale back the services/products/hours the company provides. Severe economic conditions force companies to rethink their core missions and often that rethinking can be a good thing. Rather than being open seven days a week with all the staffing issues that entails, perhaps the local bakery is closed two days in the middle of the week. Rather than offering four models with 10 options each with all the manufacturing costs all of those alternatives offer, perhaps the car/cell phone/stereo company offers two models with five options each.
- Institute a mandatory one-week furlough for all employees, with no pay.
- Shut the company down while there is something still left to split among those who are still left. There is some of the "creative destruction" that is often attributed to capitalism in this idea; some companies (horse and buggy builders) need to be moved aside to allow the new engines of change (automobiles in the early 1900s) to take their place.
- Embrace telecommuting solutions for some staff as a way to reduce the cost of office space.

Of course, these are not things you can implement on your own. You'd have to get buy-in from senior management and other departments. But these ideas do show that there are alternatives in tough times. For additional discussion in managing during challenging economic, see the section **"Managing the Money during Difficult Times"** on **page 179** in **Chapter 6, Managing the Money**.

It can also help to remember that more than one employee has looked back after a period of time and said: "You know, getting laid off was the best thing that ever happened to me. I had the opportunity to give thought to what I wanted to do in the future, I changed industries, I started taking classes in a new programming language, and landed a job that I really like where I'm learning a lot." You certainly do not want to act like laying someone off is doing them a favor, but in many cases it may turn out to be a blessing in disguise.

2.4 GENERATIONAL ISSUES AT WORK

Never before in our history have such stark differences been seen between generations in the corporate world. Think about it: There was the Baby Boomer generation, but the generations before that didn't have their own names. (At least not at that time; in retrospect they are sometimes referred to as "Depression," "Pre-World War II," "World War II," "Veteran," "The Greatest" generations, etc.)

The current generations have their own names, and they are popularly classified as shown in Table 2.3.

Table 2.3 Different Generations

	Traditionalists	Baby Boomers	Gen-X	Gen-Y
Alternate names	Veterans, Silents, Greatest Generation, Mature Generation, Forgotten Generation	Me Generation	Generation-X, Post-Boomers, Baby Bust	Generation-Y, Echo Boomers, NexGen, Millennials
Born	1925–1944	1945–1964	1965–1980	1981–2000
% of work force	10	45	30	13

Source: *Eisner, Susan, "Managing Generation Y," Society for Advancement Management, 2005 International Conference.*

As shown in Table 2.3, things get confused by using alternate names for the same item. Plus, some people like to include references to early and late components of each generation. Furthermore, the dates used in Table 2.3 are certainly not universally accepted identifiers. While there have always been multiple generations at work simultaneously, it is getting so much attention at this point in time because of the degree of difference in attitudes, behaviors, values, and styles among them. And, of course, people are living much longer now, so more generations are alive at the same time.

These differences between the generations are associated with several factors that include:

- Economic circumstances that have forced older generations to stay in the workforce longer
- Advances in technology
- Changes in approaches to parenting, including greater involvement
- Increased resources (schooling, medical, household income)
- Faster paced lifestyle
- Greater access to media and information
- Increased expectations

Of course, there is debate as to which of these are causes and which of these are effects, but that is for a different book. In this book, the important point is that the generations are different, people's attitude and behaviors can vary greatly among them, and you as a manager will be severely challenged if you don't recognize the importance of this, demonstrate flexibility, and adapt your behaviors accordingly.

Table 2.4 provides greater detail into the differences attributed to the different generations.

As you can see, the different generations can have very different ideas, perspectives, and attitudes. The simple issue of what is considered "professional behavior" can be like night and day. The same can be said regarding their differing views about policies, rules, boundaries, work hours, tools, and, of course, proper attire in the work place. In short, you cannot expect all employees to march to the beat of the same drummer.

Managing across Generations

Having multiple generations on your team should be considered an enormous asset. It gives you a greater diversity of thinking, views, style operating, and knowledge base. In a 2010 study by the staffing firm Robert Half (www.roberthalf.us/workplaceredefined) there were some very positive findings:

- 43 percent of workers surveyed say multigenerational teams bring together people of varying experience levels to provide knowledge in specific areas.
- 27 percent of those surveyed say working with multiple generations allows for greater diversity of project teams so all points of view are heard.
- 35 percent say working on multigenerational teams has led to increased productivity.
- The top benefits of working with multiple generations are (1) bringing together people of varying experience levels, (2) greater diversity of project teams, and (3) mentoring opportunities.
- Communication styles may vary, but ultimately, multigenerational teams learn from each other, and bringing together diverse groups increases productivity.

However, that doesn't mean you can just kick back, put your feet up, and let that diversity do its thing. As a manager, you have to be aware of how best to manage that diversity and the pitfalls to be aware of. For example, a 2010 Accenture study and report found that "Millennials are likely ignoring or violating your IT policies right and left, using non-standard applications and improvising where they think it makes sense." In addition, the Accenture study found several important trends about Millennials:

- Many expect to use their own technology and devices rather than those supplied by employers.
- But they also want employers to provide the latest technologies.
- Awareness of or adherence to corporate IT policies is limited. Millennials routinely bypass corporate approval when it comes to downloading and using technology.

Leveraging a Multigenerational Workforce

Taking advantage of a multigenerational workforce requires some tuning and stretching of fundamental management skills. First and foremost you don't want to ignore the fact that differences exist among the generations. As such, when you create project teams, you can (and should) include individuals from the various generations so that everyone can leverage the best of what each generation has to offer, while also learning from each other. This includes allowing members of one generation to mentor and coach members of another—yes, that may mean members of the younger generations coaching the older. Don't let age define roles and assignments—look first to skill sets and strengths. You should also respect and recognize the preferences of each generation. For example, with the younger generations, consider flex hours or some telecommuting options.

Factor the generational issues into your recruiting practices. (See the section **"How to Get Help with Your Hiring"** in **Chapter 3, Staffing Your IT Team, on page 66.**) Ask the candidates about their background and experience with working on teams made up of several generations and how it impacted the project, the other team members, and so on. Similarly, take pride in your own multigenerational teams. When recognizing team accomplishments, be sure to include members of all generations. This is particularly well done when there's a newsletter with a photo of the team and it's obvious at first glance about the team's multigenerational makeup. Also look to tailor recognition to each generation's preferences. For example, a traditionalist may like a lunch with the boss, whereas a Gen-Xer might prefer a gift certificate for music downloads.

You should always make sure that each generation feels valued. Look out for your own subconscious biases in soliciting input, making assignments, and such. Go out of your way to ensure that everyone feels included. Also, just because someone works in a different manner than how you work doesn't mean their way is wrong. Be open-minded about new ways of working and doing things, which includes embracing but not forcing technology.

Table 2.4 Generational Differences

	Veterans	Baby Boomers	Generation X	Millennials
Work style	By the book—"how" is as important as "what" gets done	Get it done—whatever it takes; nights and weekends	Find the fastest route to results; protocol is secondary	Work to deadlines—not to schedules
Authority/leadership	Command/control; rarely question authority	Respect for power and accomplishment	Rules are flexible; collaboration is important	Value autonomy; less inclined to pursue formal leadership positions
View of authority	Respectful	Love/hate	Unimpressed	Polite
Relationship with authority	Seniority and titles are respected	Desire flat organizations that are democratic	Competence and skills are respected over seniority	Flips traditional roles by the young teaching seniors (e.g., technology skills)
View toward change	"Something's wrong"	Caution	Potential opportunity	Improvement
Communication	Top down; formal and through standard channels	Guarded; somewhat formal and through structured network	Casual and direct; sometimes skeptical; hub and spoke	Collaborative; casual and direct; eager to please
Feedback	No news is good news	Once per year	Weekly/daily	On demand
Problem solving	Hierarchical	Horizontal	Independent	Collaborative
Decision making	Seeks approval	Team informed	Team included	Team decided
Recognition/reward	Personal acknowledgment and compensation for work well done	Public acknowledgment and career advancement (money, title, corner office)	A balance of fair compensation and ample time off as reward; freedom is the ultimate reward	Individual and public praise (exposure); opportunity for broadening skills; meaningful work
Work/family	Work and family should be kept separate	Work comes first	Value work/life balance	Value blending personal life into work
Loyalty	To the organization	To the importance and meaning of work	To individual and career goals	To the people involved with the project
Relationship	Personal sacrifice	Personal gratification	Reluctant to commit	Inclusive
Technology	"If it ain't broke, don't fix it"	Necessary for progress	Practical tools for getting things done	What else is there?
Training	The hard way—learn by doing	Too much and I'll leave	Required to keep me	Expected and continuous
Learning style	Classroom	Facilitated	Independent	Collaborative

Sources: *Zemke, Rob, Raines, Claire, and Filipzcak, Bob, "Generations at Work: Managing the Clash of Veterans, Boomers, X-ers, and Nexers,"* American Management Association, 2000. Ngenperformance.com. Lancaster, Lynne C., and Stillman, David, *When Generations Collide: Who They Are, Why They Clash, How to Solve the Generational Puzzle at Work,* HarperCollins, 2002.

The younger generations were brought up with technology. Older generations have certainly learned technology and adapted to it, but not to the same extent or at the same pace. While the younger ones are Tweeting, Facebooking, blogging, texting, and so on, the older generations may be a step or two behind. Encourage the use of alternate solutions, but allow everyone to come up to speed with it at a pace they are comfortable with. This also means that you as a manager should not limit your modes of communications. While the older generations may prefer face-to-face chats, your younger generations may prefer instant messages or text messages (perhaps at 2 AM on a Sunday!).

Finally, work with your HR department to help ensure that the entire organization is recognizing the multigenerational issue and addressing it carefully. Does the break room have beverages and snacks that appeal to all generations? One good example is employee benefit plans: different generations generally have very different priorities and those can be addressed through different options and choices.

Table 2.5 Advantages and Disadvantages of Experienced Workers and "Newbie" Workers

Some Strengths of Experienced Workers	Some Strengths of "Newbie" Workers
Their time in the office is fully focused on work, as opposed to trying to blend work with their personal lives by Facebooking in the middle of meetings. They focus better. Eric Schmidt, former CEO of Google, recalls "that shortly after joining the company . . . he was frustrated that people were answering e-mail on their laptops at meetings while he was speaking. 'I've given up' trying to change such behavior, he says. 'They have to answer their e-mail. Velocity matters.'" Maybe. But attention to the speaker/presenter/teacher/group leader certainly matters too. Until society figures out which cell phone and PC behaviors in public are acceptable, it will be incumbent upon managers to make their standards known. "Because you can" check your e-mail during a meeting or text your colleague during a conversation with your boss does not mean it's the right thing to do. And many newbie workers have never been told which behaviors are acceptable (and which are not) because the technology is often so new.	Those who are newer to the workforce generally have less personal demands outside the office and find it easier to put in that extra weekend needed to complete the upgrade.
Thinning or gray hair often mean wisdom, experience, and perspective to your team.	Relative newbies grew up with technology and constantly had to learn new tools and new ways of doing things. It is never a challenge to convince them to let go of the old method and to try a new approach, such as send and receive e-mail from their cell phones and use social networking at work. They are less likely to be in a position where they are stuck in a particular technology and cannot be dislodged. It comes naturally to them to use any technology available in new and innovative ways. They can answer e-mails without feeling that they have to be in front of a PC, for example.

Continued

Table 2.5 Advantages and Disadvantages of Experienced Workers and "Newbie" Workers—Cont'd

Some Strengths of Experienced Workers	Some Strengths of "Newbie" Workers
New technologies are often little more than variations on old technologies, and having someone who has already climbed the steepest parts of the learning curve can be a distinct advantage.	Relative newbie workers have spirit and energy and zip—and they know almost everything! Of course, they *don't* know almost everything, but they *think* they know almost everything, which sometimes can be a great advantage.
They have perspective. They have the background of having lived and worked through huge problems, such as national recessions, complete company backup failures, and having the corporation bought out, as well as smaller issues, such as new product rollouts.	IT projects are often complex endeavors that get people down; they take a long time to start, take a lot of energy to maintain, and the end can seem unattainable. Relative newbie workers often add the blind enthusiasm necessary to get over the last 20 yards to the finish line. They don't know that failure is an option so they work over the weekend and get all of the new servers installed.

Note that when we say "experienced" and "relative newbie" workers, we mean "individuals who have more and less than (respectively) approximately 10 years of corporate experience." Of course the number varies from industry to industry, and organization to organization, but in general, we are referring to the amount of time an individual has spent in a formal organizational setting.

Your job as a manager—regardless of whether you are young or old yourself—is to make sure that every member of your team understands the importance of communication: not only communicating with people in other time zones and cubicle farms across the company, but listening and speaking to people right in front of you. This can be startling news to some workers. The importance of communications has been discussed throughout this chapter—and for good reason. In addition to communications, being flexible, avoiding stereotypes, and encouraging collaboration can help to minimize the generation gaps. The best teams, of course, have the energy of youth and the wisdom of age.

2.5 Further References

Websites

www.accenture.com/SiteCollectionDocuments/PDF/global_millennial_generation_research.pdf (generational issues at work).

www.amanet.org (American Management Association).

www.changingminds.org/disciplines/leadership/articles/manager_leader.htm (leadership vs. management).

www.humanresources.about.com/od/360feedback/360_Degree_Feedback_Process.htm (360 reviews).

www.managementhelp.org (Free management library).

www.microsoft.com/presspass/download/features/2011/05-18Remote.pptx (report on U.S. telework trends).

www.roberthalf.us/workplaceredefined (generational issues at work).

www.teleworkresearchnetwork.com/costs-benefits (telework programs).

www.trwib.org/agingtoolkit/documents/Multigenerational%20Diversity%20in%20U.S.%20Workplaces%20Eliminating%20I.pdf.

www.worldatwork.org/waw/adimComment?id=48318 (telework programs).

Books and Articles

Bacal, R., 2008. How to Manage Performance: 24 Lessons to Improving Performance. McGraw-Hill.

Casselberry, R., 2008. 30 Skills Every IT Person Needs. InfoWorld August 13.

Eisner, S., 2005. Managing Generation Y. Society for Advancement Management, International Conference.

Greengard, S., 2011. Managing a Multigenerational Workforce. CIO Insight Magazine May/June.

2011. Harvard Business Review's 10 Must Reads on Managing People. Harvard Business Press.

Jaffe, B.D., 1998. Following a Few Simple Rules Can Ease the Pain of Employee Reviews. InfoWorld January 26.

Jenkins, T., 2010. A Commonsense Approach to Dealing with People: Managing People Made Easier. iUniverse.

Kluger, J., 2009. Why Bosses Tend to Be Blowhards. Time Magazine March 2.

Kotter, J.P., 1990. A Force for Change: How Leadership Differs from Management. Free Press.

Kouzes, J.M., Posner, B.Z., 2008. The Leadership Challenge. Jossey-Bass.

Lancaster, L.C., Stillman, D., 2002. When Generations Collide: Who They Are, Why They Clash, How to Solve the Generational Puzzle at Work. HarperCollins.

Nazarian, A., 2010. Technical Minds: Leading and Getting the Best Work from Your Technically-Minded Team. CreateSpace.

Orrell, L., 2008. Millennials Incorporated. Wyatt-MacKenzie.

Richards, T., 2010. Self-Confidence…for Managing People at Work. Outskirts Press.

Society for Human Resource Management, 2005. Generational Differences Survey Report.

Tulgan, B., 2009. Not Everyone Gets a Trophy: How to Manage Generation Y. Jossey-Bass.

Violino, B., 2011. Workers without Borders. Baseline Magazine July/August.

Waxer, C., 2009. Clash of the Generations. Computerworld February 16.

Zemnke, R., Raines, C., Filipzcak, B., 2000. Generations at Work: Managing the Clash of Veterans, Boomers, X-ers, and Nexers. American Management Association.

Staffing Your IT Team

3

The key for us, number one, has always been hiring very smart people.
Bill Gates

CHAPTER TABLE OF CONTENTS

3.1 Why IT Managers Need to Deal with Hiring People 65
3.2 Write a Position Description 74
3.3 Recruiters 79
3.4 Selecting Candidates 83
3.5 Further References 101

Your success or failure as an IT Manager is based almost entirely on the people that work for you. Every time you hire a new employee, you have an opportunity to add value to your team, to your company as a whole, and to adjust the balance of skill sets and personality of the team. Therefore, each hire should have your full attention and not be dismissed as another administrative chore. This chapter discusses the important details associated with the various elements involved in hiring for your team.

Hiring a few years ago was difficult because there weren't enough well-qualified candidates available for the open positions. More recently, hiring has been difficult because there are now too many well-qualified candidates. The reasons will change, but the difficulty—and importance—of hiring the right people for the right jobs will never change.

3.1 WHY IT MANAGERS NEED TO DEAL WITH HIRING PEOPLE

You need to deal with hiring carefully because the people on your staff are the single biggest factor in determining whether you're going to be successful at your job.

Hiring means dealing with recruiting agencies and your Human Resources (HR) department, reviewing résumés, conducting interviews, and negotiating offers. If you secretly wish that the first candidate you meet is *the one* and you're glad your job isn't in personnel, don't worry: you're not alone. That means you feel the same way as every other IT Manager.

It's precisely this urge to "hire first, ask questions later," however, that can easily lead to a decision that you and your company will come to regret. This chapter details some of the issues to watch out for, the questions to ask (both of yourself and interviewees), and other issues you should be concerned about when considering bringing someone new onto your team.

Human Resources Department's Role

Because recruiting for an IT position usually involves dealing with a lot of technical terms, skills, and résumés with acronyms and buzzwords, many HR departments that normally lead recruiting efforts for all other departments will take a back seat and let you drive when it comes to IT recruiting. But just because you are driving does not mean they can't help with the logistics of the process. Talk to HR and discuss the following:

- Is there an approved list of recruiters to use? What is the company's policy on their fees?
- Can you find and use your own recruiters?
- Who is responsible for placing ads on websites? Who pays for the ads?
- Is there a careers section on the company website or a mechanism for alerting employees at subsidiaries and sister companies?
- Will HR perform the initial screening of applicants' résumés?
- Will someone (either you or HR) use social networking tools like LinkedIn to proactively go out and find possible candidates?
- Who evaluates the salary range for this position and what is the evaluation process?
- Who should be the internal point of contact for agencies and applicants?
- Who does background and reference checks?
- What is the time frame for the process?
- Who is in charge of the process?

As stated earlier, many HR departments recognize that IT recruiting is a special skill and one that they might not be particularly good at. Accordingly, they may ask you to take as large a role as possible. If this is the case in your company (and don't assume it is), HR may only want to get involved during the initial screening process, help you with scheduling interviews, and then help at the end with background checks and offer letters.

How to Get Help with Your Hiring

If you're working for a small company, you'll probably have to assume some HR duties, just like you have to assume some administrative, accounting, or travel duties. But once the company reaches a certain size, it should get someone to help with the hiring duties. They don't have to take care of all the hiring, but they certainly can help.

In particular, you can get the HR department to help you with the screening and recruiting processes:

- Once you have written the position description (see the section **"Write a Position Description"** later in this chapter on **page 74**), they can post it for you. They can work with you to figure out where the position should be posted—general job sites, industry-specific sites, etc.
- Have them identify someone in their department as a contact point. Let them field the initial calls and e-mails. Have them narrow the initial responses (which can be in the hundreds, even for specifically worded technical jobs) down to a manageable size. Give them strict guidelines ("The candidate must have 5 years of programming experience and must know at least Perl, C++, and Java") to use to perform the initial screening. Give them a number: you want to *look at* 15 résumés max and *talk to* five candidates max.

- If the job requires writing skills, HR can ask for writing samples.
- If interpersonal skills are important, HR can save you valuable time by eliminating those candidates who are simply poor communicators, or don't take pride in their appearance, etc. The buzz word is "client-facing," as in: "This position is client-facing; its primarily role is to interact with executives and support their use of technology." For this position, the company (and the department) needs to be represented by a professional-looking individual. Some companies will also refer to this as an individual's "presentation."
- Once you have done the interviewing and chosen the candidate you like, hand the ball back to HR. They can call the candidate's references and draw up the offer letter. Finally, you or HR can make sure there is a place for the candidate when he first arrives, that he has work to do, is introduced to his coworkers, and also that the associated new-hire materials (such as the benefits package and company policies) are covered.
- Your HR representative can also be an effective liaison between you and the candidate when the offer is extended and/or negotiated. They have the experience to know how to handle these situations, how to respond, etc. They will check with you before committing to anything and offer you guidance.

Justifying a Hire

Before you hire someone, though, you may need to get approvals to do so. Whether it is simply replacing someone who recently left or adding to staff, you may need to convince others that this hire is necessary. If it's a new position, you'll have to explain why this role is needed and what benefit it will deliver. Sometimes the position description (discussed later in this chapter) has enough information; other times you may need to go into more detail. Some examples of justification include:

- The department's workload has grown by X percent in the past year, and additional staff is needed to keep up. Sometimes you can justify the workload with metrics such as the number of calls to the Help Desk, number of new projects, and the company's growth. Also, consider losses due to previous downsizing (the "falling further behind" syndrome).
- The department has brought in new technologies and you need to hire people who are already skilled and experienced in order to use the product effectively. However, be careful with this as it is often said that it is cheaper to train an existing employee than to recruit a new one.
- The company can save time and money if certain processes are automated, but you need staff to implement and support this.
- You will be able to respond to your users/customers X percent faster if you expand your staff.
- The company has decided on an initiative (e.g., a new major application, or expanding into new markets) and expanding technology is a critical factor for success.

Be as specific as you can with your estimates, but also note that they are only estimates. No one expects you to be able to determine to the dollar or to the hour how much savings or productivity improvement a new hire will generate so note that these are your estimates. But use numbers in your request. Numbers represent facts, and presenting facts is better than presenting an opinion—don't just say "it would be good to get another guy." Plus, you don't want to be perceived as an "empire-building" manager who thinks he can increase his own status (or boosting his own ego) simply by managing a larger staff.

IDEAS FOR MANAGING IN TOUGH TIMES

Justifying a new hire was never easy, but it has gotten radically more difficult over the last couple of years due to the global economic downturn. Here are some things to keep in mind before you ever start to seek approval for a new hire.

- Decide if you want to hire a full-time person or a contractor. This issue is discussed more fully in the section **"Should You Hire a Full-Time Employee or a Consultant?"** later in this chapter. Because companies have become more and more resistant to the idea of bringing someone on full time, if a contractor can fill the need you will generally have an easier time justifying the expense.
- Be ready with the answer if you are asked if this job function can be outsourced—either to a company specializing in this function or to a resource/location that can perform the job for less money. Outsourcing has serious benefits and liabilities (discussed in **Chapter 6, Managing the Money** on **page 161**), but be ready with both when you are asked, as you most assuredly will be asked.
- Be ready to explain why no one else in the company cannot perform this function already. (See the next section **"Start with Internal and External Referrals."**) You may have already run through the potential candidates in your head and dismissed each one, but that kind of quick analysis might fail you in the heat of a job-justification conversation. Be ready with specifics.

Start with Internal and External Referrals

Looking inside is the best method to start your search for a candidate. Does anyone in your department/ company/personal network know of a candidate who matches your criteria? Coworkers, other managers, and internal job-posting boards all can provide valuable names. You should *always* start here.

The quality of people you contact through these referrals is generally higher and the candidates are generally better suited for the position. Most people are conscious of putting their reputation on the line when recommending another person and will do so only if they have some level of confidence that the person merits the recommendation.

Be sure you don't make any promises though. Ask everyone if they know of someone, but be careful not to make any assurances up front. The most you should promise is that you'll look at their résumé or that you'll make sure the right person looks at the résumé. Some internal referrals can be radically mismatched ("I thought you said you were looking for a C++ programmer, not a Web development person"). Aside from the occasional courtesy interview, you shouldn't waste your time, or theirs, by interviewing candidates who are never going to get the job.

Of course, make sure the candidate is treated with respect. If they're referred to you and aren't right for the position, make sure they're contacted with that information. You want to be able to reuse your internal contacts, and leaving their recommendations in limbo is a good way to make sure they don't help you next time.

You can go further than looking at their résumé if that is called for. Often called "courtesy interviews," these are interviews with a candidate that you perform as a favor to someone. If the CEO calls and asks you to hire his nephew, you can certainly agree to talk to him. Not necessarily *hire* the person, but you can talk to them.

Internal versus External Hires

An internal hire is when someone from within the company, or perhaps even from within your own department, is selected for an opening. In some cases it might be a promotion, and in other cases it might just be a lateral change. Hiring individuals from within your own department or your own company presents its own challenges. Like many other issues dealt with in this book, there are good and bad reasons for hiring inside (see Table 3.1).

Table 3.1 Pros and Cons of Internal Hires	
PRO	**CON**
The candidate is known. Her strengths and weaknesses have been seen by other people you work with so there shouldn't be many surprises.	**Hiring an internal person may anger other people you work with.** If the person has talent and is a contributor to his group, his boss may be reluctant (or downright furious at the idea) at one of their workers transferring within the company. For personal reasons, many managers are angrier at a worker transferring to another department or division than they are at a person leaving the company altogether. It doesn't make a lot of sense (a lost worker is a lost worker, and going to another department still might benefit the previous manager in some small ways), but it's a fact. Try to determine what the reaction of the manager of the candidate you are interested in will be before you start talking to people. This can range from a simple and casual request at a meeting you are both attending to a formal, preinterview notification.
Many companies aggressively promote the concept of hiring/promoting from within so you can get some kudos from upper management for adding to the company's internal hire list.	**People who have worked for the company for a while know "where all the bodies are buried."** They arrive with many preconceived ideas—maybe even some about your department. New people to the company generally come with their eyes and ears open, ready to absorb and learn. Some internal people arrive like that, whereas others arrive with many hard-to-shake prejudices.
Other employees will appreciate seeing that there is an opportunity to move up. Too often, staff members leave a company simply because they don't believe they see much opportunity for their own growth. **There will be a radically shorter introduction term;** the candidate knows how the company works, is familiar with the organization, terms, and processes and can start being productive much sooner.	

> **THE FOUR C'S OF INTERNAL VERSUS EXTERNAL HIRES**
>
> When considering whether to hire an external vs. internal hire, your assessment regimen is as critical as any other step in the new hire process. Following the four C's can provide a guide to making a more informed decision:
>
> - **Circumstance:** What are your needs? Do you require a short-term win or can you afford to wait a little longer for someone to get up to speed? Consider specific vs. general, strategic vs. tactical, etc.
> - **Cost factors:** We know the expense tied to hiring new employees, but what about calculating your opportunity costs—the cost of choosing one candidate over another?

Continued

THE FOUR C'S OF INTERNAL VERSUS EXTERNAL HIRES—Cont'd

- **Chemistry:** Will your team like him or her? How will morale be affected? It is difficult to predict how a person will mesh with others, yet it can significantly alter the effectiveness of a team. To that end, I would always have the managers on my team (with strong personnel evaluation skills) interview all candidates.
- **Continuity:** How long will you need this person? If you get a superstar, don't expect to hang on to them too long and if you get a dud you might end up having to manage them out sooner than later.

I hired five new managers over a two-year span (due to rapid department growth), which gave me a unique perspective on internal vs. external hires. Two were hired from the outside, while three were promoted from within. These were managers who would need to possess a range of experience in managing people and in understanding the financial sector, as well as the ability to grasp both branded and proprietary systems and technology.

External vs. Internal Hires: The Experience Gap

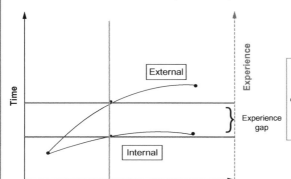

The External hire will have a steeper learning curve while the Internal candidate will typically enjoy a shorter time to get "up to speed." Oftentimes the reason for going outside is the need for more experience. The second y axis plots "Experience" and one can see the trade-off (gap) between a quick learner vs. what an outsider might bring to the table, even early on in the assimilation process.

There were significant learnings from this (real life) exercise, which I apply to each and every hiring situation I encounter. In the end, the two external hires were successful and stayed well after I moved on while two of the three internals became protégés, one eventually succeeding me in the position (the third was a dud, proving you can't nail it every time, despite a rigorous hiring gauntlet!).

There is no magical formula that will tell you whether to promote the familiar (internal) candidate vs. bringing in a veteran (external); however, it's a safe bet that with strong due diligence you can rest easier knowing you did your homework.

—Tim Holtsnider
Project Manager, Global Customer Service Business Integration
Monster, Inc.

Should You Hire a Full-Time Employee or a Consultant?

The answer, of course, is "it depends." It depends on what your needs are. Both types of staff have their strengths and weaknesses.

Full-time employees are individuals who work for your organization. Some are paid by the hour and some are salaried, but in either case, they are hired by, paid by, and report to someone in the organization. In addition to salaries, full-time employees receive additional benefits that can take the form of health insurance coverage, vacation time, retirement plans, etc. To your Finance and HR people, these individuals are sometimes referred to as W-2s because they get a W-2 tax form at the end of the year.

Most full-time employees are hired on an "at-will" basis, which means that either the employee or the company can terminate the arrangement at any point for any nondiscriminatory reason. However, this can vary from state to state, and certainly country to country. Regardless, your Legal and HR departments will probably insist on sufficient reasons and due process, though, if you're the one looking to end someone's employment. The alternative to at-will employment is when an employment agreement/contract is signed by both employee and employer.

Consultants (also referred to as contractors), however, are brought in on a temporary basis by companies. They're generally paid by the hour or day, receive no benefits, and aren't on the company's payroll. They aren't employees of your organization and are often responsible for handling not only their own benefits and insurance, but also their own taxes. You may find an independent contractor through an agency or consulting firm or you may find them directly through Web searches or personal referrals. Online job sites are popular methods of finding qualified contractors. These individuals are often referred to as 1099s because instead of receiving a W-2 tax form, they get a 1099 tax form (either from your company or their agency).

Which type of employee should you hire? See Tables 3.2 and 3.3 for the pros and cons of full-time employees and consultants.

Along those lines, it is important to note that IT is a strenuous world and that IT projects are often complex, multi-person, multi-year adventures. You'll need to get buy-in from everyone on your team for many of the issues you address; contractors may or may not be there for you in the crunch.

Determine Which Type Is Best for Your Job

To best determine whether you should hire a consultant or a full-time employee, think about why you're seeking new staff. Do you need someone for a few months in an area of technology that your team has no expertise in and probably won't need in the future? If so, you should hire a contractor. Do you need someone to fill a gaping hole in your team or replace an employee who is leaving? If so, you should hire a full-time employee.

Financial considerations may also play a role here. Not only does the actual cost enter into it, but, as mentioned before, sometimes an organization doesn't want to add head count, and would prefer you bring someone in as a consultant instead of as a full-time employee.

Consultant or Employee: You Can't Have It Both Ways

Regardless of whether you decide to hire an independent contractor or a full-time employee, make that determination *before* you open the req. In the past, several companies have tried to have it both ways. That is, even though individuals were brought on as contractors, the employer was essentially treating them as full-time employees. These companies have lost lawsuits as a result of this kind of situation. As such, the individuals were entitled to those things that true full-time employees enjoy, like participating in stock purchase plans (www.bizjournals.com/seattle/stories/2000/12/11/daily7.html).

Worker status is a tricky issue with many potential legal ramifications. If you have any concerns about the status of your workers or potential employees, take them up with your HR and Legal departments as soon as possible.

Timing Considerations

The circumstances and requirements of the hire will often help you with this decision; if you're looking to fill an entry-level position, the spring is a good time to get this semester's graduates. And if your company follows the academic calendar (for example, textbook publishing and school supplies

Table 3.2 Pros and Cons to Using Consultants

PRO	CON
In general, contractors may have more diverse experience. You can find independent contractors with backgrounds in most, if not all, of the obscure corners of technology. Because they aren't locked to one desk and to one organization, they're free to roam and learn what new projects and new companies can teach them.	**Consultants often cost more than full-time employees.** Even counting benefits, etc., that a full-time person is paid, contractors can easily cost you more. This is particularly the case if the contractor is hired through an agency, as the pay rate will include the agency's markup. (Contractors have to pay their own Social Security taxes, among other things, so their rates will generally be higher than a full-time person's wages.)
Because contractors often have such varied expertise, they usually require little or no training to become productive. You can see results from contractors in a relatively short amount of time.	**If you hire a consultant, for budgeting purposes you will need to estimate how long the contract will be.** This is sometimes very hard to do; if you are finishing off a companywide operating system upgrade, you know (roughly) how many machines are involved, how long it will take to do each one, etc. But if you are helping the Development team implement a new Accounts Receivable system, there are many variables that affect the outcome. That process could take anywhere from a few months to much longer, and sometimes factors nowhere near your control can influence that figure.
Consultants don't add to head count. When companies are trying to save money, it looks poorly if they are adding to staff. Although the actual costs may be more expensive, upper management and the Finance department frequently would rather pay a contractor as opposed to increasing the employee head count.	**It is easy (and potentially disastrous) to forget that contractors aren't employees of your company: Their loyalty, in the end, is to themselves.** This isn't to say contractors do a poor job; some do spectacular jobs (while others don't, of course). But they care about getting paid and recording hours; their interest in the long-term growth of your department or your company isn't all that high. If a contractor feels that he may not have much of a future with your company, he may start looking for a more reliable revenue stream, and possibly leave you at his convenience, not yours.
Consultants can usually be dedicated to a particular project, whereas full-time employees have many other responsibilities.	
You can terminate a contractor quickly and easily when you need to. Sometimes this is the most significant benefit of a consultant. This might be because the need for the contractor is for a specific time period, or because you want to be able to end the relationship easily (without interference from HR) if the person doesn't work out. Various states have various laws about what you must do in those situations. (And the laws for these kinds of actions vary radically overseas.) While professional courtesy says you should give at least two weeks' notice when terminating a full-time person, in general, you can fire a contractor the same day.	

Table 3.3 Pros and Cons to Using Full-Time Employees

PRO	CON
In general, full-time employees are more committed. They're more loyal to your organization because they have a vested interest in its success. They have a better understanding of the context of the work they're doing; they remember the project when it was done five years ago, and they understand why this particular VP's needs are being given priority.	**Full-timers can sometimes be less deadline driven.** They know there is always tomorrow, and many aren't shy about reminding you. Many full-time employees are dedicated, hard-driving workers, but some are not.
Full-time employees are cheaper in the short term. When you calculate the cost of a worker, you need to include the benefits the employee receives, the cost of office space, etc. But in the short term, even the total of these costs can be less than a pricey consultant.	**Terminating full-time employees is much more complicated than terminating contractors.** There are many laws and policies surrounding the termination of a full-time employee, and this is one area where you are much better off having your HR department deal with the issue.
Sometimes, full-time employees are better suited for the specific task at hand. Sometimes the learning curve for a consultant can be severe, whereas a full-time employee brings critical legacy knowledge about the processes, people, and organization that can radically affect the time it takes to complete that process. It may be wiser to get an employee up and trained about a new technology, rather than to try to get a contractor fully versed in the organization and processes of your company.	

companies), you'll be on a more defined schedule. Summertime (due to vacations) and the holiday period at the end of the year are generally quieter times for staffing. This is because people aren't generally looking to make potentially career- or life-altering changes during these times. Similarly, at the end of the year, some companies will defer all hiring until the following year, simply for the benefit of making this year's financial numbers look better.

When is the best time to hire? The correct answer to this question is *at least one month before you need to hire*. Hiring people takes time, often more time than you expect, and it's not a decision you should leave until the last minute.

How long before this employee is producing? Bringing people up to speed takes time, too. Since you brought them on because they had a specific skill set that you needed, contractors often need less training than full-time employees. (You should think twice about paying for a contractor's training expenses. It happens, but it should be when you've exhausted all other options.)

Full-time employees that you have hired may or may not have the specific skill sets you need. Regardless, everyone needs some time to get acclimated. In addition to the logistical issues involved (the person needs a desk, a computer, a network ID, e-mail account, etc.), you need to plan for time for employees to get settled. And don't forget that their coworkers need to adjust to a new team member, too.

WHY DO SOME ORGANIZATIONS REFUSE TO INCREASE FULL-TIME HEAD COUNT?

There are reasons why a company may not want to increase its full-time head count that, strangely enough, have nothing to do with money.

- **Official Size Limits.** Companies may want to stay a certain size to qualify for specific government contracts. There is a 500-employee limit, for example, to qualify as a small business in certain industries (www.sba.gov/content/determining-size-standards). Hiring consultants or part-time employees does *not* affect this limit, but hiring full-time employees does.
- **Business Model.** Some companies are little more than middlemen, facilitating the flow of business from one sector to another, from one group of companies to another. (eBay is a such a company.) Companies like this grow or shrink quickly based on their immediate needs; they want to remain very flexible and not be burdened with a lot of overhead. Not only do they not hire full-time workers, they often lease office space on a very short-term basis.
- **Impressing Investors.** When times are tough, investors like to see a company reducing costs, and that includes staff reductions. Nonetheless, it is all too common to see individuals laid off as employees, only to be brought back very quietly as consultants.
- **Nature of the Market They Are in.** One author calls it the "Ben and Jerry's vs. Amazon" model. Does your company operate in a market with lots of well-established competitors (like Ben and Jerry's)? If so, slow, organic growth may be your best method of succeeding. On the other hand, if your company enters a new field (like Amazon was doing when it started), getting as much market share as soon as possible may be the best way to approach things. (Venture capitalists sometimes call this the "First In Wins" type of market.) In that case, adding as many employees as soon as possible may be required.
- **Seasonal Impact.** Many industries are directly impacted by the calendar. Retailers are busiest in December, beach resorts are busiest in the summer, ski resorts are busiest in winter, and florists have peaks around key holidays. In cases like these, it may not make sense to bring on full-time employees for jobs that may last only a few months.

3.2 WRITE A POSITION DESCRIPTION

Most likely you're going to have to prepare a Position Description (PD), sometimes called a Job Description (JD). A PD is a relatively detailed description of a specific role.

Your HR department may ask you to write a PD so that it can be posted internally within the company or it may be used to relay the pertinent details to agencies and recruiters. HR may also use the information in PDs to help prepare an ad for the newspaper or for a job-posting site. HR often insists that every employee have a PD so that every individual's responsibilities, accountabilities, and so on are clearly spelled out. In many organizations, the content of the PD is the basis for determining the grade, title, salary range, bonus eligibility, and so on for a position.

Even if you aren't required by your company's procedures to prepare a PD for the hiring process, it's a good idea to do so. Every member of your staff should have a PD of their own job. That way, there is little doubt as to what their responsibilities are.

A PD can also be used for performance evaluations, salary considerations, and staffing justification. If an employee becomes a problem employee, it's good to have a hard-and-fast description of what their official duties are supposed to be. HR can use this information to help resolve difficult personal situations.

Position Descriptions versus Contracts

Along these lines, it's important to remember that the PD is just that—a description. It is *not* a contract. There are several reasons this distinction is important, but the most important ones are:

- Many companies have formal contracts with some of their employees (particularly at the senior levels), and a PD is not designed for that purpose. Some companies have formal, legal contracts that they require employees to sign upon joining the organization. These contracts are generally strong legal instruments with very specific terms. They aren't good methods for determining what a person should do; they are often a list of things a person should not do (such as using company resources for personal needs, or revealing confidential information). A PD doesn't serve this legal function.
- Goals, responsibilities, and expectations are things that should be listed in a PD. These aren't legally enforceable items, but nonetheless are critical components of the position.
- Things change. Although your staff may or may not appreciate change, it's still incumbent on you as a manager to maintain your flexibility. Your boss will demand a wide variety of things from you, often adding or subtracting duties the same week. You'll need to adapt quickly to those new challenges and be able to turn your staff in the new direction. A PD that details exactly what an IT professional can do severely limits that individual's flexibility and radically constrains the manager and the department. You want the PD to be general enough to cover all aspects of the job. (You don't want to be in the position of assigning someone a task and hearing them say "that's not in my job description.")

The format of the PD can vary. Your HR department may have a standard format that it likes to use. It's often similar to an outline and is usually kept to one or two pages.

General Requirements

While PDs vary from company to company, there are many similarities. The following are common elements of a PD (see Figure 3.1):

- **Job title.** The title should be descriptive about the job and also be one that an employee will be proud to have on his business card. Something along the lines of "IT Associate II" has little meaning; "Senior Software Developer" is better. Use industry standard titles and descriptions so that both you and the potential employees can readily do comparisons of qualifications versus salary and benefits.
- **Position summary.** A high-level, two- or three-sentence description of what the job entails.
- **Scope of responsibility.** This provides more detail about the job. It may cover the number or types of systems, requirements for being on call, budgeting responsibilities, personnel responsibilities (hiring, management, performance reviews, etc.), requirements for doing high-level presentations or low-level documentation, etc. This section usually has the most information about the job and what is expected of the employee.
- **Immediate supervisor or manager.** Identify the title of the individual the person will be reporting to. This will help give some perspective to where the position is in relationship to the entire IT organization.

Job title: Senior Java Developer

Position summary: Writes application code for company's commercial Web site

Scope of responsibility: Work with systems analysts, customer service, and marketing teams to develop and maintain code for company's e-commerce Web site. Will be responsible for developing, testing, documenting and maintaining code in an environment consisting of approximately 30 systems with 100 modules, 50 servers, two data centers, and receiving approximately 200,000 hits per day. Employee will participate in a rotating on-call schedule to insure that systems are available and reliable on a 24/7/365 basis.

Immediate supervisor: Robert Smith, Manager of E-commerce Development

Number of direct reports: None

Travel: 10–15% travel required

Specific requirements: Minimum 3 years Java development, 10+years development in another language (C, C++, Perl, SQL)

Education: Four year college degree preferred

Experience required: Minimum 1 year experience in supporting a high-volume retail e-commerce site.

Salary: $75,000–$95,000

FIGURE 3.1

Sample position description.

- **Number of direct reports.** Indicate the size of the staff that reports to this position. It might even help if you provide some simple description of the staff (operators, programmers, other managers, etc.).
- **Minimum versus specific requirements.** For all critical issues, list the minimum requirements (and name them as such), as well as any specific requirements. If you must have a programmer with at least three years of development experience, say so clearly. If you need someone with SAP in their background, be clear about that.
- **Education, training, and certification requirements.** If these are a requirement for the job, specify what they are.
- **Experience required.** If formal training isn't required, companies often ask for a minimum number of years of "real-world" similar experience in a given field. Sometimes you may want to identify the type of experience that is required. For example, you may want someone with experience in a similar industry or with very large organizations.

- **Travel.** If there is travel required in the position, it's important that it be identified. Traditionally, it's identified as a percentage of time. It's important to be as honest here as possible. Since most candidates look negatively on travel requirements, you might want to be extra careful and overestimate the amount of travel. You may also want to describe the travel in more detail (local/domestic/international, or short trips of two or three days vs. weeks or months at a time).
- **Salary.** If you include a salary in a PD, give a range. If there is a bonus, simply say "bonus eligible."

Advertising Options
First, Post Internally

In some companies, you *must* post open positions internally first. Find out if your company requires you to do so or allows you to do so only if you wish. Typically HR feels that existing employees should have the first shot at any new openings, and it is bad form for employees to find out about an opening through external sources. And sometimes you may want to let people within your department know a job opening is about to be created, but other times you may not want that information known until the last minute. Whatever you do, don't try and have it both ways; employees will find out that you are advertising behind their backs and your reputation (deservedly) will suffer. In short, don't advertise (inside or out) until you're ready for everyone to know about it.

Popular Websites

There has been a tremendous shakeout in job sites, and after many sites merged, there are only a few left standing. Monster.com, Dice.com, CareerBuildeer.com, and your local craigslist.org are the most popular. There are also site aggregators, such as Indeed.com and Jobster.com, that scour all of these sites and consolidate the results. In general, job posting sites are free to the candidates, but require the hiring firm to pay a fee to post the ad.

There are a small number of sites that also require the candidate to pay a fee, such as TheLadders .com and ExecuNet.com. However, there is no consensus among either candidates or recruiters that sites like these offer any real increased value.

In addition, social networking sites geared toward professionals, such as LinkedIn, have also become very popular, not only for posting job ads, but for actively searching for candidates that meet your criteria. In addition, websites for trade journals and professional associations very often have job postings.

Web Posting Issue to Think About

The good news is that your job will be shown to millions of people; the bad news is that your job will be shown to millions of people. And most jobs in IT can't be filled by millions of people.

Be prepared for a large number of responses. It sounds like a nice problem to have until it happens to you. Online postings routinely generate hundreds of responses in the first few days—even if you have the job sites filter the results.

Networking

Filling a job via networking can be a very rewarding process. Start by talking to your professional contacts (peers, subordinates, HR representatives, coworkers from former jobs, sales representatives, contacts you meet at conferences and seminars). You don't have to go into great detail, just briefly mention the type of job you have open, along with a brief description of what you're looking for.

Your network of contacts, though, extends far beyond the people you currently work with, as well as those you used to work with. Some people are ferocious networkers, tracking every contact made at a social setting in a complex database. You don't have to be that person, but know that your range of contacts is much larger than you might think; imagine talking to people at your church, or neighbors, Little League coaches, people you meet at trade shows, and so on. A little word of mouth can go a long way.

As mentioned before, social networking sites such as LinkedIn.com, Plaxo.com, ZoomInfo.com, and Facebook.com have become valuable tools for developing networks and contacts for both job seekers and job providers. A 2010 survey by Jobvite.com of HR and recruiting professionals found that:

- 92 percent currently use or plan to recruit via social networks
- Of this group, 86 percent use LinkedIn, 60 percent use Facebook, and 50 percent use Twitter for recruiting
- 50 percent of hiring companies plan to invest more in social recruiting, while only 17 percent will spend more on job boards and 36 percent will spend less on job boards
- 58 percent have successfully hired through a social networking site
- Of those that have hired through social networking, 89 percent did hires from LinkedIn.com (source: recruiting.jobvite.com/resources/social-recruiting-survey.php)

Professional Contacts
- The HR department may have recently interviewed someone who was rejected for a position in another department, but perhaps fits your requirements better.
- Members of your, or other, departments may know of people at their former jobs.
- Your vendor representatives, who are probably already familiar with your environment, may know individuals at their other customer sites who would be a good match.
- Perhaps someone who was a close second for a previous open position can be called back in for this position.
- Professional organizations that either you or one of your staff belong to can be a good resource.
- Local schools and universities may provide contacts.

Personal Contacts
- People on your staff may have friends and colleagues who they can vouch for and know are looking for jobs. This connection brings a real bonus: What higher compliment is there for you as a manager than for one of your subordinates to recommend a friend to work for you?
- Your community can provide you with a rich source of potential job leads. Let the word get out to your friends, to fellow community members, to neighbors, and to fellow squash players that you're looking to hire someone.
- For all you know, the next person you meet at a Fourth of July barbecue softball game could know the ideal candidate for you.

Effectiveness of Networking
Does networking work? It sure does. Does it work every time? No. It's a matter of luck and timing, the people you contact, and the way you talk about the job, as well as other factors that you can't always identify. You never know the chain of connections that will lead you to the right contact. In fact, one of

the coauthors found a job via someone he went to Sunday school with and hadn't spoken to in over 15 years. One of the nice things about networking is that it can be the least expensive way to find candidates, but it may not be the fastest or most effective. However, you can always use networking in conjunction with other recruiting methods.

Job/Recruiting Fairs

The value of job fairs has always been debated but its value has radically diminished for IT jobs in these everything-is-online days. There are job fairs that still work for some jobs, but in the relatively specialized world of IT, weeding candidates (and companies) online is much more efficient for both parties. Some companies still attend job fairs, but these jobs in IT tend to be "client-facing"; that is, there will be some contact with customers and companies want to see how potential employees present themselves. There is also concern that job fairs are more likely to bring the more desperate candidates (i.e., those willing to wait in long lines) as opposed to the most qualified.

The (Limited) Value of Print Advertising

The days of choosing one type of job ad over another are fading; newspapers, as part of their push to move online, have partnered with job websites. Many newspapers are offering print as well as online listings. Although print ads are a dying breed, they aren't dead yet. Very senior positions still often appear in "display ads" in the business section. Some companies choose to use print ads *in addition* to online ads, and some choose to use print *instead* of online, perhaps as a way of attempting to reach a different demographic. As recently as 2011, one of the coauthors spotted an ad for a CIO in the classified job section of the *New York Times* amidst several columns of IT job listings. Perhaps since the company was obviously looking for a seasoned executive, they thought that the newspaper might be a more targeted medium (maybe assuming that the type of candidate they're looking for probably grew up in the days when newspapers were pretty much the only venue for job advertisements). Or perhaps they were looking for a candidate who was thinking a bit outside the usual box of job search methods.

3.3 RECRUITERS

Whether you call them recruiters, agents, or headhunters, they are a fact of life in the modern corporate hiring world. Recruiters generally don't have a great reputation. Sometimes that poor reputation is deserved; many other times, however, a recruiter can mean the difference between success and failure of a project that is relying heavily on very specific types of employees. Using a recruiter has both advantages and disadvantages. Weigh them carefully before deciding. The costs for making the wrong choice can be high.

In truth, a recruiter is probably going to use some of the same methods (the Web, networking, etc.) that are discussed in this chapter, which you could easily use yourself.

Another factor to consider is that recruiters' roles have shrunk dramatically in direct relation to the rise of job sites. The recruiting industry has also suffered from the recent economic downturn that saw more layoffs than hires. Finding a candidate on Monster.com may be the right method for you, but using an old-fashioned recruiter has some positives and negatives, too. Details for each option are discussed in Table 3.4.

Table 3.4 Pros and Cons to Using a Recruiter

PRO	CON
Recruiters take the lion's share of the recruiting burden off of you. Your HR department may do nothing more than use one or two of the recruiting media mentioned earlier. The recruiter, however, will place the ads and work the phones. In addition, he'll do the initial screening of candidates and résumés. He will make sure that the candidates he sends you are in the right salary and skill range. Recruiters will also meet candidates before sending them to you to be sure that they have the appropriate "presentation" for you. The last four sentences state what the recruiter "will do." More appropriately, they ought to say "should do." It's the "wills" and "shoulds" that separate good recruiters from bad ones.	**Some recruiters do not listen to you and your requirements.** If they continually send you candidates and résumés that clearly aren't suitable matches, change to another recruiter. This is a very common problem. Recruiters have bodies they want to place (and often take the view that if they throw enough things against the wall, the odds are that eventually something will stick), but that isn't your problem. Demand what you are paying for. Some recruiters try to convince you to ignore your own instincts. If you reject an agent's candidate, the recruiter should ask why so that he can learn what you don't like and increase the odds of sending you people you will like. But if your agent tries to argue with you or convince you that you should consider someone you didn't like, it's time to move on. There are plenty of fish in this sea.
In large metropolitan areas where there is a large pool of talent, agents can help you separate the wheat from the chaff. In areas where the pool of talent isn't quite so deep, a recruiter may be able to help you find the oasis in a desert. If your marketplace is a difficult one to recruit in, agents can help. For example, many downtown metropolitan areas have an intensely competitive hiring IT environment. Qualified IT professionals know they can find a job easily and are generally very savvy about doing so. Are you prepared to find the right avenues, investigate the common sources for this position, and so on by yourself?	**Some recruiters try to increase the odds of success by overwhelming you with résumés.** One of their primary functions is to separate the wheat from the chaff; if you aren't saving time using a particular recruiter, switch. In general, working with agents is a mix of personalities—yours and theirs. And since you're the one paying, you can, and should, choose not to work with those who don't seem to work well with you.
A recruiter has his own network and contacts. In addition to posting ads on websites, an experienced headhunter will know lots of people. He will likely know people who may be interested in changing jobs, but who aren't actively searching the job sites. This network will also help him match up the right personality and attitude with the culture of your organization.	
If the job you're hiring for is a complex one with very specific requirements, a recruiter can take on the burden of finding those candidates. If the job you're hiring for is a popular one, that a lot of people will be interested in applying for, a recruiter can help narrow down the field.	

If a headhunter's less-than-stellar reputation is deserved, the way in which they are compensated may be one of the reasons. Agents generally receive up to 25 percent of the annual starting salary of the person they place. With high commissions, coupled with weeks or months between placing a candidate successfully, a headhunter has high incentives to do his best to succeed at every opportunity. However, his definition of success may vary from yours. You want the *best* candidate, he wants you to hire *any* candidate—as long as it is his.

You should also talk to your HR department. There may be specific policies against using head-hunters unless all other avenues have been exhausted or they may have negotiated rates with specific recruiters that you can use. Many companies now have a short list of approved recruiters that every hiring manager within the company *must* use.

WHAT RECRUITERS DO THESE DAYS
IDEAS FOR MANAGING IN TOUGH TIMES

Some companies have adopted policies that forbid the use of recruiters. The reason for this policy is that senior executives imagine that the high fees that recruiters charge can be avoided by doing the work without them.

In some cases, that is certainly true. There are many candidates looking for jobs in challenging economic times. However, as discussed several times in this chapter, making a good hire is a series of steps in an often complex process, not just a matter of finding the right person.

However, like all other middlemen in a business process, the Internet has radically altered their business model. A recruiter whose value was based solely on "secret information" (which person was looking, what company was hiring) is probably out of business by now. Recruiters not only have to find the right candidate, they often have to vet that person (sometimes doing several prescreening interviews), coach the candidate before and after the interview process, negotiate with the company regarding short- and long-term compensation, and manage the candidate's progress for a period of time.

Finding the Right Recruiter

Finding good recruiters is more of an art than a science, but probably not terribly different from how you found your accountant or dentist. You probably took a recommendation from a friend or relative the first time you needed an accountant. Later, you may have changed accountants, perhaps based on another recommendation, because you weren't 100 percent comfortable with the first one. You may have gone through a few options before finding one you're comfortable with. In essence, you net-worked. Finding a good agent to help you find a job or to help fill an open position is the same process.

You can start by asking people you know which headhunters they've used. Ask who they liked, disliked, and why. Your company's HR department can probably offer you some references of agents they've worked with in the past, as well as those they've had bad experiences with. You can also ask others in your department about agents they've used. If you really don't know where to turn, you can always look on the Web for local agencies; there are several large international recruiting agencies that have offices in most major cities. Regardless of how you find them, be sure and check out their references before you start using them.

You want to find agents you like working with. You may prefer agents who are fast paced or those who are more laid back. Because they often conduct their business over the phone or via e-mail, it is entirely possible that you may never meet some of the agents you work with. As such, you'll have to rely on your instincts to judge them as you work with them and speak to them on the phone. As complicated as the world gets, and as competitive as recruiters are, it's somewhat surprising to know that many agreements with recruiters are done verbally. And, if you don't meet them in person, you won't even have the proverbial handshake.

You may not even have to find recruiters, because they'll often be looking for you. Headhunters earn their keep by establishing contacts with hiring managers, companies, and candidates. Sooner or later (probably sooner) they'll learn that you're a manager and that you have responsibility for staffing. They may hear this from existing contacts they have (such as others at your company) or simple cold calls to your switchboard ("Can you transfer me to the IT Manager?"). Once they establish a beachhead, some resort to time-worn techniques such as bringing donuts to meetings to further cement their hold in your department.

Technical Abilities

Many recruiters don't have the technical depth required to adequately help you with your search. Recruiters are no different than the rest of the population in this regard: There are many people who are very ignorant about technical matters, there are those who know enough "to be dangerous," and there are truly knowledgeable people. Your concern should be twofold: how much do they understand and how honest are they about their abilities.

Remember that sometimes you will be trying to fill positions that require skill sets that are still being developed. IT is a constantly changing industry. If you want to hire someone with word-processing skills, those metrics are well defined. But you might be trying to find a .Net programmer or Flex programmer. Those technologies are only a few years old.

This means you may only find a few recruiters who understand your requirements. What you will be looking for is a recruiter who is honest enough to admit what they don't know and willing enough to listen to you tell them what they need to know.

Things to Keep in Mind

Some important things to remember when dealing with recruiters:

- Fees generally run up to 25 percent of the annual salary that is offered and are almost always negotiable—in tough economic times, everything is negotiable. Agree on the fee up front and preferably in writing. Include terms about when the fee is paid and what happens if the employee is fired or quits soon after being hired.
- Often a recruiter will ask what your company normally pays as a finder's fee. If they do, this is a great time to offer a lower number. Recruiters know that if you use them once, you may use them again so they may be willing to give up a few percentage points in exchange for a potentially lucrative long-term relationship.
- Headhunters' fees are usually paid after a certain period of time. This is to ensure that the candidate doesn't quit or isn't discovered to be a disaster immediately after being hired. Agents often request their fees after 30 days. You can usually push that out to 60 or 90 days. Don't pay the fee early based on the promise that you'll be credited with a refund if the new hire doesn't work out before the agreed-upon period.

Using Multiple Recruiters

It's quite common, and not considered unethical, to give the same assignment to multiple recruiters. As long as you can deal with working with several agents, it will increase your odds of finding exactly the right person. On the off chance that two recruiters send you the same candidate, the professional thing to do is work with the recruiter who sent you the candidate first. (If there are two identical résumés in your e-mail in-box, use the time stamp to tell you who sent it first.)

3.4 **SELECTING CANDIDATES**

Whether candidates come to you via your own network, ads, recruiters, or Human Resources, now that you have some possibilities, the next step is to evaluate them.

Reviewing Résumés

Résumés come in all shapes and sizes, and there is no science to reviewing them well. What one manager may consider a great résumé, another may dismiss immediately. A résumé that's great for a programmer may not be great for a programmer/analyst. When candidates write résumés, they may agonize over every word, phrase, and formatting choice. There are volumes on the subject of writing résumés. This section, though, addresses the issue of *reading* résumés. Things to look out for when you read a résumé include:

- Be on the lookout for spelling and grammatical errors. Most people spend an enormous amount of time getting their résumé just right (and having others review it), so any mistakes should have been filtered out. If it contains a typo, it could mean the candidate isn't focused on detail, or is cavalier about things that most others take very seriously. These are traits you probably wouldn't want in a member of your team.
- Take note of the overall appearance. Does it seem well formatted or thrown together haphazardly? This could be a reflection of the fact that the candidate thinks that things like appearance are superficial. There are many résumé services and lots of easy-to-use résumé templates available on the Web; no candidate these days should have an ugly resume.
- Look at the job history. Is the candidate a job hopper? Are there gaps that you want to ask about? Some gaps are common—the dot-com bubble of 1999–2001, and the economic downturn of the late 2000s put many IT workers out of work. Also, many IT professionals have short or long stints as contractors and work in brief, six-month assignments and then move on to the next company. However, while many managers will reject a job hopper, they may also be concerned about those who have been in a job for an extended period of time. They may fear that a candidate with 15 years at his current job has only one view of the world and may have difficulty adapting to a new job environment.
- Does the level of detail in the résumé match what you're looking for? For example, if the résumé highlights that the candidate upgraded the operating system on a server, it may indicate he's coming from a much smaller environment compared to yours; you may have so many servers that an OS upgrade is such a common practice that the task is barely mentioned among technicians, much less seen as a résumé-worthy accomplishment.
- Does the résumé have a laundry list of technologies? For example, does it list every model of every brand of workstation and server they ever worked with (e.g., IBM PC, XT, AT, Compaq Proliant 5000, 5000R, 5500, 5500R, 6000, 6500, 7000R) along with every version of every software package (e.g., Windows 2000, XP, 2003, 2008, Vista, 7)? You may see lists like this and think, "Is this candidate really proficient in all these technologies?" You may also ask, "Why does he think I care that he knows about technologies that were discontinued over 10 years ago?"
- Notice factual claims. Résumé padding is very dangerous. (A CEO of Radio Shack resigned years ago after it was discovered that he misrepresented his educational credentials.) Don't be afraid to ask direct questions about a candidate's claims: Were there other people working on these websites

you designed or was it all your doing? Did you write most of the code for that billing system or were you a member of a team?

Résumés are rarely read from top to bottom. Typically, they are glanced over quickly (various studies show that the average résumé gets well under a minute's attention). This glancing process allows the manager to hunt for things that he's looking for, as well as to see what else jumps out at him. These are reasons why a well-formatted and carefully crafted résumé is so key.

Telephone Screening

After screening résumés, but prior to face-to-face interviews, some managers like to do telephone interviews to narrow down the list of candidates. A quick 5- to 10-minute telephone conversation can reveal quite a bit. For the more hands-on and technical positions, you can use a few technical questions to gauge a candidate's level of expertise. Telephone screening is ideally suited for customer service representatives such as Help Desk analysts, since it gives you some insight into their telephone manner, their communication skills, and how their style is when interacting with customers and users.

For the less technical and more supervisory positions, you still might be able to use a brief telephone interview as a gauge to their interpersonal skills, especially if these skills are a critical part of the job requirement. Of course, telephone screening just helps you narrow down the field, since you still need to meet with those candidates that do well on the phone.

Often the Human Resources department will do the initial screening of candidates, pass 20 résumés to the hiring manager, the manager will cut that number to 10, and then the résumés will be *sent back* to HR. They will then conduct a brief phone interview to further narrow down the candidates to a manageable number of in-person interviews. This relatively convoluted process is justified when there are many well-qualified applicants for an important position.

At What Level Should I Interview?

If the position reports to one of your managers, consider having that manager do the first rounds of interviewing. This saves your time and empowers your manager. If you have several levels of staff reporting to you, you may not feel the need to be involved in the interviews for every position in your organization. However, you should be involved in interviewing for:

- Positions that report directly to you
- Positions that report to your direct reports
- Positions in your organization that are highly visible or very critical

Even if you feel you don't need to be involved in interviewing for a lower-level position, you may want to at least meet briefly with finalists before offers are extended.

Narrowing Down the List

Like many information-based activities the Internet has streamlined, searching for a job has been radically simplified. For just a few dollars, a job seeker can send out thousands of résumés. As such, hiring managers like you are deluged with résumés. The pendulum swings back and forth from not enough candidates to too many candidates. Having too many options may seem like a desirable problem to have, but it's a difficult issue in its own right.

How to Choose from Hundreds of Candidates

First of all, get help. Ads posted on job sites often generate hundreds of responses. Of course, many are completely mismatched to your posting, but someone has to weed through the electronic stack of files (many named "resume.docx", of course) to glean the real candidates from the wannabees. Sophisticated résumé-scanning software (your HR department may already use this) can quickly scan hundreds of résumés for specific keywords. Your internal recruiters and headhunters should also be helping you narrow down the list so you don't feel overwhelmed.

Get help from HR—fast. For details, see the section **"Human Resources Department's Role"** earlier in the chapter on **page 66**. Some companies have résumé-screening software, special e-mail addresses, and third-party services to handle the first wave of responses. Give HR a list of specific requirements for the position you're looking for and a specific number of résumés you want to read: "I would like to see 30 résumés of qualified candidates—no more." If you receive fewer than five qualified candidates in a hot market, then this is a problem that points to an issue with your advertising. Did you use the right terms? Did you post in the right places? For more details about advertising, see the section **"Advertising Options"** on **page 77**.

If you receive several hundred résumés, you don't have the time to give each one appropriate consideration. To narrow down the pile, select a few criteria. You may want to eliminate those résumés that don't have a cover letter, drop those that are outside your geographic area (especially if you don't plan on paying to relocate someone, or don't have a robust teleworking environment), or toss out those that show a history of job hopping.

How to Choose from 30 Qualified Candidates

Having narrowed the initial number of résumés from the hundreds down to 30, now you must use a different set of skills to move from 30 to 5. (These numbers are approximate; decide which numbers work for you.) Your goal is to narrow the number of résumés you are reading down to a manageable number of candidates you can interview in person. As discussed before, sometimes a phone interview is an ideal method for prescreening candidates.

While grateful for help from HR, you'll probably review their selections next. You may have 30 "qualified" choices but five to 10 can be eliminated right away. You may not have specified it to HR, for example, that the person can't be entry level or must have hands-on programming experience (not just classroom time). Whatever the reason, about one-third of your candidates will probably fall to the side.

That still leaves you with 20 qualified candidates. In a hot market, it's good to remember that many candidates could fit the bill. Give yourself some room when making this decision: you aren't trying to find the *perfect* candidate (there may be five perfect candidates or, more likely, there won't be any); you're trying to hire a person who fits your requirements and your team well.

Choose five candidates to talk to in person, but keep the remaining 15 on hand just in case the first round doesn't work out.

Should You Hire an Overqualified Candidate?

The two simple answers are:

- Yes, because in a hot market (for employers) you'll get more for your money.
- No, because in a hot market (for employees) they'll jump to another company as soon as they get an offer that matches their skill set better.

Ask your HR department and fellow managers what their take is on the short-term prospects for the hiring market.

Young managers (i.e., recently appointed managers, not youthful managers) should be very careful about hiring overly qualified candidates. These individuals are often more challenging to manage; that doesn't mean they're more difficult, it means they require special attention. They didn't acquire all these skills by accident; they're probably very aware of career paths, training programs, and openings in other departments—things an employee with less experience might not know or care about. Or they may also be fully aware that they're taking a job they're overqualified for and could easily turn into an attitude problem for you and everyone else. These are all management challenges that a new manager may not yet be ready to handle.

General Interview Guidelines

Some guidelines for conducting interviews include the following:

- The candidate may be nervous (especially if he's interviewing for his first job or he's anxious to get back to his current job before his extended lunch hour is noticed). Try to make him feel comfortable with a few light comments (e.g., "I hate interviews, don't you?") or by asking a few easy questions (e.g., "How are you? Did you have any difficulty finding the office?").
- After you get started, see if you can get the interview away from the question/answer format and into more of a conversation or discussion. Both you and the candidate will benefit from a more relaxed exchange of information. Not every person can relax in an interview, however, and other factors (such as the chemistry between the two of you) may influence the tone of the meeting. Don't overemphasize this aspect of the interview, especially for individuals whose interpersonal skills aren't as critical to their success on the job as, say, their technical skills.
- Don't do all the talking! Many hiring managers spend a great deal of time talking, as opposed to listening. Don't tell the candidate too much about what you're looking for (at least not until you've heard what the candidate has to say). If you do, the smart interviewee will simply regurgitate what you say back to you. It's the candidates who should do all the talking, but they can't do so unless they are given a chance. You are there to evaluate them first; all your other responsibilities (such as presenting the position, representing the company, and so on) come second.
- Avoid asking yes/no or other short-answer questions. You really want the interview to become a discussion. Use questions that force the candidate to give descriptive answers. Questions that start with "how" or "why" are great for this. Make them think on their feet.
- Toward the end of the interview, always give the recruit a chance to ask her own questions. Most candidates are usually armed with a couple of standard questions for this opportunity. The smart candidate might ask you a question about something discussed in the interview to demonstrate that she was listening or is interested. Even smarter candidates will show that they've done their homework and ask you some questions based on researching your company.
- Many interviews are now conducted with several people from the hiring company in the room at the same time. The advantages are obvious: while one person asks the question, the other people can evaluate the candidate's nonverbal responses; and multiple interviewers can not only think of more of the key questions to ask but they can later share different perspectives on the same person. It's also an incredible time-saver.

Prepare a List of Questions

Always prepare a list of questions that you can refer to during the conversation. You can, and should, ask both technical and nontechnical questions (performing a technical interview is discussed later in this chapter). The questions will depend on the position you are recruiting for. If you're recruiting for a project manager, for example, you might be more concerned about the candidate's leadership and management skills than you would be if you were interviewing a programmer. However, if you're involved in interviewing a programmer who reports to one of your project managers, you may not have the expertise to ask meaningful technical questions. Still, your interview in this situation can be just to evaluate the individual's background, professionalism, maturity, and personality.

Once prepared, ask the candidate what they think the key issues in their field are and how well they know them. Also ask them if they can provide a specific example that can confirm what they just said about themselves.

Nontechnical Questions

Some nontechnical questions that you can ask include:

- "How was this position described to you?" (This is a great way to find out how the people the candidate met prior to you, such as the headhunter, hiring manager, and HR, view the position.)
- "What were your responsibilities at your last job?"
- "Describe a crisis that you were involved in and how you dealt with it."
- "Describe an assignment or role you really didn't like and why you didn't like it."
- "Describe the pace and culture at your previous jobs and which ones were good and bad matches for you."
- "What did you like/dislike at your last/current job?"
- "Tell me about the relationship you have with your current manager. Do you work well together? What would she say about you? Is she a good manager?" (Be careful not to tread into personal waters here. A person can be a great manager and a difficult person and vice versa, but for the purposes of this conversation, make sure to keep the conversation on a business level. If the candidate starts making personal comments, change the topic.)
- "Which industry trade journals do you read?"
- "What do you know about this company?"
- "Did you go to our website? What did you think of it?" (Every candidate should go to a company's website before an interview. You are looking for their reactions to the site, not if they looked at it. If they did not look at it beforehand, that is a bad sign.)
- "Why are you interested in this job or working for this organization?"
- "What doesn't your résumé tell me about you?"
- "What motivates you?"
- "What do you like, and not like, about working in IT?"
- "What do you want/expect to do on a daily basis at work?"
- "What do you like to do when you're not at work?"

You can also have them walk you through their job history. They can tell you why they took certain jobs, why they later left them, their accomplishments at each one, and what they took away from each job (regarding learned experiences).

Remember, you're listening to *how* they answer, as well as to *what* they answer. You may not agree with everything they say, but if they can convey their answers clearly, with confidence, and back them up with sound reasoning, it demonstrates a certain level of professionalism, maturity, communication skills, and analytic thinking. One technique is to look for people who are hungry (eager to learn and execute), humble (modest), and honest.

It's a good idea to have a set of questions that you ask all candidates. This allows you to have a common frame of reference. Also, take plenty of notes during the interview. After just a few candidates, you'll have difficulty remembering who is who. Good notes can come in very handy a few days later when you're trying to decide who to bring back for a second interview or when you're trying to explain to a recruiter why their candidate isn't qualified.

What Not to Ask

Court decisions and legislative statutes have placed some topics off limits in interviews: race, gender, marital status, age, handicap, sexual orientation, and religion, among others, are topics to be avoided. Not only should these items never be discussed in an interview or any other job-related discussion, you can't use them as factors in making decisions.

For example, if a petite woman applies to be a PC technician, you may doubt her ability to do the lifting of equipment that the job requires. However, you cannot dismiss her out of hand. What you *may* be able to do is say to her that "the job requires you to unpack, move, and lift PC equipment that weighs up to 25 pounds; are you able to perform these tasks?" Similarly, if the same small woman applies for an operations position in the computer room, you may be concerned about her ability to reach the tape cartridges stored on the top shelves. If she is otherwise qualified, the courts would probably tell you to hire her and to make "reasonable accommodation" such as investing in a step stool. *These are all very sensitive areas. Before asking any list of questions, consult with your HR or Legal department. You may be putting your company and yourself at risk of litigation.*

Some interviewers like to ask particularly tough questions and conduct interviews more aggressively. Sometimes this is for sound reasons (e.g., you want a sales rep who can handle all kinds of customers and prospects and difficult situations). Other times it could be because the hiring manager has a large ego and seeing others squirm reinforces his status (at least to himself). If candidates are wiping their forehead and saying "whew" when they finish an interview, you may want to ask what value you get from that interview style.

Who Else Should Interview a Candidate?

Allow others to interview the candidate, whether it's for technical reasons or to compare personalities and demeanor.

- You can have your own peers interview the candidate.
- You can ask individuals who are at peer level to the open position.
- You may want to have your boss meet the recruit.
- If the position requires interaction with other departments, they may want to have a representative involved in the interviewing process.
- The HR department, if they haven't done the initial screening, will also be able to provide an alternative view.
- If you're interviewing someone who will have management or supervisory responsibility, it isn't unheard of for them to meet with some of the people who will be their direct reports.

Including other interviewers makes the process more complicated and adds more time, but it's well worth it. You'll find that multiple interviewers, collectively, are more selective than any one of you individually. That's a positive thing. It increases the chances that when you do agree on a candidate, it will turn out to be a good one. Also, allowing other members of the department to participate in the interviewing process demonstrates to your team that you respect their opinions and that you're interested in hiring someone who will fit well into the team. Lastly, anyone you involve in the decision is less likely to criticize the choice later.

You may not want to bring in other people (or be directly involved yourself) until a certain stage in the process; some job postings generate hundreds of responses and require an aggressive filtering process before the first interview is held. If you are going to have people help you with interviewing, plan *when* you want their help before you contact them.

A DIFFERENT PERSPECTIVE ON THE SAME CANDIDATE

One of the coauthors was interviewing a candidate who seemed to be a good fit for a position. The candidate was brought back to meet several of his peers-to-be for interviews. On this second round, all the male interviewers thought favorably of this candidate, but the one female interviewer had misgivings and thought that something was amiss. She suggested that the candidate may have a problem working with women. The candidate was brought back to meet with another female interviewer who took an instant dislike to the candidate. It will never be known if the candidate did indeed have a problem with women. But, the important thing here is that different people do have different perceptions and insights. Consider that an asset and tool at your disposal. The candidate was rejected.

Key Concepts for a Good Technical Interview

Technical interviews are needed to help judge if a candidate has the appropriate skill level for the job. However, it's quite common for IT Managers to lack the knowledge base for conducting in-depth technical interviews. This is most frustrating if you're interviewing for a position that reports directly to you. In some cases, you can have others within the IT organization conduct technical interviews. Also, it's common to hire a consultant to conduct technical interviews with candidates you're interested in.

Don't be ashamed that you don't have detailed technical expertise. You're *never* going to have all the expertise that your team does—the IT world is changing too fast. Also, because you're a manager, you may no longer be spending your days doing the hands-on work you did just a few months or years ago. Find out what the key issues are for the technical area that you're interviewing for. Talk to some of your other employees; they may know some of the key topics.

Do Some Preliminary Reading

Research particular topics of concern on the Web or in print materials. Even if you don't ask specific technical questions, you can ask a candidate about important issues associated with his area of expertise. What does he think of a particular vendor's support or quality assurance? What does she think of competing products? What about open source software? What is her prediction of the future of Linux?

Let Them Explain Technologies to You

A clever way to hide your ignorance, as well as get an education, is to ask candidates to explain certain technologies to you. "What is a subnet mask? What is meant by object-oriented programming? What do you think if IPv6? What are the pros and cons of Java versus C++?" Of course, you may not know if the candidate's answers are correct, but you'll probably be able to judge if he's just "winging it" or really has an understanding of the matter at hand. You'll also be able to determine what type of interpersonal skills he or she has: Can she articulate complex thoughts clearly? Does he come across as condescending? Are his opinions so strong that you worry he may prove to be inflexible?

Testing Candidates

You may also consider giving the employee a formal test. This could be one you develop yourself or done with the assistance of testing software. Of course, many candidates may not like taking a test because they realize that it may show particular skill deficiencies or they may be poor test takers.

But more important, testing may create an impersonal atmosphere that places more value on specific knowledge than on the individual person and their ability to contribute, accomplish, and succeed on a team. Also, testing only evaluates the mechanics of a skill. It doesn't evaluate the employee's aptitude with it nor does it evaluate the employee's other qualities, such as dedication, ability to juggle multiple priorities, and interpersonal skills.

Nonetheless, testing can be an effective technique for some positions. Jobs that have very specific and easily quantified requirements (specific software application experience, for example, or words-per-minute typing skills) are good candidates for screening tests. In addition, many jobs now get many qualified candidates and many of those candidates are willing to fudge their abilities; testing can level that playing field.

You should have a standard test with an answer key. If you have a very small department or company and you can't develop your own test, call in a consultant to help you craft one. Having the test results readily available can also give your technical staff something concrete to discuss with the candidate—it forges an instant bond if the chemistry is there.

ARE "PROFILE" OR "PERSONALITY" TESTS USEFUL?

"I have found these tests—which we call 'Profile tests,' by the way, because 'Personality tests' are not what they are—to be an extremely useful hiring and management tool.

Here are some things to consider if you are going to try them:

- *The 'softer' aspects of a person can be difficult to evaluate in a two-hour interview process. These tests often reveal information that we would not have figured out until later, after the person was hired.*
- *While these tests are very accurate about some items, the final decision is still up to you on how to use the information they provide. They measure raw intelligence power well, for example. However, not every job needs to be performed by a very intelligent person; at the same time, some jobs are complex, analysis-driven positions that require high IQ power just to understand. These tests can help you make that determination.*
- *When we decided to use these tests, we tried them on everyone in the company first. We found them to be very good predictors of corporate behavior.*
- *We use them on the second interview; the first interview is a general one, where we try to keep our commitment level and the candidates' to a reasonable level. Sometimes, despite all the paper, it only takes a few minutes for a person and a company to figure out they are not a good match. Profile tests (which take about 45 minutes and are administered by an outside firm) are done once the first hurdle has been passed."*

—Cathy Thompson
Cofounder and Principal
Thompson, Hennessey & Partners,
Commercial Real Estate
Boston, Massachusetts

One final note of caution: some companies have strict guidelines against testing candidates. The legal implications of testing are unclear; be sure to verify with your HR department what your company allows you to do.

Interviewing Candidates over the Web

With the growth of remote workers through telecommuting and work-from-home programs, it is becoming increasingly common to first interview candidates who are not geographically close to your office location via technology before bringing them in for a face-to-face interview.

Remote interviews can be done using the web-cam capabilities of a number of different applications, everything from instant messaging (like Microsoft Live Messenger, Yahoo, Google Talk), to web-conferencing products (like WebEx, Adobe Connect), all the way up to full video-conferencing setups (like those from Polycom and Tandberg). All of these options provide voice and video capabilities, although you're always free to use traditional telephones for the voice portion.

While interviewing a candidate over the Internet is extremely cost-effective and efficient, it is not without its challenges. To ensure that the process is as smooth and effective as possible for you and the candidate, there are some guidelines to keep in mind.

- **Widely used technology.** Try to use web communication/conferencing tools that are already widely used (e.g., Skype). Not only will this minimize the chance of any technical gotchas, but it also increases the chance that the candidate already has it and is familiar with it.
- **Prep/practice time.** Be sure you give the candidates sufficient time to get familiar with the technology before the actual interview. If you will be using free software solutions from the Web, invite the candidate to try it out with family and friends to get a comfort level with it.
- **Getting started.** Encourage the candidate to relax and just be himself. Invite him to keep a glass of water nearby. If chatting for more than 30 minutes, suggest a break.
- **Appropriate environment.** Both you and the candidate should select a setting that will be away from background noise, distractions, and interruptions. Also, be aware of what will be behind you and on camera. Better that you should be sitting in front of a solid-colored wall as opposed to a window where the background activity may be distracting, or the light impacts the quality of the video image.
- **Distracting habits.** Be conscious of your own behavior. If you tend to tap your fingers, click your pen, or shuffle papers, it cannot only be a distracting visual, but the microphone will pick up the noise and add to the distraction. If you find the candidate is doing something like that, let him know that the microphone is picking it up. He'd probably rather know about it so he can stop as opposed to finding out that you were distracted during the whole interview by it. (If they do not preemptively prevent screaming children and barking dogs from the session, take that as a clear sign of how much they care about the interview.)
- **Making eye contact.** The tendency is to look at the screen image of the person you are talking to. However, when you do that, the person on the other end feels like you are not making eye contact with them. Remember to periodically look directly into the camera, both when you are talking and listening to the other person. This will help establish eye contact and a greater sense of connection. Otherwise, the candidate may get a sense that you are not terribly interested in what they are saying.

- **Speaking clearly.** Because of the limitations of audio over Internet, be sure that you speak in a manner that is easy to understand. This is especially important for those with accents, or those who are not native speakers of the language they are interviewing in.
- **Time delays.** A video or voice call over the Web can have a slight delay in the audio (similar to a cell phone call) and the video. Keep this in mind and be careful to avoid speaking at the same time the candidate is speaking. And, before responding to something a candidate has stated, take a moment or two to first see if he is actually done with his thought, or just taking a pause.
- **Making allowances.** Most candidates are nervous during an interview, and they are likely to be more nervous with a video conference. Be sure to take that into consideration if their speech and body-language aren't what you would normally expect in an interview.
- **Picture-in-picture.** Most of the Internet video-chat tools have a picture-in-picture capability so that you can see how you look on camera while you're seeing the other person. It is a good idea to use the feature to help ensure you're seen the way you want to be seen.
- **Traditional interview practices.** Just because you're interviewing on video-over-the-Web, don't forget standard interview best practices: careful listening, asking good questions, giving the employee an opportunity to talk and ask questions, etc.
- **Wrapping up.** As you wrap up the interview, ask the candidate what he thought of interviewing this way. You may get some good feedback that you can use to improve the use of the tool in the future.
- **Being sure to exit the call.** When the interview is over, be sure to exit and close the software. Otherwise, you risk the session being open and the candidate seeing and hearing what you do and say next.

A video conference over the Web is no substitute for a face-to-face interview. However, for candidates that are distant from your location, it can be an effective tool for the initial interviews and screening of candidates before going through the effort and expense of bringing them into the office.

If the candidate will be working remotely once they get the job, the video-call interview can give you good insight as to what it will be to interact with them and "meet" as employees once they have the job.

The Right Skill Set for the Job

Have a well-defined list of criteria before you start recruiting. Use this list to weed out résumés and then use a fine-tuned version of that list to interview candidates. Bring the list to the interview itself—you are running the show, so worry more about being thorough and complete and less about appearances.

Keep in mind that you're interviewing for two skill sets. One is *technical* skills and the other is *everything else*: their attitude toward work, ability to juggle multiple priorities, ability to work with others, general intelligence, resourcefulness, potential for growth, dedication and commitment, professionalism, and maturity. You may also be looking for project management skills, supervisory skills, and interpersonal skills, as well as the ability to write reports or give presentations.

When to Accept Similar Experience

Should you accept similar experience? It all depends on how similar the experience is to what you're looking for. It also depends on your needs. If you need to put someone to work on the first day, to be productive on a critical project, your definition of similar might be quite narrow. However, if you can afford to invest time to bring an individual up to speed, then your definition of similar may be more forgiving.

If you like a candidate, but have concerns that his experience isn't similar enough, share your thoughts with him directly. "I like your background, Patrick, you have excellent experience, you'd be perfect for the job, but I'm concerned that you don't have enough experience with X technology." At the very least, by doing this you're being honest with the candidate and letting them know why there is a chance they won't get the job. More important, you're giving the candidate an opportunity to respond. For all you know, Patrick may have something in his background that wasn't mentioned on his résumé that will make you feel a lot more comfortable about his experience or about his ability to compensate for the gap.

With your responsibility as an IT Manager revolving around technology, it's easy to get caught up in specific technology experience when recruiting—hardware models or software version numbers. Of course, these skills are important, but the technical skill set is only a portion of the qualifications. Softer skills such as interpersonal interaction, writing, attention to detail, and ability to function in a team environment can be just as vital.

Rank Criteria

Have a well-defined list of criteria for a job established *before* you go into the interview. As part of the definition process, you can rank each criterion in terms of importance. These rankings will vary from department to department and company to company. Some organizations rank teamwork way ahead of technical skills, whereas others place a much higher value on technical competence than they do on the ability to work well with others.

You may find that an interviewee is a bit weaker in one area than you would like, but significantly stronger in another area. Also, more than likely, you'll see résumés and candidates who have similar experience to what you're looking for. You may find that a candidate's technical expertise is weaker than you would like, but they strike you as someone who is very bright, picks up new skills quickly on their own, and is a very hard worker.

It is pretty common for a manager to value softer skills (personality, intelligence, interpersonal, resourcefulness, etc.) over specific technical skills. The idea behind this is that technical skills can always be learned (and in the ever-changing field of IT, picking up new skills is an ongoing requirement for success), but teaching someone how to be responsible, likeable, or intelligent isn't as easy.

In addition, the priority you assign to these skills will vary on the job in question; because many technical jobs require relatively little personal interaction, a candidate's ability to "work well on a team" may not be of much value.

In the end, as you weigh all of these issues to make your choice, don't be surprised if you feel you're making a judgment call—you are.

Other Requirements That You Might Be Flexible About

- **Years of experience.** What's more important than the number of years is what the candidate did in those years.
- **College degree.** Perhaps this is more important for a manager, but it's less so for a technologist. And the more years since that college degree, the less it adds value as opposed to experience.
- **Training.** Pertinent training? Fundamentals or advanced? How long since the classes were taken? Have the skills been used out in the real world?

- **Specific hardware and software technology.** Is a dot version or two behind in software truly a disqualifier? These days, everything gets outdated quickly.
- **Environment size.** This can be measured in terabytes of storage, users, number of applications or servers, or number of locations—whatever is appropriate for your needs.
- **Certification.** It may not show anything more than they can cram and memorize to pass an exam. See the next section for a separate discussion of this issue.
- **Industry experience.** Frequently, IT workers don't see enough of their company's business environment to really have a legitimate feel for the industry they're in. While similar industry experience is nice, you may want to broaden it to a more macro level, such as manufacturing or services, for example.

Ability to Learn

When considering prerequisite technical skills, remember that virtually everyone in IT must be at least smart enough to master new skills and adapt to changes in technologies and products on a regular basis. If you have faith that a person is smart enough to learn new skills, you may want to consider trusting that faith with someone who might have to take some time to come up to speed on the specific technology set in your environment.

The Value of Certification

The IT world has gone a little crazy with certification. Chances are that if you've heard of a particular hardware or software product, the vendor is offering some type of certification for it. There's an alphabet soup of available certifications, including CCNA, CNE, CNA, MCSA, MCSE, CCIE, CCNP, A+, CCIP, MCAD, MCT, CISSP, PMI, MCSD, MCP, MCDST, MCDBA, OCA, OCP, OCM, CLS, and CLP, to name just a few.

Certification really hit the front pages with Novell's Certified Netware Engineer (CNE). In the late 1980s and early 1990s, everyone wanted to be a CNE. To many it seemed like the passkey to dream jobs. However, by the mid- to late 1990s, a new term was coined: "paper CNE." This term referred to people who took crash courses, studied intensively, and passed the CNE exams, but had virtually no experience to go with the new accreditation on their résumé. Novell's restructuring of their certification program helped deal with this. It's an interesting commentary that 10 to 15 years later, having a CNE was considered of minimal value since Novell had lost so much mind and market share.

Vendors must monitor their certification programs like the Federal Reserve monitors interest rates to balance between too much and too little growth. Vendors don't want their certification program to be so easy that it has no value or prestige, but at the same time, they don't want the programs to be so hard and elitist that too few people are able to pass the tests.

Test-Taking Skills

Whether it was in high school, technical school, or at the Department of Motor Vehicles, we all learned that a passed exam only represents knowledge at that particular moment, which may only in itself represent the ability to study prior to the exam. The same can be said of technical certification. If someone is certified, you know what their knowledge set was at the moment they were tested, which could mean they have the ability to study very hard, have a steel-trap memory, or have information that was ingrained during years of experience. While many IT Managers recognize this, many also look for certifications on résumés. Similarly, many managers looking for programmers prefer individuals with four-year college degrees, even though a college degree may add no value to a programmer's skill set.

Value of Commitment

One aspect of accreditation that's often overlooked is its representation of commitment and persistence. Getting certified usually means passing a series of exams. For many, it also means taking a series of classes. Doing this takes time, energy, and motivation. When you see someone who has been certified, perhaps the first thought you should have is "here's someone who can stick with something and see it through to the end." Not a bad trait for someone who will be managing projects. The same can be said about college degrees, especially if they're obtained while working full time.

When you see a candidate with certification, be sure to consider how long it's been since that accreditation was obtained and to what degree those skills have been used since. If required, ask them if they have kept their certification current with continuing classes and exams.

Checking the Value of a Certification

There are a number of steps you can take to check the value of a certification:

- Talk to your own network of contacts.
- Contact the technical area's association (if there is one). Ask them about the value of certification; they might be also able to point you to a source that can either verify or deny their claims.
- Contact the product manufacturer. Companies such as Cisco, IBM, and Microsoft have extensive certification programs and local contacts. Again, they will tout their own benefits, but they might also be able to point you to specific individuals who benefited from or are looking for those skills.
- Scan the Web. Are other employers asking for this in their ads? If the certification appears often, that is a good sign.

Education

Education has changed radically in the last 20 years. Now there are online paper mills, rock-hard certification courses, distance learning, for-profit colleges, and $200 K tuition bills. The simple criteria of yesterday ("a four-year education is invaluable these days") have changed.

Bill Gates is the richest man in the world according to Forbes, and chairman of one of the world's largest and most successful companies, yet he never finished college. Neither did Steve Jobs of Apple, nor Mark Zuckerberg of Facebook. However, Larry Page and Sergey Brin, cofounders of Google, met while they were pursuing doctorates at Stanford. According to a Bureau of Labor Statistics report released in 2010 (www.bls.gov/spotlight/2010/college), the median weekly earnings of workers with bachelor's degrees were 1.8 times the average amount earned by those with only a high school diploma, and 2.5 times the earnings of high school dropouts. And, even though the IT industry is filled with stories of those who have succeeded without a college degree, the economic downturn has increased preference for graduates—it's easy to understand why a hiring manager will choose a graduate when faced with a high-number of quality candidates.

When looking at the value of an education for a new hire for your company, consider three things:

- Type of education
- Direct value to the job
- Indirect value to the job

Direct Value to the Job

As a rule, the more hands-on and technical a position, the less *direct* value a typical four-year degree has for you as the employer. This is even truer for a graduate degree. Is a Java programmer with an MBA a better programmer than a Java programmer who only finished high school? Some might argue that the programmer with only a high-school degree might be better since all those years went toward actual experience rather than the more theoretical academic experience. Notice the emphasis on the word "direct." Of course the MBA may serve the programmer well as he moves up in his career.

A college education is of more value to a position that involves supervisory or management responsibilities. Also, a college degree is often a prerequisite to getting a supervisory or management role. As a general rule, actual experience and skill should always carry more weight than any educational requirements. And even for someone who has significant educational credentials, the value of that education generally decreases with time. The most important point here is: How easily can the candidate learn new things? The world and the marketplace we work in change quickly and significantly. Has this candidate shown the ability and interest to learn new tools and skills as they become the new standards? Lifelong learners are often the most productive employees in an organization.

A four-year degree will also sharpen skills for writing, analytic thinking, reading comprehension, and so on. Sometimes the value of those skill sets is often overlooked until you see that first horribly written e-mail from a staffer.

Indirect Value to the Job

However, a college-educated employee can provide several important *indirect* benefits to a position. Pursuing a four-year degree can be a difficult and complex task; it can show the individual's willingness to make a commitment and follow through. It can be a financial challenge; many people have to pay for a portion, or all, of their college education themselves. It can be intellectually challenging; a person may be pursuing a programming career now, but 10 years ago chose physics as a major in college.

At the minimum, you should seek a high-school degree for virtually all positions. This should at least give you an indication (although no guarantee) that the individual has the fundamental skills to operate in a job (reading, writing, basic math, etc.). As you move up the education ladder (two- and four-year degrees, graduate degrees, etc.), look to it as an indication not necessarily of a higher degree of technical skill, but of more skilled analysis, comprehension, and verbal skills.

Business-Related Degrees

If their degree is in a business-related discipline, it may indicate that they've been exposed to many ideas and concepts that they'll encounter to various extents within IT. This exposure may be valuable for someone who does systems analysis or is involved with management. It can also be valuable to have a person with these skills on your staff; they can serve as a kind of liaison or translator to the Sales and Marketing departments.

Hard Sciences-Related Degrees

If the candidate's degree is in one of the hard sciences (physics, mathematics, chemistry, e.g.), it may show that they have a stronger ability for logical and analytical thinking. Candidates from these fields may also have greater focus on detail, documentation, procedure, etc. Start with this assumption and verify it with further questioning.

Soft Sciences-Related Degrees

If the person has a degree in one of the social sciences (psychology, sociology, e.g.), they may have greater skills in user-oriented activities (support, training, process improvement, user interface design, etc.). They may have a greater ability to see things from a different perspective and not be limited by the idea of "only one right answer." Start with this assumption and verify it with further questioning.

Technical Courses

Many candidates now list on their résumé individual technical courses they have taken, even if they haven't received any certification. If the skill in question is one you are interested in, ask about the courses, how far into the course had the candidate gone, and why did he stop?

Checking References

References are too often overlooked. Some employers ask for them (especially on the application) but never check them. Some employers check them after the candidate starts, and some check them before the offer is made. Most HR departments handle the reference-checking aspects of hiring; confirm with your HR department to see how your company handles this process.

There are two types of references to check: background checks and professional references.

Background Checks

This is the validation of the accuracy of what the candidate says on the application or résumé. This usually includes contacting schools to see if the person did attend and received the degrees and certifications he claims. This is also for confirming his past employment to see if he did indeed work at the companies he claims for the time frames he claims. The background check may also include a review for any criminal record.

Doing background checks can be tedious and time-consuming, and many companies outsource it to firms experienced at doing it. Some organizations contacted for this information may first ask for authorization from the individual (such authorization is usually included in the fine print of many employment applications). Some organizations (particularly former employers) may only give out limited information. They will typically confirm the dates of employment, but won't provide title, salary, or any comment (good or bad) about their performance.

Professional References

This is the opportunity to speak to individuals that the candidate has worked for and with to get some more insight into the candidate. It's quite common to ask for three references. If the candidate can't provide them, an immediate red flag should go up.

You should assume that any references the candidate gives you will only have positive things to say—he'd be crazy to put you in touch with people who thought otherwise about him. It's for this reason that some people place little value in calling these references or simply think of it as clerical work that HR can do.

However, there is still some value to be gained by making these calls, and making them yourself. While you're unlikely to hear anything negative about the candidate, you should ask open-ended questions to see what the references say about the candidate. Are they using similar adjectives, describing the same traits and characteristics? Does the information provided by the references match what the candidate said? Some questions you can ask include:

- "When, and for how long, did you work with John?"
- "What was his role?"
- "How would you describe him as a worker?"
- "Why did he leave your company?"
- "What types of work does he enjoy?"
- "What types of work does he excel at?"
- "How would you describe his relationships with coworkers and his manager?"
- "What types of work does he enjoy least?"
- "Is there anything else you'd like to tell me about him?"
- "Would you want to work with him again?"

With luck, the references will give you feedback that matches your own perception of the candidate (and validate what he's told you and put on his résumé). If there is a disconnect, you have to try to gauge how big a gap there is and what that might mean.

It is also becoming increasingly popular to include an Internet search when checking the references of a candidate. This may be something that the hiring manager or HR does somewhat informally or may be a specified part of the process when checking references. Very often the results may give some insight into the candidate's personality. Trade journals are filled with stories of hiring managers who found something offensive about the candidate when doing an online search or learned enough to determine that the candidate may not be a good fit with the culture of the organization.

Hiring managers have even made decisions by what they can assess about the candidate's judgment by what they've found on the Internet. For example, if a candidate has pictures of himself passed-out drunk on his Facebook page, the hiring manager may wonder about the professionalism and judgment of the candidate in keeping those pictures online (especially during a job search) and what that may say about the candidate's professionalism and behavior in the workplace. Much more problematic are hiring managers who may consider factors unrelated to job performance (e.g., political views) about a candidate that they find on the Internet.

Common Hiring Mistakes

At some time or another you'll probably discover that you misjudged a candidate. You may discover that someone you thought would be fine doing program maintenance is a stellar performer and has great potential or you may find that the candidate you thought was ideal turns out to be a dud. Hopefully, your errors in judgment will be more of the former than the latter. To avoid out-and-out mistakes, be on the lookout for:

- **A poorly defined position.** If you don't describe the position accurately (the good and the bad), you may end up getting bad résumés and selecting a candidate who doesn't fit.
- **Hiring for the wrong reasons.** Because you dislike the entire hiring process, you only meet with two people and pick one quickly.
- **Not getting enough input.** As suggested earlier, it's a good idea to have other people meet with strong candidates. Every interviewer has a different approach and perspective and asks different questions. It's entirely possible that someone else may notice something that you didn't.
- **Talking too much (or too little) during a job interview.** The best interviews occur when both the candidate and the interviewer have a chance to learn about each other. If one party does all the talking, there will be a large information gap when it is over.
- **No reference checks.** Not every company does these (because the responses are often so rote or because they add time to the hiring process). Many companies are now outsourcing this function, so it might be worthwhile to alert your candidate to the fact that their references will be receiving a call.

Offering the Correct Salary for an IT Position

When you start to recruit for an opening, you should have a salary range in mind. This range can come from several key sources of salary data:

- The HR department of your company
- Recruiters
- Web and computer magazine salary surveys (e.g., salary.com, payscale.com, wageweb.com, and salaryexpert.com)
- Other individuals in your company doing similar work
- Salary levels that you're seeing from candidates who apply
- Salary of the previous individual in that job
- Salaries of the staff members, if any, who report to this position

Before Making the Offer

Make sure that HR and whichever other upper management individual(s) need to approve the final offer are in agreement on the specified range. You'll know if your range is too low based on the response you get to your recruiting efforts. If only a handful of people apply, you're probably offering too little. Although it is not uncommon for someone to change jobs for the same salary, most people expect at least a 10 percent increase. This increase compensates them for the risk that is inherent whenever someone changes a job, but it also entices them to take your job. Nonetheless, you can't offer more than you, or your company, can afford to pay. And you're probably not the only person who decides that figure. If the last individual in the position was a poor performer, that might be justification to convince yourself, HR, and the powers-that-be that you need to offer more money to attract better talent. An extended search that doesn't find any reasonable candidates can also be a justification for reviewing the salary range.

Using Agencies

Be careful when you share the salary range with any agencies you use. Because their commission is based on the annual salary, they have a vested interest in placing someone at the highest possible salary. It makes their job easier to find good candidates if the salary you are offering is competitive. If the recruiter winces when you tell her the approved salary range, don't take it too personally—she's just doing her job.

Because the agent's commission is based on the salary of the person you hire, they may be tempted to inflate the salary of the candidates they send you. As a check, ask the candidates themselves about their salary. The written application that the candidates fill out (with the usual legalese about misinformation being grounds for immediate dismissal) can also help you get a true sense of what their current compensation is.

Other Ideas besides More Money

Invariably, the candidate you like the most will be the one that stretches the envelope of your salary range. If you don't think you'll be able to attract this person with your salary offer, there are a few things you can try.

- Consider promising a salary review (not a guaranteed increase, but a review) six months after the person starts. Don't commit to a specific increase amount (after all, the candidate may not work out or the company may change its salary ceiling). But the chance of an increase in six months may be just what you need to attract the person. (Make sure to get approval from HR/management before you promise anything.)
- Make the position and environment sound as exciting and attractive as possible. Naturally, remain truthful about it. Making something exciting doesn't mean lying about it. You want the person to be as motivated to take the job as you are in offering it to him; that will make finding a middle ground much easier.
- Get the candidate to look at the entire package. Today's competitive IT environment has spawned a wide range of noncash incentives that can be far more lucrative than "mere money." Emphasize those to the candidate. Does the position have bonus potential? Make sure the candidate includes that figure in her consideration. Does your company offer a stock purchase plan? A profit-sharing plan? A matching 401(k) plan?
- Many workers today are enticed by work-style options that match their lifestyles. Working from home, telecommuting, and flextime are all options that can be very important to some candidates. (Sometimes it can be a personality issue—many programmers are not "morning people," for example—but often it can be a family issue. People with small children or elder-care responsibilities have enormous time management challenges and respond favorably to companies that offer them options in this regard.) Many IT jobs are—although many are not—suited to alternative work arrangements.
- Also, make sure that the candidate is fully aware of your company's benefits programs; health and insurance benefits can have very important positive tax benefits. Stock options should also be clearly specified if you are making them part of your offer. Originally a benefit only for the upper reaches of a corporation, stock options have now become a part of many workers' pay plans throughout the ranks of an organization. Companies are offering employees a more direct participation in the profits of the organization as a whole. Is it a good working environment, with little demands for overtime and being on-call? If so, it could be a key selling point. If there is an on-site gym, make sure to mention that.
- Don't forget to talk about vacation time. With today's society, particularly in the IT world, it sometimes feels like the workday never ends. It's not uncommon for people to leave the office, go home

for dinner and time with the family, and then log on to the office to answer e-mails and do more work. Many people read e-mail and do work 7 days a week, regardless of whether they are "at work" or not. If the position you're hiring for doesn't require much off-hours attention or allows for some working at home or if your company has specific policies or practices in place to minimize over-work, be sure you mention that as part of the overall package—they can be very attractive to individuals. (An animator at a studio was told that employees could only work until 6 PM—after that the boss turned off all the lights. In the interview process he did not believe this claim, but soon experienced it firsthand (www.gumbydharma.com/).)

3.5 Further References

Websites

www.adobe.com/ConnectWebConference (web conferencing solution).
www.bizjournals.com/seattle/stories/2000/12/11/daily7.html ('permatemps').
www.bls.gov/spotlight/2010/college.
www.destinationcrm.com/articles/default.asp?ArticleID=4354 (outsourcing discussion).
www.facebook.com (social networking site).
www.hireright.com (background checking company).
recruiting.jobvite.com/resources/social-recruiting-survey.php (recruiting via social media).
www.linkedIn.com (professional networking site).
www.naceweb.org (National Association of Colleges and Employers).
www.payscale.com (salary survey information).
www.plaxo.com (networking site).
www.polycom (video-conferencing solution).
www.salary.com (salary survey information).
www.sba.gov/content/determining-size-standrds (business size determinations).
www.tandberg.com (video conferencing solution).
www.webex.com (web conferencing vendor).
www.zoominfo.com (professional networking site).

Books and Articles

Bradt, G.B., Vonnegut, M., 2009. Onboarding: How to Get Your New Employees up to Speed in Half the Time. Wiley.

Brown, J.N., 2011. The Complete Guide to Recruitment: A Step-by-Step Approach to Selecting, Assessing and Hiring the Right People. Kogan Page.

Erling, D., 2010. Match: A Systematic, Sane Process for Hiring the Right Person Every Time. Wiley.

Herrenkohl, E., 2010. How to Hire A-Players: Finding the Top People for Your Team - Even if You Don't Have a Recruiting Department. Wiley.

Jones, D.P., 2011. Million-Dollar Hire: Build Your Bottom Line, One Employee at a Time. Jossey-Bass.

Meister, J.C., Willyerd, K., 2010. The 2020 Workplace: How Innovative Companies Attract, Develop, and Keep Tomorrow's Employees Today. Harper Business.

Miller, G., 2010. Hire on a WHIM: The Four Qualities That Make for Great Employees. Dog Ear Publishing.

Shamis, B., 2011. Hiring 3.0: New Rules for the New Economy. Leverage Press.

Smart, G., Street, R., 2008. Who: The A Method for Hiring. Ballantine Books.

Yeung, R., 2010. Successful Interviewing and Recruitment: Structure the Interview; Identify Exceptional Candidates; Hire the Best Person for the Job. Kogan Page.

Project Management

CHAPTER TABLE OF CONTENTS

4.1 Projects and Project Management: A Quick Overview 104
4.2 Phase One: Scope the Project 106
4.3 Phase Two: Develop a Project Plan 111
4.4 Phase Three: Launch the Project 116
4.5 Phase Four: Track the Project's Progress 117
4.6 Phase Five: Close Out the Project 121
4.7 Decision-Making Techniques 122
4.8 What to Do if/when the Project Gets off Track 123
4.9 Useful Project Management Techniques 126
4.10 Funding Projects 130
4.11 Multiple Projects: How to Juggle Them Well 132
4.12 Dealing with Non-IT Departments on a Project 133
4.13 Further References 134

As an IT Manager, your life will revolve around projects—some small, some enormous. Projects are an integral part of corporate life. This chapter discusses how they are conceived, organized, funded, tracked, and executed.

Project management is a complex and formal management science, although it is often more art than science. While you probably won't need all that complexity and formality to run most successful IT projects, it's essential to your success as a manager to understand not only the basic principles but a few of the advanced concepts of project management.

If you have been assigned the project of installing an e-mail upgrade for the company, for example, and you are working for a 400-person company, you need to carefully plan how you're going to accomplish this task, who is going to help you, how much it's going to cost, and when is it going to be done. While it may appear a simple task to someone outside the department, anyone with much experience in IT knows an upgrade project such as this can take an enormous amount of time, planning, money, and effort. Careful project management can be the key to accomplishing this task successfully.

4.1 PROJECTS AND PROJECT MANAGEMENT: A QUICK OVERVIEW

You won't go too long as an IT Manager without hearing the word "project"—you probably heard it a lot even before you became a manager. "Project" is a catchall word.

Different Kinds of Projects

The range of activities defined as projects is very wide:

* It could be a relatively simple activity such as purchasing and installing new PCs for all the company's administrative assistants. It might be a more complicated venture, such as deploying a system-wide application or an operating system upgrade. Or it could be a monumental task, such as implementing an Enterprise Resource Planning (ERP) application throughout the company.
* It might be highly complex and involved (ERP applications are notoriously difficult to implement) in nature, or not at all (getting the latest tablet device for all the executives).
* It might be staffed by a single person in your office or manned by a team of 75 people from five different departments in three different countries.
* Simple projects may require only a little planning and all the key information is maintained in someone's head. A complicated project may need special project management software along with group calendaring and scheduling to keep it all on track.
* It might have a very tight and immovable deadline (e.g., installing a new tax package before the start of the fiscal year) or the time frame may be much more forgiving (e.g., "as long as it gets done sometime this year").

Your ability to manage a project so that it meets its goals, within the defined time frame and within the approved budget, will be one of the single most important skills you can develop as an IT Manager.

The Value of Project Management

Project management has become a formal discipline and a widely practiced part of today's corporate life. While it isn't necessary for you to become an official "project manager" (PM) and get certified by the Project Management Institute (PMI), it's useful for you to know some of the important principles of project management to help you in your role as a manager. Every manager has some PM responsibilities, regardless of how those needs are defined; it can be critical to your success to not only accept, but embrace these responsibilities. Take control of the projects in your business life and manage them properly—it will be well worth your effort.

Five Key Phases to a Project

Starting with **Section 4.2, "Phase One: Scope the Project"** on **page 106**, the five key phases of a project are discussed:

1. Scope the project.
2. Develop a project plan.
3. Launch the project.
4. Track the project's progress.
5. Close out the project.

Various companies and organizations define these phases of projects differently. However, these particular five stages are taken from the PMI's *Project Management Body of Knowledge* (PMBOK), the standard text for project managers. The PMBOK is the PM community's bible; according to the preface, it's "the sum of knowledge within the profession of project management." Many companies use PMI-trained PMs (who have been taught using the PMBOK) to develop projects.

Do You Have to Be a Certified Project Manager to Run a Project?

No. Being a certified PM is definitely an advantage when running large and complex projects, but it isn't a requirement—this issue is not too different from the discussion on technical certifications in **Chapter 3, Staffing Your IT Team** in the section **"The Value of Certification" on page 94**.

There are many common pitfalls that anyone running a project faces and we'll discuss some of them in this chapter. One common problem, for example, is that most project managers may be tasked with managing the project but don't have formal authority over project team members from other departments. This issue can make managing individuals a difficult challenge. But that particular difficulty isn't solved by *certification* of the project manager.

The Project Management Institute (PMI)

The PMI (www.pmi.org) is the international organization that trains and certifies project managers. Unlike many certification organizations, PMI is the real deal. Its main certification, a Project Management Professional (PMP), requires "A four-year degree . . . and at least three years of project management experience, with 4,500 hours leading and directing projects and 35 hours of project management education" (www.pmi.org/Certification/Project-Management-Professional-PMP.aspx). If you see a PMP certification on a résumé, it means the individual has spent a lot of time and effort achieving these goals.

IT Managers may or may not need all the experience that a certificate from the PMI implies (although some IT Managers now have, and more are pursuing, a PMP; the organization now has over 400,000 members). However, it's important for you to know that the science (and art) of project management has become much more formalized in the last 10 years and that the PMI has been at the center of that change.

The PMI and its PMP certification are certainly well regarded in the industry. However, like other certifications and educational backgrounds, the story doesn't end there. It all depends on how these skills are put to use.

WHY I CHOSE PMI

I have been a project manager for many different companies in many industries all over the world for over 40 years. A long time ago I decided to get certified as a PM and, after careful study, I chose the Project Management Institute. I picked PMI because:

- They are by far the largest organization of its kind in the world.
- They are truly a worldwide group; there are many PM groups, but they are recognized more by the countries where they are located.
- PMI's requirements for certification are very rigorous.
- You must pass a thorough exam.
- There is a significant cost involved (to deter people from doing it on a whim).
- It requires a demonstrated depth of experience.

—George Puziak
Area Project Manager
Davai International, Inc.

A Project Management Office

In larger organizations, the volume of project activity is so large that it may warrant the creation of a Project Management Office (PMO). In its simplest form, the PMO watches over all projects via the individual project managers and acts to ensure that projects are progressing effectively and that project managers are being vigilant. The PMO also serves as a traffic cop to ensure that projects aren't interfering with each other, overusing resources, and leveraging from each other's efforts, spending, etc. Depending on the organization and its size, a PMO may be specific to IT or it may be a resource for the whole company. In the latter situation, a PMO could be overseeing all sorts of projects—everything from re-IP-ing a network to redecorating the cafeteria.

In addition to overseeing the projects, the PMO also sets standards for project methodology within the organization. It can define best practices for project management within the organization; this can include project methodologies that are used, processes for determining justification, return on investment (ROI), formats for common types of documentation used within a project, metrics, and more. In highly regulated industries, or particularly complex organizations, the PMO can help ensure that projects are being handled in a consistent manner and adhering to compliance requirements.

4.2 PHASE ONE: SCOPE THE PROJECT

A project generally starts as an idea—either yours or someone else's. At the very beginning, a project is usually short on specifics. There's no framework for costs, time frames, or the resources required. In fact, as these areas begin to get quantified, potential projects often get killed because they will take too long, cost too much, require too many staff members to implement, the benefits just aren't worth the cost or risk, or their goals are too elusive.

Once you have a project, whether you gave it to yourself or someone else gave it to you, it's your job to manage it properly. Obviously, projects of different sizes aren't all managed the same way. As mentioned earlier, the size and complexity of projects can vary tremendously; the approach you take to implement a three-year, 75-person project will vary greatly from the way you give a single subordinate an assignment to accomplish in a week.

Clearly Define the Project's Objective and Scope to Avoid Scope Creep

First and foremost, the project needs a clearly defined objective. Objectives can take all kinds of shapes. One effective way to think of the objective is to ask yourself, "What is the achievement that will most clearly show that this project is completed and successful?" The objective should also reference the justification, the ROI, company savings, improved efficiencies, increased functionality, and so on. Setting a *project's* goals are not very different from setting an *employee's* goals. (See the section **"Development Plans and Goals"** on setting SMART goals on **page 52** of **Chapter 2, Managing Your IT Team**.)

A project objective must have several important characteristics. It must be:

- Clearly defined
- Agreed upon by the important people related to the project (see the discussion of stakeholders in the section **"Identify the Stakeholders"** on **page 108** of this chapter.)
- Documented
- Measurable

Other issues need to be considered, but you must first define your objective, get it agreed to, and put in on paper. Document not only goals but also decisions so that you won't hear "I never agreed to that" or "we decided to only allow 50 users into the system." You want to be able to reply, "No, actually, the number we agreed to was 150 and I have the meeting notes to show you."

PMI's definition of "scope creep" is right to the point: "adding features and functionality (project scope) without addressing the effects on time, costs, and resources or without customer approval." Hallway conversations, side notes in a mid-status report review, and meeting asides are ways that new responsibilities can sneak into your project without you realizing it. If your objective is clear, agreed upon, and documented, you will go a long way toward avoiding scope creep.

Very often, when a project's scope is documented, there is a section identifying what areas are considered *out of scope*. For example, a project team may be formed to implement a new application, but the team will only be implementing the core modules and not other ancillary modules. Similarly, the scope may only be for domestic use, and international use is out of scope for the project.

Also, be prepared for radical changes in project direction—projects seldom progress as planned. It is important to plan—you need an intelligently designed structure to work within—but be ready when the plan needs to be changed. In addition, be ready with a rough cost/benefit analysis if new features are suddenly required.

A TYPICAL CHANGE IN MID-PROJECT OBJECTIVES

When Rob Letterman and Conrad Vernon signed up as directors of *Monsters vs. Aliens*, a computer-generated spectacle from DreamWorks Animation, they were jittery about all the usual things: telling a good story, rounding up the celebrity vocal talent, and surviving a four-year production process without suffering a nervous breakdown.

Then Jeffrey Katzenberg hurled a curveball at them. After work on the movie was well under way, Mr. Katzenberg, DreamWorks Animation's chief executive, informed the pair that they would also need to deliver the movie in 3D.

"We were totally taken aback," Mr. Vernon said, sitting in a conference room at DreamWorks headquarters here.
—Barnes, Brooks, The Creatures That jumped off the Screen, www.nytimes.com/2009/03/22/movies/
22barn.html?_r=1&scp=1&sq=3-d&st=cse

Department versus Company Objectives

Carefully match your project's objectives to the company's overall objectives. Don't think of yourself or your department as an island, but instead think and act as if you are part of a dynamic, constantly changing organization. As a consequence, define your project's objective within the company's overall goals. This step may sound obvious, but it often isn't done.

Sometimes the connection between your project and the company's overall direction is *not* obvious: it is then your job as the manager of the project to formulate this connection and state it clearly. If your company is an auto parts dealer and you are installing a new upgrade for the phone system, many people in the company might wonder why they have to help and how that activity helps them. You need to have the answers to those questions ready.

Get Proper Sponsorship for the Project

Along with clearly defining the project's goals, you need to carefully define the sponsors of your project. A project sponsor is someone who can:

- Champion the project at higher levels
- Clear away organizational obstructions

- Provide resources (people, budget, software, hardware)
- Communicate with key stakeholders
- Keep the project alive by providing funding, authority, and influence
- Protect the project from those who don't support it and turf wars

Very often, a project sponsor will send a communication out to everyone involved as the project gets launched. Typically, this communication identifies the overall objectives, the importance to the company, and thanks everyone in advance for their cooperation. A simple communication like this can help pave the way to success for the project and can eliminate the chance of someone saying "this project is news to me."

Other examples of sponsorships include:

- Perhaps your boss handed you the project; make sure that you clearly inform her that you will need her support soon.
- Maybe your boss's boss came up with this clever idea, and it was passed down to you. If that happens, find out as quickly as possible from the source of the idea how much help you're going to get when it comes to issues such as funding, personnel, and so on.
- If you created the project yourself, after clearly outlining its goals, set about finding out how much help you're going to get from others in the company.

You will almost assuredly need help from people outside your department, and you'll probably need help from people higher up the corporate ladder. Find out how much help there is going to be before you start making any significant decisions or commitments. Your project may actually be a pet project of the company president or some other high executive. If so, having this type of sponsorship and backing can be enormously helpful to you in eliminating roadblocks, particularly as you try to make use of resources from other parts of the company. If somebody "upstairs" wants everyone to have access to all business applications from mobile devices, you're going to need a lot of personnel, time, effort, and money to make it happen.

Identify the Stakeholders

"Project stakeholders are individuals and organizations that are actively involved in the project, or whose interests may be affected as a result of project execution or completion" (PMBOK, p. 24). The key word here is the first "or." Obviously, people and groups working on a project will be affected by its outcome. But stakeholders are also individuals who don't work on the project but who are affected by it directly. You need to identify *all* the stakeholders in a project. Sometimes this task is a difficult one.

Examples of potential stakeholders in IT projects include:

- **The departments and end users that will be directly impacted by the new system.** An example of stakeholders would be the Accounting and Finance users when the new General Ledger system is put in.
- **Those that will be indirectly impacted by the new system.** Although the warehouse may be the primary beneficiary of the new inventory system, the way it improves efficiency may also have an impact on Sales and Shipping and Receiving, as well as the Procurement Group. Further down the chain it could impact Accounts Receivable and Payables.

- **Oversight groups.** Some departments such as HR and Legal oversee activities of the entire company. A project to scan old personnel records into a new document management system is generally a good idea. However, HR may be concerned about the sensitivity of those documents, who gets assigned to that task, and who gets proper training, whereas Legal may have thoughts about what it means for records retention policies.
- **Direct and indirect sources of funding.** Those that are paying for the project have a vested interest in it. Maybe your department is paying for the required hardware, but other departments are picking up other project costs (software, consultants, training, etc.).
- **Outside vendors.** Maybe your company's adoption of this new software is a bigger deal to the vendor than you realize. You might be able to wangle better maintenance agreements as a result.
- **Government agencies.** Your company's expansion into a new country may trigger all kinds of regulatory issues that will have to be addressed. In software companies, for example, what constitutes "non-exportable software" is a big issue. Some cryptographic techniques are prohibited from being shipped outside of the United States.
- **Those further up the corporate ladder.** Your bosses' superiors may be using the success of this project as part of a means of evaluating your boss, or the department, so the reviews of both you and your manager may be on the line.

Identify the Constraints, Interdependencies, and Risks

Projects aren't easy to manage. If they were, everyone would do it. There are many factors to consider, many of which are discussed in this section. But note that although some of these factors are under your control, many are not.

Potential Variables

Going into a project, make sure that all the issues and variables that are still uncertain are identified to all members of the team. Examples of these include:

- Approval of associated costs such as travel expenses for contractors from out of town
- Availability of identified required resources
- Risks such as uncertainty of vendor deliveries or implementation of new technology
- Interdependencies such as the inability to move to a new data center until construction is complete
- Constraints such as the unavailability of resources from Accounting at the end of the year because of the priority of year-end closing activities

Possible Solutions

You'll also want to indicate how you're dealing with those issues. Potential solutions include:

- Associated costs might be shared with other departments that stand to benefit directly from the project but who aren't formal members of the team.
- Resource availability might be less of an issue if multiple resources for the same task can be identified. It sounds easier to do than it is, but sometimes you can find others to cover your bases.
- The risk of implementing new technology can sometimes be mitigated with adequate training and testing time.

- Interdependencies can sometimes be addressed by simply alerting the various parties that they are part of a larger schedule.
- The constraint of resources during the year-end closing can sometimes be addressed via juggling the scheduling in ways that don't affect the final deadline.

The Project Charter

The Project Charter is the document that really launches a project and covers everything addressed in the previous sections:

- Scope
- Objectives
- Sponsors and stakeholders
- Constraints, interdependencies, and risks

The Project Charter may also have a formal signature line for sign-off. In addition, it often provides estimates of the items discussed later in this chapter:

- Time frame estimates
- Resource estimates
- Cost estimates
- Roles and responsibilities

Depending on the project, it may warrant investing some time to determine these so that the estimates just listed are more than educated best guesses.

As mentioned earlier, in addition to identifying what's in scope in the Project Charter, it could be very valuable to also identify in this document those areas that are out of scope. When complete, the Project Charter often becomes the "bible" for the project. It's the document that everyone references throughout the life of the project. When there are issues of scope creep, the Project Charter can serve as a reference to determine what's in and out of bounds for team members to work on.

Get Historical Perspective

Some projects are brand new events with no precedent. But these are the exceptions. Most projects have some history to them—some kind of background that can help you put the entire venture into perspective.

- Was a project similar to this one undertaken by the company before? If you are installing the servers for the new office in London, see if the notes and personnel for the expansion across the street that was finished last year are still available.
- Do some of your team members have comparable experience you can leverage? If the two technicians who installed the phone system last month are available, can you get them on this team to help with the network installation?
- Does the executive management of the company remember similar work? Does your boss recall the two previous laptop upgrade projects? If he doesn't, remind him that in 2011 (and way back in 2008) it took twice as long as anticipated to get machines in from the field.

Steps like these can help smooth your project planning and management considerably. For a further discussion of the value of historical perspectives for projects, see the section **"Time Estimates"** later in this chapter on **page 112**.

4.3 PHASE TWO: DEVELOP A PROJECT PLAN
Three Critical Components to Any Project

Every project has three critical components: time, money, and resources. You will also see this concept displayed as a triangle (see Figure 4.1).

The point of this graphic is that the *interplay* of the three characteristics of a project—time, money, resources, and how each relates to the other—directly affects the quality of a project.

For example:

- You might have plenty of time to install a new server (the application it will run won't be installed for another month), but if you don't have enough money (your boss doesn't want to pay for the high-end configuration you recommend) or the resources (both technicians who do this work routinely are gone—one has left the company and the other has been reassigned), the quality of the project will suffer.
- Money may not be an issue ("spend whatever you need" was the instruction you heard from your boss on the new "mission critical" Sales force automation deployment), but if it's only one person doing all the work for 200 users and the work must be done "yesterday," the quality of the project will suffer.
- You might have all the resources you need (you have five people of your own plus two from the vendor for installation of a state-of-the-art video conferencing facility), but you haven't been given enough money (the whole budget for the setup only included the cost of the hardware and didn't consider the cost of installing it) or enough time (people are moving in on Monday—*this* Monday), the quality of the project will suffer.

Think about each critical component of a project carefully when developing a project plan.

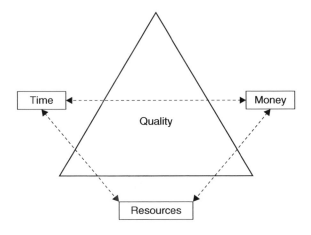

FIGURE 4.1

Three key components of a project.

Write the Project Plan with the Closeout Report in Mind

It sounds contradictory to plan the beginning with the end in mind, but in fact, that's exactly what you should do to achieve maximum project success. Everything you do, from the first planning meeting to the final celebration party, should be executed with the final result in mind. If you plan this way, the end result will force you to constantly act in certain ways, making decisions based on certain criteria. And that way of working will result in a far better outcome. Specifically, write your Project Plan with what you want to say in the Closeout Report; see the section **"Writing a Closeout Report" on page 121** later in this chapter.

Now that you know what you'll say at the end of the project, prepare to be ready to say it at the beginning. Be as specific, actionable, and quantifiable as possible. "Make the Sales department happy" isn't actionable, specific, or quantifiable; you may (or may not!) make them happy by executing this project. Regardless, it will be hard to quantify. In your plan, write a goal such as "install, upgrade, or refurbish all laptops in the Sales Department by January 1." When the new year rolls around, you will be able to say that you have achieved the goal of that project. The guidance given in the section **"Development Plans and Goals" on page 52** in **Chapter 2, Managing Your IT Team**, for developing staff goals can be very helpful for project goals.

Another useful suggestion is to include how much money you will save the company: "upgrading the Web-hosting facilities will cost the company $10,000 a quarter, but initial estimates are that faster processing time, more availability, and larger storage capacity will save the company a minimum of $25,000 per quarter for the first year alone."

Time Estimates

Next, determine how much time this project will take. Determining how much money and how many people you'll need is hard, but figuring out how long a particular project will take is even harder. Most people don't estimate time well. Some people are excellent at determining the approximate length of a project, but keep in mind that estimating is a poorly practiced art. Knowing this fact in advance will help you evaluate not only your skills in this area but estimates you receive from others.

The best place to start with time estimating is to find out if there is history: Has a project like this been done before? If so, how long did it take? That doesn't mean that if it took two months to install a previous version of the operating system across the company that it will take two months this time. (OS upgrades have gotten much more efficient and people are much more familiar with the process. But still . . .)

It may not take you the same amount of time as before, but it gives you a framework to operate under. You have a general idea of how much time this will take. And, when you present your project plan, you can add that historical data to your report. ("In 2010, it took us two months to get everyone up and running with Windows Vista. We propose to do this new Windows version in three weeks maximum.")

Sometimes, however, you won't have a historical record to work from. You will be executing a project for the first time. In that case, be sure to do two things:

1. Have *some* basis for your estimate. If you're essentially guessing that something will take two years, it should be based on estimates of the time required for the component tasks.
2. *Overestimate*. You're working with the unknown and you should estimate accordingly. Most people usually plan for things to go well. You also have to try to account for unforeseen problems, conflicting priorities, and "unreasonable" demands.

A helpful way to estimate a project is to get all the key participants in a room to talk about all the things that have to be done, the order in which they have to be addressed, and approximately how long they will take. Ask questions such as "And after that will we be done?" or "What *exactly* do we have to do to get that task done?" Continue to drive things to a finer level of detail and help get all the requirements and tasks out for discussion.

It's common to come up with a time estimate as a group—members of your project team (see the section **"Decision-Making Techniques"** in this chapter on **page 122**) will all have opinions about how long a project will take. Some managers take the number proposed and double it. That may sound devious, but as mentioned before, time estimation is a notoriously difficult thing to do. You'll be much happier overestimating than you will underestimating. It seldom occurs that more time is given to an IT project than is required. It happens, of course, but not very often.

Also remember that when time is estimated, everyone has to factor in that all team members are seldom working on only one project. They are usually working on this project as well as several others, in addition to everything else that they have to deal with on a day-to-day basis. For example, a certain task may only take a few hours to complete, but the employee won't be able to get to it for a week because they are already committed to another project.

Resources Required: Employees (Internal and External to IT)

For team members who report to you, it's easy enough to assign them to the project, but you can't simply go into other departments and assign individuals to your project. You need to meet with their department heads and explain your project to them and what resources you're coming to them for. This may take a great deal of diplomacy, especially if the various department heads don't have much of an interest in your project. It is at times like this that you'll need to call on your well-defined objectives, explain how those objectives fit in with the overall company goals, and be ready with an explanation of how your project positively affects the person you are talking with. When the objectives don't convince them, you can either reevaluate your project and objectives or call on your project sponsor to place a phone call or write a quick e-mail to help dilute the resistance.

Full-Time versus Consultant Employees

For a full discussion of the reasons to hire a full-time employee or a consultant, see **Chapter 3, Staffing Your IT Team** on **page 65**. The short story is that each has its advantages and disadvantages, depending on the circumstances and need. The nature of the work also helps you determine which kind of worker is your best choice. One of the advantages of consultants for projects is that they will usually be dedicated solely to the project, whereas full-time employees usually have many other responsibilities in addition to your project. Also, if a consultant is only needed for the duration of the project, their assignment can be terminated easily when the project wraps up.

Vendors and Service Providers

You may have vendors involved in this project, perhaps on a consulting basis, to implement a new application or on a support basis. You may also have service providers, such as telecom carriers, that are critical for getting certain components implemented.

It's important that you identify all the resources required and identify constraints and parameters of their involvement. In some cases you may have a resource completely under your direction (such as an employee or consultant) or you may have limited access (such as a vendor's technician only being available to you for two weeks). In some cases you may feel almost helpless regarding certain resources, such as waiting for your ISP to deliver a new circuit or a hardware vendor to ship a particularly constrained item.

Money

Chapter 6, Managing the Money on **page 161** offers a full discussion on what you need to know as an IT Manager about budgeting. But for project management, you want to be able to identify different types of costs:

- One-time costs
- Ongoing costs
- Hidden costs
- Consultants
- Internal resources
- Capital versus operating expenses

See the section **"Justifying the Costs"** on **page 132** later in this chapter.

One-Time Costs

As the name implies, one-time costs are incurred for those items that require a single outlay of money. For example, new hardware and software licenses generally represent a one-time cost. Of course, if the hardware is leased (and there are monthly payments), then it wouldn't be considered a one-time cost.

Ongoing Costs

Ongoing, or recurring costs pertain to those items that are paid for continuously. For example, the monthly cost for a new telecom circuit is an ongoing cost, as are the maintenance and support costs related to hardware and software (even though the hardware and software themselves are a one-time cost). Cloud-based services generally have ongoing monthly costs. Salaries for employees and the costs of contractors are also ongoing costs.

Hidden Costs

In addition to the visible costs of a project, there are many "invisible" costs that will serve you well to consider. This chapter discusses "hidden" items, such as unnecessary meeting attendance, but there are others. Consider the loss of productivity the company suffers when an employee is suddenly transferred to a new project and can no longer work on the tasks he had been doing. Other types of hidden costs can include costs for certain items that were not fully disclosed by the vendor (e.g., activation fees), or unplanned items, circumstances, or requirements that impact the cost of the project.

Consultants

The cost for consultants is often broken out separately for accounting purposes. As with the aforementioned costs, consultants may be a one-time cost (e.g., six months of time during implementation) or perhaps an ongoing cost (e.g., for ongoing support and training).

Costs of Internal Resources

In many companies, the costs of internal resources, primarily staff salaries, are factored into the total cost of the project. The decision to do this is essentially a policy set by the Finance department, if they want total project costs to be treated a certain way in the accounting. You should check with them to see if they want these costs included. If so, you need to determine how far these costs go (e.g., in addition to salary do they include benefits and cost of overhead such as office space?). Generally, if you have to account for these costs in your project, there are rules of thumb available from Finance for calculating them.

Capital versus Operating Expense

As a general rule, one-time costs are considered capital expenses, whereas ongoing costs are considered operating expenses. There may be exceptions to this; for example, one-time costs under a certain threshold aren't capitalized. In addition, there may be gray areas as to whether certain costs should be capitalized. For example, Finance may elect to capitalize the cost of training if it's exclusively needed for the project. However, if it's training that would've been taken anyway, it may get treated differently.

Work with Finance on these issues. You won't be the first person to ask these questions, and they'll understand that they are new issues to you in your new role. Get a good understanding of these policies the first time and you'll make everyone's life easier.

For a further discussion of capital versus operating expenses, see the section **"The Difference between Capital Expenditures and Operating Expense Items"** in **Chapter 6, Managing the Money** on **page 167**.

Roles and Responsibilities

A critical element to the success of any project is the clear definition of roles and responsibilities from the outset. In as much detail as possible at the start, work with everyone on the team to define all the roles.

Defining everyone's roles doesn't mean *dictating* to people what those roles will be. There will be times where power plays occur or where one person doesn't want to assume the role that he should. Plan for the more common occurrence—every player on the team wants to know exactly what their role is and what they are responsible for accomplishing.

Confusion about roles is a real project killer. The question, "Who is in charge of the project?" is a common source of problems, as well as, "I thought I was doing testing." You won't be able to answer every question at the beginning of the project, but you should spend as much time as possible trying to anticipate any potential trouble areas.

Multiple Projects

To further complicate the issue, it's entirely likely that you, and many others on your team, will be involved with several projects simultaneously, each of a different size, each at a different point in its life cycle, and each competing for resources. Not only will you be coordinating the companywide upgrade to a new accounting system, for example, you may also be overseeing the new operating system installation for a server, be involved in the purchase of a new phone system for the organization, and serve on a cross-functional team implementing a new work-from-home program. And every member of the various projects you're working on is also working on other multiple projects themselves.

Not only should you be identifying everyone's roles, but you should also be estimating what portion of their time will be expected on your project. In some cases their involvement in the project may come in batches. One example might have one person with virtually no involvement for the first three months, but then they will have to give 50 percent of their time for four weeks.

4.4 PHASE THREE: LAUNCH THE PROJECT

You have scoped the project and developed a formal project plan; now it's time to get the project off the ground.

Range of Launch Options

The range of options for launching a project is quite varied. Some projects start off with a brief memo passed down from your boss: "We are starting a project to upgrade our web site to allow online shopping." Not an easy task, but a project has been initiated.

The other extreme might be one of Microsoft's product launches. Microsoft announced it spent over $100 million on marketing Windows Vista. Launching a new operating system is a monumental task, but in a similar way, a formal project has been initiated.

Your projects will probably fit somewhere in the middle: You might get more formal notification of its beginnings ("Let's meet Friday to discuss the request from Accounting to upgrade their database") and a little less than Microsoft's billions to work with ("We have to keep this project under budget, too, so let's make sure the $15,000 number is on everyone's mind").

Stage a Kick-Off Meeting

It may be wise to enlist your boss when trying to demonstrate the value and importance of your project to other department heads. Often the senior-most executive who is sponsoring the project will call for a meeting, along with various department heads, at the beginning of a project. The purpose of a meeting like this is to (1) make sure that all the various department managers are aware of the importance of the project and (2) encourage them to commit resources to it as needed. A meeting like this, often called a kick-off meeting, can be a critical success factor in a project.

A good kick-off meeting will have every member of the team in attendance. The roles and responsibilities can then be defined—ideally in front of the sponsors. Goals, schedules, budgets, and so on can also be presented to everyone—again in front of everyone. This public accountability (if appropriate for your project) can be a very effective method to solidify your team's goals.

Goals of Your Kick-Off Meeting

At your kick-off meeting set some ground rules, establish some administrative procedures, and make sure that everyone is on the same page. Make sure everyone is very clear about the project's objective and scope. This is the perfect time to discuss the project's goals. You have already written them down, and this first meeting is the place for you to distribute them and make sure everyone buys into them.

At this same meeting you may want to establish how often and where the project team is going to meet. A regular schedule of a weekly meeting at the same time, in the same room, is helpful—it sets a valuable routine.

4.5 PHASE FOUR: TRACK THE PROJECT'S PROGRESS

The bigger your project, the harder it is to keep track of who is doing what, how long different tasks will take, and so on. Several techniques for project management (project meetings, minutes, etc.) are discussed throughout this book, but these techniques provide more snapshot-type information and fall short of giving any perspective about the "big picture." Although many software tools are available for project management, one in particular, Microsoft Project, has become the predominant choice. It has become very popular for managing projects of almost any size.

Microsoft Project

There are many project management software tools, but Microsoft Project is the most popular. It has legions of users who would never dream of using any other product. And they can't imagine why you would consider using anything else, either. In some companies, using Microsoft Project has achieved a near-religious status. If you're working for one of those companies, get used to receiving .mpp files.

Simply entering your project's information into Microsoft Project is a valuable exercise in itself. It forces you to think of the specific tasks needed, their dependencies on other tasks, and the times and resources needed. As you do this, Microsoft Project will alert you when the left hand doesn't know what the right hand is doing. For example, if you've over-allocated resources, or if time constraints are exceeded, Microsoft Project will let you know.

By defining to Microsoft Project which tasks can occur simultaneously and which must be done sequentially, it's easy to make changes to any portion of the project and have all the dates and resource allocations updated automatically and see what the impact is.

Microsoft Project also allows you to integrate your data with other time tracking and office productivity tools relatively seamlessly.

Remember, however, all the power that Microsoft Project provides can overwhelm you and you can forget that *you* are running your project, not Microsoft Project.

HOW FORMAL DO I HAVE TO GET?

Focus your time, energy, and money tightly. You don't have to be very formal about it—not every good project manager uses Gantt charts, for example. But you have to manage your project carefully, regardless of how formally you do that.

Whether you are installing a new phone system, taking over the management of a building, or deploying a fleet of brokers to evaluate a potential new marketplace, you have to *systematically schedule your efforts and the team members'*.

By managing your time lines, you can anticipate when your resources will be slack or overdrawn, when the project will slow down or intensify, and when you need to step in and rearrange things. You need this kind of information, or the project will overwhelm you.

—Peter Hansen
Principal, Hansen Realty, Berkeley, CA

Other Project Management Tools

One reason you might consider using a different tool is that Microsoft Project is a sophisticated product. It has many features and capabilities, many more than the average person managing projects would ever use. However, there are many companies that use *enterprise* project management tools, which can track multiple projects and resource assignments across all of those projects. These tools can provide the manager with a high-level view of the status of all projects and identify opportunities to reassign resources among different projects. Examples of enterprise project management tools include:

- Planview
- Computer Associates Project and Portfolio Management
- Oracle Project Portfolio Management
- Microsoft Project EPM
- IBM Rational Portfolio Manager
- Hewlett-Packard Project and Portfolio Management

Also, Web-based project management tools (Redmine, Tenrox, and KForge are examples) are gaining popularity. Rather than e-mail files back and forth, users are making changes using their browser to access an application provider via the Internet, update project plans, and post and share project-related files. It's more efficient and convenient. More and more work activities are moving "to the cloud" in this way. See an extensive discussion of the Cloud in **Chapter 11, Connectivity: Social Media, Handhelds, and More, on page 287**.

Gantt Charts and Time Lines

A Gantt chart allows you to quickly see what is supposed to happen and when. It tracks time along the horizontal axis. The vertical axis lists all the tasks associated with the project, their start and end dates, and the resources required.

For an example of a Gantt chart that can be generated from Microsoft Project, see Figure 4.2. When you generate the Gantt chart for a particular project, you and every member of the project team (along with anyone else who is interested) can see the true scope of it, the time frames, tasks, dependencies, resource assignments, and such of the entire project. Gantt charts rarely fit on a single page, by the way, so it is common for the entire report to require a whole wall to view when all the printed pages are taped together.

PERT Charts and Critical Paths

Program Evaluation and Review Technique (PERT) charts or PERT diagrams are graphic representations of the dependencies between tasks in a project.

PERT is basically a method for analyzing the tasks involved in completing a given project, especially the time needed to complete each task, and identifying the minimum time needed to complete the total project.

In Figure 4.3, a circle represents a task start or end and a line between two circles represents the actual tasks and how they're related.

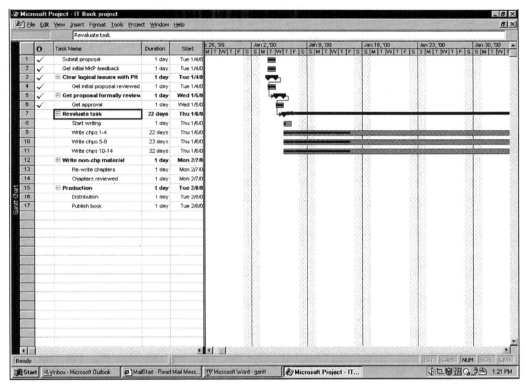

FIGURE 4.2

Sample Gantt chart.

Critical Path

One of the more helpful pieces of information from a PERT chart identifies the *critical path*. The critical path is the series of tasks or events that determine the project's total duration. In other words, if any of the tasks on the critical path take longer than expected, then the entire project will be delayed by that amount of time. Tasks that aren't on the critical path won't have the same influence on the overall project for various reasons (perhaps because they're done in parallel, as opposed to sequentially).

In Figure 4.3, the critical path consists of tasks A, C, and F. If any of these tasks takes longer than expected, it will delay the project as a whole. Activities outside the critical path can change (up to a point) without impacting the entire project. "Slack time" is the term used to indicate how much a non-critical path task can be delayed without impacting the project as a whole.

Project Milestones

Both Gantt and PERT charts allow you to identify and track your tasks. Creating a milestone in your Gantt chart allows you to add a very useful level of functionality to your project tracking.

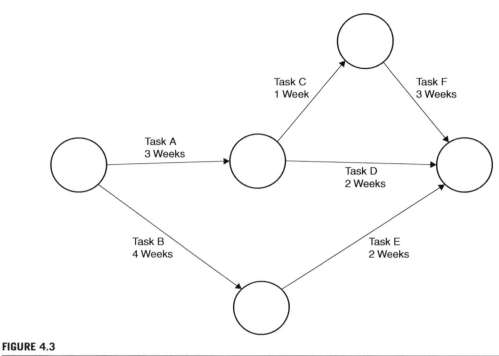

FIGURE 4.3

PERT chart.

A milestone is a major event in the life of a project. A large project can have many milestones: Moving your company's offices from New York to Raleigh will not only have many individual tasks, but it will also have many milestones. When the decision is officially made, for example (it might have been bandied around for years), is a milestone. But that will be only the first milestone; when the new site is selected, when the lease for the new building is signed, when the phones and wiring are complete, when the data center is ready, when the telecommunication lines are turned up, when office construction is done, when the first people start working in the new building, and so on, are all milestones.

Think specifically about what needs to be accomplished to reach your project goal. Begin by breaking the objective down into a few milestones. You don't need a lot of detail here, but divide the project into a few chunks so that you can begin thinking about the kinds of people you want on the project team, and maybe begin to develop some perspective on time frames, costs, and other resources.

Updates to Management and the Team

One of the things that everyone wants to know about a project is: "How is it going?" Certainly your boss and the project sponsor want to know this, and the project team needs to be told as well. Oftentimes a project is so big that team members are only familiar with their own piece and aren't aware of the overall project as a whole.

Regular project meetings (discussed in the section **"Productive Project Meetings"** later in this chapter on **page 128**) can be helpful for keeping members of the team up to date. But these meetings may not be sufficient for everyone; some people are only involved in the project during certain periods, for example, and therefore don't attend every meeting. Sending out project status reports and posting meeting agendas and minutes, as well as a current version of project plans, are two ways of making sure that everyone has access to data they need.

Summary Updates

Gantt charts, PERT charts, critical paths, and so on are useful tools, but the chances are that your manager, the project sponsors, and the stakeholders may not want to see that level of detail. Even your own team members may not want to wade through all of that just to see if things are on track. Providing regular updates that summarize progress can be valuable to all. These summaries can include the following topics:

- Accomplishments since the last update
- Mention of those items in progress and whether they're going faster or slower than expected
- Upcoming activities
- Issues and concerns (perhaps vendor deliveries are taking longer than expected or a key member of the team resigned recently)
- Overall status: this is the opportunity to identify if things are going as planned or whether you're anticipating delays, cost overruns, etc.

Determining the appropriate content, who sees it, and how often these updates go out is a matter of judgment. For example, a daily report for a two-year-long project may be overkill. It may make more sense to do it monthly for the first 18 months and then switch to biweekly and weekly as the project gets closer to implementation. Similarly, the summary just given may be sufficient for your boss, but perhaps an even briefer summary is appropriate for her boss.

Red, Yellow, Green Indicators

Another technique used to keep everyone informed about project status is to use red, yellow, and green status indicators for key items. Stealing from the traffic light paradigm, they are a simple and effective way of communicating the status that might otherwise get lost in a verbose explanation. These indicators are usually included as part of other status reports and are associated with key tasks and milestones.

4.6 PHASE FIVE: CLOSE OUT THE PROJECT

Writing a Closeout Report

A Closeout Report is the report written at the end of a project. It can be a brief, three-page document or a 50-page, detailed report. It should contain, at minimum, the purpose of the project and how well the team executed that purpose. Additional components of a Closeout Report can include a brief history of the project, specific goals accomplished and/or missed, resources used, which aspects went well, and what lessons were learned from things that didn't go well.

One simple method of generating a Closeout Report is to take the initial Project Charter—the document you worked so hard to create at the beginning of the project—and compare it directly to what you accomplished during the project. Earlier in this chapter we discussed developing a plan with a Closeout

Report in mind. For example, say your plan called for the purchase and installation of six new servers in less than two weeks; you accomplished that, so identify the goal, the step, and the accomplishment. Name names, specify how much money and time you saved, give credit where it's due, and pat your team on the back.

Additional Accomplishments

If relevant, add the new uses or new procedures that your project uncovered. Maybe the new system you installed caught the attention of another department and it's now serving two purposes. Maybe the automating of the sales process saved more money than expected, as well as reduced errors. Point these successes out.

Dealing with Bad News

If your Closeout Report contains bad news, be clear about it. Compare it to the Project Charter and try to identify how things could have been different. Were the goals set too unrealistically? ("Purchase and install six servers by COB Friday.") Were you given enough resources? ("You can use one person from Accounting, but that's it.") Don't point fingers at individuals, but try and learn from the problems: What are the lessons the company can learn from this project's disappointment and failures? ("In the future, changes to the time reporting software will require the involvement of someone from HR.")

The Need for Follow-Up Activities

It's pretty rare that a project finishes with every loose end tied up. There are often a number of items that require follow-up. These could be items such as making sure ongoing maintenance is done, the contractors complete all the documentation they promised, and so on.

The completion of projects—the installation of a new billing system, for example—often generates the need for more training. This training can be identified either while the project is being worked on or as it's completed. If the project completion is going to get a critical function working (such as a billing system), training should be scheduled well in advance to have users ready.

4.7 DECISION-MAKING TECHNIQUES

One way to think about the decisions you'll have to make in your role as a PM is to think about the four types of decision-making mechanisms you can use. These mechanisms are, naturally, only one of many ways to approach the issue. How and why people make decisions is a giant field of research. But these approaches are fairly common methods used to look at the issue.

Four Types of Decision-Making Methods

1. **The Majority Wins.** You take a vote and whichever side of the issue gets the most votes wins. This is certainly the most democratic method, it makes team members feel the most involved, and is often the perfect solution to some clearly defined, black-or-white types of problems. However, it can lead to strange decisions (do you really want the team to meet off-site every week?) and is often not the right method for solving very complex problems. Also, commonly, the *most popular* approach may not be the *best* one. Some people may opt for it because it's the simplest, quickest, or least expensive.

2. **An appointed subcommittee decides or recommends.** This technique is good because the committee can gather and analyze detailed facts and present a recommendation to the group as a whole. It is bad because not everyone is involved in the decision and because even small committees can get locked up. This approach is excellent for problems that have many components that need to be researched before a decision is made or for issues that need to be decided quickly and outside of the large group. The U.S. Senate, for example, has many committees and subcommittees whose function is to do the often critical preliminary work before presenting an issue to the Senate as a whole.

3. **You decide with help from your team.** This is often the most efficient and most popular method. Many decisions on a project don't lend themselves to group dynamics; there is either not enough time or the issue isn't all that important to the group (does everyone really have to weigh in on the font choice for the input screen?), but you can solicit opinions from team members that you know care about the issue, and are knowledgeable, and then decide. It's not 100 percent democracy, but it's not 100 percent dictatorship, either.

4. **You make the decision by yourself.** A manager will make plenty of decisions by himself and no one will care. To keep a project moving along, sometimes it's critical simply to make a decision and move on. (The team lost two programmers on Friday, for example; you decide to contact HR that afternoon to begin to fill those positions. You know other people in the group feel the positions should be filled with analysts, but you don't, and time is ticking away. Make the decision and go forward.)

Some decisions made unilaterally won't be popularly received, of course, by team members who perceive these as decisions "imposed upon them." When that happens, you'll be well served to have a history of democratic decision making behind you, as well as an explanation about how this particular decision was made with the project's ultimate goals in mind. You may not make everyone happy, but if you do it well, you will be respected.

With the difficult decisions, you may not be sure that the right decision was made, but you can be sure it was a good decision if:

- All views, concerns, and issues were voiced and discussed
- All alternatives were considered
- You can explain (when questioned in the future) the factors and reasoning that led to you deciding the way you did

Once a decision is made, you shouldn't feel compelled to revisit it unless some of the key factors related to it have changed.

4.8 WHAT TO DO IF/WHEN THE PROJECT GETS OFF TRACK

Managing time and money are your biggest opportunities to succeed in project management—and your largest possibilities for failure. Watch them both carefully. This section provides suggestions for how to deal with the inevitable problems associated with managing time and money.

Regardless of how or why your project is taking more time or money than expected, it's imperative to keep the stakeholders (particularly the sponsor and your boss) informed. If you try to cover up the problem, it will almost assuredly come back to haunt you. Invariably, the problem will eventually surface, and you'll not only be faulted for the original problem, but also for attempting to cover it up (which could do more damage to your reputation than simply being late or going over budget).

Some Issues out of Your Control

There will be events in every project that are out of anyone's control:

- People get sick
- Family emergencies come up
- Long-planned vacations arise
- Calls from other departments come in for "your" resources
- Personnel get promoted and move on to other responsibilities
- Team members move on to other positions
- Vendors fail to meet their commitments
- A corporate downsizing is announced
- Severe weather events occur
- Changes in the organizational/management/economic landscape suddenly take place

---

FOUR TONGUE-IN-CHEEK "LAWS" OF PROJECT MANAGEMENT

Managing projects can be a complex task and most projects run into some difficulty before they are completed. Before discussing how to handle some of these difficulties, it seems appropriate to let you know about the following four "laws" of project management. They are often presented in a tongue-in-cheek way. However, they prove true more often than not:

1. No major project is ever installed on time, within budget, or with the same staff that started it.
2. Projects progress quickly until they become 95 percent complete and then remain 95 percent complete forever.
3. When things are going well, something will go wrong.
   a. Corollary: When things can't get any worse, they will.
   b. Corollary: When things are going well it's because you have overlooked something.
4. The 80/20 rule: The first 20 percent of a project schedule completes 80 percent of a project's goals, but the remaining 20 percent of the project's goals takes 80 percent of the project schedule.

When a Project Gets behind Schedule

If your project falls behind schedule, don't panic. Consider the following ideas when you see a project slipping:

- **Determine exactly how far behind you are.** If you're using a Gantt chart, for example, you can track which tasks are behind schedule. (Microsoft Project calls them "variances.")
- **Try to isolate the problem.** Are you behind on one small, relatively isolated part of the project or is the entire mission going to be late?
- **Try to recalibrate.** Can the schedule be changed easily? If the task involves one person working on a single piece of the project, can you work with him to reset the timetable?
- **Gain perspective.** Reset the schedule for the offending task and the entire project may be delayed, but how big a problem is that? If you promised a completion date for a three-month project on Friday, will having things finished a few days later really matter?
- **Be open to all your team members and stakeholders.** If time is slipping away, you have a responsibility to everyone to let them know the status of the project, and that the deadline is at risk. In particular, people reporting to you (team members) need to know what's really happening. And people above you (your bosses) need to be kept informed.

- **Lead, don't just manage.** Here is a chance for you to shine as a leader. When you have to let people know about a problem with the project, make it less about assigning blame (don't say, "We'd be fine if Jack just pulled his weight," for example) and more about showing your skills as a leader ("We are two weeks behind schedule but here is my plan for how we can catch up"). See the section **"Leadership vs. Management" on page 31** of **Chapter 2, Managing Your IT Team.**
- **Involve others.** When someone alerts you to a problem or delay, ask them for their recommendations and suggestions on how to deal with it. Of course, you have to be careful with this technique. Individuals may shy away from identifying problems if they have a sense they're going to be stuck with the ownership of resolving it. Share the situation with the whole team and invite suggestions on how to address it.
- **Do some research on the reasons for the delay.** The schedule might have been set unrealistically (by you or someone else) at the beginning; if you look into delays as they occur, and you carefully track them, you will be able to better anticipate problems in the future.
- **Be aggressive in solving the problem.** If you need more time to complete a project, tell people and get more time. Hoping no one will notice isn't a strategy for continued success.

Perils of Adding Staff

Consider, but don't automatically decide, adding resources. Some projects are either understaffed from the outset or suddenly develop a need for further resources in mid-project; adding staff to these tasks often results in accelerating the project. When adding resources, consider how long it will take a person to get up to speed and productive on this project.

Other types of projects, however, aren't well suited to the additional staff fix. Software development, famously, rarely benefits from adding developers. Fredrick Brooks, in his groundbreaking book, *The Mythical Man-Month*, states his famous law: "Adding manpower to a late software project makes it later." Keep in mind that some tasks just can't be sped up by adding staff. For example, no matter how many women you assign to the task, it will still take nine months to produce a baby.

Your Project Is Costing More Than Expected

Projects run over budget all the time. How *far* over budget is often the most important issue. Consider these solutions:

- Determine exactly how far over budget you are: $5,000 over on a $300,000 project is not that important; $5,000 on a $15,000 project is a problem you have to address immediately.
- Do some research on the reasons for the budget overage. The budget might have been set unrealistically (by you or someone else) at the beginning; if you look into the overages as they occur and you track them carefully, you'll be able to better anticipate problems in the future.
- Be clear to your boss (and other stakeholders involved in the money side of the project) that there is a problem. A 5 percent variance on dollars can be trivial or critical (depending on the size of the budget), but most bosses will want to know about that discrepancy.
- Adjust the project deliverables. Many projects are redefined as they progress: If your initial project goal called for all 14 satellite offices to get individual servers, and installation costs on the first five sent you over budget already, it is time to reevaluate your project goals. All the offices may get their own servers, but that may not happen until next year, instead of this year.

- Look for "hidden money." Your project budget may have a contingency budget or your boss may have money from another project you can use.

Avoid falling into the trap of thinking that you'll save money later in the project and in the end you'll be okay.

4.9 USEFUL PROJECT MANAGEMENT TECHNIQUES

As you gain experience for managing projects, you'll find, discover, and adapt a variety of techniques that you find helpful. Each project manager does this, and many have adopted styles and techniques unconsciously, barely aware of how effective they are.

Project Teams

Formalizing a group of individuals working loosely together toward a common goal can have tremendous benefits. Calling these people a special group or telling them they are all now members of a "project team" or a "task force" can solidify a project's goals and make progress toward those goals much more evident. When people feel identified with a project, they are much more likely to feel responsible and accountable for it.

The size and complexity of your project will determine how formal you need to be with assigning teams: getting three new sales people up and running with laptops, for example, may take a day or two and involvement from several different people in IT at various times, but the task probably doesn't need a formal team.

Moving your company's offices, however, is a classic project that benefits from formalizing a team. Each member has specific tasks, and everyone can have a clear idea of what the goal is and how they can help with that goal.

Candidates for the Project Team

Who are candidates for your project team? Individuals' involvement on the team can be quite varied. Some people may be dedicated nearly 100 percent to the project throughout its life. Others may spend only a small portion of their time on the project. Still others may only be involved with the project during certain phases. In addition, a project team will probably consist mostly of employees, but there may also be outside consultants if special expertise or additional resources are needed.

The first people you'll include on the team are the ones you think it will take to achieve the project's goal. As you talk with these people, they will offer up suggestions of others that need to be involved. They will also offer you different perspectives on what it will take to make the project succeed. Some of the project's team members may be on your staff. Others that you'd like to include might be your peers, direct reports of your peers, and individuals from other departments—perhaps some that are senior to you.

While it's tempting to pick the best and brightest for your project, you may want to temper that instinct. Projects are great mechanisms to allow others on your staff to shine and to give them the opportunity to show what they can do. Since the best and brightest are always in high demand, give careful consideration to balancing your project team with a mix of people that deserve the opportunity to show they can contribute.

Create a War Room

For some projects, it has become trendy to have a project room or "war room." (A movie about Bill Clinton's 1992 presidential campaign—a project that used a project room to great effect—is called *The War Room*.) This room provides team members a place to work on the project that is separate from their regular work area. The idea of the war room is to keep members from being distracted from the project by their regular duties and to increase communication (and hopefully productivity, quality, etc.) by having the team members near each other. Lately, war rooms aren't complete unless they also include a whole host of toys (Koosh balls, hacky sacks, Nerf games, etc.), a whiteboard, an endless supply of munchies and soft drinks, and "open" seating so that team members can communicate easily.

Formalized Project Frameworks

Chapter 8, Security and Compliance, has a section called **"Methodologies and Frameworks"** on **page 238**. A number of these, such as IT Infrastructure Library (ITIL), ISO 9000, Six Sigma, and Capability Maturity Model Integration (CMMI), have aspects and techniques that you can apply to your projects to help ensure quality and that goals are met and for managing/tracking progress.

Participate in the Project Yourself

Consider participating in the project yourself—give yourself tasks to do besides managing the project. While managing the project is often a full-time job, if team members see you working on the project, it inspires them. Plus, it gives you greater insight to the project, as well as your staff's activities. Until the late 1990s, for example, Bill Gates contributed directly to Excel's code.

Offer Project Perks

Group lunches, team T-shirts, coffee mugs, or milestone achievement awards—think of ideas to keep your team active and involved. Consider small rewards along the project timeline (weekly team meeting small prize drawings, for example) instead of awards at the end. Company-paid doughnuts have a very attractive cost-in-exchange-for-information ratio and often get people to meetings.

THE FLYING PIG AWARD

At our company, we have a challenging project—one that some people say we will complete "only when pigs fly."

Every month we have an all-hands meeting where we present a "Flying Pig" award and certificate. The flying pig is a ceramic pig that the winner is allowed to keep for a month—until someone else "wins" (earns) it. Team members nominate potential awardees. People post the certificate in their cubes and sign and decorate the pig when their month is up.

—Karen Hitchcock
Business Analyst

Give Your Project a Code Name

"Operation First Falcon" sounds a lot more exciting and important than "Operation General Ledger." For projects that are large enough, create a code name and a project logo, put them on polo shirts, and you'll be flooded with requests for people to join your project. (Not necessarily the people you want on the project, but that's a different problem.) Use the logo and name on documents pertaining to the project to help create a sense of identity and branding.

Productive Project Meetings

Okay, now you have the project team, or at least the first cut at the project team. The next thing you want is to get all the team members together. Work to make sure every one of your meetings is as effective as it can be. Information should be shared, issues discussed, decisions made, and action items determined.

- Set clear goals in your first project meeting: document the objective and scope of the project, how frequently meetings will be held, have minutes taken, and so on.
- Holding a successful project team meeting involves several simple but effective meeting techniques. These methods are discussed here; use them to increase the productivity of your meetings and your team.
- Don't forget that you're in control, and therefore responsible, for the success of both the meetings and the overall project. Watch both carefully.

Meeting Agendas

Typically, each project meeting will follow a consistent format. Develop one that seems to work well for you and your team and that everyone is comfortable with. Typical areas for a project meeting agenda might include the following:

- Status review of open items and action items from previous meeting
- Decisions and agreements from previous meeting restated
- Review of overall status of project and discussion of any major issues
- Updates from each subteam or team member
- Accomplishments of note
- Key tasks and milestones coming up

You will also want to use the meetings for special events. For example, it may be an opportunity to demo a recently completed application component or it may be the right place for a vendor to demo a product that may be appropriate for the project. Alternatively, if the project hits a snag or a particularly important decision needs to be made, the agenda can set aside time for an in-depth discussion of the issues.

Minutes of the Meetings

Have minutes taken so that there is no disagreement on items that were decided, tasks that were assigned, etc. Minutes should also include accomplishments, areas of concern and problems, updates on time frames, and so on. The minutes should be distributed to all team members and project sponsors as soon as possible after the meeting occurs—and certainly before the next meeting. Taking and distributing minutes can be painful tasks that can be easily forgotten or ignored; they can also be critical to the long-term success of the project.

As manager of the project, it's your job to make sure these tasks get done. You may get volunteers to take minutes or you may not get any. A popular technique is to rotate this assignment each meeting or decide that the person who shows up *last* for the meeting is the one assigned to take minutes. (This can be a clever way of making sure people arrive on time.) Among other things, the minutes ensure that everyone is aware of how the project is progressing.

The minutes may also give senior executives an idea of when they need to get involved; they may decide to rally the troops, motivate, or buy lunch for everyone because a milestone is met. Minutes can chart the progress of activities and tasks from week to week and serve as a reminder of things that need to be done. The minutes can also document who is responsible for each item. Too often, especially in large project teams, it's too easy for everyone to think "someone else" will take care of it. Although several people may be working on an item, it's important to identify a single person as the one to take the lead.

The minutes should reflect the key items of the meetings, such as decisions, issues, and project status. For the meeting minutes, consider using the ideas discussed in this chapter and in the section **"Updates to Management and the Team"** on **page 120**. Each meeting's minutes should follow the same format so that people know where to look to find the information they need.

The Hidden Cost of Meetings

There are, of course, the visible costs of meetings: booking rooms, video conferencing, maybe you all will have to fly to a common city to meet, the cost of setting up and training on the Web conferencing software, doughnuts, and so on.

But the largest cost of meetings isn't often calculated. One way to think about meetings is to *total up the hourly wage of every person attending the meeting*. This cost is seldom considered, but it should be computed every time. If it were done each time, far fewer meetings would be held and far fewer attendees would be invited. Right now, you are inviting the VP from Sales because she is a stakeholder and you want to do the correct political thing; she may be attending because it allows her to meet with your boss before the meeting. In fact, perhaps she shouldn't be invited and wouldn't miss attending; if properly informed, she can get the status of your project from your weekly update e-mail and you can get more done with fewer (non-contributing) people in the room.

Next time, run the numbers and see how much the company is paying for everyone to be in that room. If the meeting has to be held out of town, these calculations are routinely (in these more ROI-conscious times) done. However, "inside the office," far too many meetings with too many non-essential personnel are still held.

Project Meeting Options

There are now a variety of ways for your entire project team to meet:

- **Face to face.** While this is still the most common and often the best option, it is sometimes completely impractical. Even people down the hall from you can't always attend meetings in person, much less the Help Desk team in India (with your group in New York).
- **Videoconferencing.** The price for this option has plummeted. Many companies now have web cameras and speaker phones available for employees. Even an occasional videoconference at a rental facility can save radical money over airfare and hotels for all participants. Larger companies often have their own video conferencing facilities.
- **Conference calls.** This is now a very common and more accepted alternative to other types of meetings. Cell phones now come equipped with "conference" buttons. Conference calls, however, have two drawbacks: they tend to drag on, and because people aren't being watched, they can do other things while in the meeting. "Do other things" often means checking e-mail, but it can mean other, more distracting things, too. Some conference calls participants are 100 percent there; some aren't even 25 percent engaged.

- **Online meeting services.** Tools such as Cisco's WebEx, Citrix's GoToMeeting, Adobe's Connect, and Microsoft's Live Meeting, used in conjunction with a conference call, can help facilitate online meetings and training, allowing you to do presentations, demo applications, poll attendees, whiteboard, and more. These tools allow you to do real-time collaboration so that you can pass a document (or control of your desktop) over to another participant on the call. Because these services are available from many resellers, you don't need to build your own infrastructure to host them.

Useful Meeting Techniques

At each meeting, review the minutes of the previous meeting. It's a good way to remind everyone about accomplishments and to re-review any action items that were still pending or unresolved at the end of last week's meeting.

- Stating the desired length of the meeting up front can be an effective technique for getting people to participate. If everyone knows that the goal is to finish the meeting in one hour, people will make more of an effort to get to the point (and will try to force those who don't to cut things short).
- Meetings held earlier in the day are more productive than those when people are tired after a full day's work; however, many critical project meetings are held at the end of the day to have a daily project meeting update.

4.10 FUNDING PROJECTS

In general, when it comes to IT projects, the concerns are primarily about "hard" dollars. Hard and soft money are economic and budgeting concepts. The definitions may vary from organization to organization, but for the most part, "hard" costs are those that the company has to write a check for (hardware, software, outside consultants, etc.). "Soft" costs refer to costs that are less concrete (office space, use of existing staff, time, etc.). When corporate management wants to know how much a project is going to cost, they often only care about hard costs. However, at times, it may be advantageous to add in the soft costs (e.g., when you're trying to make a project look more impressive in a press release or on your resume). In addition, referring to the soft costs will demonstrate to management that you're aware that the use of existing resources costs the company money as well.

Your best source for determining a project's costs might be the members of the project team. It was their expertise that led you to select them for the team; tap this same expertise to evaluate costs. However, it's very possible that team members may only be able to provide you with information about the technologies that will be required, but not the costs of these technologies. This isn't unusual. Many technical personnel aren't interested in, or aren't exposed to, the business side of the technology. When you face this situation, you may have to go on the Web or contact the vendors and manufacturers directly to get estimates on the products your team members identified. In some cases, a project team may include someone solely dedicated to tracking the project's budget and other administrative activities.

Estimating Costs: Go High

As a general rule, projects always exceed their initial cost estimates. As a result, it's common for project managers to inflate their cost estimates by factors of 10 percent or more, sometimes a lot more. There are several reasons for this. When estimating costs, it's not unusual for smaller, miscellaneous items to be overlooked as everyone focuses on the big expenses. However, these miscellaneous items can add up to a significant amount.

- If management balks at the total cost, the inflation factor provides you with some room to revise the estimate downward without (in theory) impacting the success of the project.
- If the cost estimate is going to be wrong, err on the side of making it too high rather than too low. If it ends up too low, you will end up in the embarrassing position of having to admit your poor planning and shortsightedness and asking for more money.

The inflation factor gives a PM an opportunity to look like a hero if he can complete the project for less than was estimated. Then again, wildly padding your estimate simply to ensure that you come in under budget can negatively impact your credibility in the eyes of management, as well as the credibility of the IT department.

Projects Always Cost More Than Estimated

There are many costs to include within any IT project. In addition to the obvious costs of hardware and software, others common costs to consider include vendor support costs, travel, installation costs, annual licenses and maintenance, physical plant expenses (raised floor, air conditioning), training, telecommunications, books and manuals, user group fees, trade shows, software utilities, test equipment and environments, parallel testing, integration costs, incentives for project team members, consultants, and so on. Also, don't forget some money for the Nerf balls, munchies, sodas, and pizzas for working during lunch or late into the night.

Exactly Who Is Going to Pay for It?

If the company is going to pay for all the costs you've estimated for this project, someone has to figure out where the money is going to come from. More than likely, the company's budget, as well as your department's budget, has already been set. And unless someone built enough padding into either of these to cover your new project's expenses, it's likely that your project may cause your department, as well as others, to go over budget.

This dilemma may not be as big a problem as it initially seems. If corporate management approves your project and costs, then the various department heads will have your project as a ready justification when they have to explain their overruns. If the project is sponsored or initiated by a very high-level executive, she may direct you to charge all the project's costs to a special department code that she is responsible for, which alleviates everyone else's concerns about their own budgets.

Some companies may choose to set up special "chargeback codes" for projects so that it's easier to track the total costs. This is especially true for very large projects. This means that other departmental budgets aren't impacted by the project, and it also presents a convenient way to track the project's costs. Then again, when such a special code exists (sometimes jokingly referred to as a "slush fund"), it can be very tempting to use it for items that have only a tangential relationship to the project. For smaller projects, individual departments may be instructed to "eat" the costs as part of their regular budget. It's important that you know how upper management wants to pay for the costs associated with your project so that there are no surprises and that your project doesn't make enemies among other department heads at the same time you're trying to develop allies.

Justifying the Costs

No matter who initiated the project, sooner or later you're going to have to defend the costs. If you're the one who initiated the idea for the project, you may have to justify the project even before you know the costs. The most efficient means of justifying your costs is to try to show a clear Return on Investment (ROI) for your project. For example, if you wanted to implement a pool of shared printers, you could easily justify the costs by demonstrating that the company will no longer have to pay for individual printers at each desk and workstation. Keep in mind that justifying the costs is usually very closely aligned with justifying the project. Very often, when trying to justify the costs, you have to look no further than the project objective and its justification to find what you need.

Often, the justification may consist of a variety of intangibles that are hard to quantify. In the printer pool example used earlier, you could also cite that it would simplify the inventorying of toner and spare replacements parts.

First, here is a list of the more tangible benefits:

- Improved productivity and efficiencies (faster and/or less expensive)
- Reduced costs (fewer dollars/resources needed to accomplish the same task)
- Increased revenue
- Meeting changing demands of the marketplace
- Less waste (materials, time, resources)
- Reduced head count (in these more politically correct times, it's better to phrase this in more sensitive terms: "reallocation of existing staff to other company areas" or "eliminate the need to add to staff")
- Compliance with legislative regulations (tax laws, environmental issues, safety regulations, etc.)

Next is a list of the less tangible benefits:

- Increased advantage over competition
- Improved customer relations
- Better company/product/brand awareness
- Higher quality
- Improved staff morale
- Greater convenience (for staff, customers, business partners)

Both of these lists can come in handy when defining your project charter. Think of the project's justification as the answer you give to people when they ask, "Why should we do this?" and later when they ask, "Why are we doing this?", and finally when they ask "Why did we do this?"

4.11 MULTIPLE PROJECTS: HOW TO JUGGLE THEM WELL
You Will Have Multiple Projects

There are some IT Managers who work on a single project 40 hours a week, but they are the exception. Almost every manager, and certainly almost everyone in IT doing project management, has to juggle multiple projects. Some may be small, some may be due later in the year, but almost everyone is juggling more than one project. You may decide that an enterprise project management tool (discussed on **page 118** of this chapter) is the sort of thing you need to help manage multiple projects.

Prioritize by Time and Money

Some projects are huge. "Huge" depends on the size of your organization, of course, but if they need 75 percent of your time, be clear to yourself and others that this is where you'll be spending most of your time and effort.

Sorting tasks by time is a common technique: if you have a relatively low priority task that is due tomorrow but a high-value task that is due in two months, you can accomplish both by doing the lower priority one first. But that is the simple case. More often the problem is juggling two competing projects, both "due yesterday." You'll become a radically better manager of projects if you can take situations like this and convert them to your advantage: evaluate each project and determine which one has the highest priority. Make that determination and act clearly upon it.

Prioritize by Politics

Why kid around? Some projects are simply more important because they are politically more important. If your boss wants all of his executives to have webcams, you are going to do this before you install the new network printer downstairs. Be clear about your tasks and tell your boss about your other priorities; often they won't care, but sometimes they'll adjust their needs when informed of your conflicts—the new network printer required downstairs may be for a department he's trying to appease.

4.12 **DEALING WITH NON-IT DEPARTMENTS ON A PROJECT**

It's important to remember that IT is a service organization: it exists not to test out the latest hardware and software (although that is definitely a perk), but to provide computing capabilities to other groups within the company.

Working with other groups in the company is inevitably going to mean having non-IT members on a project. In that situation, three basic issues will arise: how do you motivate individuals you aren't managing, which department is in charge, and how do we charge our time?

Motivating Employees outside of Your Department

This situation isn't always a problem: most project members are willing and capable performers. Many see the task defined, see their roles as part of the bigger picture, and perform admirably.

Others, however, do not. Also, employees that don't play well with others are hardly unique to IT-managed projects. There are two actions you can take in this situation: emphasize the company's overall goals to that individual ("when this project wins, we all win") and, if more drastic measures are required, speak privately with the person's manager. If more direct managerial actions are required to get the desired employee performance, let the correct manager handle the situation. You wouldn't want some other manager "handling" your employees.

Who Is in Charge?

Some projects will never resolve this issue, but most will. And you can save everyone a lot of headaches by addressing this issue as quickly as possible. Bring the point up in the introductory meetings, at the funding meetings, and at the kick-off meeting. Get the issue settled as fast as possible.

One common scenario is one department (e.g., IT) working with another (e.g., Sales). Both departments have vested interests in the success of the project and the time and money investments are the same. But one of the department heads has a much more domineering personality; this individual is very vocal about his needs and those of his department.

If you find yourself in this situation, *from the beginning* you must be clear to your team members, his team members, and the two or three people up the ladder that you both report to that this will be a 50–50 project in terms of decisions. When you're clear to everyone about that, be clear that you will "go upstairs" as required, and the people upstairs know it and everyone on the team knows it.

4.13 Further References

Websites

www.ca.com/us/project-portfolio-management.aspx (enterprise project management tool vendor).

www.hp.com (enterprise project manager tool vendor).

www-01.ibm.com/software/awdtools/portfolio (enterprise project manager tool vendor).

software.isixsigma.com/newsletter (Six Sigma—quality control implementation methodology).

www.kforgeproject.com (web-based project management tool).

www.mercury.com/us/products/it-governance-center/projectmanagement (enterprise project management tool vendor).

www.microsoft.com/project/en/us/solutions.aspx (enterprise project management tool vendor).

www.oracle.com/us/solutions/project-management/index.html (enterprise project management tool vendor).

www.planview.com (enterprise project management tool vendor).

www.pmi.org (Project Management Institute).

www.redmine.com (web-based project management tool).

www.tenrox.com (web-based project management tool).

Books and Articles

Berkun, S., 2008. Making Things Happen: Mastering Project Management. O'Reilly Media.

Brooks, F., 1995. The Mythical Man-Month. Addison-Wesley Professional.

Geracie, G., 2010. Take Charge Product Management. Actuation Press.

Kendrick, T., 2010. The Project Management Tool Kit: 100 Tips and Techniques for Getting the Job Done Right. Amacom.

Marchewka, J.T., 2009. Information Technology Project Management. Wiley.

Philips, J., 2010. IT Project Management: On Track from Start to Finish, third ed. McGraw-Hill Osborne Media.

Project Management Institute, 2008. A Guide to the Project Management Body of Knowledge: Pmbok Guide. Project Management Institute.

Roberts, P., 2011. Effective Project Management: Identify and Manage Risks; Plan and Budget; Keep Projects under Control. Kogan Page.

Simon, Bruce, Webster, Phil, F., 2010. Why New Systems Fail: An Insider's Guide to Successful IT Projects. Course Technology PTR.

Swanborg, R., 2011. Winning Ways to Project Success. CIO Magazine August 1.

Wysocki, R.K., 2009. Effective Project Management: Traditional, Agile, Extreme. Wiley.

Software, Operating Systems, and Enterprise Applications

A computer will do what you tell it to do, but that may be much different from what you had in mind.

Joseph Weizenbaum, Artificial Intelligence Pioneer

CHAPTER TABLE OF CONTENTS

5.1 Types of Software..135
5.2 Operating Systems..137
5.3 Open Source 141
5.4 Managing Software 142
5.5 Cloud Computing...148
5.6 Enterprise Applications..152
5.7 Enterprise Resource Planning (ERP) 157
5.8 Further References 159

Although software has never been a simple item to categorize, these days there are many more types of software and many more methods of managing them. This chapter discusses some of the major types software: operating systems (OS), database management systems, enterprise applications, business applications, middleware, productivity tools, utilities, and security. It talks about how to manage them successfully (including purchasing, management, licensing, and tracking), as well as computing in the cloud.

5.1 TYPES OF SOFTWARE

In general, software is categorized according to its use.

- **Database Management Systems (DBMS):** Data are the heart and soul of IT, and its most valuable asset. While all data are in a database, a DBMS is used for administering data. The DBMS is the interface to the database and can control access, maintain integrity to minimize corruption, adjust the structure of the database to match changing business needs, perform transaction processing (Online Transaction Processing; OLTP), and generate reports (Online Analytical Processing;

135

OLAP). Enterprise DBMS solutions include MySQL, Oracle, Microsoft's SQL Server, and IBM's DB2. There are also small-scale DBMS offerings such as Microsoft's Access and FileMaker Pro.

- **Operating systems:** There are now essentially three main operating systems: Windows, MacOS, and the family of Linux/Unix variants. For a full discussion of operating systems, see the section **"Operating Systems"** on **page 137** later in this chapter.

- **Business applications:** This is a catchall term to refer to those software packages that allow the users and the business to do their job(s). This might be a warehouse inventory system, the payroll application, or a simple application that allows administrative assistants to print mailing labels.

- **Enterprise applications:** These applications are those that are used by virtually every part of an organization and act as a way of integrating systems, users, and functions. Enterprise applications may include business applications (such as an ERP system from SAP or Oracle), as well as something like companywide e-mail. They're discussed in detail in the section **"Enterprise Applications"** on **page 152**.

- **Middleware:** This software connects other software. This type of software can encompass everything from formal middleware products (such as Oracle's Fusion, IBM's WebSphere, and Red Hat's JBoss software) that are packaged, sold, and installed as distinct units, to a few hundred lines of code custom written to connect one proprietary piece of software to another. Middleware is sometimes referred to as an "interface" or a "hook."

- **Client/server:** This is a reference to an application's architecture, not to its function. A client/server application has two pieces of software associated with it: one that sits on the server and does the vast majority of the processing and the other piece that the user (or client) accesses that serves as the user interface. E-mail (such as Microsoft's Exchange or IBM's Lotus Notes) is an example of a client/server. The client portion is the software that allows users to read, write, and manage their e-mails. The server portion is the part that moves mail along between users, provides administration tools for the IT staff, controls security, allows for the creation of policies (such as mail retention), etc. Enterprise resource planning (ERP) applications are also examples of client/server-architected solutions. It should also be pointed out that very often the "client" is only a browser.

- **Productivity tools:** This industry-accepted term refers to common desktop applications such as word processing, spreadsheets, and presentation. Productivity tools are either sold in suites or as stand-alone components. Microsoft Office is the best known of these, but alternatives include Corel's WordPerfect Office, Apple's iWork, and the free open source software from OpenOffice and KOffice.

- **Utility tools:** This large category can include items for tasks strictly associated with the IT staff (e.g., backup, monitoring, management, and administration), as well as those that might be used by the end users (e.g., file compression, file conversion).

- **Security:** This category of software can refer to a variety of solutions that protect the environment (firewall, antivirus, anti-spam, user authentication, encryption, VPN).

- **Development tools:** These items include all elements of software used to create other software, such as compilers, linkers, debuggers, source code control systems, and languages.

As you can see, some of these categories overlap. A solution such as Oracle Financials could be simultaneously categorized as an enterprise application, a business application, and a client/server solution.

5.2 OPERATING SYSTEMS

Without an OS, a computer isn't much more than a door stop. Operating systems have a long and interesting history that includes some familiar names (Unix, Windows, Linux, Mac OS) and some forgotten ones (DOS, CP/M, VMS, Netware, TRS-DOS, OS/2). A particularly exciting new area of the OS market is the handheld industry with offerings from RIM, Apple, Hewlett-Packard, Microsoft, Nokia, and Google; these are covered in **Chapter 11, Connectivity: Social Media, Handhelds, and More** on **page 287**.

There are three major offerings for desktop and server operating systems: Windows, Mac OS, and Linux/Unix variants.

Windows

Microsoft's offerings dominate both the server market (Windows Server 2003 and 2008) and the desktop market (Windows XP, Vista, and Windows 7). Windows has also made inroads in the smart phone market with Windows Phone, but has not been as successful here. The lion's share of the workstations on the planet are using some version of Windows. Version 1.0 of Windows was released in 1985 and there have been many versions released since. Because it's so popular, most application vendors will first write their software to support Windows; many won't even consider writing their application on any other OS platforms. However, because of its prevalence, it is also the preferred platform for hackers and virus creators to go after.

Mac

The long-time, though distant, runner-up to Windows for the desktop is the Macintosh operating system. This operating system has many die-hard adherents; its demise has been predicted unsuccessfully for many years. Mac is the de facto OS used by certain industries, primarily those associated with audio/video media, design, graphic arts, and so on. Since 2001, with the release of version 10 (code-named "Cheetah") of the Mac operating system, Apple has been using Unix as the underlying foundation of its graphical user interface. Although mostly known as a desktop operating system, there is a server version of the Mac-OS as well.

The Mac platform's percentage of market share has always been in the single digits, but it has been growing steadily. IDC Research showed that in 2010 Apple's shipment to enterprise customers was only 2 percent of all enterprise PC shipments. In addition, many people look to Apple as the leader in hardware, software, and user-interface design and innovation. Some of Apple's challenges with making further inroads into the enterprise environment include:

- Lack of tools for managing in large environments
- No product roadmaps to help IT managers make decisions
- Mac versions of enterprise applications may not exist, or lag behind the Windows versions

Apple has also produced the iOS operating system, which is for its handheld and tablet devices. See **Chapter 11, Connectivity: Social Media, Handhelds, and More** on **page 287** for further discussion on the Apple OS (iOS). The success of the iPhone and the iPad have radically changed the discussions about which is the dominant operating system.

Unix Variants and Linux

Unix and its variants have quite a history, which started in the 1960s and 1970s at AT&T's Bell Labs. Big names in this market include HP-UX from Hewlett-Packard and AIX from IBM, but it's Linux that has made real headway in gaining market share. Both IBM and Hewlett-Packard now sell and support Linux running on their hardware and with many of their application offerings.

Linux is an open source operating system developed by Linus Torvalds in 1991. The system is a Unix variant and has been distributed freely since its creation, although "free" in this context is a complicated concept. For a further discussion of free software known as Open Source Software (OSS), see the section **"Open Source"** on **page 141** later in this chapter.

Choosing an Operating System

You probably already have multiple operating systems in your environment. Although it would be nice to standardize on one, it is rarely possible anymore. It's important to keep in mind that you really don't "choose" operating systems directly. It's a decision that is made almost indirectly based on other factors and issues. Specifically, which applications your company uses, which hardware (workstations, servers, handheld, and mobile devices) you need to support, and what the specific needs of your users are often determine which operating system(s) you're using.

Applications in Your Environment

Many major desktop business applications are now available on all three platforms. There are equivalent open source applications for Microsoft's Office suite, as well as applications available "in the cloud." MS Office itself has a version for the cloud, known as Office 365. (For more about cloud computing, see **Chapter 11, Connectivity: Social Media, Handhelds, and More** on **page 287**.) Server applications may run on only one or two platforms, though. For example, the server software for SAP is available to run on Unix or Windows, but not Mac. However, the client front end for SAP *is* available for Mac desktops. Sometimes you hit brick walls like Apple's iOS not supporting Adobe Flash, or Microsoft's Internet Explorer 9 not supported on Windows XP.

The key issue here is which *nonstandard* applications are you going to run? Many companies run large collections of custom software applications to run their business. Situations like these make keeping the previous operating system preferable because changing to a new operating system, or adding another one to the environment, can be a significant undertaking.

Typically, most of the operating system choices you face will be related to the server side of the environment and will come about when consideration is given to bringing a new application into the organization. Factors to consider here include:

- The skill set of your staff, along with the cost, effort, and time involved to develop expertise in a new OS.
- Which business applications you will be running and which operating system(s) they run on.
- Performance/cost concerns: The application may run faster on one operating system as compared to another, but that performance difference could be mitigated with the choice of hardware.
- Compatibility with the rest of your environment: If the tools you use to maintain your environment (backup, antivirus, encryption, monitoring, etc.) are operating system specific, the cost and effort of having to support another operating system could be enormous.

A 2011 *InformationWeek* survey of IT professionals showed that the top criteria for choosing an operating system were:

- Support for existing applications
- Security of the operating system
- Specific functionality of the device and operating system
- Integration with existing security and management tools

Customers' Needs

As discussed in **Chapter 1, The Role of an IT Manager,** in the section **"Determine Who Your Team Members Are"** on **page 11**, determining who your users are (and who *their* customers are) will make you a much more productive IT Manager. Choosing operating systems is no exception to this rule. Consider what the de facto standard is for your customers. If a user community (e.g., the graphic arts department or the elementary school you are supporting) runs on the Mac platform, it will be much more efficient in both the short and the long term if you choose Macs for everyone. This will eliminate problems with sharing files, compatibility, and so on. It will also radically cut down on your training and equipment costs, as users can share their knowledge and their machines among each other.

Multiple Operating Systems

It's common now to have multiple OSes in one company, despite corporate efforts to keep everyone on one platform. A 2011 *InformationWeek* survey showed that 85 percent of IT organizations officially support more than one OS (with the average supporting three), and 65 percent of IT organizations allow one or more additional OSes that are not officially supported. A big part of this has been the growth of mobile devices with their own operating systems. Users sometimes go their own way. Supporting three platforms in one environment, of course, can be a difficult task. Here are some ways of dealing with mixed environments.

Operating System Emulators

A number of tools and products have been developed to allow applications developed for one operating system to run on another operating system. This can help eliminate the need for users to have two different workstations. While emulators are very convenient, they can create additional challenges for support. Just as there are nuances and idiosyncrasies with applications and operating systems (version, components, setting, hardware, etc.), an emulator can complicate things further by adding another layer into the mix. For example, when an application isn't working right, is it because of the application, the core operating system, or the emulator? Perhaps it's how these are configured or how they interact with each other.

Virtual Machines

Virtualization allows you to take a single physical device (e.g., one workstation or server) and run multiple instances of operating systems. Each of these instances looks and operates as its own device, but because they coexist on a single physical device, they are considered to be *virtual machines*. Even if one of the instances should crash, the remaining operating system instances will continue to run. With virtual machine technology, all instances of the various operating systems run simultaneously, and switching among them is fast and easy.

Uses

The virtual machine offerings designed for clients are convenient for a number of scenarios. If your environment has to support multiple operating systems, virtual machine software can be used by:

- Your Help Desk and support staff so that they can use a single piece of hardware to run different operating systems comparable to what different users have. In this way, the support staff can replicate the user's environment when providing support.
- End users during operating system migration. If a particular business application isn't yet supported by more current versions of an operating system, it can challenge efforts to move the whole organization to the later OS version. By using virtual machine software, all users can be migrated to the new OS, and legacy applications can be run on an instance of an older OS.
- The training room PCs can run various instances of operating systems, each configured similarly to various user scenarios. This allows the trainers to easily provide training that replicates the various user environments.
- Software developers and testers can use virtual machine technology to test their applications easily from varying workstation configurations and environments.

Virtual machine offerings for servers also have distinct benefits and are quickly being embraced by organizations as a way to efficiently consolidate servers. By consolidating servers, the investment in hardware can be reduced. But, perhaps one of the most significant advantages is that it requires less physical space in the data center, and also less cooling and electricity. Virtual machines also let IT quickly create new environments for testing and development without having to buy new hardware. Server environments that are virtualized can be moved easily and quickly to different hardware, which greatly simplifies the effort of optimizing the resources and moving applications to more current hardware.

Also, legacy applications can be run on virtual servers without having to set aside dedicated hardware environments for them. It is important to note that with the growing popularity of virtualization, many software vendors have included specific references to this technology in their licensing agreements so that if you have multiple copies of their software running on virtualized servers, you need to be sure that each instance is licensed properly. The most popular solutions for virtualization are VMware from EMC and Hyper-V from Microsoft.

Virtual Desktop Infrastructure (VDI)

An offshoot of the virtual machines is the virtual desktop infrastructure (VDI). With VDI, end-users are given "thin" clients (e.g., low-end workstations, netbooks, and even tablet devices). The real horse-power resides on the VM sessions that have the tools and software the users need. They use these devices to access a virtual workstation environment that is hosted in the data center in a server farm. The benefit behind VDI is that the user-devices are inexpensive, with little configuration and software associated with them, almost like dumb-terminals of mainframe days, and the VMs are more easily managed since they are centralized. The user has the identical experiences with access to files and programs regardless of where they are, and the device in front of them. The number of VMs can be easily scaled to adjust to a changing workforce so that the environment and investment is optimized.

However, so far the ROI on VDI has been somewhat illusory. Case studies have shown that the upfront costs can be very high, and that there have been problems with user acceptance, performance, and issues with software application compatibility in virtual environments.

5.3 OPEN SOURCE

For many, many years, there was the Microsoft world of software and then there was everyone else's world. While the Redmond giant still owns a large portion of some very large markets, and many individual companies have made inroads into individual markets, it's the Open Source movement that has the largest impact on Microsoft's share of the operating system market in recent years.

Definition

Open Source Software (OSS) is software (both operating systems as well as applications) created by the worldwide user community. It isn't owned, developed, or supported by any one company, much less one person. Many individuals, organizations, and companies around the world develop, install, and support OSS, but the software itself isn't theirs and they don't charge anything for it.

Because the source code for OSS is available for all to see and change at will, there is a certain fear of "who is in control?" In the Open Source movement, the concept of a "benevolent dictator" is recognized as the person in control. While there could be hundreds or thousands of people suggesting fixes and enhancements to the product, it's the benevolent dictator that evaluates them and makes the determination as to which will be adopted and when. Of course, that won't stop people from making their own fixes and enhancements; it just means they won't be part of the "official" code. Linus Torvalds is generally recognized as Linux's benevolent dictator. For the pros and cons of Open Source, see Table 5.1.

Table 5.1 Pros and Cons of OSS

PRO	CON
Initial cost is low or nonexistent.	Depending on how it's obtained in your organization, there may be no formal support for the product.
Adherents claim many open source products are simpler and easier to use.	Many companies are afraid that without an "identified" owner, or if they haven't paid for the software, there will be no one to turn to when they need help (i.e., vendor support). That's why purchasing "distributions" of Open Source (such as the one from Red Hat) is a common option—the vendor also can provide support (for a fee, of course).
Major corporations, such as IBM and Hewlett-Packard, are supporting and offering Linux solutions, bringing legitimacy to the once fledgling movement.	Detractors of OSS say the software is often harder to use and missing important features.
Because the source code of OSS is available to all, there are more eyes looking at it, which increases the chances that bugs and security flaws will be found (and fixed). In theory, this makes OSS more reliable.	Some are concerned that since OSS code is free (i.e., no "profit"), there is little incentive for anyone to enhance it, add features, etc.
	The success of the product depends on the collaboration of hundreds of people around the planet. This is too much risk for some companies to accept. There are many conflicting studies as to which OS is more reliable and secure.

Cost

All OSS is "free." That is, there is no charge for the software itself. However, within the OSS genre there are "distributions" (or "distros") that cost money to buy. In the OSS world, a distribution is a collection of OSS software already configured, compiled, and ready to install. These distributions are put together by a third party and are sometimes preferred to the original OSS code because the third party is willing to provide support. Red Hat is the best known example of a Linux distribution. Many companies prefer to use distributions because there is comfort in knowing that an identifiable party (as opposed to the "OSS community") is responsible for support.

However, whether free via OSS or paying for distribution, the costs of software are much more than the initial expense; when evaluating the purchase of software, you must consider Total Cost of Ownership (TCO). Typical TCO considerations include the long-term components of a purchase, such as installation, training, and financing.

5.4 MANAGING SOFTWARE

Managing software is a critical component of an IT Manager's work. There are several key issues and some very useful tools to help the manager cope with those issues. With the pace of advances and the development of software applications, features, and functionality, software is becoming more of a dynamic asset.

Total Cost of Ownership (TCO)

Purchasing software is an activity that can range from a simple retail purchase of a graphics tool or a download of a file compression utility to a complex, months-long, meeting-filled, companywide process of buying an Enterprise Resource Planning solution. However, the purchase price isn't the only cost associated with software.

The TCO concept is this: When you are considering buying an asset (e.g., a computer, a car, a house) you should consider not only the initial purchase price—for example, say a business application will cost the department $10,000—but all the costs associated with that purchase over the life of the asset. There will be costs associated with the time to install the application, as well as hardware associated with it, vendor maintenance/support fees each year, staff salaries, training costs, and so on associated with running that application. TCO is as applicable to hardware as it is to software. TCO is discussed in more detail in **"TCO and Asset Management: What Are They?"** in **Chapter 7, Getting Started with the Technical Environment** on **page 196**.

Software Management Techniques
Deployment
One of the most complicated issues related to desktops and laptops in the large corporate environment is the deployment of software. When there is a new software package to be implemented or an update (no matter how minor) to an existing application, the manual distribution and installation can be a very tedious and labor-intensive process. Ensuring that all workstations are comparably set up and maintained can drain a great deal of IT's resources.

To streamline this situation, there are several concepts that many environments (small and large) have seized upon. They're gaining in popularity and quickly becoming standard practice:

- Developing a standard disk image
- Selecting a disk cloning package
- Implementing a software deployment tool
- Users download from the IT intranet site
- Locking down the desktop

Develop a Standard Disk Image

Every organization should create a disk image that will essentially serve as a way of ensuring that each workstation's software is set up and configured as similarly as possible. This can reduce a technician's troubleshooting time significantly. Ideally, there will be only one standard image in an environment, but it is common to have more than one for different department needs, types of users, and so on.

Select a Disk Cloning Package

A disk cloning package uses very sophisticated techniques to quickly copy large amounts of data in a fraction of the time it would take to use conventional methods. Once the master disk image is made, it's possible to duplicate it to other workstations in a matter of minutes. In larger environments, where there is a constant influx of new computers arriving at the loading dock, a disk cloning package can save an enormous amount of time in putting your standard disk image on new computers (or when you redeploy computers). Also, because it creates an identical duplicate, it virtually eliminates any errors that might creep into a manual effort. Popular disk cloning solutions include Ghost from Symantec, and Snap Deploy from Acronis.

Implement a Software Deployment Tool

While a standard disk image, along with a cloning tool, ensures that everyone has a similar software configuration when a new workstation is deployed, it does nothing to help with updating software or adding software. Numerous tools are available to help with the deployment of software (e.g., LANDesk, Symantec's Altiris, Microsoft's SCCM, Casper from JAMF). These tools operate in a very similar fashion by allowing you to "script" the installation process for a software update—be it as complex as a new companywide application or as small as an updated printer driver. Other alternatives for deploying software include running scripts when users login, and features of Microsoft's Active Directory.

Users Download Software from an Intranet

A very common method of deploying software—and one that allows for the user to "pull" the software at their own convenience rather than have it "pushed" to them when they don't need it—is to have users download software from an intranet. This method is particularly useful for software that not every user needs; every user will need Microsoft Word, for example, but most won't need MS Project, much less that $5,000-per-seat tool the Finance department bought.

You can direct users to your IT intranet site to install these packages. A script or installer program you configure will ensure that the software is installed the way you want. This method allows IT to very efficiently deploy software that only a percentage of the entire user base will need. Some of the deployment tools mentioned earlier provide for this sort of self-service functionality for software installations.

Locking down the Desktop

Many organizations now try to limit a user's capabilities to make troublesome changes by "locking down" the desktop. Typically, this may mean that the user can't install new programs, alter network settings, or change the way the operating system is configured. Similarly, it prevents the user from deleting key programs and files and from stopping vital operating system services. However, even with a locked-down desktop, you can still give the user the flexibility to alter personal settings, such as selection of wallpaper, default printer, screen saver, colors, and fonts. A number of applications, such as the Group Policy feature of Microsoft's Active Directory, let you define and manage these policies centrally. There is additional discussion on flexibility related to standards and the locked-down desktop in **Chapter 10, Working with Users** on **page 263**.

Software Licensing

There are two general types of software licenses: free and for-profit. Initial portions of examples of both types, the GNU and Microsoft licenses, are shown in the boxes.

HOW GNU DEFINES FREE SOFTWARE

"Free software" is a matter of liberty, not price. To understand the concept, you should think of free as in free speech, not as in free beer.

Free software is a matter of the users' freedom to run, copy, distribute, study, change, and improve the software. More precisely, it refers to four kinds of freedom for the users of the software:

- The freedom to run the program, for any purpose (freedom 0).
- The freedom to study how the program works and adapt it to your needs (freedom 1). Access to the source code is a precondition for this.
- The freedom to redistribute copies so that you can help your neighbor (freedom 2).
- The freedom to improve the program and release your improvements (and modified versions in general) to the public so that the whole community benefits (freedom 3). Access to the source code is a precondition for this.

A program is free software if users have all of these freedoms. Thus, you should be free to redistribute copies, either with or without modifications, either gratis or charging a fee for distribution, to anyone anywhere. Being free to do these things means (among other things) that you do not have to ask or pay for permission.

Source: *www.gnu.org/philosophy/free-sw.html*

SCOPE OF LICENSE SECTION FROM A MICROSOFT END USER LICENSE AGREEMENT (EULA)

"The software is licensed, not sold. This agreement only gives you some rights to use the features included in the software edition you licensed. Microsoft reserves all other rights. Unless applicable law gives you more rights despite this limitation, you may use the software only as expressly permitted in this agreement. In doing so, you must comply with any technical limitations in the software that only allow you to use it in certain ways. You may not

- work around any technical limitations in the software;
- reverse engineer, decompile or disassemble the software, except and only to the extent that applicable law expressly permits, despite this limitation;
- use components of the software to run applications not running on the software;

Continued

> ### SCOPE OF LICENSE SECTION FROM A MICROSOFT END USER LICENSE AGREEMENT (EULA)—Cont'd
>
> - make more copies of the software than specified in this agreement or allowed by applicable law, despite this limitation;
> - publish the software for others to copy;
> - rent, lease or lend the software; or
> - use the software for commercial software hosting services."
>
> **Source:** *Microsoft Windows 7 Home Premium EULA*

As you can see, even from these small portions of these agreements, some software licensing terms can be rather complex and also quite lengthy.

Licensing Issues

In general, corporations seldom consciously engage in illegal activities. They also generally respect intellectual property copyright laws. However, due to complexities of licensing agreements and the volume of purchase activity, it can be difficult for an IT Manager to fully know if his company is licensed properly for all its software.

There are numerous cases of small companies being subjected to a software audit based on a call from a single disgruntled employee to one of the software industry trade groups (e.g., Business Software Alliance or the Software and Information Industry Association).

Countless hours and resources have been expended by companies to deliver the documentation and proof of appropriate licenses requested. Companies consider themselves fortunate if it's determined that the illegal licensing discovered was unintentional and that the company had been making a good faith effort to be legal. In cases like this, there may be no fines or punitive damages. However, the company will have to pay the license fees for all the unlicensed software that was discovered or agree to delete all the unlicensed software.

In fact, it isn't unusual for a company to find out that it's over-licensed on some products and under-licensed on others. Under-licensing usually occurs with software that isn't "standard" on every PC. For non-standard software, it's very easy for the purchase of the license to be overlooked and forgotten by the administrative staff. In such a case, the technical staff may seek to satisfy a user's request and install an unlicensed software copy and neglect to inform the administrative staff to purchase the license.

The process of keeping track of software licenses is often referred to as "software metering." There are some general guidelines that you as an IT Manager should be aware of to avoid putting your company at risk for copyright infringement.

- Understand that when you buy a software license, what you're usually buying is the right to use a copy of the software; the vendor usually remains the actual owner of the software.
- Read and understand the licenses that come with your software. Because license terms can change, review them periodically. If they're complex (and most of them today are very complex), pass them along to the Legal department for review. Your vendor and software reseller can also help explain the terms.

- Don't expect to be able to negotiate a change with your software's vendor (although larger organizations may have some success here). If the software you're buying isn't an off-the-shelf or shrink-wrapped package, you'll have better chances. See the section **"Negotiating Licenses"** on **page 147**.

Licensing Models and Types

To complicate matters further, there are several different licensing models and types of licenses that a vendor may offer. Vendors may define these differently from one another, and may not offer all types. The most common are discussed here:

- **Concurrent user licensing.** With this type of licensing, you only have to buy enough licenses to match the number of users who will be logged into the application at the same time. If you have 100 users that use the warehouse inventory application, but only 20 are using it at any one time, you'd only have to buy 20 licenses.
- **Per seat licensing.** With per seat licensing, you have to purchase a license for each user who has access to the application. In the warehouse inventory example just given, you'd have to buy 100 licenses.
- **Per server licensing.** With per server licensing, you license the server software, not the users. There may also be tiers of server licensing; for example, some sever products are licensed based on the number of processors installed on the server or on the number of users who will access it.
- **Multiple tier licensing.** In some cases, you may need to buy licenses for both the server and the user(s). For example, with Microsoft's SQL licensing with per server licensing, you license the server software as well as the users. But a different offering for SQL requires only the server to be licensed. With Microsoft's Exchange, you have to buy an Exchange license for the server, Outlook licenses for the desktop client, and an Exchange CAL (client access license).
- **Multiple use or home use licenses.** Some licenses allow a single license of the software to be used on each user workstation (e.g., the one in the office, the one at home, and the one on her laptop in her briefcase), as long as these copies aren't used by others, or concurrently.
- **Internal or external uses.** Depending on your planned use for the software, there may be different types of licenses. For example, if you're buying software to host your company's intranet, that may be one type of license. However, if you're hosting data for others to access, it may be a different license.
- **Virtual machines.** When using software in a virtual environment, be sure that your software is licensed properly for each virtual machine. This is a relatively new area for software licensing, and many vendors are still clarifying their licensing requirements here.
- **Non-perpetual licensing.** Most software licenses are perpetual, which means you pay for it once and then you own it. With non-perpetual (sometimes known as subscription, annual, or renewable) licenses, you pay a fee each year to use it for the next 12 months. Once you stop paying, you have to stop using the software. With these licenses you are essentially renting the software, as opposed to owning it. When computing in the cloud (see the section **"Cloud Computing"** on **page 148** of this chapter) you are usually renting the software.

The issues around licensing are growing very complex as vendors simultaneously tighten the terms and conditions and offer different options and alternatives. When trying to determine the different types of licenses you have to buy, be sure to ask lots of questions and ask the vendor to show you where their verbal answers are documented in their licensing agreement(s).

Maintenance and Support Plans

In addition to buying a license, vendors also sell upgrade or maintenance plans that entitle you to upgrade (at little or a reduced cost) to newer versions of the software as they come out. The value of these plans depends on how often the vendor expects to provide new versions and how often you expect to be interested in these newer versions. Keep in mind that a vendor may also offer a support program, which entitles you to technical support on a product but doesn't include providing you with upgrades. Alternatively, buying into a plan for upgrades may not include support. Check with your vendor and make sure you understand what you're buying before you buy it.

Negotiating Licenses

While you probably won't be able to negotiate the specific terms of the license, it's entirely likely you can negotiate a volume discount based on the license quantities you intend to buy. Use your network of contacts to find out what other organizations are paying. The larger your purchase, the more room you have to negotiate on price. You may also have success negotiating additional licensing rights (such as home use) with your purchase. You may also be able to negotiate some free training from the vendor in order to seal the deal. Remember to look at the total purchase of licenses, support maintenance, training, and any professional services and negotiate. You may be able to upgrade or extend your support from the vendor (e.g., from "bronze" to "silver") at no cost.

Be wary of agreements that automatically renew support and/or maintenance services unless you notify the vendor in writing. You can usually ask to have this provision removed. If the vendor refuses, you can get around the issue by handing him a written notice that you don't intend to renew at the same time you give him the original order.

Let your company's legal resources review the terms of any software license you buy. In all likelihood, your company's lawyer will say that the license has numerous unfavorable terms and that he recommends against entering into such an agreement. However, he is also likely to add that he recognizes that there is no real alternative. Negotiating with vendors is also discussed in the section **"Reviewing Contracts with Vendors"** on **page 175** in **Chapter 6, Managing the Money**.

Get Organized

Whenever possible, consolidate all your software purchases. Many large software retailers have systems in place designed to help companies keep track of their license purchases, their obligations, expirations, and so on. In a crisis or emergency situation, you may feel that the only solution is to install a copy of a software package that hasn't been paid for. If you choose to go this route, you should ensure that a proper license is ordered and purchased at the same time.

With all the licensing options and permutations available, it can be an administrative chore to track the licenses you have and to make sure that when you're buying additional licenses, upgrades, or software and maintenance plans that you're doing it for the licenses you actually own.

Keep records of your license purchases: quantities, dates, vendors, and so on. For licenses that need to be renewed periodically, keep track of the start and end dates, and the same for support and upgrade plans. It is not unusual for organizations to get letters and inquiries from their software vendors' compliance department, or from a software vendor association, about the legitimacy of the licenses in use. Having good documentation readily available can go a long way to help ensure a simple inquiry doesn't turn into an audit or legal matter. Make sure that everyone in IT is fully aware that it's against the law and company policy to pirate software. Advise users that it's against company policy to bootleg software, and any unauthorized software will be immediately deleted when found.

5.5 CLOUD COMPUTING

"Cloud computing" or "computing in the cloud" refers to making use of resources on the Internet (i.e., the "cloud"). These resources can include servers, data centers, storage, and applications. Also, these resources can generally be accessed only using a web browser. The advantages of cloud computing is that it dramatically reduces, sometimes even eliminates, associated infrastructure costs. While cloud computing is often quickly adopted by small start-ups that don't have the capital to invest in IT resources, it has made significant inroads into established organizations as well. Cloud computing is also seen as a solution that will help control internal IT staffing levels, although 49 percent of IT leaders in a 2011 *CIO Magazine* survey said that cloud deployments wouldn't affect IT headcount.

The Many Flavors of Cloud Computing

If you are familiar with any of the Internet e-mail solutions (e.g., Yahoo, Gmail, HotMail) you already have a sense of cloud computing. For these, all you need is a web browser and an Internet connection and you have full access to your e-mail. Everything else you need to be fully functional with these vendors' e-mail solutions exists on the Internet. These solutions have grown to include address books and calendars. Google also has its Google Docs and Google Apps offerings, to include the ability to create, store, edit, and post spreadsheets, presentations, and word processing documents online. Take a moment to note how significant this is. Using Google Apps, a user can do most of the most common productivity tasks without having to purchase any end-user software. Not only does this reduce the software costs, but it also eliminates all the tasks and costs traditionally associated with end-user productivity tools (e.g., deployment, upgrades, patching, licensing, purchasing). It also reduces the burden of IT regarding centralized storage, servers, backup, and so on.

However, it's important to note that cloud computing does not always refer to free solutions. Sometimes it's free, and sometimes it isn't. Generally, cloud computing offerings are free for individual personal use, but come at a cost for business uses. One example is the Google Docs offering mentioned earlier. While all those features and functions are free, Google also offers a premiere edition (Google Apps), for business users at a cost of $50/year/user with additional features and functionality targeted to a business (e.g., more storage, data migration, phone support, shared e-mail distribution lists, greater access control options, shared calendaring). The list of vendors in the cloud computing space is growing dramatically with various offerings from names such as Microsoft, Amazon, Oracle, Rackspace, Salesforce.com, and IBM.

Taking things to the next level are business apps that are available via cloud computing. Best known here is Salesforce.com, which has a suite of business applications for sales, customer service and support, sales analytics, marketing, and so on. These apps are all accessed using only a browser from Internet-connected devices (including smart phones and tablets). All of the usual infrastructure requirements (servers, data centers, management, upgrades, security, backups, databases, etc.) become the responsibility of the provider. Other applications that are making inroads into cloud computing are Human Resources Information Systems (HRIS), payroll, accounting, and content management.

Because managing e-mail can be so mission critical, burdensome, and complex, many companies are now offering Microsoft's Exchange e-mail solution via the Internet as a way to shift that burden away from individual IT departments.

As a fairly new industry, cloud computing comes in different flavors, with different terms—some of which overlap:

- **Infrastructure as a Service (IaaS)** refers to offerings of servers, storage, Internet connectivity, firewalls, routers, switches, etc.
- **Platform as a Service (PaaS)** refers to a solution that not only provides the hardware infrastructure, but also the software and development platforms for your team to build, install, and maintain applications. PaaS offerings also include version control, testing tools and environments, and ability to roll out and roll back different versions.
- **Software as a Service (SaaS),** software may be browser based or installed on workstations. However, the distinction with SaaS vs. traditional software is that you pay for actual use as opposed to individual licenses. This shifts software to more of a variable operating expense, as opposed to a fixed capital expense. Google Docs and Apps, Salesforce.com, Success Factors, NetSuite, and Microsoft's Office 365 are popular providers of various SaaS offerings. SaaS may not always be for end-users; back-end services (like e-mail anti-spam/anti-virus) can also be an SaaS offering.
- **On-demand computing,** a catchall term that refers to the concept of providing computing resources as they are needed, as opposed to the traditional full-time basis. Also sometimes referred to as "utility computing." Amazon's Elastic Compute Cloud (EC2) is a popular vendor for on-demand computing.
- **Grid computing** refers to leveraging the processing power of a large number of networked computers for large-scale computations. This usually has the most relevance in the scientific communities. Also sometimes referred to as "distributed computing."

There can be overlap in some of the terms and models presented here, and definitions may be slightly different among providers. The coauthors of this book used cloud computing—they built a web site on Google Sites—to collaborate on manuscripts.

For some of the pros and cons of cloud computing, see Table 5.2.

Many of the same considerations and factors associated with choosing an outsource provider (see the section **"Outsourcing and Offshoring"** in **Chapter 6, Managing the Money** on **page 182**) go into decisions about computing in the cloud.

Private versus Public Cloud

The cloud solutions that were described earlier are examples of public clouds—they are there for anyone or any organization that wants to pay. An alternative is a "private cloud." Private clouds are attempts by very large organizations to leverage their significant IT resources to essentially offer on-demand/cloud-like offerings to their internal customers and subsidiaries, as a way to provide services in a more efficient, flexible, and scalable manner.

A hybrid of the public and private clouds is the virtual private cloud (VPC). The VPC essentially uses the public cloud model, but the cloud provider logically segregates your resources from its other

Table 5.2 Pros and Cons of Cloud Computing

PRO	CON
Pay only for services you use.	Tied to the vendor. Raises concerns about vendor's viability or issues if you need to change providers, migrate data, etc.
No capital outlay for software and/or hardware. No direct costs associated with maintenance, upgrades, support, etc. (All of these are generally bundled in with the service cost.)	Lack of control. You may have little or no say regarding operations, future direction of software, etc.
Vendor's dedicated staff for service and support around the clock. Because the vendor is directly vested in the success of this model and their offerings and are able to leverage resources and tools on a grander scale, they may be in a better position to monitor/manage the resources than you could internally.	Resources may be configurable by you, the customer, but not entirely customizable.
Shifts a great many of IT traditional responsibilities (deployments, upgrades, patching, monitoring, etc.) to the vendor.	Long-term ongoing costs may approach costs for maintaining in-house resources.
As a result of the vendor's focus on reliability, availability, and redundancy, it may often provide built-in business continuity and disaster recovering solutions for your enterprise.	May be complex options to choose from (e.g., dedicated vs. virtual resources), making the cost analysis difficult to evaluate.
A variety of offerings giving you a great deal of flexibility.	Could be complex (or impossible) to integrate across multiple on-demand/cloud-computing vendors, systems, applications.
Since you're generally just paying for use of the application, which the vendor is monitoring, the concerns of licensing and auditing are almost eliminated.	Concerns about security, privacy, and meeting your organization's compliance and requirements needs.
Easy to adjust to changing needs, cycles (e.g., when additional storage is needed, it is available virtually immediately).	With all resources managed and operated by a third party, you have no control over availability and reliability.
	Who actually owns the resources, particularly the data?

customers using technologies like VLANs and other security solutions so that the resources from the cloud provider seem like an extension of your own network.

Some organizations are more comfortable using a VPC model, since it offers additional security provisions for their initial forays into cloud solutions.

Considerations When Moving to the Cloud

While the cloud solution for IT resources can be very attractive, it is not without potential hurdles and pitfalls. The industry is still very new, and everyone is learning as they go. In time, things will stabilize and become more standardized, but until then make sure you do careful investigation and evaluation before moving to the cloud:

- **Data Retention for Software as a Service (SaaS).** Is your data being kept indefinitely? Or will it be archived/purged after a period of time?
- **Backup for Infrastructure and Platform as a Service (IaaS and PaaS).** If you have an application or database in the cloud, you may be the one responsible to make sure it gets backed up. If you accidentally delete a file, you'll be the one to do the restore. Typically, backups for IaaS and PaaS are done by using additional storage from your cloud vendor.
- **Licensing.** Which software and licenses are you responsible for, and what is your vendor providing?
- **Data location.** In which country will your data be stored? This may be an issue for some regulatory and privacy concerns as well as which encryption software you use.
- **Vendor support.** What sort of Service Level Agreements (SLAs) will your vendor commit to? If there is an extended outage will you get a credit? Is their support team responsive? What kind of tools do they have to help you manage, monitor, and troubleshoot? For SaaS models, will your end-users be calling the cloud provider for support or your IT team?
- **Term of agreement.** Do you have to commit to a multiyear contract upfront? What if you want to get out early? If you do want to leave your cloud provider what about issues of migrating/transitioning data, applications, services back to your organization or to another provider?
- **Organizational.** What impact will it have on your team? Will roles be eliminated or changed? Will new positions be needed to focus on cloud operations and activities?
- **Standardization.** If your environment has unique requirements, or nonstandard/traditional configurations, will you be able to replicate that in the cloud? Most cloud vendors allow you a very defined degree of flexibility—will that be sufficient?
- **Operations tasks.** Who is responsible for installing software? Applying patches and upgrades? Monitoring and management of the resources? These can vary greatly between the IaaS, PaaS, and SaaS models.
- **Billing and invoicing.** Does the provider offer sufficient detail and reporting so that you can fully understand the bills? Which tools are in place for you to ensure that your team isn't using on-demand services needlessly (like the programmer who requests some virtual servers and storage for some testing in an IaaS model, but then forgets to delete them, incurring 10 months of usage fees)? What happens if you are late with a payment—is your service cut off?
- **Liability for breeches.** What responsibility will your provider agree to in case there is a security breech?
- **Recovery/redundancy.** What sort of capabilities/facilities does the provider have in case of failures/outages?
- **Protection of data.** Most cloud vendors consider data security to be a top priority. But how can you be sure they are doing everything they say they are doing, or that you need them to do? For example, if they say that firewalls are configured to prohibit certain types/sources of traffic, will they show you those configurations?
- **Network connectivity.** Do you have sufficient bandwidth at all your locations if your applications are moved to the cloud?
- **Return on Investment (ROI).** It's entirely possible that a long-term cloud-based solution may be more expensive that hosting the solution yourself. However, cloud-computing still offers great advantages in terms of flexibility, scalability, and other conveniences that make it worthwhile. In fact, a 2011 *CIO Magazine* survey found that 48 percent of IT leaders are evaluating cloud options before making any new IT investments.

Table 5.3 Benefits and Challenges of Cloud Computing

Top Benefits and Challenges of Cloud Computing from 2011 *Baseline Magazine* Survey (in order of importance)		
Benefits	*Challenges*	
Increased flexibility/versatility	Preventing unauthorized data access	
Increased scalability	Preventing data loss	
Lower fixed costs for whole organization	Service costs that are rising or may rise	
Reduced demand on IT staff	Risk of occasional data unavailability	
Reduced maintenance/migration costs	Handling risk of slower applications	
Increased data security	Makes regulatory compliance more difficult	
Reduced demand on hardware	Less ability to customize	
Increased user productivity	Uncertainty of cloud vendor's staying power	
Happier users	Possibility of data being stored offshore	
Centralization of organization's fixed costs	Risks of higher migration costs	
More user access to high volume IT resources	Legal risk of losing document versions	
Easier compliance	None of these	

Source: *Currier, Guy, Speeding the Cloud,* Baseline Magazine, *May/June 2011*

Some of the concerns on this list will vary (or even disappear) depending on the model of cloud service you're using (e.g., SaaS, PaaS, IaaS). However, the list should give you a sense of the issues associated with cloud computing.

Cloud computing is a very new area, and most organizations are just beginning to explore and think about how it can be used. A 2011 industry survey by *Baseline Magazine* shows that the cloud is viewed with many benefits as well as challenges (see Table 5.3).

5.6 ENTERPRISE APPLICATIONS

An "enterprise application" is an application that is widely used throughout the organization and integrates the operations of many different departments and functions. Enterprise applications are very valuable but can be very complex pieces of software. They require extensive planning to implement and can be very expensive.

For large companies, with hundreds and thousands of users, the value of connecting all of their functions is enormous, but so are the tasks of implementing and administering the software. This chapter discusses several enterprise applications: e-mail, directory services, and enterprise resource planning.

E-mail

When organizations are doing their disaster recovery planning, one of the applications that is almost always deemed mission critical is e-mail. E-mail has become the lifeblood of communications for virtually all organizations. For a task as simple as seeing if a colleague is free for lunch, many will reach first for the keyboard as opposed to the telephone.

Usage Statistics

A report by the Radicati Group published in 2011 revealed some interesting information about e-mail:

- There are 3.1 billion e-mail accounts around the world.
- Corporate users send and receive 105 messages per day on average (33 sent, 72 received).

Educate Your Users on the Key Principles of E-mail

You (or the Training department, if you have one) can offer a class on the e-mail system you use and tips for effective communication. What you need to get across to all your users are some simple principles of using e-mail that are less software oriented and more usage oriented.

- **Keep it brief.** If you don't like reading long e-mails, what makes you think others do?
- **Make the subject line count.** Be as clear in this line as possible. Instead of using "meeting" as your subject line, use something more meaningful, such as "operations review status meeting."
- **Reply to all e-mails that expect one.** Not every e-mail that is sent needs a reply, but many do. If you send something to somebody, you expect a reply. Provide the same courtesy.
- **Differentiate TO: and CC: recipients.** As a general rule, people on the TO line are people who need to know and/or have to take action with the content of the message. People who are CC'd (which stands for carbon copy, a technology that predates photocopy machines) are generally getting the information on an FYI basis.
- **Use the Reply All button with extreme caution.** This button is probably the largest contributor to e-mail waste.
- **Spell-check all e-mails.** All e-mail programs have a function that allows e-mail to be spell-checked automatically. Activate it.
- **When stressed or angry, don't press the Send button.** Wait until you've had a chance to cool off so that your e-mail isn't overly emotional.
- **Define policies and guidelines for saving e-mail.** How do you want users to save their e-mails? Is there a company policy? Provide your users with a specific plan. Do you want them to store up a month's worth on their hard drive or archive to the network? Your e-mail system has features to help you manage this. You can automatically purge e-mail that reaches a certain age and limit the size of a message, as well as the size of a user's mailbox.

In addition to telling users that they can delete their old e-mail, you should tell them that their e-mail is backed up daily so that they don't feel the need to save every minor note.

Managing E-mail

Because e-mail can quickly get out of control, it needs to be managed aggressively. Managing it can become a large part of your day; if you have a large company, it can become the sole responsibility of a team of people. A number of vendors offer solutions for monitoring e-mail and addressing issues such as spam and viruses. In addition to the following ideas, important aspects related to e-mail are discussed throughout **Chapter 8, Security and Compliance** on **page 205**.

Junk Mail (Spam, Chain Letters, Phishing, Jokes, etc.)

Although e-mail can be a very valuable tool for circulating vital information very quickly, it can distribute junk just as fast. If someone receives an e-mail of a joke or a spiritual message that they like, they can circulate it to one person—or thousands—with just a few clicks of the mouse. Although it may seem innocent at first, the growth can be exponential, resulting in massive storage requirements for e-mail servers. It can slow down the delivery of mail because your servers are backed up distributing hundreds or thousands of messages unrelated to work.

Statistics about spam vary from 70 to 90 percent of all e-mail. E-mail packages now let the user identify which e-mail is spam or junk. With a feature like this, once a source of junk mail is identified, any future mail from the same source is immediately deleted. There are also a variety of anti-spam solutions that are implemented at the e-mail gateway so that spam never reaches your users' mailboxes. But even these anti-spam solutions, which are designed to help you mange e-mail, require their own management. Because they aren't foolproof, there may be some issues of false positives (legitimate e-mail identified incorrectly as spam) and false negatives (junk mail identified incorrectly as a legitimate message). These issues can lead to more calls to the Help Desk, and your staff tracking down misdirected e-mails. You may also need to maintain white and black lists for your anti-spam solution. White lists identify senders whose mail should always be treated as legitimate, whereas black lists identify senders whose mail should always be treated as spam. These lists override the determination that the anti-spam solution would make based on its own algorithms.

Harassment

Although e-mails with jokes and spiritual messages may seem innocent, they can easily cross the line and some may be seen as offensive or harassment. Your organization should have a clear-cut policy (from senior management, not from IT) that indicates a zero tolerance for any material (including e-mail) that can be construed as offensive on grounds of sexual harassment, racial discrimination, and so on. It isn't uncommon for e-mail messages to be included as evidence in various types of litigation. One of "investor" Bernard Madoff's alleged co-investors was indicted using some of his firm's e-mails (online.wsj.com/article/SB123903070566093099.html). Work with your Legal and HR departments to define, if you haven't done so already, a clear e-mail policy.

Viruses

Although you should certainly educate your users about messages from unknown sources, a more aggressive posture is also called for. All your workstations and servers should run anti-virus software. In addition, you should have anti-virus software on your e-mail servers that scans messages and their attachments for viruses. Products from Trend Micro, Symantec, McAfee, among others, are relatively inexpensive for the protection they provide. Anti-spam and anti-virus solutions for e-mail are also available in the cloud as an SaaS offering (e.g., Google's Postini and Cisco's IronPort). See **Chapter 8, Security and Compliance**, on **page 205** for more information regarding viruses and how to defend against them.

Data Size and Retention

Because e-mail is so often used to distribute big files, such as large presentations and videos, as well as games and jokes, the amount of storage required to keep it all can be massive. As such, it isn't unusual to have a corporate policy that sets limits on the size of messages, the size of mailboxes, and the age of messages. These limitations are available with the most popular e-mail packages. It's important that users be made aware of these policies, and that the limits are set after considering users' needs.

Users should also be aware that size limits may be in effect regarding external users with whom they exchange mail. Be clear to your users that just because your company's e-mail size limit is large, that doesn't mean other companies have the same limit. As such, if you allow your users to send messages of a certain size, there is no guarantee that the message will get through since the recipient's mail environment could very well have a lower limit.

Appropriate Use

Just like with the use of the company phones, it's reasonable to expect that not every message your users send will be work-related. There will be an occasional personal message. Most organizations expect and tolerate this as long as they aren't oversized and don't contain offensive e-mails. However, it's wise to have a formal policy (just like the one that probably exists for use of the company phones) saying that e-mail is for work-related use only. Some organizations will explicitly state that some personal use of e-mail is okay, as long as it's limited, inoffensive, and so on. Similarly, most companies state that the e-mail environment, and its content, are owned by the company, and reserve the right to review e-mail messages that their employees send and receive. The company usually will only invoke that right, though, when a problem or policy violation is suspected.

Along these lines, many organizations automatically add disclaimers to any e-mail messages that are sent outside the company. These disclaimers often assert the confidentiality of the message. But, many industries (e.g., financial, legal) may add statements pertinent to their field.

E-mail Archiving

With regulatory requirements like Sarbanes-Oxley, HIPAA, along with discovery of electronic documents in litigation, finding and accessing specific e-mail messages is becoming a growing requirement. It's becoming increasingly common for the Legal department to contact IT and make a request such as "we need to find all the e-mails that anyone in the Comptroller's group sent or received during 2011 about the merger plans."

Although that seems like a simple request to the Legal department, it's a monumental amount of work for IT. First, they'll need a list of everyone in that department (don't forget people that might have left during the year). The users' online mailboxes are of no use since they no longer contain the items that were deleted. So, the backup tapes have to be recalled, individually restored, and then searched. And, to do the search, someone in Legal is going to have to come up with a list of keywords that might indicate a message about merger plans.

Archiving solutions can greatly reduce the complexity of requests like the one used in this example. These solutions keep copies of all e-mails sent and received (based on rules you define), and they can easily be searched en masse. While the previous example could easily take week or months to fulfill with the restoration and search of backup tapes, the same request could be done within a few days using an archiving solution.

In addition to a sophisticated indexing and searching mechanism, archiving solutions rely on "single instance" storage to reduce the amount of storage required. For example, if HR sent an e-mail to all 1,000 employees, the archiving solution would recognize this and store only a single copy of it (and the same is true of attachments) in the archive.

Unified Messaging

Unified messaging is the term applied to integrating your voice mail and e-mail systems. In short, you can use your e-mail system to access your v-mail (messages appear in your inbox as audio files or as text using a speech-to-text solution) and use your v-mail system to access your e-mail (a synthesized voice reads your e-mail messages to you). Unified messaging can also allow you to send and receive faxes from your e-mail inbox and can greatly reduce the amount of paper associated with traditional faxing. This technology is just beginning to gain acceptance and is still maturing.

It's also important to note that there are several ways to approach the integration:

- Your v-mail vendor may sell a system that integrates to your e-mail environment.
- Your e-mail vendor may have an add-on to integrate with your v-mail.
- A third-party vendor may offer a product to tie the two messaging systems together.

Unified messaging can be complex and may be costly. It also increases the storage requirements greatly, as users will have a greater amount of flexibility in saving and forwarding voice mail messages. Even if you aren't planning to implement unified messaging immediately, however, you may want to consider it as an issue if you're evaluating new e-mail systems. As voice-over-IP (VoIP) grows, both for consumer and for corporate use, unified messaging is growing as new features, functionality, and vendors are emerging.

Directory Services

When new users join an organization, it's common to find that they may need access to 10 or 20 applications. Sometimes, this means creating a separate account for each application—oftentimes, each with a different ID and password for the user to deal with.

Not only does this become an administrative nightmare for IT (going to each individual application to create the appropriate IDs) and a burden for the user (remembering the different IDs and passwords, changing them, etc.), but it can be a security risk to ensure that all the appropriate IDs are deleted when the user leaves the organization. The issue related to accounts and IDs is referred to as identity management.

Moving toward a Single ID and Password

The goal of directory services is to greatly reduce the administration, user burden, and security risk that can be associated with multiple IDs.

A directory service is essentially a system application and database that is used by all other applications. By using just a single set of ID and password credentials, called single sign on (SSO), users can sign on to the network, e-mail, and all the business applications they need to access.

Single sign on and identity management are also discussed in **Chapter 8, Security and Compliance** on **page 205**.

Directory Structure

Directories are set up in a hierarchical or tree fashion, very similar to an organizational chart. Some of the elements found in a directory include the following.

- **Objects (directory entries).** Virtually everything in a directory is an object. An object could be a person (i.e., user), a computer, or a device. A directory "container," which can hold a collection of objects, is also an object. Objects are often referred to as directory entries.
- **Organization unit.** This is comparable to a folder in a file system. It simply holds other objects and may also hold other organization units.
- **Attribute.** This provides some specifics about an object. For example, if the object is a user, there could be an attribute for the user's phone number. If the object is a printer, there might be an

attribute for the printer's IP address. Some attributes may have more than one value. In the case of a phone number attribute, it's entirely possible that someone may have more than one phone number. An attribute type is the kind of information (e.g., phone number), whereas the attribute value refers to the specific content (e.g., 212-555-1212).

- **Object class.** This defines which attributes are required/optional and allowed in an entry. For example, the object class for a printer may indicate that the IP address attribute is allowed and required. Essentially, the object class defines the rules associated with different types of objects. A directory entry may be assigned to more than one object class. For example, a directory entry for a user may be assigned to object classes for an e-mail user, an employee, a T&E user, etc. Also, each of those object classes would have attributes appropriate for its need.

5.7 ENTERPRISE RESOURCE PLANNING (ERP)

ERP has a broad definition; it's used in a variety of ways to mean the set of activities that a company engages in to manage its resources across the entire enterprise. This can mean activities as diverse as product planning, sales programs, materials purchasing, maintaining inventories, and performing classically defined HR functions. Major software companies in the ERP space include SAP, Lawson, SSA Global, and Oracle. ERP is a very hot topic in corporate circles.

Prior to ERP, companies would use different packages for various business functions: inventory, sales and distribution, financials, HR, and so on. Different packages were used simply because no vendor had a product offering that could cross all these various disciplines. The various packages might be purchased or homegrown. To pass data among the various functions, a company would write numerous interface programs (middleware) to extract data from one application's database for use in another application.

The Value of ERP Software

With the introduction of ERP, a company can essentially have a single application (or a single set of applications provided by a single vendor) and database for all its vital business functions. The value of this can be enormous. Because all the applications are integrated, a change in activity in one area of the company ripples through the system to all affected departments so that they could react accordingly. A sudden spike in sales notifies the Purchasing department to increase orders of raw materials, the receiving department to look out for these deliveries, the manufacturing department to gear up for increased production, HR that more labor will be needed to fulfill the demands of the increased sales, and so on.

ERP solutions for the supply chain (manufacturing, purchasing, logistics, warehousing, inventory, distribution, etc.) are a large portion of the market. Solutions for the supply chain often extend to include links and interfaces with suppliers and partners. ERP vendors also have different offerings for different industries.

General ERP Implementation Issues

There are several elements of ERP to keep in mind when considering implementing an ERP system.

- ERP isn't a trivial-sized activity. True ERP systems run across the entire enterprise and, as such, literally affect every aspect of a company's business.

- Because the scope of an ERP implementation can be so far-reaching, it acts as a magnifying glass. Problems are quickly seen throughout the organization. Also, problems no one knew about suddenly become very exposed.
- Implementation of an ERP system is a gut-wrenching experience for a corporation. Some companies thrive on the new system, embrace it as the salvation of their business, and explode forward. Others find the difficult medicine of ERP a very hard pill to swallow and eventually bail in midstream, leaving unhappy employees, customers, and vendors screaming in their wake (to say nothing of opening the gate to lawsuits). Trade journals are equally filled with success and failure stories of companies that have gone through ERP implementations.

Costs of Implementing ERP

In addition to the upheaval an ERP implementation can cause, the cost of implementing ERP will easily be in the hundreds of thousands of dollars and could go to the tens of millions for larger and more complex environments. Usually, the biggest costs of an ERP implementation are the consultants that you will need to assist in the implementation. Because of the complexity of installing an ERP package, it's common for consulting costs to total two to three times the cost of the actual software package. Many very large consulting firms (e.g., PricewaterhouseCoopers, Deloitte, Accenture, Ernst & Young) have entire divisions dedicated to ERP implementations.

In addition to consultants, a good portion of the budget will also go to training, support, and a large investment in additional hardware.

Major Changes Required

In many cases, the organization may find that it actually has to change the way it does business in order to implement an ERP package. While the traditional approach of implementing a package is to tailor it to your organization's needs, it's not uncommon to have to use the reverse approach when implementing an ERP package.

Many core activities associated with ERP are software related, although the thrust of the implementation is often not only software. It can include changing the way departments function, organization, procedures, employees' roles, and a sea change in the way the company operates.

As the person responsible for a large part of the software and hardware health and well-being of the corporation, your job, your responsibilities, and your entire skill set are going to be radically affected by any ERP motions your company undertakes.

It Isn't Only IT's Decision

It's likely that you won't be the only one consulted before your company decides to implement an ERP system. Most likely, you will be part of a group or committee making that decision. Because implementing an ERP system is almost always a multiyear adventure, you may join a company in mid-implementation. Your decisions won't be "Should my company do this?" as much as "How can I help my company do this in the most efficient manner possible?"

ERP may be the single largest IT project your company has ever undertaken. Its success or failure may lead to the success or failure of many executives and departments. Stories abound of ERP implementations that led to enormous cost overruns, 20-hour days, 7-day weeks, loss of key team members, implementation delays, and more.

If you're involved in an ERP implementation, chances are you will be making more use of some of the topics in this book (project management, budgeting, etc.) than with any other project you'll ever be involved in.

You, as well as everyone else involved, should look at an ERP implementation as the single greatest opportunity to reengineer the way your organization works and to have a huge beneficial impact that will probably live on for many years.

Disadvantages to ERP

ERP isn't without its risk and detractors. There can be disadvantages and pitfalls to it.

- The very rigid structure of an ERP solution oftentimes makes it difficult to adapt to the specific needs of individual organizations.
- Because ERP software is enormously sophisticated, there is often a tendency to implement more features and functions for a particular installation than are actually needed. This drives up costs and may reduce usage if the system proves too complex to use.
- The cost to implement and maintain ERP systems is very high and can challenge ROI calculations.
- Some departments and users may be hesitant to agree to the implementation if they feel they're giving up control of their data by switching from a department application to an enterprise-wide solution.

As the name implies, an ERP implementation is a decision that needs to be supported and embraced by the entire organization. If not, the odds of success will be severely limited.

5.8 Further References

Websites

aws.amazon.com (cloud service provider).
online.wsj.com/article/SB123903070566093099.html (use of e-mail as evidence in financial fraud).
www.lawson.com (ERP vendor).
www.acronis.com/enterprise/products/snapdeploy (disk cloning tool).
www.altiris.com (software deployment tool).
www.apple.com/iwork (productivity tool vendor).
www.bsa.org (trade organization for software publishers).
www.cisco.com/web/about/ac49/ac0/ac1/ac259/ironport.html (cloud-based offering for e-mail security).
www.cloudtimes.org/25-cloud-vendors-to-watch-out-for (25 leading cloud vendors).
www.corel.com (productivity software vendor).
www.gnu.org ("free" software site).
www.google.com/postini/ (cloud-based offering for e-mail security).
www.jamfsoftware.com (software deployment tool vendor).
www.koffice.org (Open Source productivity software).
www.landesk.com (software deployment tool vendor).
www.linux.org (Linux).

www.mcafee.com (antivirus software vendor).

www.microsoft.com (software deployment, cloud, virtualization, and productivity tools).

www.openoffice.org (Open Source productivity software).

www.oracle.com (ERP vendor).

www.rackspace.com (cloud service provider).

www.radicati.com/wp/wp-content/uploads/2011/05/Email-Statistics-Report-2011-2015-Executive-Summary.pdf (e-mail usage study).

www.salesforce.com (cloud service provider).

www.sap.com (ERP software vendor).

www.siia.net (trade organization for software publishers).

www.ssaglobal.com (ERP software vendor).

www.symantec.com (antivirus software and deployment tool vendor).

www.trendmicro.com (antivirus software vendor).

www.tumbleweed.com (e-mail management vendor).

Books and Articles

Babcock, C., 2010. Management Strategies for the Cloud Revolution: How Cloud Computing Is Transforming Business and Why You Can't Afford to Be Left Behind. McGraw-Hill.

Bradford, M., 2008. Modern ERP: Select, Implement & Use Today's Advanced Business Systems. Lulu.com.

Brousell, L., 2011. Putting the Cloud First. CIO Magazine June 15.

Carter, J., 2008. Unified Communications 100 Success Secrets Discover the Best Way to Unify Your Enterprise, Covers Unified Messaging, Systems, Solutions, Software and Services. Emereo Pty Ltd.

Currier, G., 2011. Speeding the Cloud. Baseline Magazine May/June.

Flynn, N., 2009. The e-Policy Handbook: Rules and Best Practices to Safely Manage Your Company's E-Mail, Blogs, Social Networking, and Other Electronic Communication Tools. Amacom.

Haletky, E.L., 2008. VMware ESX Server in the Enterprise: Planning and Securing Virtualization Servers. Prentice Hall.

Hugos, M.H., Hulitzky, D., 2010. Business in the Cloud: What Every Business Needs to Know about Cloud Computing. Wiley.

McHoes, A., Flynn, I.M., 2010. Understanding Operating Systems. Course Technology.

Meeker, H.J., 2008. The Open Source Alternative: Understanding Risks and Leveraging Opportunities. Wiley.

Mitchell, R.L., 2011. Big Business Takes a Small Bite of the Apple. Computerworld August 22.

Menken, I., 2010. Virtualization—The Complete Cornerstone Guide to Virtualization Best Practices. Emereo Pty Ltd.

Rashid, F., 2011. Cloud Security Services Can Reduce Malware. eWeek July 18.

Rhoton, J., 2010. Cloud Computing Explained. Recursive Press.

Rustad, M., 2010. Software Licensing: Principles and Practical Strategies. Oxford University Press.

Silberschatz, A., Gagne, G., Galvin, P.B., 2011. Operating Systems Concepts. Wiley.

Sosinsky, B., 2011. Cloud Computing Bible. Wiley.

Vaman, J.N., 2008. ERP in Practice: ERP strategies for steering organizational competence and competitive advantage. McGraw-Hill.

van der Hoeven, H., 2011. ERP and Business Processes. Llumina Press.

Winkler, V., 2011. Securing the Cloud: Computer Security Techniques and Tactics. Syngress.

Word, J., 2011. Integrated Business Processes with ERP Systems. Wiley.

Wagner, B., Monk, E., 2008. Enterprise Resource Planning. Course Technology.

Managing the Money

6

Budget: A mathematical confirmation of your suspicions.

A.A. Latimer

CHAPTER TABLE OF CONTENTS

6.1 The Budgeting Process 161
6.2 The Difference between Capital Expenditures and Operating Expense Items 167
6.3 Lease versus Buy: Which One Is Better? 168
6.4 Other Budgeting Factors to Consider 170
6.5 Managing Vendors 173
6.6 Managing the Money during Difficult Times 179
6.7 Outsourcing and Offshoring 182
6.8 Further References 187

As a manager, one of the things you have to manage is money and how your department spends it. Also, because IT departments often have one of the largest budgets in the organization, many eyes will be on your budget. This chapter will help you minimize, and deal with, the raised eyebrows over all those eyes. In the pages that follow, we discuss the issues behind a variety of topics, such as how and when a budget is generated, capital versus operating expenses, leasing versus buying, key factors you need to watch out for when developing your department's budget, managing the relationships with your vendors, outsourcing, and managing the money in difficult economic times.

6.1 THE BUDGETING PROCESS

The budgeting process assigns specific amounts of money to specific departments within a company for a single period of time called a "fiscal year." Sometimes a company's fiscal year is not the January–December calendar year. The year that the budget tracks can be any 12-month period, although it generally begins on January 1, April 1, July 1, or October 1 (the beginning of a quarter).

Regardless, the 12-month period for your budget is called the "fiscal year." If the fiscal year isn't the same as the calendar year, you identify the fiscal years by the year in which it ends. For example, if your fiscal years go from July 1 to June 30, you would refer to the budget that covers July 1, 2013, through June 30, 2014, as the 2014 budget, or sometimes as "fiscal 2014."

In general, the budgeting process begins two to three months before the start of the fiscal year. At this point, you begin to develop your first draft of the budget, estimating the amount of money you plan to spend during the upcoming 12 months. You prepare this budget based on the past year's spending as well as factoring in future plans and expectations such as growth, consolidation, new initiatives and projects, etc.

In your planning, you should have discussions with other department managers to learn about their upcoming needs and projects that might impact your department's spending. Depending on your company and the business that it is in, you may also want to include discussions with key partners, clients, suppliers, and customers. Similarly, it would be wise to take a look at your company's chief competitors to try to learn about their use and plans for IT to help gauge your own plans.

If you are new to management, you will quickly discover that the budget process and all its associated processes are critical to you and your department's success. Regardless of how important your role in the company is deemed to be, unless that importance is backed up with financial support specified in the budget process, you will find getting anything done to be a very difficult task.

Possible Budget Items

The first place to get started with a budget is to review the previous years' budgets for your department. Budgets are historical records and are (in most cases) carefully tracked—somebody in your company is always watching the money.

Every company keeps track of budgets and spending a bit differently and may use different names, categories, and groupings from the ones given here. Find out how your company budgets and then customize the concepts and techniques described here to meet your needs.

Which Items to Track

The following is a list of potential items for your department's budget. Check each item to see if you are tracking it in your department and if not, why not.

Personnel
- Staff compensation (salaries, overtime, bonuses, etc.)
- Benefits
- Recruiting (agencies, ads, etc.)
- Bonuses/overtime
- Education/training
- Consultants/temporary help

Hardware
- Upgrades
- Maintenance and support
- New equipment
- Leases/rentals
- Replacement components

Software
- New software (applications, operating system, utilities, etc.)
- Vendor maintenance and support

- Upgrades
- License renewals

Telecommunication Services
- Service fees for handheld devices, cell phones, and tablets
- Telco lines (point-to-point, MPLS, voice-trunks, ISDN, etc.)
- ISP connections and services

Supplies
- Printer consumables (paper, toner)
- Backup tapes
- Miscellaneous hardware items (keyboards, mice, flash-drives, cables, etc.)
- Basic office supplies

Travel and Entertainment
- Conferences
- Off-site travel to branch offices and new sites
- Lunches and dinners for staff working late or through the weekend

Miscellaneous
- Books and subscriptions
- Membership dues for professional organizations
- Postage
- Duplication

Depreciation
- Hardware
- Software

Physical Plant
- Data center services (cabinets, raised-floor, HVAC, electrical)
- Cabling (fiber and copper)
- Furniture

Outside Services
- Disaster recovery
- Off-site tape storage
- Service bureaus
- Consultants
- Service providers (Web hosting, application providers, services in the cloud, etc.)

Overhead
- Rent
- Utilities

Chargebacks—Who Really Pays?

In some companies, the budget for IT is used for all technology costs. In other cases, each department must budget for the technology it buys, such as computers and printers, as well as for specific projects and applications. Sometimes IT's budget for items used across all departments (IT staff, servers, Internet connections) is prorated and charged back to each department. These are commonly called "chargebacks."

The benefit of charging expenses back to individual departments is that those departments become more cost conscious of their IT uses and requirements. They better understand the costs of making everyone's e-mail accessible on their cell phones, for example, if they have to pay for that functionality. The downside is that it can create a tremendous amount of administrative overhead to calculate the chargebacks and process them. It can also create additional headaches for you if department heads think the chargebacks are too high. "I saw an ad in the paper for a $500 PC, but the ones we're buying are $800—my team doesn't need a brand name or fancy configurations, so we'll take the $500 one," for example. It can also create IT challenges if some department heads are very cost conscious about their spending on IT, while other department heads are less concerned. Situations like this mean that there can be distinct technology differences/capabilities from one department to another.

Although chargebacks don't alter the budgeting process dramatically, they may have an impact on how you approach it.

Reviewers for Your Budget

Most likely you'll be reviewing the first drafts of your budget with your director or vice president. In general, it's a good idea to get as many eyes and minds involved with your budget as possible. You don't want to overlook anything. This includes getting your direct reports involved in the process. Solicit from them ideas about projects they know about, things they'd like to get done, hardware and software that needs to be replaced or upgraded, and so on.

In all likelihood, involving your staff in the budget process will benefit both of you—not only will they appreciate the opportunity to be involved, they will most likely offer up some items that you had neglected to think about. At the same time you're collecting the expected dollar amounts for your budget, you want to make sure you're collecting the associated explanations and justifications. You will have to refer to this information when it comes time to explain, justify, and defend your budget. See the section later in this chapter entitled **"Getting Approval and Defending Your Budget"** on **page 165**.

Try to keep as much detailed information as possible, not just high-level summaries. For example, instead of putting $500K in software maintenance, identify the various applications that you pay maintenance for, how much the maintenance is, and when the maintenance comes up for renewal. Having this information readily available makes it that much easier if you are asked to explain your budget. Also, it helps identify those items that should be removed from the budget because they are no longer in use.

You need to thoroughly understand and know your material before making a formal presentation. You should be fully versed in how you came up with your numbers, what assumptions were used, and so on. Many managers, IT and non-IT alike, don't do their homework before making a formal budget presentation. This lack of preparation clearly shows during the meetings. The more knowledgeable you are, the more confidence they'll have in what you say.

In general, the budget may be approved by your CFO or executive committee around the start of the fiscal year. However, it's not unheard of for the final approval to be delayed until a month or two into the new fiscal year.

Estimating (and Overestimating) Your Numbers

It's general practice to overestimate your budget to a certain degree. While this style sounds questionable from a practical and ethical perspective, it's so widely practiced and accepted that you need to address the issue directly when you present your budget. Most experienced managers expect an overestimation.

It's important to understand that the practice of overestimating is very common and well understood by both sides. If you consciously do *not* overestimate (and many managers don't), make a point of bringing this up during budget discussions with your supervisors.

There are several reasons for overestimating:

- It gives you room to cut if upper management asks to reduce spending.
- It gives you room for those unanticipated expenses that invariably crop up.
- It increases the likelihood that you'll be within budget for the year, which could be a critical factor in determining your bonus or merit increase.

Of course, the downside of overestimating your budget is that if you don't use all the money allocated to your department, you may not get approval for such a large budget in future years. A large surplus may also give the impressions that you don't do a good job of planning. Very often, the end of the budget year has department managers either shifting some of next year's purchases into this year's budget (trying to use up unspent funds) or shifting some of this year's purchases into next year's budget (trying to avoid going over their budget).

Getting Approval and Defending Your Budget

As you work to develop your budget, it is likely that you'll have to present it or defend it in some manner. While there may be great temptation to review each item line by line, this isn't a common practice. Summaries are generally the expected norm for discussions with management and the finance department, but have the details ready in case you need them.

You'll probably have to give a high-level overview of your budget to your superiors—using more words than numbers. You may end up presenting this to your manager, to Accounting, or to some sort of company budgeting committee. You'll be better off couching these explanations in business terms, as opposed to IT terms. Don't try to explain why three programmers are needed for the Web analytics project. Instead, explain the value of delivering the project to the company in time for the holiday shopping period, and that the cost of the programmers is the means to that end.

Also, be prepared to explain how budget reductions will impact various goals and projects. For example, a time frame for a project may need to be extended or functionality will be sacrificed. (See the section **"Three Critical Components to Any Project"** in **Chapter 4, Project Management** on **page 111** about " ... the *interplay* of the three characteristics of a project—time, money, resources . . . .")

It may be appropriate to make references to last year's budget and projects as a comparison. You should also be prepared to explain large variances from year to year. For example, if you're queried as to why you're expecting a 25 percent increase in supplies, you can explain that the new document imaging system will greatly increase the amount of data that is stored online and has to be backed up so you'll need to buy more tapes. When presenting your budget, not only are you providing information and letting your audience see what they're getting for their money, you're also trying to make them feel confident in your abilities.

Remember to keep in mind that you are probably presenting to an audience who has little understanding of the technical details behind your job and your budget. They don't know the difference between a mega*bit* and a mega*byte*—and they don't want to know. That is your job. In your budget presentation, act as you always do when presenting to a nontechnical audience: recognize they are experts in their own field who deserve respect from a fellow professional. You don't like being demeaned because you don't know what an "indemnification clause" is when Legal mentions it, so don't demean non-ITers because they ask what a KVM switch is.

Don't be surprised if your budget goes through several iterations. The powers that be may kick it back and ask for reductions or more explanation. You may be asked to eliminate certain projects so that those costs can be recovered or you may simply be asked to reduce it by a fixed amount or percentage. If so, be sure that you explain the consequences of those reductions.

During the Year: Tracking and Revising Your Budget

During the year, your Accounting department will probably furnish monthly or quarterly reports of your department's year-to-date spending. Look closely at these reports. It's not uncommon for data entry errors to occur where another department's purchase is charged to your cost center or for one of your own purchases to be charged to the wrong category.

The report you get from Accounting will probably have several columns for each category:

- Budgeted amount
- Actual amount spent for the month
- Actual amount spent year to date
- Variance against budget (an over/under amount indicating how well you are doing compared to the expected amount based on your original budget)
- Variance against last year (an over/under amount indicating if you are spending more or less for the same items as last year)

Your Accounting department may be able to give you reports with different formats based on your needs. Detailed reports can usually be requested if you have questions about information in summary reports. But don't get too caught up watching pennies. As a general rule, your primary concern is the total budget for your department. If your overall spend is well under budget, no one is likely to care if you overspent within the supplies category, for example.

Revising Your Budget

During the year, you may have one or two opportunities to revise your budget. These revisions are often referred to as forecasts, reforecasts, revised estimates, or updates. These revisions can be used to:

- Include projects that weren't expected during the initial budgeting process.
- Eliminate or reduce costs for projects that were canceled or scaled down since the initial budget was proposed.

- Update/refine projections based on actual spending and other changes (e.g., vendor pricing, expansion, size of projects).
- Demonstrate anticipated cost reduction as a result of belt tightening.

Each opportunity to revise the budget is a chance to deliver a more accurate estimate. Your initial budget is essentially a 12-month projection. However, a midyear revision is 6 months of actual costs and only 6 months of projection.

6.2 THE DIFFERENCE BETWEEN CAPITAL EXPENDITURES AND OPERATING EXPENSE ITEMS

A budget usually consists of two sets of numbers: one for capital expenditures and one for operating expenses. Typically, these are considered separately, with different amounts of scrutiny. IT is a bit of an odd duck department in the budgeting process in that it usually has a significant capital budget. After all, most of the traditional corporate departments (Marketing, Finance, HR, etc.) usually don't have much need for acquiring assets.

- Whenever you spend money on something, you'll have to consider if an item is a capitalized or operating expense so that it can be treated accordingly in the accounting process. A capital expenditure is for an item that will have a useful life of several years, such as a piece of hardware. Examples of capital expenses would include most hardware, software, Enterprise Resource Planning (ERP) solutions, furniture, physical plant items (e.g., cabling, data center cabinets), and so on.
- Alternatively, an operating expense item is something whose value is gone in a shorter period of time. Operating expenses are the cost of resources used to support the ongoing operations of a business. They often recur, in that they have to be paid each month or quarter (e.g., the electric bill or salaries). Operating expenses are for items that last for a short time and have no residual value after that period. Examples of operating expenses would include salaries, telecom lines, software and hardware maintenance agreements, equipment rentals, etc. A software support agreement, for example, is an operating expense item. The value of the money spent each year lasts only for the 12 months of the agreement.

Capital Expenditure Details

If the useful life of a $10,000 router is expected to be five years, accounting principles of capital depreciation allow you to spread the cost over the life of the equipment—in this case five years. So, even though the company may have to write a check for the full amount when it buys the equipment, the impact of this purchase on the company's books, and your department's budget, may only be $2,000 that first year and in each of the subsequent four years of the device's expected life.

Because there is more paperwork involved in tracking a capitalized expense for each year of its useful life, there is generally a minimum dollar amount for capitalizing items. For example, a computer cable might be useful for 10 years, but because it only costs $25, it would not be capitalized. The minimum amount for capitalizing varies from company to company. Figures of $500, $1,000, or $1,500 are common—check with your Accounting department.

Although the useful life of a connection to the Internet might seem to be quite long, in reality its useful life is only as long as your last payment to the carrier. Stop paying the carrier and its life drops to zero. Since you're really just renting it from the carrier, it can't be considered an asset on the books of your organization.

Check with Your Company's Policies

You'll do yourself a big favor by checking with your Accounting and Finance departments to get an understanding of your company's policies regarding capital expenditures, depreciation schedules, and so on. Armed with this, it's within your best interest to group projects' costs into three categories: capital expenditures, expense items, and any recurring costs that will continue after the project is completed (e.g., maintenance contracts, telecommunication costs, etc.).

Gray Areas

There are several gray areas regarding capital and expense items. Typically, assets are tangible items. However, software and applications aren't things you can touch. There used to be a lot of variance in the treatment of software costs, but now it is generally capitalized—but not always. Some organizations will capitalize a vendor's consulting services if they're bundled with the sale of hardware. Similarly, there may be justification to capitalizing the staff salaries, or training, associated with a particular project.

Interpreting accounting regulations can be as difficult as interpreting any other legalese. It's always best to check with the experts. For accounting issues, the experts are your Accounting department.

Another issue related to the consideration of capital versus operating expense is your company's sensitivity to each. Some companies are particularly sensitive to capital expenditures, whereas others are more sensitive to operating costs. You probably won't find any official statement or policy about this, but you're likely to get a sense of it fairly quickly.

For items that are capitalized, you will see the cost for each year of the item's useful life charged to your budget (usually in a category called "depreciation"). The Accounting department has software called a "fixed assets application" to track the cost and depreciation of capitalized items.

The example given earlier said that a $25 cable wouldn't be capitalized because the cost was too low, even though it had a long useful life. If you place an order for 1000 cables, you still wouldn't capitalize the cables (even though the order totaled $25,000) because *individually* they cost so little. However, some companies still choose to look at the total order so that it can be capitalized.

6.3 LEASE VERSUS BUY: WHICH ONE IS BETTER?

One of the discussions you're likely to have about acquiring hardware is "lease versus buy." Leasing computer equipment carries with it essentially the same pros and cons as leasing a car (see Table 6.1).

When you lease something, you're essentially renting it for a specified period of time. In general, you make arrangements to purchase a piece of hardware, but the leasing company makes the actual purchase. The leasing company is then the owner and they lease it to you. Over the period of the lease, the total lease payments will be higher than the purchase cost. This difference is a result of the rate charged by the leasing company (essentially interest).

During the term of the lease, which is generally several years, you're responsible for the hardware, its maintenance, upkeep, and so on—just as if you owned it. You will make monthly or quarterly lease payments. It's important to note that lease payments are generally treated as an expense item, not as a capital asset. The reason is simple: you don't own the leased equipment. However, it is also possibly for a lease to be treated as capital—see the sidebar on page **169** about Operating versus Capital leases.

At the end of the lease, you usually have several choices:

- Terminate the lease by sending the equipment back to the leasing company.
- Extend the lease (although you should be careful that the new lease payments are based on the unit's current market value, not the original purchase price).
- Buy the equipment. Often you can do this for a very low cost ($1.00) or for its current market value.

Keep in mind that you generally have to inform the leasing company of your plans 90 days prior to the end of the lease.

OPERATING VERSUS CAPITAL LEASE

Some leases are essentially rentals, whereas others are really purchases that happen over a long term. For example, if you rent office space for a year, the space is worth nearly as much at the end of the year as when you started; you're simply using it for a period of time. This is an operating lease. If you lease a server for five years, at the end of the lease the computer is worth a lot less than it was when the lease started. The leasing company doesn't want the unit back at the end of the lease because it's highly unlikely to find a customer that will be interested in a five-year-old piece of computer equipment. The company you leased it from has to account for this and charges you a payment that will recover all of the lease's costs, along with their margin for profit. At the end of the lease, ownership of the unit transfers to you. This type of lease is referred to as a capital lease and is really a purchase with a built-in loan. According to Financial Accounting Standards Board (FASB) Statement 13, a lease is considered a capital lease if it meets any one of the following criteria:

- The lease transfers ownership of the property to the lessee by the end of the lease term.
- The lease contains an option to purchase the leased property at a bargain price.
- The lease term is equal to or greater than 75 percent of the estimated life of the leased property (e.g., the lease term is six years and the estimated life is eight years).
- The present value of rental and other minimum lease payments equals or exceeds 90 percent of the fair value of the leased property less any investment tax credit retained by the lessor.

Leasing

Should you lease an item or buy it? As Table 6.1 shows, there are pros and cons to each choice.

Table 6.1 Pros and Cons of Leasing

PRO	CON
Predictable payments for the life of the lease could ease budget projection and administration.	Extra effort during purchasing to coordinate activities between the leasing company and the equipment vendor. During the life of the lease there is ongoing administrative work to process the invoices and payments.

Continued

Table 6.1 Pros and Cons of Leasing—Cont'd

PRO	CON	
Allows companies with limited cash flows, or lines of credit, to obtain expensive equipment.	Complications arise if equipment is upgraded during the life of the lease: Should the upgrade be leased or purchased? If leased, it needs to be co-terminus with the original lease. If purchased, you have to remember not to send the upgrade back to the leasing company at the lease's end. Also, some leases have provisions in them that stipulate that any upgrade will invalidate the lease.	
Allows for predictable and planned turnover of equipment that's replaced regularly (e.g., PCs, servers, printers).	If you're leasing a high volume of equipment (such as PCs in a large environment), there is additional effort to track inventory precisely so that equipment can be located at the end of the lease to be returned.	
Many businesses have discovered they don't need to own the equipment they use.	The packing and shipping of equipment returned at the end of a lease could be burdensome.	
Depreciation and interest on debt may produce potential tax/financial benefits.	If you charge equipment to the department where it's used, it could require extra effort to code each lease invoice properly.	

Who Makes This Decision?

Lease versus buy isn't a decision that IT should make alone. In fact, it's a decision usually made by the financial departments with input from IT. Very often, the decision will be based on whether the company can better accommodate the costs as a capital expense or an operational expense.

6.4 OTHER BUDGETING FACTORS TO CONSIDER

There are a number of key factors that you should consider when budgeting:

- Growth of your department's workload
- Technological change
- Staff
- Software maintenance
- Hardware maintenance

Growth of Your Department's Workload

In general, the IT workload grows each year. Even if the company's growth is flat and the general cost of technology continues to decline, in most companies, the need for IT resources continues to grow exponentially. This growth includes items such as faster line speeds, more powerful corporate smart phones and other mobile equipment, additional applications, more server horsepower, greater redundancies, and more disk space. (Even with the recent trend of companies "outsourcing" IT work to data centers, IT departments within corporations continue to grow. As you know, *someone* has to make all this stuff work together.)

It's hard to determine an exact figure for each year's growth. Often it's no more than a best guess. Before making your guess, however, you should examine how the IT workload has grown in the past and learn about upcoming activities and projects that the company has planned that might impact the demand on IT.

Technological Change

Technology changes fast. This is a fact of life in the computer world that makes this industry so fascinating and frustrating at the same time. When you buy a new piece of equipment (e.g., a server), it's safe to say that you'll need to upgrade it over time to get more out of it as growth demands. You'll need to add memory, disk space, and perhaps additional processors. Eventually, there will come a time when it really doesn't pay to invest more money into this device, either because the technology has changed (e.g., new generations of processors) or because the cost of new equipment is relatively inexpensive.

Regardless of the specific reason, you need to anticipate this fact. While technology does change quickly, you need to be able to forecast the need to upgrade it and its eventual obsolescence and replacement. As equipment gets replaced, you're likely to be questioned for the need of the replacement. Be prepared to explain to users who have little understanding of technology why you're buying a new piece of equipment to do the same job as the piece of equipment you bought three years ago.

Staff

Growth of staff salaries (annual merit increases, promotions, bonuses, etc.) should be routinely factored into each year's budget. A more significant budget factor is staff turnover.

The turnover rates of IT personnel vary tremendously. Those individuals that enjoy always working with the latest and greatest technologies may not last more than a year or two before they're off to greener pastures. PC technicians may also last a short time as they seek to find opportunities beyond the Help Desk. Your company, salary, and benefits, each employee's goals and objectives, and their overall happiness with the company—and with you as their manager—are all factors that will influence your staff members' decisions to stay with the company.

Even though your staff may seem quite content, you should assume that there will be some turnover. You may not be able to predict who and when, but you can probably estimate the number of people that will leave. As you try to best guess the turnover, you need to estimate what it will cost to recruit their replacements: headhunters, Web postings, and so on. And when you're thinking that some employees may actually leave, you might want to also throw some money into your consulting budget to provide for interim staffing while you recruit new employees. Finally, the new staff may need some training to bring them up to speed on some of the technology solutions you're using. As a manager it's always best to remember that it is generally less expensive to train staff than to recruit them.

Software Maintenance

No one knows everything there is to know about technology, and that's why vendors offer maintenance agreements. This can be a significant factor for software—annual fees of 20 percent of the purchase price are fairly common. Some packages are so critical to your environment that you can't even consider forgoing support. Other packages may not be as important.

Keep in mind that sometimes software vendors differentiate between *maintenance* and *support*. Maintenance may be limited to your ability to get upgrades for the product. Support, however, generally refers to your ability to get assistance (phone, Web-based, etc.) when you have a problem or question regarding use of the software. Make sure you understand what your vendor means by maintenance and support. Also, for some vendors, maintenance only covers interim releases and patches, while major upgrades have to be paid for separately.

Hardware Maintenance

Like software, some critical hardware (e.g., a production server) may have very high levels of formal maintenance arrangements, whereas other devices (e.g., a printer) may go without formal support for a variety of reasons (it may be just as easy, or inexpensive enough, to simply keep a spare around). You may choose a hybrid solution by having formal service arrangements for your more vital devices and using less expensive coverage (or no coverage) for less critical components.

While software support and maintenance are often only provided by the original manufacturer, there are numerous sources for hardware maintenance. Factors to consider when looking at maintenance agreements for hardware include:

- Days and hours of coverage required (9–5, Monday–Friday; 24/7/365; etc.)
- Response time guarantees (keep in mind that frequently the response time refers to how long before the vendor calls you back, not how long it takes for a technician to arrive on site and certainly not how long it takes to repair the device)
- Plans for spare parts (some vendors you contract with may offer to keep a locked cabinet of parts in your computer room so that they are always available to them)
- Whether the vendor and/or its technicians are certified
- Pricing: standard versus premium for extended coverage, or escalated response times
- Consequences or remedies if the vendor fails to meet promised service levels

Time-and-Material (T&M) Contracts

Alternatives to maintenance contracts are Time-and-Material (T&M) arrangements. With these arrangements, when you place a service call for a piece of hardware, the vendor will bill you for the technician's time and the parts that are needed—similar to a repair on your car after the warranty expires. Because of the high degree of reliability of today's technology, it's entirely possible you'll save money by forgoing hardware maintenance contracts and rolling the dice on T&M.

Risks with T&M

There are two risks associated with T&M:

- The repairs could be costly and it's likely that the cost of a single site visit for a repair will be more than the cost of an annual contract.
- Vendors usually give greater priority to calls placed by customers with service contracts than to calls for T&M service.

If you go with T&M, make sure you set up the account with the vendors you'll use. By establishing a relationship in advance (knowing your customer number and site number and having the right phone number to call), you will expedite the process when you need to make a call.

Vendors' T&M Policies

To make sure you fully understand what you're entering into with a T&M policy, be certain to ask about the vendor's policies regarding:

- Hourly rates, overtime
- Minimum time charges
- Charges for travel
- Credit for defective parts that are swapped out
- Availability of parts

Warranties

The last choice for hardware support is the warranty that comes with new equipment. Warranties of up to three years are common. However, sometimes the warranty requires that you send the unit back to the manufacturer or bring it to an authorized repair center (although some equipment does come with an on-site warranty). But it's important to realize that most on-site warranties generally provide for a "best effort" for a next business-day response. Generally, vendors and/or their resellers offer upgrades for new equipment warranties to provide for higher levels of coverage.

When you're thinking about skipping a maintenance contract on a piece of hardware because the price seems too high, be sure to think about the cost to your environment and its impact on customers, users, clients, and business partners if that unit should go down. Consider a situation where a piece of equipment fails after business hours on a Friday. Your call may not even be handled until the following Monday, and a next business-day response would get you a technician on Tuesday. She may diagnose a faulty part, and its replacement has to be sent overnight from the warehouse for delivery on Wednesday. In this case, you've been down for five days. Throw a few wrinkles into the situation—a technician who doesn't show, a misdiagnosis, out-of-stock parts, a holiday, delayed deliveries—and your downtime could easily be a week.

6.5 MANAGING VENDORS

Purchasing IT equipment has become more complicated as time has passed. The reasons for this complexity are because the players have changed, the metrics have changed, the information changes quickly (new versions no longer come out only once a year), and the sources for purchasing items have changed (nobody sends you catalogs in the mail anymore).

As an IT Manager, you will be buying a lot of hardware and software. You have a complex matrix of responsibilities that includes saving money for your company, getting the right resources to make the projects work, giving your employees the right tools, and meeting a series of overlapping deadlines that occasionally seem hopeless.

Establish a Relationship

Relationships between IT buyers and their vendors have now reached the level of maturity that buyers from other well-established industries—clothing, merchandise, food, and so on—have enjoyed and suffered from for a long time. Gone are the days of get-me-the-latest-as-fast-as-you can. Very few companies automatically upgrade to every new version of every product they use. Companies now make a determination whether an upgrade is worth the expense and effort and may choose to skip a version and wait for the next.

As a consequence, IT buyers get to enjoy, and suffer from, all the aspects of a more well-defined experience with their vendors. Companies don't buy as quickly or as blindly, nor do vendors come out with major upgrades quite as frequently. New versions are released, but the real functionality change often isn't as great as it once was (security and antivirus patches are notable exceptions).

Add to the mix the fact that the amount of money involved is exponentially higher than it ever was (and budgets on both sides of the table are tighter than they ever were), and you have the elements of a combustible experience. Your job is to make sure that if anyone gets burned, it isn't you.

Another complicating factor is the move to "computing in the cloud." Well-accepted definitions of this term are still evolving, but it essentially means that your applications and data exist on the Web with a service provider. You buy (or rent) and run software over the Web. When new software is released, you do not get CDs, you get a link. The service provider takes care of everything related to the servers and also deals with the backups, application upgrades, redundancies, etc. Managing the costs and vendor relationships in such a virtual world is a new challenge. For a fuller discussion, see the section **"Cloud Computing" on page 148** in **Chapter 5, Software, Operating Systems, and Enterprise Applications.**

Help Your Vendors

There is a second principle at work here: Put yourself in the vendor's shoes. In any conversation, trying to imagine what the other person is thinking can help your thinking. In buying situations, try to imagine what the vendor is thinking. Sometimes it can be obvious; he is trying to nickel-and-dime you and that's all there is to it. But sometimes you can guess his next move; if he drops his initial asking price, for example, he may have chopped a year or two off the length of the service contract.

Along those lines, make sure your vendors get paid. Track big invoices through your Accounting department so that you know your vendors are happy. Someday you'll need to ask them a favor, such as needing immediate delivery on an item that usually has a long lead time.

Remember that a vendor/client relationship is a two-way street. It may appear to be one-way, but it is in fact two-way. There will be times when you will be able to make or break a vendor's monthly quota, but there will also be times when you will need a server delivered over the weekend or a trial of the latest hard-to-find tablet device. In both situations, it helps both parties to view the relationship as one that can help each other rather than an adversarial one where only one wins at the expense of the other. Think of your primary vendors as strategic partners.

Request for Proposals

In many cases you know exactly what you want and you just want to order it, which is more often the case with purchasing specific hardware and software. In other cases, there may be special requirements. These can include things like installation, setup, configuring, and custom coding, etc. Or, you may have special needs, such as the work can be performed only after hours.

In these cases you would prepare a Request for Proposal (RFP) or Request for Quotation (RFQ). An RFP is essentially a document detailing your requirements and asking specific questions. RFPs can be a single page in length or run up to 50 pages or more. They vary depending on the scope of the project and the number of concerns you have. They are an excellent way of ensuring that both you and your vendor(s) are on the exact same page as to what is expected, what's provided, what the costs are, and so on.

Similar to an RFP is a Request for Information (RFI). An RFI is generally used to gather preliminary information about a vendor in order to see if they meet some basic requirements. The RFI helps narrow down the list of vendors that would get the RFP. For example, you may want to use an RFI to ensure that the vendor has a minimum amount of experience in a certain area, has a global presence, or has the sort of products and services you are looking for. Of course, you can ask RFI-type questions in an RFP, but there's no point in making a vendor fill out a lengthy RFP only to find out that they don't meet your minimal requirements.

Get Multiple Bids

If the product you're evaluating has competitors, you should always get multiple bids. Even if you know the exact make and model of the product you want, you should still get multiple bids from different resellers. Some organizations—government agencies, for example—are *required* to get multiple bids. In most cases there may not be a legal requirement, but it certainly makes sense in many cases to get more than one bid, especially for larger purchases. When you get multiple bids you're keeping everyone on their toes and showing others that you're conscious of costs.

Be warned if a vendor reacts negatively when you talk about getting multiple bids. It's a common sales technique to try and get the customer not to look at other options; any vendor worth their salt is going to understand you're shopping around. They will tailor their sales approach to your actions and not overreact when you bring it up.

When evaluating multiple bids, make sure you're comparing apples to apples. Are the part numbers the same? Are the maintenance contracts for the same duration and include the same level of support? Do the professional services cover the same items? (Note: This is very hard to do, but very important. One common technique for vendors is to blur categories to make their bids appear more competitive; don't take offense at this tactic, just take it into consideration—be very aware of it—when making your buying decisions.)

As mentioned in the previous section, RFPs are used frequently for getting multiple bids (especially on larger purchases) because they help ensure that each vendor is being told exactly the same information and being asked to provide the same information.

Set Up a Trial

In some cases, you may not want to make the purchasing decision until you've had hands-on experience with the product so that you can do a thorough evaluation. Many software vendors allow you to download 30-day evaluation versions of their product right off their website. Hardware vendors are also eager to deliver a device for you to try for yourself. In some cases, the vendor will work with you to set up the product or service. This works to your benefit as well as his—it reduces the learning curve and setup time and the vendor is sure that the product is performing optimally for you.

Reviewing Contracts with Vendors

Depending on the size of your organization and the size of the contracts (in monetary terms), getting formal legal help can be of great assistance in this situation. If your company isn't big enough to have an in-house lawyer, have the contracts reviewed by a legal consultant. Regardless, you should read the contract and be able to understand the following:

- What exactly am I agreeing to?
- How much am I actually paying?
- What are my liability and rights?
- What are the vendor's liability and rights?

In many contracts, the up-front portion contains some standard legalese that may go on for pages: issues of confidentiality, warranty, liability, applicable laws, and so on. This is the part you really want the legal experts to look at. They know if anything here is putting the company at risk. They will alert you to:

- Any wording that they're virtually forbidding you (i.e., the company) to agree to
- Terms that they're uncomfortable with (for these they should suggest alternatives)
- Terms that they're uncomfortable with, but recognize you're unlikely to get changed (although they will suggest you at least ask)

You need to turn your attention to the section called Terms and Conditions (also called "Ts and Cs"). As an IT Manager, this section of the contract deals with items that you're concerned about. This section might cover areas like:

- Service level guarantees or agreements (SLAs)
- Specifications of hardware and software
- Support, maintenance, upgrade terms
- Automatic renewals
- Ability to return/cancel if not satisfied
- Specific deliverables
- Associated costs, time frames, and so on

Everything is negotiable. Don't feel that just because it is on a form that you have to accept it. You may end up accepting it, but at least know that you can ask for changes. Remember that whatever promises your representative gave you are of no value unless they're in writing. If it is important to you, ask to have it included in the Terms and Conditions. Also, remember that by the time you get to the negotiating, your representative can virtually taste the commission he's making from this sale. At this point he almost becomes an advocate for you to his own Legal department. Take advantage of this ally.

Evaluating Alternatives

Today's technology environment is so complex and so charged with money that the number one rule of buying any technology product has to be: "Be prepared." Products have gotten so complex—and systems they are designed for have gotten so complex—that a simple "Yeah, this server can handle 1000 e-mail users at the same time" kind of statement no longer flies. You need benchmarks, you want other clients' stories, and you have to have objective data; in other words, when it comes to functionality, you have to do your homework.

For important purchase decisions, set up a simple matrix that allows you to compare all of your requirements and options. An evaluation matrix, as discussed in the next section, doesn't make the decision for you, but it clearly outlines your options and locates them conveniently next to each other. A formal matrix is not required for every buying decision, and the cost and the importance of the purchase will naturally dictate how much effort you want to put into analyzing things before actually buying.

However, seeing all the criteria and the items listed right next to each other can be of tremendous value when trying to determine how important the issue is for you, which vendor to use, and which equipment to buy. It also helps to ensure that you are using consistent criteria for evaluating all the vendors. Some buyers then share that matrix with the winning vendor.

With larger purchases, an evaluation matrix can help document (perhaps to your boss or to Finance) why a particular item was purchased instead of a competing item.

Set Up a Matrix

There is a relatively standard set of metrics you can use to evaluate most technology products. Typical evaluation matrices include:

- Functionality
- Price
- Performance
- Vendor viability
- Training required
- Vendor services
- Scalability
- Support and service
- Interoperability
- Product's position in the market

Functionality

The most obvious question is: "Does this product do exactly what you need it to do?" These days, you need to ask that question of a vendor several times. Yes, the data sheet on the network switch claims it can handle speeds of up to X, but is that in the vendor's perfectly controlled test environment? Is that performance available "out of the box" or is it only available with some upgrades to the base model? How fast can it handle real-world traffic, that is, your data center backbone?

If it's something for your end-user community, they may be the key players in determining if the product does what it needs to do, does it well, is easy to use, etc.

Price

Although important, this generally shouldn't be your only criterion. Rank other criteria for each purchasing decision. This is good information to have on hand when someone from Accounting asks why you purchased brand X over Y, or used vendor Z.

As discussed earlier in the chapter in the section **"The Difference between Capital Expenditures and Operating Expense Items"** on **page 167**, there are two components when evaluating the cost of a technology product:

- Capital Investment
- Operating Expenses and Total Cost of Ownership (TCO)

Capital Investment

This is the short-term, up-front cost of an item. It includes the hardware and/or software and all the associated components to make it do what you need it to do. For software, in addition to volume discounts, you want to consider how the product is licensed (see the section **"Licensing Models and Types"** in **Chapter 5, Software, Operating Systems, and Enterprise Applications**, on **page 146**).

Operating Expenses and TCO

In addition to the up-front capital investment, think of the costs for ongoing support and maintenance, implementation, training, prerequisite hardware and software, conversion/migration, and so on. TCO has become a much more popular method of evaluating products in the IT world. Competing platforms vendors, for example, try to justify higher initial prices by claiming their TCO is lower when compared over a several year period.

There are products where TCO isn't relevant. If you are buying a server rack, there isn't going to be much maintenance, training, and so on required. But most other products you buy in IT *do* require some TCO evaluation.

TCO analysis is a large and complex field, filled with vendors, consulting companies, and competing theories. Depending on the size of your purchase, you may want to create your own TCO analysis sheet. Include costs for capital investment, maintenance, support, training, consumables and supplies, installation, and any other either company- or product-specific costs. See the section **"TCO and Asset Management: What Are They?"** in **Chapter 7, Getting Started with the Technical Environment** on **page 196** for further discussion of TCO.

Vendor Viability

Is this vendor one that is likely to be around for a while? Are they at risk of going under because they're a fledgling start-up or are they ripe for acquisition or merger? Depending on the type of purchase you're considering, this may be a key issue.

Training Required

Will your staff need to be trained on this new product? Or is it something they can pick up on their own? If training is required then this cost has to be considered. Is training readily available or is it offered only twice a year and only in one location? Can the training be done at your site or via the Web?

Vendor's Services

Do you need, or will you want, professional services from the vendor to customize the product or help with its installation or integration into your environment? This could be an important factor to help ensure success, but it could also be a considerable cost. Use of a vendor's professional services can raise the cost of an implementation considerably, but also can help ensure success.

However, the vendor may be so eager to make the sale that he is willing to offer assistance, or training, at no charge. Similarly, will the vendor provide you with an opportunity to evaluate the product at no charge?

Performance

Hardware performance is often easily quantifiable. In addition to processor speed, a variety of other issues can impact performance: type and amount of memory, how the device is configured, number of processors, bus speed, amount of level-2 cache, among others. Performance benchmark standards are common. Also, if a vendor starts touting the performance of his equipment using standards other than those used in the industry, take it as a sign that his equipment may not perform as well. If everyone knows throughput is the standard and you start hearing about duration, be wary. Ask about the machine's throughput and be ready for a quasi-explanation about why that standard may not be correct.

Scalability

Will the product *scale* to meet the size of your environment? When considering an enterprisewide application (e.g., e-mail), your test bed will probably be quite small. However, the results may be very different when the product is deployed throughout your organization. Does the vendor know of another company your size using this product?

Support and Service

These can be critical components of an IT purchase. Products are getting more complex and their maintenance requirements are getting larger. Treat the item and the service options or contract as equally important elements in the buying decision. One may appear to cost more than the other, and be more important in the short term, but over time, the value of each can even out.

Also consider serviceability. Are parts easy to get? Does one vendor have long hold times on their support line? (This can be easy to verify with a call from your office.) Will you be able to find staff or training that can help maintain this item? Are technicians and parts available 24/7? How is the quality of their tech support?

Interoperability

Does the product *integrate well* into your environment or will it require specialized interfaces? Does the product adhere to industry standards or is it based on proprietary technology?

Product's Position in the Market

Is this a mature product? Are others using it? Is it considered a proven solution or is it more leading or cutting edge? Neither one is better than the other, since its importance and worth depends on circumstances, needs, and tolerance for risk. You may be interested in a brand-new solution or technology as a way of being innovative, differentiating yourself from the competition. However, if reliability and stability are top priorities, a more seasoned and proven product will be the better choice.

6.6 MANAGING THE MONEY DURING DIFFICULT TIMES

After years of incredible growth and economic expansion, 2008 and 2009 saw the greatest downturn in the economy since the Great Depression. With layoffs and cutbacks, and with a global reach, virtually no person, no company, and no country was spared its impact. It is also safe to say that your organization will again suffer difficult times in the future—cyclical swings, new competition, deteriorating revenues, increased costs, and so on. As manager of the IT department, you will be called upon during tough times to be involved in making sure that the company gets through it in one piece. During the difficult times, you should be looking at three areas:

- Managing costs
- Looking for opportunities to leverage IT for increased business value
- Demonstrating leadership

As is usually the case, flexibility will be key. Management will not take kindly to resistance to change during tough times. This will be a time when your leadership and your ability to maintain calm and motivate your staff will count and be noticed.

Managing Costs

Since IT probably has one of the largest budgets in the organization, it's no surprise that management will look there for significant cost-savings opportunity. There are tough choices to be made; in some cases you may have to incur smaller short-term costs as temporary work-arounds while you delay larger projects.

Usually, one of the first places considered for cost savings is labor. Can employees be cut? Although terminating anyone's employment is a difficult thing to do, it is always a stark economic possibility. (See the section **"Layoffs and Terminations"** in **Chapter 2** on **Managing Your IT Team** on **page 55**.)

Look carefully at your team. Are there any weak performers who aren't carrying their weight? Are there people assigned to projects that will be canceled or postponed? If other areas of the company are cutting staff, that may be justification to reduce your support staff. Also, as discussed later in this chapter, outsourcing may be a cost savings. Related costs such as contractors, seminars, and training are easy costs to cut before having to look at trimming the staff.

Consider staff-related expenses. Can you use videoconferencing solutions (or other technology offerings) to reduce the cost of travel? Is telecommuting an option to help reduce office costs?

What about IT's current and upcoming projects? What can be delayed or canceled? Do you really need to do that ERP upgrade this year—can't it wait? What about your technology refresh plans? If you currently refresh your workstations every three years, can you push it out to four years? Is there any waste going on? Are you replacing monitors every time you buy a new workstation, for example? Can't they continue to use their old monitors? Perhaps that SAN upgrade can be delayed another year. Examine any project that was going to put in a new system or application. If you've done without that application up until now, perhaps you can do without it a little longer.

What processes does IT have that are labor-intensive and can be automated? This can include workstation imaging, software distribution, and patching. Can you use remote-control software for user support instead of visiting users' desks? This may not impact costs directly, but it will make your team more efficient and productive, and no one will fault you for doing that in tough times.

Call in your suppliers and explain the situation—they are mostly likely in the same situation themselves. Tell them that you'd rather not have to look for other, less expensive suppliers, but that is what you'll have to do if they can't give you better pricing. Since they don't want you to look into other suppliers, much less switch to one, there's a good chance that they will do something to keep you. This is especially true of telecom and cell-service providers. You can also consider alternatives to standard technologies, such as sending phone calls over the Internet (VoIP) to reduce traditional phone charges.

Immediately cut some of the niceties, such as team lunches and noncritical travel. These may not amount to much in terms of your overall budget, but they help send a signal to the team about how serious things are. Expenses related to training and consultants may also be initial targets when costs have to be trimmed.

Leverage IT for Increased Business Value

IT should always be looking to align itself with the business, but that is especially important during difficult times. IT has a dual role here in that technology can help reduce costs, as well as support business development activities.

There are some quick hits for IT to help reduce costs to the business. When the business cuts back on travel, IT can deliver relatively inexpensive solutions to help mitigate the impact. This can include videoconferencing (from vendors such as Polycom and Tandberg), Web-based conferencing (with solutions such as Skype, webcams, Cisco's WebEx, Adobe's Connect, Citrix's GoToMeeting, Microsoft's Live Meeting), instant messaging, audio-conference call solutions (which you may already have with your existing phone system), remote access solutions, among others.

IT can also help automate procedures that are currently heavily dependent on manual effort and moving paper around. This can include items such as purchase/budget approvals, T&E processing, and online report distribution/viewing. Are there systems that can be put in place to help reduce error and improve quality so that time isn't wasted redoing work?

Work with the different business areas to see how IT can help them. Are the customer service phone systems, websites, and tools as effective as they can be? Are there tools that can help Marketing and Sales mine existing data for increased business opportunities? What tools and technologies are available to help the business areas innovate and differentiate themselves from the competition (as well as reduce costs)? In tough times, the company may be looking to reinvent itself; make sure you are prepared to show how IT can help make that happen.

Take a look at how different business areas are interacting. Is there sufficient collaboration and sharing of information? Are the Engineering and Research and Development teams aware of the complaints coming in on the support lines? IT can help implement tools and solutions to help ensure that people have access to the information that they need and that different areas aren't duplicating each other's work because everyone is operating in a "siloed" (isolated) fashion.

Solutions here probably won't be free. However, if you can show clear value by either reducing costs or helping the business gain/retain business and customers, management will be more than happy to make an investment now for a payoff to come. However, during tough times, management will probably want to see that payoff coming as soon as possible, not in five years.

Demonstrating Leadership

Often IT is looked at as a cost center and a rather expensive cost center at that. Having a reputation like that during tough times can hurt you and your department, which will in turn end up severely hurting the business. As the IT Manager, you want to be sure that your department's value is recognized by management and the rest of the company. Make it clear that IT is fully aware of the difficult times the organization is going through and is fully involved by making sacrifices, proactively suggesting changes, and helping other departments achieve their goal and cut costs.

Your leadership (discussed in the section **"Leadership vs. Management"** on **page 13** in **Chapter 1, The Role of an IT Manager**) is more important when the going gets tough than it is during times of growth. Your company's management and business leads will be looking to you for cost cutting and for new solutions to help drive the business. Show them that you are proactive and creating opportunities, that you're coming to the table with ideas, and that you are adjusting priorities properly. Where possible, investigate how your competitors are doing during these times and what steps they are taking. Stay on top of what's going on by reading more than IT journals. Be aware of what's going on in your company's industry and the business world in general. You need to know how different events affect the economy, your company, your department, and your job.

At the same time, your team will be looking to you for guidance. They'll be nervous and uncertain and will look to you for your calm (at the very moment that you're trying to hide your own sense of uncertainty, of course). These are great times to increase your visibility to your team and the department. Be open and honest with communications, acknowledge that things are tough, but also talk about the steps the company is taking and the ideas being considered. You won't completely eliminate your employees' nervousness, but if they feel fully informed, you can certainly mitigate it to a great extent. Nothing helps reduce panic more than showing that you're aware, concerned, and taking action.

Finally, solicit feedback from everyone—your team, your peers, your management, and your suppliers and vendors, as well as colleagues at other companies.

6.7 OUTSOURCING AND OFFSHORING

Managing your staff and your resources is a major task of an IT Manager. Outsourcing in all of its forms can be a very effective tool for helping you accomplish that task. But as you can imagine, outsourcing is not without its own associated costs (see Table 6.2 for definitions).

There are many tasks that you and your department perform. There are some that you perform because you *have* to, but you would gladly assign them to someone else given the opportunity. Perhaps doing these tasks chews up valuable skilled resources that you could use better somewhere else, perhaps your department doesn't do them well because they fall outside your core competencies, or perhaps no one likes doing them for other reasons.

Companies outsource a wide range of tasks; some send their Help Desk departments or their entire application development and maintenance. Others may use third-party services for their data center or to monitor the network.

One way to think about outsourcing is to think of one company with one kind of expertise—developing software, for example—hooking up with a company that has a different kind of expertise, such as accounting. Could the first company build its own billing system if it wanted? Yes. But it might be less expensive, get better results, and have fewer headaches if it contracted to have another company do it.

There are entire companies dedicated to the process of helping you outsource your tasks.

Offshore Outsourcing Overview

Sending work overseas is a much more drastic method of outsourcing—"drastic" both in a good and in a bad sense. We'll outline the positives and negatives of doing this (see Table 6.3), but keep in mind that offshore outsourcing is a *very* controversial idea. The decision whether to contract with an offshore company (some people would call that "sending local jobs overseas") isn't likely to be made entirely at the IT level, but here are some things to think about if you are called in and asked for your recommendations.

Table 6.2 Outsourcing Definitions	
Term	**Definition**
Outsourcing	When one company makes an agreement with a second company to provide services that the first could provide, but chooses not to. IT companies often outsource portions of their software development, for example. They might do this for various reasons (see the discussion later in this chapter), but the important point is that they *could* perform that task if they chose to. Using a third party to perform a task your company doesn't normally do—say you develop software but you need your new offices wired for electricity, so you hire an electrical contractor—is *not* outsourcing.
Offshore outsourcing	Arranging with a second company to provide services that the first company could provide but chose not to—and the second company isn't located in your own country. A common example of offshore outsourcing is a company in, say, Redmond, Washington, USA, contracting with another company in, say, Bangalore, India, to help it with its software development or customer support.

Table 6.3 Pros and Cons of Offshore Outsourcing

PRO	CON
Many of the tasks that Americans have traditionally performed, especially in IT, can be done for less money in other countries. Americans have a high standard of living compared to the rest of the world, and programmers overseas aren't paid at near the same rate. This is also true for Help Desk workers, data center employees, and software testers (among others).	The first negative is morale: If word gets out that you are replacing local jobs with overseas work, there will be significant employee issues to be dealt with. Among the public, not everyone agrees that globalization is inevitable and that the march of jobs to the lowest paying corporation (wherever they may be) is the most efficient, let alone the most moral, course to take. Many companies now go out of their way to hide their offshore outsourcing agreements.
In addition to cost, another often-cited benefit of outsourcing work overseas (to India and Russia in particular) is that your company gets the benefit of a 24-hour work cycle. Once your Help Desk is finished with their workday in the United States, for example, they can then send calls to the second company located in India or Russia. Since these countries are virtually on the other side of the world, their workday is only beginning. This allows calls to be answered, open tickets investigated, etc., around the clock.	The overhead costs involved in establishing a smooth relationship overseas are significant. It still may eventually be worth your company's while to do this, but there will be a steep cost curve at first.
It's common now: By 2015, 3.3 million jobs will have been sent overseas, according to Forrester Research. As the offshoring trend matures, U.S. firms will contract out increasing amounts of white-collar work such as accounting, drug research, and technical R&D.	There will be cultural considerations. While many IT workers overseas speak English, for example, and although many are trained in the United States, many workers are not. Different cultures have different laws about hiring, about contracting workers, different holiday schedules, etc. There will be some learning involved before both companies are comfortable with the arrangement and working together effectively. With the focus on security and compliance issues (see **Compliance and IT** in **Chapter 8, page 226**), many companies have concerns about exposing sensitive data to third parties in another country.

Outsourcing and offshoring can be very challenging, and while it can save money, companies have to be careful about what it means to the quality of work and impact on customers and operations. In a 2007 global outsourcing survey by KPMG LLC, 60 percent of the respondents said that problems with outsourcing are related to people. In 2005, Sears, Roebuck and Co. ended a $1.6 billion/10-year outsourcing agreement it had signed with CSC Corporation just a year earlier for "failure to perform certain of its obligations" (www.computerworld.com/industrytopics/retail/story/0,10801,101774,00.html). J.P. Morgan Chase & Co. abruptly canceled a $5 billion outsourcing arrangement with IBM Corp. Dell decided to return to U.S.-based call centers for its corporate customers when it was deluged with complaints after shifting its support operations to India (http://www.techedgeezine.com/112603_dells_service_dehli.htm). The list goes on and on.

Which Functions to Outsource

At some point, your organization is likely to ask you to consider outsourcing. One of the first steps is to consider which function(s) in your department is a candidate for outsourcing. While outsourcers will tell you that they can run the entire IT department, that might be too big of a first step. An easy way to dip your toe into the outsourcing waters is to first try functions that require minimal, or absolutely no, knowledge of your company's industry and/or operations.

For example, printer maintenance is something that is often outsourced. Just like you probably have a third party taking care of your copiers, you can have a third party take care of your printers (consumables, maintenance, repairs, monitoring, etc.). After all, a printer is a printer, and the outsourcer and their technicians really don't need to know anything about your company or your business (except where the devices are and who the VIPs are). The same can be said for the routine functions of workstation moves and setups. Other areas to consider outsourcing are shrink-wrapped software support for those how-to questions about Windows, Excel, PowerPoint, etc.

When these functions are outsourced, not only are you freeing up your internal staff for those tasks that require specialized knowledge of your industry and organization, but you may also be delivering a higher level of service, as the outsourcer is well versed in that function. For example, if your existing Help Desk gets a call from a user wanting to know how to do footnotes in Microsoft Word, there's a pretty good chance that your staffer would first do some investigating to figure out how to do footnotes and then walk the user through it. If that call had gone to an outsourcer with a support staff that only does MS Office support, there's a good chance that the user would get a quicker and more comprehensive answer.

More complicated areas for outsourcing are those that require more specialized knowledge of how your company operates or that involve functions that deal with sensitive or confidential areas (e.g., application development, network security, HR or finance data). Not only will it take additional time to outsource these areas (particularly for bringing the outsourcer up to speed), but many companies get nervous about having some of the functions outside of their own control. However, there are still some ways to find reasonable middle grounds. For example, instead of outsourcing network security and operations, perhaps only outsource network monitoring. Instead of outsourcing applications development, perhaps only outsource application maintenance. Some companies would prefer to keep their outsourcing to those items that are behind the scenes, and are less comfortable in outsourcing functions that will have direct interaction with users and customers, such as Help Desk or customer service functions.

Another flavor of outsourcing is when companies "operate in the cloud," which was briefly mentioned earlier and is discussed further in the section **"Cloud Computing"** on **page 148** of **Chapter 5, Software, Operating Systems, and Enterprise Applications.**

Does Outsourcing Make Sense?

Although there are a number of factors to consider when deciding whether to outsource, as a general rule, determining if it makes business sense is the overriding concern.

The Business Consideration

How will outsourcing benefit the company? Will it lead to cost savings? Will it provide better service delivery, perhaps in terms of quicker turnaround or better quality? Will it somehow improve relationships with customers or users? Will outsourcing improve the company's image?

Answering these questions takes some careful evaluation and judgment. As mentioned earlier, many outsourcing deals have been canceled because they didn't yield the expected results. The following steps are key in evaluating an outsourcing agreement:

1. Seek involvement of your user community at the outset. If you're considering outsourcing the maintenance of your HRIS application, for example, make sure that representatives from HR are involved at the very beginning to participate in the evaluation of outsourcers and buy in to the decision.

2. Carefully articulate to the outsourcer as much detail as you can about the environment and your expectations. The more information you can give your outsourcer, the better they'll be able to understand the requirements and to provide a more accurate proposal. For example, in the earlier example of outsourcing printer maintenance, you would want the outsourcer to know:
   a. How many printers of each model you have
   b. The physical layout (separate buildings across town, a campus environment, or in a single building)
   c. Space you can provide for stocking parts
   d. What your expectations are for response and resolution times
   e. Requirements to provide loaner equipment if a printer can't be repaired in a defined amount of time
   f. Requirements to provide updates on outstanding items
   g. Reporting requirements
   h. Requirements for any certifications of the outsourcer's staff or operations
   i. Integration with, or use of, your internal call-tracking system
   j. Executive requirements (for escalated service levels)

3. Determine your own costs for currently executing this function (otherwise, it will be difficult to know if outsourcing will save you money). These costs can include:
   a. Labor (salaries, contractors, training, benefits, recruiting, etc.)
   b. Office space for employees
   c. Related hardware and software (purchase, maintenance, depreciation)
   d. Third-party costs (for suppliers, vendors, partners)
   e. Connectivity/network costs

4. Understand the specifics of the outsourcer's terms. For example,
   a. Are they operating 24/7 or 8 AM to 5 PM?
   b. What about holidays? Which holidays?
   c. What happens if you have occasional special requirements for off-hours work? What are the costs?
   d. What are the specific service-level agreements and what metrics are used to determine if those SLAs are being met?
   e. What happens if an SLA isn't met? Do you get a credit?
   f. What about less quantifiable items, such as "quality of work," "professionalism and courtesy," and "language skills—written and oral" (these areas have been cited as the downfall of many offshoring arrangements)?
   g. What is your say in determining which of the outsourcer's staff is assigned to your organization? You probably don't want the outsourcer rotating people through your organization, but if one of

them gets into an altercation with a VIP, you want to be sure that you won't be seeing that person again.

h. Are you responsible for providing the outsourcer with anything? Seating space? Phones? Computers? Network connectivity?

i. If your outsourcer is going to be involved directly with your organization's partners and suppliers, who will be signing those contracts and who is responsible for those obligations? What happens if those relationships begin to deteriorate as a result?

j. What are the outsourcer's responsibilities regarding confidentiality, security, and regulatory requirements?

k. If there are hardware/software requirements involved, who will be responsible for the purchases and support contracts? Will the hardware and licenses be purchased in your name or the outsourcer's?

5. Carefully check the outsourcer's references.

a. Speak to their customers who are similar to you (industry, size, requirements, etc.).

b. Understand what things they would have done differently. What were the good and bad learnings?

6. Make sure you factor in the effort to transition to an outsourcer, as well as what's involved in ending the arrangement (either at contract's end or earlier).

a. There will certainly be a start-up period in transitioning responsibilities to the outsourcer as their team begins to understand your environment. Is this factored into the proposal and the costs?

b. During a start-up period you may need the outsourcer to have a project manager assigned to ensure a smooth transition and to provide reports and updates on the transition's progress.

c. Your staff will probably be upset about having to do their regular work, as well as train what may very well turn out to be their own replacements. Are you prepared for the upheaval if key members of your team start to leave?

d. What happens if the transition is not meeting your expectations? Can you back out?

e. When the outsourcing arrangement comes to an end, regardless of the reason, the outsourcer may not be as responsive or eager to assist in transitioning those functions back to you or to another outsourcer.

These days there is an equally important factor: the political consideration.

The Political Consideration

Outsourcing when jobs are scarce is a very controversial idea: outsourcing *and* offshoring can be downright dangerous. Backlash against companies sending domestic jobs overseas is often visible and embarrassing; be aware that even *investigating* the idea of offshoring can be politically sensitive.

Conclusion

As you can see, digging into this topic is not easy and can take some time. It's not unheard of for large outsourcing deals to take 6 to 12 months or longer to be evaluated and put in place. However, armed with all this information, you should be able to start doing a benefits analysis to determine if outsourcing makes sense and what the risks and benefits are. Of course, it's unlikely you'll be deciding this alone. You can expect your management to be involved, as well as Legal, Finance, HR, and, as mentioned at the very beginning, the users.

Remember, outsourcing generally doesn't eliminate headaches, it often only swaps one type of headache for another. Instead of the headaches of managing that function directly, you now have the headache of managing the outsourcer—to say nothing of handling the negative PR.

6.8 Further References

Websites

www.aicpa.org (American Institute of Certified Public Accounts).
www.fasb.org (Financial Accounting Standards Board).
www.megameeting.com (Web conferencing solution).
www.microsoft.com/livemeeting (Web conferencing solution).
www.polycom.com (videoconferencing solution).
www.tandberg.com (videoconferencing solution).
www.webex.com (Web conferencing solution).

Books and Articles

Barrow, C., 2008. Practical Financial Management: A Guide to Budgets. Kogan Page, Balance Sheets and Business Finance.
Beulen, E., Ribbers, P., Roos, J., 2010. Managing IT Outsourcing. Routledge.
Bulkeley, B., 2011. The Budget Conversation. CIO Magazine June 15.
Cone, E., 2009. Managing Through Tough Times. CIO Insight January/February.
Droms, W.G., Wright, J.O., 2010. Finance and Accounting for Nonfinancial Managers: All the Basics You Need to Know (Finance & Accounting for Nonfinancial Managers). Basic Books.
Garland, P., 2011. The CIO Imperative: Do More. Spend Less, Baseline Magazine July/August.
Hirschheim, R., Heinzl, A., Dibbern, J., 2009. Information Systems Outsourcing: Enduring Themes, Global Challenges, and Process Opportunities. Springer.
Kimball, G., 2010. Outsourcing Agreements: A Practical Guide. Oxford University Press.
Lewis, B., 2011. Outsourcing Debunked: What's real and what's baloney in IT's longest-running controversy. Amazon Digital Services.
Nash, K., 2009. The Complexity of Reduction. CIO Magazine April.
Perkins, B., 2009. Take Advantage of the Recession. Computerworld March 9.
Pratt, M.K., 2009. 5 Recession Survival Skills. Computerworld March 2.
Ramsden, P., 2010. Finance for Non-Financial Managers (Teach Yourself Business Skills). Hodder & Stoughton.
Rustad, M., 2010. Software Licensing: Principles and Practical Strategies. Oxford University Press.
Stedman, C., 2009. Hard Times Hard Decisions for IT. Computerworld March 9.
Tollen, D., 2011. The Tech Contracts Handbook: Software Licenses and Technology Services Agreements for Lawyers and Businesspeople. American Bar Association.

Getting Started with the Technical Environment

The most successful people are those who are good at Plan B.
James Yorke, Mathematician

CHAPTER TABLE OF CONTENTS

7.1 The Technical Environment..189
7.2 Understanding the User Environment 196
7.3 TCO and Asset Management: What Are They?...196
7.4 Standards 199
7.5 Technology Refreshing 201
7.6 Further References 202

In IT, it is too easy to be distracted by the exciting developments in hardware, security, networking, mobile devices, and apps. However, as a manager, you also have to keep your eyes on those areas that aren't quite as alluring. While activities like tracking your total cost of ownership (TCO) and inventorying your environment may be items you're tempted to put off, you must not do this. In fact, taking a formal inventory can be one of the activities that gives you an excellent understanding of what's in your environment, and how it operates—and is particularly valuable if your move to management came with a change in companies. A first-hand knowledge of the IT environment, its history, the users, and operation can help you to better define needs and future plans, as well as avoid repeating mistakes that were made in the past.

7.1 THE TECHNICAL ENVIRONMENT
What Do We Have Here?

You probably have more technology in your environment than you realize. And it can be very difficult to get a handle on it all. The value of carefully determining everything you are responsible for, however, cannot be overestimated. Not only does it help you figure out your role, but it helps you understand the amount of resources you have. In addition, an inventory gives you a sense of scale about the environment, and a feeling for whether resources are under- or overutilized—although you're likely to find it's a combination of both.

Completing an inventory not only provides you with a frame of reference for what you've become responsible for, but it is excellent information to include in a disaster recovery plan. (For more details on developing a disaster recovery plan, see **Chapter 9, Disaster Recovery** on **page 247**.)

Don't be surprised if the existing infrastructure documentation is out of date (or nonexistent), with the latest version in the minds of your staff. Your promotion is as good a reason as any for getting current with documentation.

Making sure there is a complete inventory can be a very valuable tool for a wide range of different projects. For example, when it's time to do budgeting, and you need to determine how much to budget for support and maintenance, a complete inventory can be very valuable. Similarly, when it's time to do something like an upgrade of an operating system, an inventory will let you see the range of hardware and applications you need to test it with.

Define Your Scope

In order to avoid being overwhelmed with information, you should start at the highest levels and work your way down to the detail you think you'll need. The level of detail you need as a manager varies and generally depends on the size of your organization and the size of your staff. As a manager, you probably don't need to be tracking nitty-gritty inventory details like serial numbers, firmware versions, room and rack locations, etc.—but you want to make sure that someone on your staff is doing that.

An excellent way to determine the scope of your inventory is to think about a disaster recovery scenario in which you have to bring the entire IT infrastructure up after a major failure (such as a fire, earthquake, or hurricane). If you can walk your way through the entire recovery scenario, then your scope is complete. If you find yourself guessing at some of the elements of your IT infrastructure, then your scope needs refinement.

In this situation, a picture can be worth a 1,000 words. Very often the easiest way to get a clear view of an environment is with a schematic diagram. Not only do they convey a great deal of information, but your technical staff will probably find a diagram easier to create (and maintain) than the equivalent material in text.

The Elements
Wide Area Network (WAN) Environment

A typical WAN schematic (see Figure 7.1) includes site locations, types of connections (VPN, leased-line, MPLS, frame relay, Internet), backup communication facilities, carriers, bandwidth, firewalls, DMZs, etc. You may also want to include types and number of servers, number of users, IP addressing, key contacts, and street addresses. In many cases, you may have connections to third parties such as service providers (e.g., payroll) or partners (e.g., suppliers or distributors). Not only do you want to make note of the connections, but you probably want to indicate who is primarily responsible for the connections and the hardware: sometimes you are, sometimes the third party is.

The WAN schematic should be updated regularly and distributed to members of the IT department. It should be posted on the wall of the data center for easy reference. The network manager should have it posted by his desk. It takes work to create one of these, and more work to keep it current. But it is an invaluable aid to the entire department. If you do not have one, go make one. Many network management tools have features to help you generate a WAN diagram.

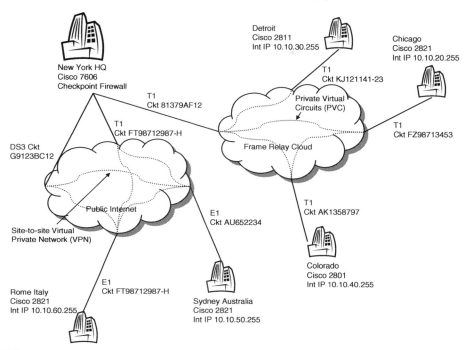

FIGURE 7.1

Example of a WAN schematic.

Local Area Network (LAN) Environment

The LAN schematic is the next level of detail. A typical LAN schematic (Figure 7.2) drills down into some of the detail of a particular site. It should include the topology, location, and connectivity of switches, and routers. It should identify different types of cabling (copper, fiber). It can also include room locations for various network equipment, model numbers for key components, IP addresses, wireless capabilities and so on. Like the WAN schematic, the LAN schematic should be regularly updated so that it is always current, and distributed widely so it is available for easy reference to all who need it.

If your responsibility includes the phone system, it may also be appropriate to include information about the voice environment on the LAN schematic, especially if you're using VOIP. This data will include information about the switch, the voice-mail environment, trunks, and so on.

Carrier Connections

The carrier connections inventory goes into the details of the WAN connections that were defined in the WAN and LAN schematics. Items to track here include circuit numbers, circuit endpoints (including building and room numbers), carriers, type/speed of line (T-1, analog, ISDN, etc.), and phone numbers for reporting problems. Although telecommunications in the United States is very reliable, problems

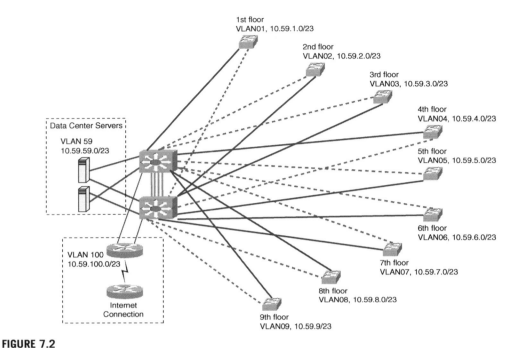

FIGURE 7.2

Example of a LAN schematic.

still come up. When a line goes down, you don't want to find yourself asking, "Which line?" and scrambling to find the circuit number or who you have to call to report the problem.

In larger environments, there are so many lines and so much activity with regards to adding, changing, and canceling them, it is quite easy to lose track. It is not unheard of for large IT environments to discover that they've been paying the bill on a line that they didn't know they had, and had stopped using years ago.

Server and Storage Environment

The documentation for the server environment drills down further and starts to give insight into how the applications work. In many cases, you may not be able to get all the detail you need into a single diagram. For example, you may find that you need one diagram just to indicate the basics, and others to talk about how key architectures (e-mail, active directory, storage area networks, etc.) are set up (e.g., indications of flow of data, like inbound and outbound mail, or servers that are operating in a cluster, etc.).

The documentation should also include which servers have Virtual Machine (VM) environments and some information about them. Of course, since VMs can be created, moved, and removed so easily, the value of detailed documentation for them could be short-lived, and it may be better to just refer to the information available from the VM management tools.

Mobile Equipment

Because mobile devices are so frequently purchased, lost, stolen, and replaced, this is a challenging list to compile and keep current if ever there was one—challenging, but important. The replacement costs in dollars aren't always high, but the security and manpower costs can be large. Spend some time now to save yourself a lot of heartache later.

Sample items to track include:

- Cell phones (company-owned ones only—you'll raise eyebrows by asking about personal ones)
- Netbooks, laptops, etc.
- Tablets

Information here should include carrier, model, OS, and so on. Tracking mobile devices can be very difficult. Some of the carriers and vendors have reports and tools to help, and some third-party vendors are also starting to provide offerings. Some mobile devices now come with (or you can easily install) tracking capabilities.

Workstations

Keeping track of workstations can be an enormous headache because there are so many of them and there is a lot of activity with regards to refreshing, upgrading, and physical movement. As a manager, you should really be keeping track of only summary information (and leaving the details of the inventory to your staff and automated tools). Important summary information can include:

- Device make and model
- OS platform and version (Mac, Windows, Unix)
- Date acquired
- Configuration (processor, RAM, disk space)

You may also want this information broken down by department or location.

An often-forgotten portion of the total number of workstations are the ones that are remote: users who travel, users who have company equipment at home, etc. These often fall into the out-of-sight, out-of-mind category. It is important that these devices be treated like any other company workstation so that they can be tracked, maintained, and updated properly. And when an employee leaves the company, you can expect HR to ask IT if that employee has any computer equipment at home. Some asset management tools can track when a device last connected to the network. If a device hasn't connected in an extended period of time, it can mean the device has been lost or stolen, or perhaps just isn't in use and can be repurposed for use elsewhere in the organization.

Application and Software Inventory

We've suggested diagrams for getting an understanding of some of the components of the infrastructure environment. For the applications, it may be best to resort to a good old-fashioned list (although for complex applications with lots of data flowing in and out, a diagram can be very helpful).

When thinking of applications, we generally think of the big business applications (such as supply chain, HRIS, payroll, accounting, e-mail, etc.) But as long as you're developing an inventory, you should also include all the tools in use—application development tools, desktop tools (e.g., word processing, Internet browsers, etc.), infrastructure tools (e.g., backup and monitoring, etc.).

An application inventory can include items such as:

- Application name
- Brief description
- User community (departments, number of users)
- Current version number
- Vendor
- Number of licenses purchased
- Terms of support and maintenance agreement
- Database environment
- OS environment
- Integration to other applications
- Support/maintenance arrangements in place (and expiration)
- Whether the application is considered critical
- What server(s) the application runs on
- What IT team is responsible for support
- Where to find a copy of the current version
- Installation information
- Special considerations
- Special backup requirements
- Peak periods of use
- Executive usage
- Who needs to be notified when scheduling downtime, or when there's an unexpected outage

Vendors

You're going to deal with lots of vendors, and each will have several contacts for sales, billing, technical support, and so on. It's important to keep track of who you're dealing with and any special arrangements you have. Some vendors you'll call so often that you'll be exchanging stories about vacations. For others, like vendors of legacy environments that you speak with only once a year or so, this inventory will be very helpful.

This vendor inventory should also include information about your support arrangements with the vendor. When there's a problem you should know immediately where to turn to find out how to call for service, including phone number and account number, and what levels of coverage you're entitled to, when your support contract expires, etc.

It is particularly important that the information be current and available to all who need it. You don't want to wait until there's a component failure to learn that the support provider's phone number changed, or that your contract expired.

Tools for Tracking the Technical Environment

There are a variety of tools out there that can you help you (and your team) track what's in your environment. Hardware vendors in particular have tools available to help you track and manage their devices. In some cases, the tools will also integrate with other vendors' products. Some tools can track and inventory, some can do management and alerting, others will do configuration management.

Many software vendors market management tools to integrate with products from a broad spectrum of hardware vendors:

- Cisco
- Hewlett-Packard
- Dell
- IBM
- Symantec
- Microsoft
- LANDesk
- NetSupport
- Absolute Software
- Computer Associates
- JAMF Software
- Remedy
- Sunflower Systems

The cost and licensing of these tools can vary widely. Sometimes, the product (or a "lite" version) may be included when you buy the vendor's hardware. In certain cases they may have to be licensed on a per-seat or per-device basis. Some of these tools for gathering information about the environment are stand-alone and others are part of larger suites. Many of these tools can integrate with some of the others, some tools are more proprietary.

Most of these are really designed for your staff to use, but they can be a great start for assembling the information you need. You probably won't find the exact tools to assemble the information together in the exact format you'd like (particularly those schematics), but you can use tools like Microsoft Excel, Access, PowerPoint, and Visio for massaging and diagramming.

Oftentimes (e.g., the vendor list or application and software inventory mentioned in the previous sections), the best route may be developing your own simple tool for doing it. Whether a small spreadsheet or database, it may prove to be the best, quickest, and cheapest way, and allows you to set it up exactly as you need it.

The Value of Good Infrastructure Documentation

The documentation about the environment should be in a very readable format. The use of diagrams, charts, schematics, and so on is very effective. Infrastructure documentation should be updated and available to all (ideally in a shared directory on a server, or better yet, your IT intranet). Although this type of documentation is considered valuable, many environments don't have it because IT workers often have little interest in creating documentation. However, not only is the documentation important, but the process of having your staff collect the information and create the documentation can be of value in itself. Naturally, you should work toward making the process of collecting this information as efficient and as natural to your organization as possible.

In addition to putting them on your intranet or a shared drive, there will be other valuable places for them. Hard copies (at home and the office) can come in handy for disaster recovery; your engineers will probably appreciate some of the schematics being posted in the computer room. Your Help Desk staff may value some of the information being posted on their cubicle walls for immediate reference.

Show your staff that you use it and rely on it. Use the materials in your memos and presentations to corporate management. And when your staff is discussing various plans and issues with you, bring out the documentation and refer to it. Ask them to explain what they're talking about using the documentation they've given you.

What You May Find

An inventory can uncover under- or overutilized resources, potential problem and risk areas, and resources and facilities that were assumed to be working but may not be. It may uncover technology that is outdated and no longer needed, or that needs to be upgraded. Or it may uncover resources providing similar or identical functionality that can be combined. It can also help you to feel comfortable that your staff has a good perspective on their environment.

7.2 UNDERSTANDING THE USER ENVIRONMENT

One of the recurring themes in this book is the importance of understanding who your users are, what they need, and what are they doing that could impact or benefit you. We discuss these issues in detail in other parts of the book:

- The section **"The First 100 Days"** on **page 20** in **Chapter 1, The Role of an IT Manager,** explained that you need to determine who the members of your team are and who your customers are; and that there are different user areas that will require your attention, and different user areas whose attention you require.
- The section **"People to Meet and Know"** on **page 24** in **Chapter 1, The Role of an IT Manager,** identifies many people you should establish relationships with, including your staff, your peers, and your boss, but it doesn't end there.
- As discussed in the section **"Communicate with Your Team"** on **page 32** in **Chapter 2, Managing Your IT Team,** communicate your vision for the department to your staff. They should understand both where you want the department to go and the plans you have for getting there.
- Users of different generations may have different priorities, styles, and preferred ways of dealing with others, which is discussed in the section **"Generational Issues at Work"** in **Chapter 2, Managing your IT Team** on **page 57**.
- All of **Chapter 10, Working with Users,** on **page 263,** is devoted to the relationship you and your team have with the user community, and why it is one of the most important relationships you will have to maintain.

7.3 TCO AND ASSET MANAGEMENT: WHAT ARE THEY?

Two phrases that have garnered a lot of attention for IT managers over the past few years are asset management and total cost of ownership (TCO). Many people use these phrases synonymously; although they are similar, they are not identical.

Both of these phrases are most often used in reference to laptops and desktops. IT people certainly realize that with a population of several hundred or several thousand desktop computers in a company, it takes an enormous amount of resources to support, manage, and track them. On the one hand, there are many hidden costs associated with these devices, their use, and their support. On the other hand, there can be significant savings in effectively managing these devices.

Although TCO and asset management are most frequently used in conjunction with devices like desktops and laptops, the concepts are readily applicable to other equipment types, like servers and network gear, as well as software applications.

Total Cost of Ownership

Total cost of ownership is a term used for the sum of all the costs associated with a computer, in addition to the obvious costs of hardware and software. There are many published studies about the true cost of a personal computer; annual TCO figures range from $3,000 to $12,000. There is endless debate about the true number, and of course, the figure can vary significantly from company to company.

The discussions around TCO are usually very controversial. Although it can be easy to total the hard costs of the hardware and software, the softer costs are much more difficult to calculate.

In addition to the cost of the hardware and software, items that factor into the TCO include:

- Cost of support (staff, consultants, vendors)
- Network facilities (servers, applications, cabling, routers, hubs, etc.)
- Training
- Administrative (purchasing, inventory, auditing, etc.)
- Money costs (capital, depreciation, etc.)

Some analyses have taken TCO to a very detailed level and have included:

- Consumables (toner, paper, etc.)
- Wasted user time (surfing the Web, looking at their Facebook page, playing games, and tweaking settings of fonts, colors, screen savers, etc.— referred to as "futzing" among those who study TCO)
- Downtime from problems like viruses, crashes, etc.
- Coworkers' time (when user A has to stop doing his job because user B asks him a question)

Calculating the TCO

At some point, someone may ask you about your organization's TCO. Calculating it is not for the faint of heart.

First, you have to calculate the current TCO—if you don't, you'll never know if the cost was reduced. Capturing these costs isn't easy because you frequently have to make assumptions, define rules-of-thumb, and do some educated guessing. For example, if your Help Desk also takes calls about problems with the phone system, you may need to subtract that portion of their time for calculating the support costs for your computers.

Once you know what the costs are, and what they are being spent on, you have to evaluate which ones can be reduced, and how much effort is required to reduce them, and ironically, how much it costs to reduce those costs. For example, you may be able to reduce the hardware costs by negotiating better pricing, or finding a new vendor. You may be able to reduce Help Desk costs by providing better training for the users—but how much will that additional training cost?

Once you've decided where you want to reduce costs, and the steps to do so, you then have to implement them. But things are seldom as simple as they seem. You may find that the new hardware vendor's equipment is cheaper, but the quality isn't as good, necessitating a lot of returns and calls for service and repair. Or, it turns out that you can't get users to show up for the training classes because they are busy with other activities.

After doing all that, you now have to go back and remeasure your TCO. Having done it once, it should be easier the second time. The most important consideration is to be sure to measure it using the same sets of assumptions, educated guesses, and rules-of-thumb that you used the first time—otherwise, you're not comparing apples with apples.

The whole TCO process can be quite arduous and tedious and easily take a year. However, the findings can be eye-opening. There are many consultants willing to help you with the process, of course. How these consultants' fees enter into the TCO equation (not to mention the cost of your time on the project) also raises some interesting discussions.

The important thing to take away from this is that there are a lot of costs and factors associated with information technology. As such, there are opportunities for tremendous savings by managing these costs well—enter asset management.

Asset Management

With all the cost variables mentioned in the previous discussion of TCO, it is critical for an IT Manager to keep a careful watch on costs. If TCO is the costs associated with computers, then asset management refers to what you do to keep those costs down. These actions can include everything from policies and procedures to technology issues. Like TCO, asset management usually focuses on desktop and laptops. However, many of the same principles can be used with other resources. Some of the most popular asset management techniques include the following:

- Maintaining hardware and software standards. The fewer the number of technology products in your environment, the easier it will be to support, maintain, and administer, although this is becoming increasingly more difficult to do for handheld devices.
- Outsourcing functions that can be done less expensively, or more effectively, to others.
- Using tools to automate manual and repetitive procedures.
- Investing in software distribution tools so that the technical staff doesn't have to visit each workstation to deploy software and/or upgrades.
- Employing disk cloning technology so that newly purchased computers don't have to be loaded manually with software.
- Proactively checking for problems (e.g., virus checking, system monitoring, etc.) and performing preventive maintenance (e.g., disk defragmenting).
- Having your hardware reseller preload your standard disk image on your workstations when they ship, so that they can be deployed to users right out of the box.
- Using inventory tracking software.
- Implementing restrictions so that users can't change system configurations and cause adverse impacts.
- Proactively deciding on upgrades, and replacements, as opposed to waiting for the unit to fail (or the vendor to discontinue support).
- Defining and setting appropriate hardware and software defaults.
- Providing support personnel with resources (training, reference materials, vendors' support agreements, etc.) to help them do their jobs.

- Tracking software usage (frequently referred to as license metering) to ensure that you're not paying for more licenses than you need, nor risking being under-licensed.
- Performing upgrades only when they are deemed necessary and worthwhile, and you've tested them to be reliable, instead of installing them every time the vendor releases one.

As you can see, most of these techniques and ideas are designed to reduce the demands on the support staff and the number of interruptions that users encounter. This is because the most expensive factor related to desktop computers is the *labor*—whether it's the cost of the support team, or the cost of the users' time when system problems prevent them from working.

Of course, if you're going to be implementing asset management techniques to reduce your TCO, you'll want to know if you're having any success or not. Most of the asset management techniques listed earlier have an implementation cost, either in terms of hardware/software or staff time, and so on. At some point you'll have to make some value judgments to decide which to implement, figuring out which might be the most worthwhile for your needs for the least cost. See the section **"Software Management Techniques"** in **Chapter 5, Software, Operating Systems, and Enterprise Applications**, on **page 142** for additional discussion.

7.4 STANDARDS

One of the classic jokes in this industry is the IT manager who says "yes, we're a firm believer in standardizing, that's why we have so many different standards."

The benefit of standardizing on your technology is many-fold. It eases the support burden if there are fewer products for the technicians to know all the idiosyncrasies of. It also means that you don't have to keep spares for as many product types. For devices like printers, it means your inventory of consumables is simplified. And, it eases things for your procurement team and shortens your vendor list. Those features can lead to shorter delivery times and better opportunities for volume discounts.

As the discussion in the next section will show, there has to be some flexibility in standards, particularly where users are concerned. And it is important to periodically review standards—perhaps annually—to address changing costs, vendor offerings, requirements, industry directions, etc.

Issues That Users Care About

When personal computing technology first started to become popular, it was quite common for organizational users to ask for specific products like an "IBM Model 80," a "Pentium processor," or a "laser printer."

Perhaps because of the ubiquity of technology, or the difficulty in keeping with the constant stream of new products and technologies, those days have faded. Technology that users can see has changed so quickly that users are now much less specific about what they ask for. There are so many new products coming out so quickly, it takes a professional (that is, someone in IT like you) to keep up.

That's not to say that users are completely uninterested in what they use. While users are less interested in the specific processor in the laptop, they may be very interested in the make, model, and operating system of their handheld devices. Of course performance is an issue, but it is not uncommon for end users to be more concerned about things that may or may not impact performance, and are often related to "technology envy"—the phenomenon of making sure your technology keeps-up-with-the-Joneses (or coworkers). Similarly, issues related to how the product impacts their daily life, as opposed to pure performance, are also important to users.

Items that fall into these categories include:

- Cordless mice and keyboards (to eliminate some wires)
- The coolest looking cell phone/handheld/tablet device (regardless of its capabilities)
- Monitor size
- The lightest and smallest laptops (for ease of travel)
- Tower units to go under the desk (so that the valuable desk real estate is not taken up)
- Desktop units (so that users don't keep banging their knees)
- Privacy and antiglare screens (especially in cubicle farms)
- Leather laptop carrying case vs. canvas
- Preference for devices in certain colors

For situations like these, IT can have standards and still provide some flexibility for the users. For example, instead of insisting that all users use the exact same model laptop, two choices can be made available. One option can be relatively small and light, easy to carry, and functional enough for the user who just wants to do e-mail, word processing, spreadsheets, etc. when traveling; the alternative is larger with a bigger screen and keyboard for those who prefer it.

For issues like ergonomic devices and anti-glare screens, the IT department should readily provide whatever the user asks for. No one wants an employee going to the HR department complaining of carpal-tunnel syndrome or eye strain because IT's standards prohibit these relief-offering devices.

Regardless of the standards you set, you can count on exceptions as a fact of life. No matter how carefully you selected your standards, it's only a matter of time before some executive asks for something that isn't a standard. Rank has its privilege, and it would be pretty unwise for you to say no. (If you do, expect to hear from your boss informing you that he "reconsidered" your answer for you.) However, before you say no, you can certainly have a discussion with that executive, asking him what features of that device are attractive to him, and showing him that those same features are available on the device that is part of your standards. He may not care all that much because yours isn't as cool-looking as the one he wants. But, it's a small sacrifice to keep an executive happy—and customer service is what IT is all about.

Issues That IT Cares About

While IT needs to offer greater flexibility to accommodate the individual needs and preferences of users, it has greater latitude in defining the technical standards that are generally beyond a user's interest or concern.

Because technology products have a limited life span (generally 5 years or less), and product offerings are changing so fast, it's unlikely you'll ever have a 100 percent standardized environment. But that doesn't mean you should just throw in the towel. In fact, the opposite is true: this is an important issue that you will be working on continuously.

IT should standardize on:

- **Hardware configurations (memory, disk, etc.).** Most of these items are now pretty modest in cost. Choose configurations that should last the life of the machine. The cost of an additional 1 GB of RAM is miniscule compared with the effort to do an upgrade after the fact (order, receive, payment, installation, interruption to user, etc.).

- **Operating system and application software (vendor and version).** The more consistency in your software set the greater the chances of full compatibility of files among users, and the easier the support and training burden is on your staff.
- **Software configuration (options, settings, directory and menu location, etc.).** It's not uncommon for application software to have over a hundred various settings (e.g., where to store files, how often to do an automatic backup). Users are unlikely to ever know about these, and less likely to deal with them. Let IT set standards so that software operates identically for all users. Again, it will pay dividends in the future in terms of support effort.

Standards for IT

In addition to technology put into the hands of the users, there are technology products that users are unlikely to ever see (although they may hear them referenced by IT). These include products like servers, routers, switches, storage solutions, gateways, and network operating systems.

IT'ers may have strong feelings about certain products in these categories, but they are unlikely to be swayed by secondary issues such as color or packaging. Perhaps that's because IT'ers deal with so much technology that some issues are unimportant while others are paramount. Nontechnical people are often surprised by the IT department's standards for using technological products, but they forget that people in IT not only have a deeper understanding of the core technology of the product, they generally have a longer history with the issue in general. IT people know what it means to purchase and install a new product from Microsoft versus one from a startup; the startup's product may have many more bells and whistles, but will the young company offer tech support, volume discounts, maintenance upgrades—and will it even be around two years from now? Is the product stable? And how well does that startup's product integrate with everything else in the environment?

It is generally easier to define these behind-the-scenes standards by finding agreement among some of your more senior engineers. If you have consensus at the top, the rest of the team will probably go along easily. Some may disagree (making a case that choice-X is a far better solution than choice-Y), but unless they feel quite strongly about it, they will readily participate in adopting uniform standards.

And, just like workstations for the users, infrastructure technology should have standards for configuration, setup, etc. In an environment that has a large volume of servers, for example, engineers should not have to hunt for the location of log files. They should know that all servers are set up identically (including naming conventions) so that when there is a problem, they can spend their time examining the log file, not looking for it. A comparable analogy can be applied to virtually all technology platforms and makes the case for standardization pretty evident.

7.5 TECHNOLOGY REFRESHING

Different types of technologies have different lifetime expectations. Workstations may have a useful life of 3 to 4 years, as do servers. Networking equipment, like switches and routers, may easily last 5 years, printers may last even longer. On the other hand, laptops and handheld devices are on the shorter end of the spectrum simply because they physically take more abuse, are subject to being lost or stolen, and the technology for these products is still evolving rapidly.

Some organizations may set defined refresh cycles, while others may choose to use things until they simply won't operate any more.

Deciding which path to take depends on a few factors:

- **The cost of vendor warranties after a certain point.** A new server may come with a three-year warranty and service contract, but getting a contract for a four-year-old server may be cost prohibitive. To make this decision, you have to factor in how critical the device is to the environment as well as the cost of the service contract compared to the cost of a new device.
- **How easy it is to replace a device that fails.** If a printer fails, it's generally not that difficult to press another one into service. Replacing a server could require considerable effort and (down)time before the new one is up and running.
- **How Accounting depreciates IT assets.** Length of depreciation policies vary from company to company; work with your Accounting department to determine what these particular procedures are.
- **How your company views IT spending.** Some organizations see IT as critical and strategic to their operation and fully endorse having it remain current. Other organizations see IT spending as merely a cost of doing business (like paying the electric bill), or a necessary evil. See **Chapter 6, Managing the Money** on **page 161** for more information on the topics of IT spending and asset depreciation.

The most common point for refreshing a piece of technology often comes when the organization can no longer bear the cost of the existing technology:

- Vendor support is unavailable, or cost prohibitive.
- The technology is no longer meeting your needs.
- The technology presents risks to the environment (reliability, security, etc.).
- The technology is holding up other IT projects (e.g., the latest software from your database vendor won't run on your aged server).

As you can see, the costs are not always dollars and cents. It will be your job to assess these costs and move to refresh the technology *before* the cost of not refreshing becomes too high.

7.6 Further References

Websites
www.altiris.com (technology management solution vendor).
www.ca.com (technology management solution vendor).
www.cisco.com (technology management solution vendor).
www.dell.com (technology management solution vendor).
www.hp.com (technology management solution vendor).
www.ibm.com (technology management solution vendor).
www.intel.com/standards/execqa/qa0904.htm (Craig Barrett on the Importance of Global Standards).
www.ipswitch.com (technology management solution vendor).
www.landesk.com (technology management solution vendor).
www.microsoft.com (technology management solution vendor).
www.netiq.com (technology management solution vendor).
www.netsupport-inc.com (technology management solution vendor).
www.novell.com (technology management solution vendor).
www.opsware.com (technology management solution vendor).

www.peregrine.com (technology management solution vendor).
www.remedy.com (technology management solution vendor).
www.sunflowersystems.com (technology management solution vendor).

Books and Articles

Bansal, S., 2009. Technology Scorecards: Aligning IT Investments with Business Performance. Wiley.

Hasselman, C., 2011. Value Driven Enterprise Architecture. CreateSpace.

High, P.A., 2009. World Class IT: Why Businesses Succeed When IT Triumphs. Wiley Press/Jossey-Bass.

Meyers, M., 2009. CompTIA Network + Guide to Managing and Troubleshooting Networks. McGraw-Hill.

Shane, S.A., 2008. Technology Strategy for Managers and Entrepreneurs. Prentice Hall.

Turban, E., Volonino, L., 2011. Information Technology for Management: Improving Strategic and Operational Performance. Wiley.

Security and Compliance

8

If you don't like their rules, whose would you use?
Charlie Brown

CHAPTER TABLE OF CONTENTS

8.1 **How We Got Here** 206
8.2 **Managing Security** 209
8.3 **Security Solutions and Technologies** 214
8.4 **Types of Threats**...224
8.5 **Compliance and IT**...226
8.6 **The Rules**..227
8.7 **How to Comply with the Rules** 234
8.8 **Hidden Benefits of Compliance**..237
8.9 **Methodologies and Frameworks** 238
8.10 **It's Not Just Regulatory Compliance**...242
8.11 **Further References** 244

(In)security is everywhere. Security is a critical component of an IT Manager's life. Almost every decision he makes will have to be evaluated at some point for its security implications. Hiring a new programmer? How much access should that person have? Installing a new server? Who is allowed to access it? Making sure that authorized people have the access they need (and *only* the access they need), along with making sure unauthorized people are blocked from access, has become one of the many security-related themes of IT.

If confidential e-mails about unannounced merger or acquisition plans are posted on the Internet, a lot of yelling happens. But security problems do not just cause embarrassing situations. If a database with credit card and bank account information is hacked, or a laptop with employee information is lost, then there are various laws and regulations you have to deal with (particularly related to notification). You don't want your CEO furiously knocking at your door, but you *really* don't want law enforcement coming to see you.

And don't ignore the costs of exposures. In 2011, the Ponemon Institute released the results of its sixth annual survey, which showed that the average organization cost of a data breach was $7.2 million, or $214 per compromised record. The study also found that negligence was the most common cause of a security breach (41%), and another 31percent caused by malicious or criminal attacks (source www .ponemon.org/blog/post/cost-of-a-data-breach-climbs-higher).

It seems like major security breaches are a daily occurrence: Sony, RSA, Honda, the U.S. Defense Department, and so on; losses from the events number well into the billions. The costs to repair these lapses in manpower alone are staggering, let alone the price of damaged reputations, data loss, business intelligence, national security issues, etc.

The topic of computer security has grown so large and complex that a single chapter can't begin to do justice to the topic. Security concerns are now so widespread that it's essentially an industry within an industry, with its own training classes, trade journals, certifications, job definitions, books, webinars, and so on devoted to addressing the issue.

As a result, the primary goal of this chapter is to provide you with a framework to think about security, to outline the issues, and to point you to places where you can get more information.

8.1 HOW WE GOT HERE

It is well understood in the technology community that in the 1980s, but especially in the 1990s, the push was to connect everything and everybody. One of the original goals of Java was to create an operating system so basic it would allow, famously, your toaster to talk to your computer.

Well, with handhelds, social networking, wireless, and countless ways to exchange and share data, it's safe to say that almost all that connectivity has been achieved. But it has come at a giant price. Little or no thought was given back then to the consequences of allowing all those computers to connect to each other. International and domestic groups of hackers with less-than-ideal motives have joined communities, entered networks, and caused serious computer havoc all over the planet. The main challenge was once how to share things electronically. The main challenge now is how to keep everything safe—how to keep your data, your networks, and your company secure.

Get Perspective

First, don't be overwhelmed. Read this chapter to determine which issues you should start examining. Not every threat will affect you; if yours is a virtual company, for example, you may have a different set of security priorities and concerns than someone managing a traditional office setting.

The volume of threats, vulnerabilities, and risks is enormous. Even scarier is what we don't know. If you start thinking of all the ways your environment can be breached, you'll feel inundated and feel paralyzed. You need to take comfort in the fact that you're taking the right steps to best protect your environment. Remember, security protection is an ongoing and iterative process; you can never say, "Okay, it's done."

Second, read the section later in this chapter on **"Risk Analysis and Risk Management"** on **page 210** carefully. If it hasn't been done already, perform a risk analysis. Finally, read the section on **"The Rules"** on **page 227** in this chapter to help you understand what is expected in your industry, or required by different regulations. Lastly, read the sections, **"How to Comply with the Rules"** and **"Methodologies and Frameworks"** on **page 234** for ideas on ways to ensure best practices for compliance.

Computer Security Themes

Within the discussions of security, several themes appear again and again:

- Security versus privacy versus convenience
- Intention matters
- CIA (confidentiality, integrity, and availability)
- Look very closely—it may not be what it appears to be

Security versus Privacy versus Convenience

In security, the trade-off between privacy and security is a choice made all the time. Radio Frequency Identification (RFID) tags, for example, are an excellent example of this duality. RFID tags are small chips embedded in thousands—soon millions—of products.

These tags allow for the electronic identification of people, animals, and objects. A sweater you buy at the department store can carry an RFID tag, for example. With RFID tags, your entire shopping cart could be scanned in an instant at the checkout without having to remove every item to be scanned individually. This is already being done in supermarkets in Europe (news.cnet.com/Tesco-to-track-milk-deliveries-by-RFID/2100-1033_3-6079022.html?tag=lia;rcol).

However, as you go through your day, RFID scanners at other stores could also read those same tags. Perhaps these other stores do this to get a sense of whether you're a big spender or not, what your clothing sizes are, or what their competition is selling. The uses for RFID chips are multiplying at a dizzying rate.

Grocery store shopping lists are generally not held that close to the vest, but you might be surprised at what you value when it's taken away from you. During Super Bowl XXXV in Tampa, all attendees' faces were surreptitiously photographed; those photos were then scanned and compared with images in a police database of criminals and criminal suspects. Many people found news of that action profoundly disturbing because it was done without permission or notification.

The aftermath of the World Trade Center attacks implemented a lot of debate about this topic, as many people felt that some of the United States' actions and laws to help prevent a recurrence would sacrifice civil liberties and personal privacy.

The trade-off between security and convenience will only become more onerous. The long lines at security gates at airports are an excellent metaphor for modern life; you can no longer just walk up to the gate and board your plane. Nor can you just turn on your computer and start working. You need to enter a password (perhaps more than one) to a machine that may be locked to your desk. Now passwords are often six and 10 digits long and have to be changed frequently. If you require "complex" passwords (e.g., mixing upper- and lowercase, use of special characters, etc.) and those passwords can't be reused, your auditors will probably be thrilled. Finding an acceptable balance between security and convenience is one of the greatest challenges in IT security.

However, you may find that users end up writing their passwords on Post-It notes attached to monitors in order to remember them. Users complain mightily about issues like this, but the more educated they are about the risks the company faces and their role in mitigating these risks, the less they will protest. This issue is discussed throughout this chapter; in particular, see the section **"Action 4: Work with Users to Make Everyone More Secure"** on **page 212.**

Intention Matters

White and black hats, hacking, mis-configuration or mal-configuration, adware, spam, phishing, spoofing, and spyware are just some of the terms related to computer security, but one of the key points in any security discussion is what was the *intent* behind the event? The results can still be devastating regardless of intent, but knowing the original purpose can sometimes help solve the problem more quickly.

If your system has been breached by a malicious hacker, you need to take specific steps to address the problem. If your system is overwhelmed by adware, you also need to address the problem. In both cases, the entire system can come crashing down. But understanding that one event was the result of malicious intent, and the other may have been the result of innocent user activity can help determine the magnitude of the problem and how it's addressed so it does not recur.

CIA

The three basic tenets of information security are summarized with a classic acronym: CIA. It stands for confidentiality, integrity, and availability. Learning about information security means learning about "CIA."

- **Confidentiality** refers to keeping secret information secret. Techniques for keeping things secret include cryptography, access control, and others. You may be protecting customer data or files for next week's presentation to the board. In either case, you want to keep confidential material from getting disclosed accidentally or intentionally. In many cases, confidentially isn't only a professional/ethical obligation, but also a regulatory requirement.
- **Integrity** in information security means that data aren't altered, either intentionally or accidentally, without proper process and authority.
- **Availability** means the systems are running and usable as they are supposed to be.

The CIA model, adopted from the military, has its strengths and weaknesses. It is a place to start thinking about security, but it isn't the final answer. The Web is full of discussions about the pluses and minuses of the CIA security model.

Look Very Closely: It May Not Be What It Appears

Computer security now is often a matter of determining that one innocent-looking item—an e-mail, a log entry, or a file change—is actually a sign of something radically different.

- Phishing is e-mail with a well-disguised intent. If they haven't been already, you need to educate your users on how to behave when they receive those fake requests that look like legitimate queries for information from legitimate sources (like banks and financial websites), but aren't.
- See the sidebar called **Some Security Stories** on **page 225** later in this chapter for the story of how research into a $.75 accounting discrepancy led to the dismantling of an international hacking ring.
- Trojan horses and viruses are applications that appear to be something you want, but in reality they're just disguised files for malicious programs. Programs like these may be used for various things like capturing passwords, looking for (or creating) vulnerabilities on your network, or grabbing data from your servers.

- Social engineering is a technique for gathering confidential or privileged information by simply asking for it. Hackers have discovered that people have a general tendency to trust others; hackers can get users to reveal items such as passwords, or to do something that's essentially against policy, by simply phoning the user and pretending to be from tech support, for example.

If you manage the person in charge of security, or you are that person, a very close examination of the various elements of your system is required. You have to be able to tell quickly and often what is ordinary and what is even slightly out of the ordinary. See the section **"Types of Threats"** on **page 224** later in this chapter for more information on this.

8.2 MANAGING SECURITY

There are five actions that can serve as your guide to manage IT security:

- Action 1: Evaluate your environment's needs, exposures, and defenses.
- Action 2: Get upper level management buy-in.
- Action 3: Mitigate the risks.
- Action 4: Work with users to make everyone more secure.
- Action 5: Remember that security is an ongoing process.

Action 1: Evaluate Your Environment's Needs, Exposures, and Defenses

The first step in most security problems is to determine how much exposure and vulnerability you have.

Perform a Security Audit

In the world of computer security, determining your exposure and vulnerability is done by performing a computer security audit. An audit like this can range from having your network administrator regularly review logs, current levels of security patches, firewall settings, and policies to bringing in third-party security auditing companies and outside consultants. The latter is often the preferred method, because it eliminates any conflict of interest and built-in bias that could be associated with assessing your own environment. Most companies of any size will use outside firms to assess their security as a means of validation that the controls, policies, and technologies are working as the company had hoped and planned.

The magnitude of your commitment to a security audit depends on two things:

- How big your company is
- Which industry and which specific business your company is in

Naturally, a security audit for a garage-based start-up is going to take less time and money than one for a corporation with 25,000 employees. But the first point may not be *less important* than the second: In these days of intellectual property awareness, it isn't hard to imagine how valuable Google cofounders Larry Page and Sergey Brin's work was back when they were grad students just out of Stanford. And while no company wants to lose data, most would agree that losing sales figures for a small furniture company isn't as disastrous as data lost by some of the private companies doing war time security contracting for the government.

Regardless of size or industry, the first step you should take is to perform an audit. The goal of your audit should be to clearly determine the level of risk you are facing now and any potential exposures you can identify that you will face in the future.

Risk Analysis and Risk Management

Risk analysis is the process of identifying the security risks throughout your system and the potential loss for every threat that is identified. Risk management is the steps you take to address the risks identified as a result of your analysis. Most of this chapter is concerned with risk management; however, the next section discusses risk analysis.

Risk Analysis

There are two types of risk analysis: quantitative and qualitative. As their names imply, each approaches the same data in a different way.

- **Quantitative.** This method assigns numerical values to the amount of damage that would occur as well as the costs of prevention to any threats. Formulae include calculating the probability of a threat occurring and the likely loss should one occur. Despite the supposed mathematical rigor of this technique, subjective evaluations creep in.
- **Qualitative.** This method generates an analysis of the risks facing an organization and is based on experience, judgment, and intuition. While subjective by definition, efforts are made to make these analyses as objective as possible.

Regardless of which method you choose (or, if you have sufficient time and money, you choose both), know that there are many companies poised to help you conduct your analysis. As with every component of this chapter, individual companies have arisen that are devoted to even the smallest corner of the computer security world. The goal of a risk analysis is to provide a clear cost/benefit comparison. The cost of securing an item is compared with the risk of losing it.

Risk analysis is performed throughout corporate America, not only in the computer industry. It's a formal requirement of HIPAA, for example. (HIPAA is the Health Insurance Portability and Accountability Act of 1996—see more information regarding HIPAA on **page 228**). The final security rule of HIPAA requires covered entities to "conduct an accurate and thorough assessment of the potential risks and vulnerabilities to the confidentiality, integrity, and availability of electronic protected health information held by the covered entity." In addition, the rule states that the "required risk analysis is also a tool to allow flexibility for entities in meeting the requirements of this final rule..."

THREE COMMON WEAKNESSES I FIND AFTER I DO A SECURITY ASSESSMENT

When doing a security assessment, there are three major components that companies always suffer from:

#1 Weakness: Weak Internal Controls on People

Companies need stringent controls on their employees. That does *not* necessarily mean watching their every move, tracking their every keyboard stroke, or monitoring every website they go to—although it *can* mean that, depending on the organization.

What "internal controls on people" really means is careful authentication to control who/what/when and which particular people can access which information. Eighty percent of security breaches occur because of improperly screened people and poor internal controls.

Continued

THREE COMMON WEAKNESSES I FIND AFTER I DO A SECURITY ASSESSMENT—Cont'd

#2 Weakness: Mis-Configured (and Occasionally Mal-Configured) Devices

Most hardware devices, servers, routers, and desktops now come with security controls installed by default. However, these devices are often not configured properly, not patched properly, and not documented properly. Security is a 24/7/365 concern, not an "install-the-device-and-forget-about-it" type of activity.

#3 Weakness: Outside "Fingerprints"

As a computer security consultant, I am amazed that corporations don't take advantage of the large number of intrusion detection and intrusion prevention tools that are now available. Hackers are clearly studying these things, why aren't you using them?

—Mark Willoughby
Security Author and Consultant

Risk Analysis Tools

There are many risk analysis tool options, but here are links to two free methods from well-known sources (Carnegie Mellon and Microsoft):

- The Operationally Critical Threat, Asset, and Vulnerability Evaluation (OCTAVE) method. It's a complete, free, and thorough method. The method was developed by CERT at Carnegie Mellon University (www.cert.org/octave/methodintro.html) and is federally funded.
- Microsoft's Security Assessment Tool at www.securityguidance.com.

Risk Management

Once you've identified the risk using risk analysis, strategies for managing those risks can be defined. Common strategies for managing risk include:

- Mitigate the risk by implementing controls, procedures, technology solutions, etc.
- Transfer the risk, perhaps by sharing the risk with partners better able to deal with it.
- Accept the risk by recognizing that it exists, people are aware of it, and it is being watched.

Even if no immediate steps to deal with risk are taken after the risk analysis is done, just being aware of the risk can be a form of risk management as that knowledge is likely to influence future decisions.

Hire White Hats (to Manage the Threat of Black Hats)

In general, a hacker is someone who is interested in finding and exploiting security flaws of IT systems and networks. The industry has stolen a paradigm from old cowboy movies to identify the good guys and the bad guys as white-hat and black-hat hackers. Black-hat hackers are those you generally think of with the term "hacker"—they're interested in security flaws in order to take advantage and abuse them—usually for profit, but oftentimes just to see what trouble they can cause. However, white-hat hackers are interested in security flaws as a way of identifying how security can be improved and how systems can be better protected. White-hat hackers are sometimes called "ethical hackers." In 2011, the hacker group LulzSec claimed that its activities included hacking into the CIA, PBS, AT&T, and the Brazilian government's websites. The group said that its motivation, in part, is because these sorts of public attacks push websites to improve their security (www.cnn.com/2011/TECH/web/06/26/tech.lulzsec.hackers/).

Both white- and black-hat hackers have exceptional technical skills and are experts in operating systems, networks, etc. Many black-hat hackers become white-hat hackers when they realize that their skills should be put to use for good instead of evil. Sometimes, jail time or a fine helps them see the light.

Action 2: Get Upper Level Management Buy-In

Security is an issue that impacts every level and every facet of the organization. CEOs can have their core company data compromised and security guards can have their keys stolen and their offices broken into. Classically, a top-down approach works better: The security policies and procedures are better aligned with the company's overall direction. A bottom-up approach, where IT initiates the direction, will generally not be as successful. Many organizations identify an individual to function as the Chief Security Officer (CSO). Depending on the company and the industry, this role may exist within IT or may exist as part of the company's executive team. This individual may tackle issues related to physical security, computer security, IT policies, privacy, investigations, among others.

See the section **"Action 4: Work with Users to Make Everyone More Secure"** on **page 212** later in this chapter for ideas on how to get all employees in an organization to actively participate in making security a part of all corporate activity.

Action 3: Mitigate the Risks

Using the risk analysis process, you've identified certain exposures and vulnerabilities in the environment. Now you have to weigh those risks against the cost of mitigating them, along with navigating the trade-offs of security and privacy.

Some of the different technology solutions for reducing risks are discussed later in this chapter in the section **"Security Solutions and Technologies"** on **page 214.** However, many things can be addressed with simple solutions or procedural changes. For example:

- User education can go a long way: simple steps such as advising them on effective passwords or reminding them to log off when leaving for the night can be very useful. Defining company policies about security practice, safeguards, and guidelines provides additional emphasis.
- Policies to track security-related requests: asking users to submit written requests via e-mail, for example, for changes in security privileges (instead of a phone call to the network manager) is an effective tool.
- Carefully tracking all changes to the environment with a change request (CR) system.
- Periodic review of IDs and privileges, and disabling those that are no longer needed, should be a regular process.
- Being diligent about applying security patches and following vendor and industry best practices.
- Very prompt disabling of access when an employee leaves the company should become a standard practice in your department; ex-employees are a known source of security breaches. Many companies now cut off access the moment the employee is informed of their change in status. (See the section **"User Terminations"** on **page 216** for more detail.) In some organizations, employee accounts will be disabled automatically as soon as the employee's status changes in the payroll system.

Many of these items can be automated so that the manual processes, confirmations, and such can be minimized.

Action 4: Work with Users to Make Everyone More Secure

If they aren't aware of it yet (and many aren't), you must convince every person in your organization—for-profit or nonprofit—that computer and information security is *everyone's* job. It's a cliché to you—a computer system is only as secure as its weakest link—but to many other people, that statement counts as wisdom. You must take this message "to the masses."

Your users need to be made aware of security issues. For example, users should be aware of the security pros and cons associated with storing a file on the LAN versus on their local hard drive. They should be told how to password protect files that have sensitive information, and they should be aware of the risks of printing certain information to a shared printer.

Users should be in the habit of logging off at night or when they'll be away from their desk for an extended period of time—better yet, look to implement application time-outs, and screensavers, that automatically lock the screen or log out after a period of inactivity.

Finally—and often most commonly—users should be aware of the security risks associated with sending (or physically taking) company files to their home machines. All the effort you put in to safeguard the company's data can be superseded by an employee mailing themselves files to work from at home. This was a practice that was not even noticed a few years ago but is now a very large concern in today's very mobile and always connected environment.

Training Users

There are books, videos, consultants, and companies that can help you with this task. Like corporate safety, computer security has become an enormous industry in and of itself. Train users about passwords, locking their workstation when they step away, and logging off at the end of the day. Users must understand that security is not strictly about IT—your training should include topics such as notifying the security guard if they see a stranger wandering the halls unescorted, locking file cabinets and office doors, and using shredders for confidential documents. Also, don't overlook guidance and reminders about those purely innocent errors, such as leaving a confidential document in the copier or discussing sensitive information in a public area (like an elevator!). Most sales reps learn early never to discuss client names in public places regardless of how innocent the situation seems. However, non-sales people are often overheard talking about the challenges of dealing with Client X or Customer Y on subways, airplanes, etc.

Use these themes to regularly train your users in computer security. Security should be an ongoing theme in the IT department, and users need to understand it. Look to make it part of the new-hire orientation, as well as an ongoing program.

Be sure to consider generational factors when training your users, the younger generations may not take your concerns as seriously. A 2010 Accenture study and report found that Millennials are likely ignoring or violating your IT policies right and left, using non-standard applications and improvising where they think it makes sense. In addition, the Accenture study found that Millennials routinely bypass corporate approval when it comes to downloading and using technology (43 percent use non-supported instant messaging, and 31 percent rely on rogue open-source technologies). For more information about this issue, see the section **"Generational Issues at Work"** in **Chapter 2, Managing Your IT Team** on **page 57**.

Employee Impact

As mentioned earlier, in the computer security world, finding the right balance between privacy, security and convenience can be very difficult. Users need to be aware of the fact that their computer activity at work is monitored and that that monitoring is done for a variety of reasons, including security—their own security, not just the company's security.

Most companies have policy guides that indicate that company resources (such as the phone system and computers) are for corporate use only—even if some personal use is unofficially acceptable. The policies will often also indicate that the company has the right to monitor usage.

The explosion in the use of smart phones—it is the rare person in the corporate world who does not have one nowadays—has caused this line to be blurred. What are personal phones, what are company phones, what are personal calls on company phones, what is company usage on private phones? If anyone asks you—and they probably will—the cleanest solution is to have individuals carry two phones. It sounds ridiculous but is not that rare. (It is not the occasional personal phone call or the checking-e-mail-while-on-vacation situation; it is the regular habit that causes problems for both parties.) But many organizations have adopted more liberal approaches, especially those with a Bring-Your-Own (BYO) program (see **Chapter 11, Connectivity: Social Media, Handhelds, and More**, on **page 287**).

Use Care When Surfing

Make your users aware that today's computing world is a complex network that requires a more conscientious and careful computer user. Of course it's certainly possible to accidentally go to an inappropriate website—we have all mistyped an address and found ourselves on a very different page from what we were expecting. But repeated travels to those sites will be noticed and acted upon. (See the section **"Intention Matters"** on **page 208** in this chapter.)

Action 5: Remember That Security Is an Ongoing Process

You'll never be able to say: "Okay, we're done, the environment is secure." Security should be looked at as an ongoing, iterative process. The IT staff should always be on the lookout for ways to improve security. Audits and compliance activities should be viewed as welcome opportunities for continuous reviews of security.

8.3 SECURITY SOLUTIONS AND TECHNOLOGIES

With entire volumes dedicated to the subject of computer security technologies, a single chapter in an IT book that focuses on the business issues (and not the details of technologies) cannot do it appropriate justice. However, there are some basics you should be familiar with.

Tracking and Controlling Access

Carefully control and monitor who goes in and who goes out of your systems: who enters your systems, what they do there, and when they leave, as well as who enters your facilities and who and when they exit it.

Control Access

A critical component of controlling access is to follow the Rule of Least Privilege: users should only be granted the least amount of access to the system, and for the least amount of time necessary, as is authorized and required for their job. More access and longer access time allow for more potential problems. Firewalls, access control lists, and other security measures can authenticate users to authorized areas of networks without taking large risks and without spending a lot of money and time.

The rule originated in the *Orange Book* (part of the Rainbow series of Department of Defense books on computer security written in the early 1980s) and is officially defined as follows: "Least Privilege—this principle requires that each subject in a system be granted the most restrictive set of privileges (or lowest clearance) needed for the performance of authorized tasks. The application of this principle limits the damage that can result from accident, error, or unauthorized use" (csrc.nist.gov/publications/history/dod85.pdf).

The previous method of controlling access was called the "M&M model": the idea was to make your system "hard on the outside and soft in the middle." That model is being replaced by "de-perimeterization" techniques, which make your systems secure *throughout*.

One method of achieving security throughout your system is to implement secure zones. A University of California information security site defines secure zones as "a combination of policies, procedures, and technical tools and techniques that enables an organization to discreetly protect its own information assets. It's a logical and physical environment with strong visible management support in which access privileges to all information assets are clearly defined and followed without exception."

Tracking Activity

A variety of methods can be used to track activity:

* System log files
* Monitoring programs
* Network mapping tools
* Physical access

System Log Files

Almost every technology solution (both hardware and software) generates log files of activities. The level of detail that can be captured can vary tremendously from one product to another and is often configurable by administrators. Servers, desktops, business applications, operating systems, network hardware, and monitoring and management utilities—all have log files. Log files can indicate who did what, at what time, on which device, and from where. Log files can be used for basic troubleshooting or to investigate security issues. These files can be examined and monitored to track user activities.

Log files can be so voluminous that some vendors have utilities to allow for proactive monitoring of them so that pre-defined event types trigger certain types of alerts and actions.

Monitoring Programs

Similar to log files, tools exist that allow you to track all the activity of your network. In addition to the old standard of tracking sites visited, you can now monitor programs used and keystrokes typed. One example of this is a packet sniffer. A packet sniffer is a software package that can examine the data traffic on a network. Typically, a sniffer is used to troubleshoot and isolate network problems.

However, it can also be used when investigating security issues. For example, a packet sniffer can be used to "trap" data to and from a particular device or can be used to look for particular content.

Network Mapping Tools

In larger environments, it can be a daunting task just to be aware of everything on the network. While the server side may stay relatively static, activity on the user-device side can be constantly changing with printer and workstations being regularly moved, replaced, and added; to say nothing of handheld devices and wireless connectivity. There are tools that can rapidly scan large networks and identify which hosts are available on the network. These tools can usually identify some key aspects of the devices, such as what type of device it may be (printer, workstation, switch), what operating system it is running, and so on. Tools like these can help identify oddities that need to be investigated (e.g., "Why are those workstations running server software?").

Physical Access

In addition to obvious building security (door locks, access cards, etc.), physical access to IT areas should be controlled. Access to the computer room or data center should be limited to those individuals who require it. Other IT areas (e.g., wiring closets) should be locked. Because of the concerns of confidential content, printed report distribution should be controlled, and an industrial-strength shredder (or third-party shredding service) should be available to dispose of output that is no longer needed.

Traditional tools for tracking access within a facility, such as security cameras, access card readers, and sign-in sheets, should also be considered part of the arsenal. Reviewing these periodically (particularly sign-in sheets and access cards used for the data center) can be very worthwhile. Simply asking your company's security department to periodically review which employees have access cards that allow entry to the data center demonstrates that you need to partner with them as part of the overall IT security process.

Accounts and Passwords

Account Usage

There are some basic principles in setting up accounts that can help ensure that they aren't used for unauthorized activities:

- You may be able to limit an account's usage to certain days of the week and hours of the day. This can be a worthwhile option for temps and consultants' accounts.
- You can often set an account to be disabled automatically at a certain date. This is also a good feature to use for temps and consultants, as these users often leave the company with no notification to IT.
- You may want to consider limiting how many times a user can log in simultaneously, or perhaps limit it to two (so the user can log on from home even if they forgot to log out when leaving the office).
- Review accounts periodically for usage. If an account hasn't been used, for example, in several weeks, it may be worth investigating. Perhaps the employee is on some kind of leave. After a defined time, you can disable the account. If there is no further inquiry about the account after another few weeks, it may be safe to assume that the account is no longer needed.
- Unless otherwise justified and requested, new accounts should be given "plain vanilla" access privileges. Any request for additional access or privilege should be submitted in writing by an authorized individual.
- Consider using special naming conventions for temps, interns, and consultants so that security administrators can spot them easily and monitor their activity quickly.

User Terminations

Although it's generally easy to ensure that accounts are created when needed (it's easy because the user keeps complaining until it is done), it's more of a challenge to ensure that accounts are deleted/disabled when they should be. Too often when an employee leaves the company, the IT security administrator is the last to hear of it. HR should notify IT immediately of any employment terminations so that IDs can be disabled and deleted. When an employee does leave the company, there should be a procedure for moving her files, e-mail, and so on to another employee's ID (perhaps a coworker or manager) so that there is no need for maintaining the terminated employee's ID. Look to implement automatic triggers to disable user accounts when an employee is terminated, or if the account has not been used for an extended period.

Passwords

These should be at least six characters in length (many organizations now insist on passwords of eight characters), should be forced to be changed regularly (but not so often that a user has to write down her current password on a Post-It note attached to the monitor), and shouldn't be the same as the user's ID, nor be a common word. When it's time to change passwords, users should not be able to reuse the same one.

"Strong" or "complex" passwords are becoming increasingly popular. While the definitions of these terms vary, it's easy to understand them in comparison to "weak" passwords, which are easily guessed. A password that is blank, is the word "password" or a string of characters (e.g., 12345, or zzzzz), or that matches the user's ID, is considered a "weak" password. Similarly, a password that is the user's date of birth or pet's name is considered a weak password. Strong or complex passwords are those words that can't be found in the dictionary, often because they include special characters, numbers, and both upper- and lowercase letters.

A 2009 survey by Elcomsoft (www.elcomsoft.com/survey/survey2009.pdf) showed that 50 percent of respondents use more than 10 different passwords across their various IDs and accounts. But, 11 percent use only 1–3 different passwords. It is likely that this is leading to behaviors that could jeopardize IT security, as well as compliance initiatives. This was confirmed in a 2010 survey by Webroot (pr.webroot.com/threat-research/cons/protect-your-computer-from-hackers-101210.html), whose findings included:

- Four in 10 respondents shared passwords with at least one person in the past year.
- Nearly as many people use the same password to log into multiple websites, which could expose their information on each of the sites if one of them becomes compromised.
- Almost half of all users never use special characters (e.g., ! ? & #) in their passwords, a simple technique that makes it more difficult for criminals to guess passwords.
- Two in 10 have used a significant date, such as a birth date, or a pet's name as a password—information that's often publicly visible on social networks.
- 50 percent of people feel their passwords are very or extremely secure, yet:
  - 86 percent do not check for a secure connection when accessing sensitive information when using unfamiliar computers.
  - 14 percent never change their banking password.
  - 20 percent have used a significant date in a password.
  - 30 percent remember their passwords by writing them down and hiding them somewhere like a desk drawer.
- 41 percent use the same password for multiple accounts.
- Only 16 percent create passwords with more than 10 characters.

- Four in 10 people (41 percent) have shared passwords with one or more people in the past year.
- Almost half of Facebook users (47 percent) use their Facebook password on other accounts and 62 percent of Facebook users never change their password.

Configure your system to automatically lock out an account after so many failed log-in attempts. Many systems will automatically lock out an account after three failed attempts within a five-minute period. The system may then be set to automatically unlock the account after another few minutes. While these two steps may seem to be contradictory, the idea is to halt any brute-force attempts to guess a password, while still allowing a legitimate user to eventually gain access. Brute-force attacks are done with programs specially designed to try every character combination until the right password is found. Unchecked, a brute-force attempt can try tens of thousands of combinations in a single hour. With these account lockout parameters, the program might only get a handful of attempts.

Special Privilege IDs

Network and system managers usually have special IDs and passwords that provide carte blanche access to systems. These are often called "root," "supervisor," or "administrator" accounts. Because of their special access, only a handful of people should have accounts like this. System administrators tend to ignore their own security rules and often set these passwords to never expire. It's important that these passwords be changed regularly and changed immediately when someone who knows them leaves the company.

It's a common best practice for IT Managers and administrators to use two IDs. One of them has the special privileges they need for certain types of activities. The other isn't privileged and is used for routine tasks such as their own e-mail. The reason for two accounts is to minimize the amount of time an IT administrator makes use of privileges, thereby reducing the risk of their impacting the entire system by accident.

Administrators shouldn't share a common privileged account, and each should have their own non-privileged account. This helps identify actions and tasks with specific individuals and is particularly helpful when examining log entries.

Another common practice is to rename, delete, or disable the default privileged account that's installed with operating systems and applications. Since hackers assume these accounts exist on your system, they're usually one of the first paths they try to use to gain access. At a minimum, you must change the default password associated with these accounts.

Access Reviews

Large environments may have thousands of users and hundreds of thousands, if not millions, of files on their computer networks. Usually, groups of files are set up that can only be accessed by certain groups of users, and vice versa. It's important that some type of user administrator review these access privileges periodically (perhaps twice a year) to ensure that unauthorized users haven't mistakenly been given access to the wrong files.

Authorization Levels

Security administrators who process the requests to grant and revoke privileges, change access, and create IDs need to know who is authorized to make these requests. For example, the payroll manager may be authorized to determine who has access to the payroll files, and the VP of sales may be authorized to determine who has access to sales figures. It's up to the IT Manager and the security administrator to make sure it's clear who has authority over what and that these requests are documented. Most companies now require that IT be formally sent an e-mail—a trouble ticket in the IT Help System, for example, for any kind of request. A manager's request for an employee's new software upgrade, a user's request for a new printer, or a request for access to a new part of the network all now need to be formally requested, documented, and tracked. HR should alert IT of new employees in advance of their start date so that IDs with basic privileges (e-mail, etc.) can be created.

Authentication

Authentication is the process for determining if someone is authorized for access.

Challenge–Response

The most familiar and traditional form of authentication is known as challenge–response. The challenge is asking the user a question, and the response is the answer provided by the user. When you are prompted for your user ID and your password, you are participating in a challenge–response protocol.

Two-Factor Authentication

Typically, access is based on what a user *knows*—usually their ID and password. Two-factor authentication bases access not only on what the user knows, but also on what they *have*. The what-they-have component is generally a 6-digit token provided by a device that users carry with them (small enough to fit into a wallet or on a keychain). The device operates by displaying a number that changes every minute. The user types in the number when logging in, and the number is validated by a corresponding authentication server.

Two-factor authentication helps prevent unauthorized access resulting from the user telling someone else their password or by having their password guessed. Many companies use two-factor authentication for their remote access security as a way of reducing the exposure associated with connectivity from the public Internet. The SecurID solution from RSA Security is the most popular solution for two-factor authentication. (But even RSA was hacked in early 2011, although there has been no detail as to what the hackers may have done, and what information, if any, may have been stolen or compromised.)

Single Sign-On

Although the situation is slowly improving, users are still burdened by having to remember a variety of different IDs and passwords. Single sign-on (SSO) is a solution that allows users to authenticate once to the network and then have access to all applications and resources for which he has been granted permission, without having to enter additional IDs and passwords. SSO is a convenience for users as it reduces the number of IDs and passwords to remember, and it's a convenience for system managers as it greatly simplifies administration. Perhaps one of the most valuable aspects of SSO is that once an employee leaves the company, all their access can be removed by disabling their SSO ID.

The challenge with SSO is that the business applications may have to be altered to incorporate the technology. For in-house developed applications, this may be a relatively straightforward change. However, with third-party applications, it may be much more complex. A host of SSO-ready applications have sprung up, and standards like OpenID and Security Assertion Markup Language (SAML) have been developed and adopted to help facilitate SSO.

This technique is a classic case of user convenience versus security trade-off discussed in the beginning of this chapter. (See the section **"Security versus Privacy versus Convenience"** on

page 207.) Certainly the fewer things to remember, the happier most users are, but should a hacker gain access to an SSO ID, they then have access to *all* the systems the user is authorized for.

Identity Management

Identity management encompasses a variety of solutions and technologies related to user authentication. These include:

*   **Single sign-on.** This option is discussed in the previous section on **page 219.**
*   **Self-service.** Allowing users to reset their own passwords.
*   **Password synchronization.** When a user changes a password in one system, the new password is automatically replicated to other applications and systems.
*   **Account provisioning.** The process of creating new accounts and revoking them when they're no longer needed.
*   **Federated identity.** This is a single-user ID that can be used for different websites because they all belong to a common "federation." While similar to SSO, federated identities are useful when trying to manage authentication to external, in addition to internal, sites and applications. This allows organizations to share user credentials across the network boundaries that normally separate them.

Other User Authentication Methods

New methods of confirming a user is who he or she claims are being created all the time. In addition to the tried and true but sometimes fallible passwords, more advanced techniques include fingerprint and retinal scanning; and speech, signature, and face recognition. Another method gaining in popularity is referred to as "knowledge-based access"; this system is based on what information the user knows. Unlike passwords and other mechanisms, this information is not prone to being forgotten or lost. With knowledge-based access, users will provide the system with answers to various questions (e.g., favorite pet's name, mother's maiden name, place of birth, first school attended, favorite sports team). Many websites use knowledge-based access for password recovery.

Security Defenses

There is an entire industry selling security solutions—hardware, software, utilities, processes, and so on. The following are some of the more common solutions being implemented, but note that this list is certainly not comprehensive.

Firewalls

Firewalls are used to control access between networks. While firewalls initially existed just in corporate networks, they are now used on individual devices, and Microsoft Windows itself has a built-in firewall. While used mostly to protect your internal network from the public Internet, firewalls are often also used between private networks. For example, you may have a connection with a vendor or subsidiary and use a firewall to ensure that their access to your network is restricted. Firewalls are configured with rules to specify which devices can connect to each other, using which protocols and ports, and sometimes even specifying the times that the connectivity is allowed.

Intrusion Detection and Prevention

Intrusion Prevention Systems (IPS) and Intrusion Detection Systems (IDS) offer a layer of protection in addition to firewalls against the exposures of the Internet.

- An Intrusion *Detection* System identifies suspicious traffic based on patterns of activity. Similar to the way antivirus software works, an IDS compares traffic patterns against various known malicious signatures (which are updated frequently). Essentially the IDS is evaluating traffic to see if it matches known attacks. When it detects suspicious activity, the IDS system will alert the network administrator.
- An Intrusion *Prevention* System takes an IDS a step further. Not only does it detect the malicious activity but it takes action (in addition to notifying the administrator). The IPS may drop a packet from the suspicious traffic, close a port automatically, or refuse further traffic from that particular IP address. In the millisecond world of network activity, a network administrator may not be able to react fast enough to a notification from an IDS about a possible attack. An IPS can take preventive action (based on how it's set up and configured) instantly after it detects any suspicious activity.

Malware Prevention

Antivirus software has long been a cornerstone of protecting the IT environment. Antivirus solutions are available for workstations, servers, e-mail gateways, and even handhelds. By downloading the latest pattern and signature files regularly (see the section **"Ongoing Maintenance" on page 221,** later in this chapter), an organization can protect itself against the latest release and developments of viruses. Many organizations will employ virus solutions from multiple vendors as a way of strengthening their defenses further.

Antispyware solutions operate very similarly to antivirus solutions, with signature and pattern files that have to be updated regularly. However, many antivirus solutions now include antispyware functionality as well.

Antispam solutions for your e-mail gateway can do more than just reduce the amount of nuisance e-mail. These solutions can provide protection by preventing e-mails that include security risks, such as phishing attempts, worms, and viruses. Malware prevention solutions can prevent third-party tracking of user activity, as well as stopping unnecessary slowdowns in individual systems and servers.

Ongoing Maintenance

In addition to access reviews, as mentioned earlier, there are activities that should be performed regularly by security administrators to identify and minimize risks.

Log, Account, and Access Review

As stated earlier, IDs that haven't been used for a predefined period of time should be disabled or deleted. Many systems can report when unsuccessful login attempts have been made; these logs should be reviewed and investigated. System logs should be reviewed for those events and incidents that could identify security threats.

Accounts that have special privileges should be reviewed a few times a year to confirm that the need for the special privilege is still valid and justified.

After discussion with other departments (e.g., Legal, Audit), shared areas of the network (places where multiple users have read and write access) may be regularly purged of files that haven't been accessed in a while. (Not only does this free up space, but it might also remove files with confidential information that users placed there by mistake or are no longer needed.)

Software Patches and Updates

Security administrators should check with their software vendors regularly to obtain and apply any updates or patches that close security holes. Processes should exist for checking the environment regularly to make sure that systems are current and for ensuring that unpatched and unprotected systems can't connect to the corporate network.

Following Microsoft's lead, many vendors now have a set schedule for releasing patches. This allows IT departments to set schedules for testing the patches and implementations to the production environment.

Pattern files updates (for antivirus, antispam, intrusion prevention/detection) are usually released on a much more frequent basis than software security patches. It's common for these files to be updated several times a day, or more. Because of the frequency of these updates, these systems have to be set to regularly download and install the updates as they are released.

IT Managers can use various tools and configuration options to manage the distribution of updates to servers and workstations. These allow the IT department to determine if updates should be automatically installed (an increasingly popular and recommended method) or only after they've been tested and validated by the IT department. Similarly, the tools can help you see which devices have the most current updates and which are behind.

Encryption, Keys, and Certificates

Encrypting data is one of the most effective methods for keeping data secure (especially if combined with other security practices). Among the most popular solutions for using encryption are:

- Public Key Infrastructure (PKI)
- Digital certificates
- VPN tunneling
- Secure Sockets Layer (SSL)
- Pretty Good Privacy (PGP)
- Encryption standards like AES
- E-mail encryption
- Disk and tape storage encryption

Reports of security breaches due to lost backup and to missing or stolen laptops have become almost commonplace. (The website www.privacyrights.org/data-breach maintains an ongoing list.) As such, many organizations are now implementing encryption as a way to limit their exposure when data are lost. Encryption of any sort of mobile media is growing dramatically—this includes tapes, laptops, USB drives, and handheld devices. Careful testing must be done before implementing encryption solutions to see how/if it impacts users, operations, and applications.

Network Access Control

In a typical IT environment, when users are prompted for IDs and passwords by an application, they are already on your network. So even if they can't get into the application, they already have access to your very sensitive network. Network Access Control (NAC) is a technology solution that controls who gets access to your network. In short, the user/device can't access any part of your environment until the NAC confirms that it should. Some NAC tools, as well as some remote access solutions like VPN products, allow you to set policies such as requiring that devices must have current OS patches, and must be running current anti-virus software before being allowed to connect to the network.

Staffing

Because many of the IT staff have elevated access privileges, it's important to make sure that the staff members themselves aren't security risks. Many companies and organizations do background checks on IT staff members and include specific requirements, accountabilities, and responsibilities related to security in their job descriptions. Consider familiarizing your staff with various security standards and certifications:

- CISSP Certified Information Systems Security Professional (CISSP) is a certification for professionals in the computer security field responsible for developing information security policies, standards, and procedures and managing their implementation across an organization. Other security certifications include SSCP (Systems Security Certified Practitioner), CAP (Certified Authorization Professional), and CSSLP (Certified Secure Software Lifecycle Professional).
- ISO 17799 is an internationally recognized information security standard that establishes guidelines and general principles for initiating, implementing, maintaining, and improving information security management in an organization.
- ISO 270001 is the international information security standard against which organizations can seek independent certification of their Information Security Management Systems.

Additional information about security standards appears in the section **"Methodologies and Frameworks"** on **page 238** of this chapter.

Security Incident Response

You should establish procedures for dealing and responding to security breaches. Of course, the type of breach may dictate different types of responses. For example, a rampant virus is going to require a different level of response and urgency than discovering that some phishing e-mails made it past your anti-spam solution.

Many organizations create a formal Security Incidence Response Team (SIRT) to respond to security breaches. A SIRT can be composed of individuals from all areas of the organization and are often on 24-hour call. They are responsible for protecting an organization's critical IT assets.

Depending on the circumstances, the situation may call for:

- Examining log files and alerts.
- Contacting your vendors for assistance in identifying the problem and then determining how to address it.
- Shutting down certain resources, services, and network components until the problem has been identified and resolved.
- Notifying senior management and the user community. In a heavily regulated industry (such as banking) you may need to involve Legal and HR as well.
- Changing all passwords.
- Notifying law enforcement.
- Performing a security audit.

In all cases, every incident should be documented in a postmortem report. Such a postmortem will usually contain:

- A chronology of events, including actions taken, from first sign of the problem to resolution
- Identification of what procedures, tools, resources, and so on worked well
- Identification of what items did and didn't work as expected

- An analysis of the root cause of the problem
- A plan to address and correct the problems and issues identified as a result of this incident

A summary of the postmortem, without too much IT jargon, is often provided to management. This summary is usually welcomed by upper management, as it documents the how and why of what happened and an action plan to ensure that a similar event doesn't occur again. A postmortem document can be an effective summary for senior management, which demonstrates that IT security is taken very seriously by your team.

8.4 TYPES OF THREATS

The range of possible threats to your business and your information is very, very large. And it changes daily. The most important point about understanding different types of threats is to know that you must constantly stay on top of them. You must have the latest patches, and you must upgrade the operating systems to the latest versions. You don't need to become a guru, but you must either stay up to date or task others with doing this.

Malware

Malware is a category name to define software that causes problems. This can include viruses, adware, and spyware. Malware can degrade system performance, expose confidential information, distribute spam, etc. Specific types of malware include:

- **Macro viruses.** Viruses that use commands (macros) in application files (e.g., Excel and Word) to replicate themselves and do damage.
- **Worms.** Self-contained programs that replicate themselves usually via the network or e-mail attachments.
- **Adware.** Software that installs itself on a workstation for the purpose of displaying ads to the user. Users often unknowingly install adware when they download applications from the Web.
- **Spyware.** Software that monitors a user's activity, often to collect account numbers, passwords, etc. Spyware often works in tandem with adware as the ads shown may be related to the activity detected by the spyware. Like adware, spyware is also frequently installed by the user unknowingly when downloading applications from the Web.
- **Trojan horses.** Programs that appear to be legitimate, but in fact are malicious.
- **Backdoor Trojans:** Trojan horse programs that allow a hacker to control your computer remotely.
- **Page Hijackers:** Akin to the purposes of adware, they covertly redirect browsers to specific web pages.
- **Rootkits:** A set of modifications to the operating system that is designed primarily to hide malicious activity. Because the rootkit software essentially resides in a modification of the operating system, it's extremely difficult to detect, and it also continually checks on itself to see that the compromised files are still compromised and reinfects as needed. In addition to being very difficult to detect, they're equally hard to remove.
- **Key loggers:** Small applications that reside on a computer to record key strokes. These are used to capture passwords and confidential information (e.g., credit card numbers).

Of particular concern with malware is what is known as a Zero-Day attack, which is malicious code that takes advantage of a security vulnerability before there's a fix for it. In some cases, the malicious code is released even before there is public knowledge of the vulnerability.

Phishing and Social Engineering

Phishing is the process of trying to obtain confidential information (credit card numbers, passwords, social security numbers, bank account numbers, etc.) by fraudulent means. The perpetrator sends out e-mail messages that appear to come from well-known companies and websites. The e-mails will mimic the legitimate company's logos, text style, etc. Typically, the e-mail tells users that there's some problem with their account and that they need to log in to confirm or verify some information. The e-mail contains links to sites that can appear virtually identical to the site it claims to be. If successful, the user will click the link and be fooled into entering the information.

Websites that are frequently spoofed by phishers include PayPal, eBay, MSN, Yahoo, BestBuy, and nationwide banks (although the practice has now filtered down to local companies too). When phishing is successful, not only will it result in financial loss for the victim, but it could also result in identity theft. The U.S. government has developed a site, www.onguardonline.com, to help educate individuals about protecting themselves from Internet fraud.

From a technical perspective, phishing relies on spoofing e-mail. From the human perspective, phishing also relies on "social engineering." Social engineering is the practice of trying to get information from people by lying to them. Social engineering relies on the natural tendency of people to trust, to follow instructions, and to want to help. From this perspective, the adage about users being the weakest link of computer security is certainly true. Typical social engineering tricks include pretending to be an IT administrator and contacting users to verify their account or password. While pretending to be from IT is popular, so is IT as the victim. In the reverse situation, the phisher might call the Help Desk and complain that he's having difficulty logging in. By counting on the Help Desk to provide "help" (including instructions, password resets, etc.), the phisher may be able to gain access to the system.

SOME SECURITY STORIES

Grand Theft

"(CNN) – A hacker has obtained the personal information of PlayStation Network account holders and subscribers of the Qriocity streaming service, Sony said in a message to customers ... The attack also has crippled Sony's PlayStation Network, which has some 70 million subscribers ..." (www.cnn.com/2011/TECH/gaming .gadgets/04/26/playstation.network.hack/).

A Tiny Clue Leads to Giant Flaw

"What first appears as a 75-cent accounting error in a computer log is eventually revealed to be a ring of industrial espionage ... Clifford Stoll [Lawrence Livermore lab scientist] becomes, almost unwillingly, a one-man security force trying to track down faceless criminals who've invaded the university computer lab he stewards" (www.amazon.com/gp/product/0671726889/002-0037032-5296037?v=glance&n=283155).

A Classic (and Unfortunate for the Victim) Story of the Damage Lack of Understanding Can Cause

Kevin Mitnick is a famous hacker, one of the first to hone his social engineering skills to break into and acquire all kinds of technical information (including code from Nokia and Motorola). After he was arrested, he had the guards so spooked at his federal penitentiary that they put him in solitary confinement for eight months because they were convinced he could launch nuclear missiles by whistling into a phone (www.cnn.com/ 2005/TECH/internet/10/07/kevin.mitnick.cnna).

8.5 COMPLIANCE AND IT

Certainly one of the biggest changes to affect the IT industry over the past few years has been the concern for compliance of a variety of regulations and legislation. Spurred by events such as the financial scandals of Enron, WorldCom, Bernie Madoff, HealthSouth, Adelphia, Tyco, Qwest Communications, and Global Crossing (to name a few), along with the financial sector meltdown of 2008 and 2009, attention has been drawn to the integrity of financial reporting and controls. In these cases, senior management was allegedly aware of events and activities that led to the misstatement of the financials and the deception of investors.

Following this series of scandals, there was renewed interest in ensuring that sufficient controls were in place to make sure that this couldn't happen again. The most well-known legislation is the Sarbanes–Oxley Act of 2002, which was passed by the U.S. Congress and is discussed later in this chapter on **page 227**. Of course, while Sarbanes–Oxley is the best known, it isn't, by far, the only set of regulations that makes sure that data, financials, etc. are being handled properly.

"Compliance" is a broad term that can carry a lot of meanings. Is the entrance to your building ADA (Americans with Disabilities Act)-compliant? Was your television compliant for the digital TV (DTV) conversion of 2009? Is your health care provider HIPAA-compliant?

Overview

The following section, **"The Rules,"** presents some important compliancy regulations. You may have heard of some of these and are wondering if they pertain to your group or company. The goal is to provide you with a brief overview of the rule or regulation; you can then either pursue further information or decide the issue does not pertain to your situation.

For example, the HIPAA *privacy* provision took effect in 2003, but the *security* provision of HIPAA didn't take effect until 2005. You may have been working for a health care provider and heard the term "HIPAA compliant" for years but not understood what that meant. For ITers, the biggest impact of the rules and regulations of compliance generally relates to controlling, securing, and managing data. This is no small issue: Making data flow from one place to another is easy (sometimes too easy), but making it flow only to certain places and *not* to others (and to be certain of that) is much harder. In 2006, the FTC imposed a $10 million fine on ChoicePoint for failing to comply with the data protection obligations of the Fair Credit Report Act when a security breach resulted in the potential exposure of financial records for over 100,000 individuals.

Personally Identifiable Information (PII)

Many of the compliance regulations presented in the following section **"The Rules"** have specific references to individuals' personal data. Within the industry, this is referred to as Personally Identifiable Information (PII) and essentially refers to any data that can be used (either alone or with other data and sources) to identify a person. The definitions of PII vary among regulations and countries, but often include fields like:

- Name
- Government ID number (e.g., Social Security number)
- Driver's license and other identification numbers
- Birth date, place of birth

- Personal telephone numbers
- Personal e-mail address
- Home address
- Mother's maiden name
- Financial information, medical information, disability information
- Credit card and account numbers

It is this PII data that often gets the most attention and protection in laws and regulations, and that IT, businesses, and organizations will take extra steps with (e.g., policies, guidelines, security solutions, etc.) to ensure compliance.

Victims of Non-Compliance

There is a perception that the victims of non-compliance are the employees of the companies themselves. And that is true: Global Crossing's excesses affected 10,000 employees and WorldCom's 12,800. Many people lost their entire 401k savings in addition to their jobs.

However, many more people are affected by corporate perfidy than is generally understood. In HealthSouth's case, not only did the company's employees suffer, it radically affected the financial well-being of its hometown, Birmingham, Alabama. When corporate scandals took their toll on companies based in New York, the state suffered a $1 billion reduction in tax revenues (www.osc.state.ny.us/press/releases/aug03/082003.htm). The questionable practices that led to the economic crisis of 2008/2009 was felt across the country and across the globe in soaring statistics related to record unemployment, a huge number of foreclosures, and wiped-out retirement nest eggs.

The situation can easily snowball well beyond a single company or state. Depending on the type and scope of the circumstances, incidents of non-compliance (such as data breaches or lack of financial reporting integrity) can impact a company's employees, customers, suppliers, and partners; in some cases it may have an impact on the financial markets as a whole. Non-compliance can lead to media attention; lack of trust by employees, customers, suppliers, and partners; individual and organizational financial loss; and, in some cases, bankruptcy. Eroding consumer confidence leads to reduced spending, which further impacts other individuals and businesses, and causes the economy to shrink.

8.6 THE RULES

The sections that follow aren't meant to be comprehensive, but they do represent some of the more impactful guidelines under which many organizations and IT departments have to operate. This section isn't intended to be a how-to guide for ensuring compliance, but to make the new IT manager aware of the various issues and their importance.

Sarbanes–Oxley

Named for its two sponsors, Senator Paul S. Sarbanes (D-Maryland) and Representative Michael G. Oxley (R-Ohio), and frequently called by a variety of nicknames (Sarbanes, SOX, Sarb-Ox), it's formally called the Public Company Accounting Reform and Investor Protection Act of 2002 and is considered to be the most significant change to U.S. Securities Law since the 1930s.

The primary objective of SOX is to ensure the integrity of financial statements. It's interesting to note that SOX doesn't regulate information technology directly, but because IT systems are usually at the core of how a company manages and reports its finances, it is no surprise that IT is significantly impacted by it.

Although less than 200 words long, Section 404 of Sarbanes–Oxley has the most impact on IT. Of particular note is the requirement for companies to annually (1) state the responsibility of management for establishing and maintaining an adequate internal control structure and procedures for financial reporting and (2) contain an assessment, as of the end of the most recent fiscal year of the issuer, of the effectiveness of the internal control structure and procedures of the issuer for financial reporting.

In addition, Section 404 requires the auditors to "attest to, and report on, the assessment made by the management."

Those few lines of requirements have had an enormous trickle-down effect throughout companies, with a great deal of it being felt in IT. In fact, SOX has placed such an enormous burden that a study and survey by the Security and Exchange Commission (www.sec.gov/news/studies/2009/sox-404_study.pdf) released in 2009 showed that:

- The SEC's survey shows the long-term burden on small companies is more than seven times that imposed on large firms relative to their assets.
- Section 404 compliance exceeds $2.3 million each year in direct costs at the average company.
- Among companies of all sizes, only 19 percent say that the benefits of Section 404 outweigh the costs.
- More respondents say that it has reduced the efficiency of their operations than say it has improved them.
- More say that Section 404 has negatively affected the timeliness of their financial reporting than say it has enhanced it.

In the years since its passage, the regulations have received quite a bit of criticism with reference to increased costs but not delivering the intended results. While some notable names have called for its repeal, the rules still stand and should be taken seriously. Misstatement of financials under Sarbanes–Oxley can lead to jail time, fines, or both for executives.

Many other countries have their own legislation that is comparable to Sarbanes–Oxley. These include Ontario Canada's Bill 198, Japan's Financial Instruments and Exchange Law, Germany's Corporate Governance Code, Australia's CLERP9, Financial Security Law of France, L262/2005 of Italy and India's Clause 49.

Health Insurance Portability and Accountability Act (HIPAA)

HIPAA has regulations promoting the privacy and security of medical records. These regulations are related primarily to the health care industry. HIPAA's regulations directly cover three basic groups of individual or corporate entities:

- Health plans (e.g., public and private insurance carriers, employee medical plans)
- Health care providers (e.g., doctors, hospitals, or any provider of health or medical services)
- Health care clearinghouses (e.g., processors of health information, such as billing services)

While HIPAA primarily impacts those in the medical industry, it can indirectly impact organizations outside of the field. For example, nonmedical companies would need to make sure that the process of dealing with and administering employee medical benefits complies with the act.

The Security Rule of HIPAA is designed to assure the confidentiality and integrity of Protected Health Information (PHI). Protected Health Information under HIPAA includes any individually-identifiable health information (IIHI). This refers not only to data explicitly linked to a particular individual, but also includes health information with data items that reasonably could be expected to allow individual identification.

The Privacy Rule of HIPAA is intended to protect the privacy of all IIHI in the custody of covered entities, regardless of whether the information is or has been in electronic form.

Associated with HIPAA is the Health Information Technology for Economic and Clinical Health (HITECH) Act, which promotes the use of information technology in the health industry. Provisions of the HITECH act address the privacy and security concerns associated with the electronic transmission of health information, in part, through several provisions that strengthen the civil and criminal enforcement of the HIPAA rules.

Basel II

Basel II is an updated version of the Basel Accord that was adopted in 1988 in Basel, Switzerland. Basel II, formally known as the International Convergence of Capital Measurement and Capital Standards, was endorsed in 2004 by the central bank governors and the heads of bank supervisory authorities in the Group of Ten (G10). G10 refers to the 10-member countries of the International Monetary Fund (United States, United Kingdom, Germany, France, Belgium, The Netherlands, Italy, Sweden, Canada, and Japan) plus Switzerland.

The Basel II framework sets out the details for adopting more risk-sensitive minimum capital requirements for banking organizations. The new framework reinforces these risk-sensitive requirements by laying out principles for banks to assess the adequacy of their capital to ensure that banks have sufficient capital to support the risks that they undertake. Like Sarbanes–Oxley, it also seeks to strengthen the transparency and integrity of banks' financial reporting.

The Basel II Accord is built around "three pillars":

- Pillar 1 of the new capital framework revises the 1988 Accord's guidelines by aligning the minimum capital requirements more closely to each bank's actual risk of economic loss.
- Pillar 2 of the new capital framework recognizes the necessity of exercising effective supervisory review of banks' internal assessments of their overall risks to ensure that bank management is exercising sound judgment and has set aside adequate capital for these risks.
- Pillar 3 leverages the ability of market discipline to motivate prudent management by enhancing the degree of transparency in banks' public reporting. It sets out the public disclosures that banks must make that lend greater insight into the adequacy of their capitalization (Bank of International Settlements, www.bis.org).

In the United States, adoption and implementation of Basel II are managed by the four Federal banking agencies (the Office of the Comptroller of the Currency, the Board of Governors of the Federal Reserve System, the Federal Deposit Insurance Corporation, and the Office of Thrift Supervision). In 2007, these agencies issued final rulings about adoption of Basel II for the largest banks in the United States (others may opt-in). The implementation process, which includes parallel and transition periods, won't have any bank fully subject to the rule until 2012 at the earliest.

Basel III, which the United States expects to adopt beginning in 2013, primarily strengthens bank capital requirements and introduces new regulatory requirements on bank liquidity and bank leverage, and provides for an enhanced supervisory review process, and disclosures.

SB-1386

California's Security Breach Information Act (SB-1386) is a state law requiring organizations that maintain personal information about individuals to inform those individuals if the security of their information is compromised. This act stipulates that if there's a security breach of a database containing personal data, the responsible organization must notify each individual for whom it maintained information. The act, which went into effect July 1, 2003, was created to help stem the increasing incidences of identity theft. Essentially, it requires an agency, person, or business that conducts business in California and owns or licenses computerized "personal identifying information" to disclose any breach of security to any resident whose unencrypted data are believed to have been disclosed.

SB-1386 defines Personal Identifying Information (PII) as an individual's unencrypted first and last name in conjunction with at least one other piece of information, such as:

- Social Security number
- Debit or credit card number
- Driver's license number or California ID card number
- Account number in conjunction with a PIN or access code

PII data is referenced in many different regulations and laws around the globe. However, each may define PII differently. Because of the reference to unencrypted data, many organizations have taken to encrypting data that leave their custody. Interestingly enough, the California law doesn't set any minimum requirements or make any statement about the strength of the encryption.

Although it's a California state law, it doesn't mean that companies located outside of California are exempt. If your company does business anywhere in California, you are affected. Since California has the largest population of any state, it's highly likely that SB-1386 has an impact on your business.

When data are compromised, SB-1386 outlines specific courses of action that an affected company must follow.

Massachusetts Data Protection Law

The Massachusetts Data Protection & Privacy law went into effect on March 1, 2010 and applies to anyone that processes, stores, or maintains data associated with a Massachusetts resident.

The law requires that companies have a written information security program (WISP), which would:

- Designate employees responsible for the program
- Create an inventory of personal information
- Assess the risk of a breach
- Have disciplinary measures for failure to comply
- Provide for training of employees
- Define how the WISP is to be monitored

The law covers both paper and electronic records, and says that access must be restricted and that the data must be safeguarded. For paper records, this would include locked cabinets and storage rooms, for example. For electronic files this would include appropriate user authentication protocols, encryption of transmitted files and portable devices (e.g., USBs, laptops), firewalls, anti-malware solutions, operating system patching, among others.

With fines up to $5,000 per compromised record, the Massachusetts law is considered one of the strictest in the nation.

Fair and Accurate Credit Transactions Act (FACTA)

The FACTA is a consumer rights bill that became fully effective June 1, 2005, and is an extension of the Fair Credit Reporting Act (FCRA). The rule says that in regard to consumer information (such as name, Social Security number, address) you must "take reasonable measures to protect against unauthorized access or use of the information." FACTA is designed to cut down on the incidences of identity theft as a result of valuable consumer information contained in business records. FACTA also discusses destruction methods, such as shredding of paper documents and destroying/erasing electronic media. FACTA also includes the "red-flag rule" to have systems in place to identify activity that may indicate attempts at fraud and possible identity theft.

Although you might think that this act only applies to organizations such as credit bureaus, banks, and retailers, its reach is actually far greater. You could easily have FACTA-covered data if you've done background checks on your employees and job applicants.

Gramm–Leach–Bliley

The Financial Modernization Act of 1999, also known as the Gramm–Leach–Bliley Act (named for its Republican Party sponsors Phil Gramm, Jim Leach, and Thomas Bliley), or GLB Act, has provisions to protect consumers' personal financial information held by financial institutions. The act is enforced by multiple federal agencies as well as states. It affects not only banks, insurance companies, and security firms, but also brokers, lenders, tax preparers, and real estate settlement companies, among others.

The GLB Act consists of three sections:

- The Financial Privacy Rule, which regulates the collection and disclosure of private financial information.
- The Safeguards Rule, which stipulates that financial institutions must implement security programs to protect such information.
- The Pretexting provisions, which prohibit the practice of pretexting (accessing private information using false pretenses).

For IT, it's important to note that the act provides each agency or authority described in Section 6805(a) of this act to establish appropriate standards for the financial institutions subject to their jurisdiction relating to administrative, technical, and physical safeguards:

1. To ensure the security and confidentiality of customer records and information.
2. To protect against any anticipated threats or hazards to the security or integrity of such records.
3. To protect against unauthorized access to or use of such records or information that could result in substantial harm or inconvenience to any customer.

GLB also requires the safeguarding of "nonpublic personal information," which includes nonpublic "personally identifiable financial information," such as any information (1) a consumer provides to obtain a financial product or service and (2) about a consumer resulting from any transaction involving a financial product or service otherwise obtained about a consumer in connection with providing a financial product or service (www.ftc.gov/privacy/glbact/glboutline.pdf).

The act also requires financial institutions to give customers written privacy notices that explain their information-sharing practices. In 2008 and 2009, GLB received criticism as a contributing factor in the subprime mortgage crisis, as GLB repealed the Glass–Steagall Act of the 1933s, thereby allowing banks, securities companies, and insurance companies to compete with one another directly and leading to the creation of financial conglomerates such as Citigroup.

U.S. Securities

- **Rule 342 of the New York Stock Exchange (NYSE)** states that member organizations shall have "internal supervision and control of the organization and compliance with securities' laws and regulations." The rule also provides that member organizations have "reasonable procedures for review of registered representatives' communications with the public."
- **Rule 440 of the NYSE** requires that "every member organization shall make and preserve books and records as the Exchange may prescribe and as prescribed by [SEC] Rule 17a-3. The record keeping format, medium, and retention period shall comply with Rule 17a-4 under the Securities Exchange Act of 1934."
- **Rule 17a-3 of the Securities and Exchange Act of 1934** defines the requirement to keep various types of records.
- **Rule 17a-4 of the Securities and Exchange Act of 1934** provides that "broker and dealer shall preserve for a period of not less than 3 years, the first two years in an accessible place . . . originals of all communications received and copies of all communications sent by such member, broker, or dealer (including interoffice memoranda and communications) relating to his business as such."
- **Rule 3010 of the National Association of Securities Dealers (NASD)** requires that member firms establish and maintain a system to "supervise" the activities of each registered representative, including transactions and correspondence (which includes e-mail) with the public. In addition, NASD 3110 requires that member firms implement a retention program for all correspondence involving registered representatives.

Patriot Act

The USA Patriot Act (formally called Uniting and Strengthening America by Providing Appropriate Tools Required to Intercept and Obstruct Terrorism Act of 2001) was passed in the wake of the terrorist attacks of September 11, 2001. While the act provides primarily for giving greater latitude to the U.S. government, it does have its impact on the private sector.

The act has a number of requirements for financial institutions in regard to verifying customers' identities and determining whether the customer appears on any list of known or suspected terrorists or terrorist organizations (thomas.loc.gov/cgi-bin/bdquery/z?d107:h.r.03162:). The act has been quite controversial, particularly as it relates to issues of civil rights and privacy. The act's provisions have been amended over the years.

Dodd–Frank Act

This bill was passed in direct response to the massive financial collapse that occurred in 2008 and 2009. It more stringently regulates the U.S. financial system with the goal of preventing another meltdown. The Act created a host of new agencies (while merging and removing others) with a goal of streamlining the regulatory structure, and increasing oversight of specific institutions regarded as a significant risk. The Act establishes rigorous standards and supervision to protect the economy and American consumers, investors, and businesses, and eliminates the loopholes that led to the economic recession.

Office of Foreign Assets Control (OFAC)

OFAC is part of the U.S. Department of Treasury and administers and enforces economic sanction programs primarily against countries and groups of individuals, such as terrorists and narcotics traffickers. OFAC regulations prohibit individuals and businesses from transacting business with specific individuals, organizations, and countries. Compliance with OFAC regulations requires checking the names of customers against the OFAC list.

CLERP-9 (Australia)

The Australian Corporate Law Economic Reform Program (Audit Reform and Corporate Disclosure) Act 2004 (more commonly known as CLERP-9) came into effect on July 1, 2004, and is designed to restore confidence in the market after a number of high-profile corporate collapses.

CLERP-9 is a substantial piece of legislation that in many ways is comparable to the Sarbanes–Oxley legislation in that it includes reforms relating to:

- Disclosure of directors' remuneration
- Financial reporting
- Auditors independence
- Continuous disclosure
- Enhanced penalty provisions

Also, like SOX, misstatement of financials under CLERP can lead to jail time, fines, or both for executives.

Personal Information Protection and Electronic Documents Act (PIPEDA)

PIPEDA is a Canadian law that regulates the collection, use, and disclosure of personally identifiable information.

Under PIPEDA, information has to be collected with the individual's consent (and only for reasonable purposes), used only for the purpose for which it was collected, properly safeguarded, and available for inspection and correction. Organizations, including corporations, individuals, and associations, are generally subject to the privacy requirements of PIPEDA if they collect, use, or disclose personal information in the course of a commercial activity.

Privacy and Electronic Communications Directive (European Union)

The European Union's Directive 2002/58 covers many aspects of electronic communications. Some of the significant provisions that focus on the security of data and networks and guaranteeing the privacy of communications cover:

- Security of networks and services
- Confidentiality of communications
- Spyware and cookies
- Traffic data (information about a person's electronic activities, such as websites visited)
- Location data (data that identify individuals' whereabouts)
- Public directories
- Unsolicited commercial communication (i.e., spam)
- Caller ID
- Nuisance calls
- Emergency calls
- Automatic call forwarding

This directive was amended by Directive 2009/136, sometimes called the "Cookie Directive," since it included a number of changes, particularly regarding prior consent to allow for cookies to be placed on workstations when navigation the Web.

Data Protection Directive (European Union)

The European Union's Directive 95/46/EC is a component of the EU's human rights and privacy laws and for the protecting of individuals' personal data. The directive has three major principles:

- **Transparency.** The individual has the right to be informed when his personal data are being processed, by who, the intended purpose, and the recipients of data. The transparency principle ensures that data may not be processed without the individual's consent.
- **Legitimate purpose.** Personal data can only be processed for specified explicit and legitimate purposes.
- **Proportionality.** The processing of data must be in proportion and related to which it is needed. This essentially defines issues of accuracy, retention, etc.

8.7 HOW TO COMPLY WITH THE RULES

The previous pages only touched the surface of some of the rules and regulations that exist for corporations in general, and IT in particular. There are many more, and if you're in a heavily regulated industry (e.g., health care, pharmaceuticals, financials) there are yet other layers to deal with.

Obviously, it's beyond the scope of this book to provide step-by-step guidance for ensuring compliance. In fact, even among the experts there is considerable debate as to what are the best ways to address the requirements. When regulations are replete with words such as "adequate," "sufficient," and "reasonable," they're clearly open to some interpretation.

However, there are some common practices that can help get you where you need to be:

- Document the policies
- Identify control mechanisms
- Educate your employees
- Maintain evidence

Each practice is discussed in more detail in the sections in this chapter.

It can also be difficult to know when "enough is enough." When it comes to security and controls, there's always more that can be done. Also, sometimes it's easy to lose sight of the fact that the regulations are usually focused on specific areas. For example, Sarbanes–Oxley is focused on the integrity of financial reporting. Yet, in many organizations it's often used as the impetus for change in things that have only the remotest relationship to financial reporting.

Document the Policies

Unfortunately for all those ITers who hate writing, documentation is becoming more and more a fact-of-life requirement in IT. Happily, many of the IT policies required for compliance are often rather short. As the heading to this section implies, your focus should be on stating the policies, not writing how-to-manuals.

For example, a backup policy could address items such as:

- How often backup is run
- What types of backup are executed (e.g., full, incremental, differential)
- What is being backed up (e.g., servers, databases, e-mail, workstations, remote sites)
- What process is employed to ensure that the backup tapes were created successfully
- What tools are used (e.g., backup software, tape library, tape-drive format)
- What happens to the tapes after backup is complete (e.g., sent to off-site storage facility)
- Any encryption that is used
- How long the backup tapes are retained before being recycled or destroyed
- What records are kept (e.g., logs from the backup software)

A document like this might just be a few pages long but it can turn out to be very valuable. Before publishing the document, get as much input and comment as possible. Often that input and comment will only be from other ITers. In other cases, you may want to review with Legal or HR.

There are some key items that every policy document should have:

- Date it was published
- Name(s) of the author(s) and approver(s)
- Some sort of revision and review history

As a general rule, it's a good idea to review all policies at least once a year. Even if there aren't any changes, you're at least showing your auditors that it's checked and updated periodically as needed.

Finally, the policy should be publicly available to everyone who needs to know. An intranet site is an ideal location for this document to be stored.

Identify Control Mechanisms

Too often, policies are created and then universally ignored. With compliance, you want to have processes to confirm that the defined policies and procedures are actually used. A control mechanism provides the appropriate checks and balances.

For example:

- If your policy defines that only duly authorized individuals are allowed to have access to the data center, you could review the access-card logs to the data center periodically to see if any unauthorized individuals have entered.
- Similarly, in the backup policy example given earlier, a process of reviewing the backup logs regularly to ensure that that they were executed and completed without errors can serve as a control mechanism.
- If you have a policy that unused network accounts should be disabled after a defined period, you could regularly run reports to identify when accounts were last used and whether or not they are disabled.

Not only do the control mechanism(s) help you make sure that policies are being adhered to but they are also convenient for your auditors.

Educate Employees

With your policies and control mechanisms defined, you want to make sure that everyone is aware of them. Your department intranet is an ideal place for centralizing the storage of these documents. For simpler policies it may be sufficient to simply e-mail a link to the documents, not only when they are first published, but when they are changed, updated, or when reviewed annually.

For more complex policies, it may be warranted to hold meetings or small classes so that the policy can be discussed, demos conducted, and questions answered. (For a more detailed discussion of this issue, see the sections **"Training Users"** on **page 213.**)

Maintain Evidence

Perhaps the most critical item in your compliance regimen is to make sure that you're keeping evidence of your activities:

- In the example in this section about access to the computer room, a simple e-mail indicating that the access logs have been reviewed.
- In the example of notifying employees about a new policy, a copy of the e-mail would serve this need. In the case of the class for more complex policies, a record of who attended the class and the class outline shows that the class was held.
- In the example about disabling unused accounts, e-mails indicating that the report was run and reviewed and directing which accounts to disable, and evidence that those accounts were indeed disabled.

When the auditors come knocking, they'll be looking to see that you have policies that comply with the various rules and regulations and that you're actually following those policies. The steps defined earlier will put you on the right track.

8.8 HIDDEN BENEFITS OF COMPLIANCE

In terms of effort, compliance is at best a burden and at worst an enormous use of time and resources. You have employees to manage, a department to run, service levels to meet, systems to keep operating, and a company to help keep profitable. All these rules can be seen as just more obstacles to be overcome to accomplish your goal.

Nonetheless, similar to the hidden benefits of disaster recovery in the section **"Hidden Benefits of Good Disaster Recovery Planning" in Chapter 9, Disaster Recovery on page 261,** compliance activities provide a major hidden benefit: *You can do important, but potentially overlooked, portions of your job at the same time.* You can comply with regulations while simultaneously getting your "real work" done. The following sections explain how you can pull this off.

The Hidden Benefit of Documentation

The first step of compliance, "document the policies," is a perfect example. Sure, some policies you need to document are obscure, but most are policies that you want a record of in order to do your job better. You should have a clearly documented backup policy—not only for compliance reasons and not only for disaster recovery reasons, but for backup plan efficiency reasons. Also, with documented policies, it increases the likelihood that everyone is following the same policy.

If you (or one of your employees) have the entire backup plan in your head (or, just as bad, have the "real" plan as opposed to the written, outdated plan or the plan no one can understand stored in that manner), the future of your entire company's data depends on the reliability of one person. Becoming compliant may wake you up to that scary fact and cause you to do something about it.

The Hidden Benefit of Control Mechanisms

The benefit to the second method of compliance, "identify control mechanisms," is similar to the first. Your policies shouldn't be abstract documents in a file somewhere, but living items that positively affect and reflect your department's behavior. Your security policies are an excellent example. Regardless of the legal requirements, you should be monitoring your security procedures aggressively. Control mechanisms will give you (as well as the auditors) the confidence that the policies you worked so hard to define are indeed being applied.

Depending on the level of security and size of your company, that monitoring can be a daily affair. There are many companies where even access to other departments is carefully restricted. If your company isn't one of these, do you need to become one? And how did you answer that question? Off the top of your head or by understanding the latest version (not the one put together last year) of your company's security policy?

The Hidden Benefit of Educating Your Employees

Keeping your employees informed isn't only a required component of some regulations, but it's simply good business practice. It's much easier for employees to comply with the policies if they know what they are.

Many employees were hurt by the global accounting and financial scandals. Employees—and that includes you—as well as investors now want to know much more about what their company is doing.

Also, it's your responsibility, as well as the responsibility of your superiors and colleagues, to provide that information proactively. Like many problems, if you approach the issue aggressively before it becomes a problem, you can turn it into an opportunity.

A timely example of keeping employees informed is to let them know the exact financial health of their company. This information, if you work for a publicly held corporation, is clearly available in many locations. As a proactive, concerned manager you can provide that data to your employees and you can provide it in an abbreviated form. Few people want to read the entire 10-K and 10-Q forms, but most want to read a paragraph or two about the financial health of the company and where to get more information if they want to do further research. Your Finance department can either provide you with that data or, more likely, point you to where that data already exist.

If the financial news for your company isn't good that quarter, you'll have happier and more confident employees if you tell them instead of them first hearing it from CNN.

Hidden Benefits of Maintaining Evidence

Maintaining evidence might be considered a polite euphemism for the popular CYA acronym. However, in truth, the evidence proves to anyone who might ask (regulators, Legal, auditors, etc.) that you're actually operating by the established policies. Maintaining evidence is essentially good record keeping and is a good habit for all to have, especially in the business world. Also, record keeping just might get people in the habit of doing more careful documentation.

8.9 METHODOLOGIES AND FRAMEWORKS

In light of all the activity surrounding compliance, you should be aware of a number of methodologies, frameworks, and processes developed by third parties. Although these weren't designed specifically for compliance activities, many organizations have adopted them to help provide increased structure to monitor and maintain their compliance activities. Oftentimes, these methodologies, processes, and frameworks are adopted and incorporated into all projects and activities by your organization's Project Management Office.

IT Governance

IT governance is a framework to help ensure that IT's strategies are aligned with those of the business, that they are delivering value and addressing stakeholder's needs, etc. A proper framework for IT governance can identify how IT is functioning overall and how well IT is returning on the business's investment in IT. As IT spending and the department itself continue to grow, many organizations have implemented a governance framework as an effective way ensuring that IT hasn't become (or doesn't become) a large sinkhole for resources. This is done at the behest of upper management, who often feel that they don't have sufficient knowledge or insight into IT to judge its overall effectiveness, value, efficiency, and so on.

Senior IT management may also use a governance framework to help decide which projects should move forward, receive investment and resources, and which projects or functions should be cut back or canceled.

The IT Governance Institute (www.itgi.org) defines five IT governance domains:

- **Strategic alignment.** To ensure that an organization's IT investments are aligned with the organization's strategic goals and will deliver business value.
- **Value delivery.** For optimizing expenses to ensure delivery on time and on budget and of appropriate quality.
- **Risk management.** To ensure the safeguard of IT assets: security, controls, disaster recovery, confidentiality, privacy, vulnerabilities, etc.
- **Resource management.** Ensuring the optimal investment, use, and allocation of IT resources (people, applications, technology, facilities, data).
- **Performance measurement.** Tracking project progress and delivery and monitoring IT services.

Because it covers so many perspectives, different organizations may emphasize different aspects. For example, in some organizations, the governance oversight may be involved primarily with project management. In others, it may primarily be about compliance activities.

Committee of Sponsoring Organizations (COSO)

From its own website, COSO "is dedicated to guiding executive management and governance entities toward the establishment of more effective, efficient, and ethical business operations . . ."

COSO has developed a framework to help organizations evaluate and improve their risk management. The COSO framework for internal controls has several components:

- Internal environment
- Objective setting
- Event identification
- Risk assessment
- Risk response
- Control activities
- Information and communication
- Monitoring

The COSO framework has been adopted by thousands of organizations to help address their compliance activities.

Control Objectives for Information and Related Technology (COBIT)

COBIT was developed by the Information Systems Audit and Control Association and the IT Governance Institute and is essentially a set of documents that provide guidance for computer security. Much of COBIT is available at no cost.

COBIT breaks down the control structure into four major areas:

- Planning and organization
- Acquisition and implementation
- Delivery and support
- Monitoring

These are then broken down even further into 34 subcategories.

IT Infrastructure Library (ITIL)

ITIL is published by the Office of Government Commerce in Great Britain. It focuses on IT services and is often used to complement the COBIT framework. In 2008, DimensionData reported the results of a survey showing that 60 percent of U.S. CIOs and 66 percent of organizations outside the United States are working with ITIL.

ITIL consists of six sets:

1. Service support
2. Service delivery
3. Planning to implement service management
4. ICT (Information and Communication Technology) infrastructure management
5. Applications management
6. The business perspective

Within these, a number of very specific disciplines are described.

Although ITIL was originally created by a UK government agency, it's now being adopted and used around the world for best practices in the provision of IT service. The main focus of ITIL is IT service management. While not designed specifically for compliance, the ITIL is often mentioned in the same sentences as COBIT and COSO.

Capability Maturity Model Integration (CMMI)

CMMI is a framework for process improvement, developed at Carnegie Mellon University's Software Engineering Institute. CMMI is designed to achieve process improvement across a project, a department, or a whole organization. CMMI can help bring together functions that are often done separately, set goals and priorities, and be a mechanism for appraising current processes.

The CMMI is probably best known for its five maturity levels:

1. Initial
2. Managed
3. Defined
4. Quantitatively managed
5. Optimizing

Each level represents the next step toward full process maturity and is characterized by several of the 25 defined "process areas." Organizations can have their maturity level determined by using a Standard CMMI Appraisal Method for Process Improvement (SCAMPI) appraiser. CMMI appraisal results at the higher levels are coveted by many organizations and are a point of pride. Many organizations will do press releases after getting a particularly good appraisal result.

International Organization for Standards (ISO 9000)

The International Organization for Standards (known globally as "ISO") is the world's largest developer of standards. ISO standards address everything from standardization of paper sizes, credit card sizes, public information signs, performance and safety, technology connections and interfaces, etc. ISO isn't a government organization; it's essentially a network of standards organizations from over

100 countries. ISO standards are voluntary; however, they often become requirements dictated by the marketplace.

The ISO 9000 standard, originally developed in 1987 and revised every few years since, provides a framework for quality management throughout the processes of producing and delivering products and services. ISO 9000 really consists of the following three components:

- **ISO 9000 Quality management systems.** Fundamentals and vocabulary.
- **ISO 9001 Quality management systems.** Requirements.
- **ISO 9004 Quality management systems.** Guidelines for performance improvements.

ISO 9000 has five main sections:

1. **Quality management system.** Covers ensuring that an organization has established what its processes are, how they interact with each other, what resources are required, and how processes are measured and improved.
2. **Management responsibility.** It is management's responsibility to set policies, objectives, and review the systems, as well as communication to the organization about processes.
3. **Resource management.** Covers a wide range of specific resources, including human resources (such as numbers of competent workers, training, etc.), infrastructure, suppliers and partners, financial resources, and the work environment.
4. **Product realization.** Covers the processes that are needed to provide the product/service.
5. **Measurement analysis and improvement.** Collecting metrics about the products, customer satisfaction, and the management systems and ensuring continual improvement.

The continuous improvement cycle of ISO 9000 can be summed up with the popular acronym of PDCA—Plan, Do, Check, Act. PDCA was originally developed by Walter Shewhart in the 1930s and is sometimes called the "Shewhart Cycle." It was popularized by W. Edwards Deming, and some have come to refer to it as the "Deming Wheel."

Six Sigma

Six Sigma was originally developed as a process for measuring defects in manufacturing and as a way to work toward the elimination of those defects. Since its original incarnation for manufacturing, it has been adopted by many organizations across a wide range of industries.

At the core of Six Sigma are two methodologies:

1. The DMAIC methodology has five phases and is for the refinement of existing processes:
   - **Define** the project goals and customer (internal and external) deliverables.
   - **Measure** the process to determine current performance.
   - **Analyze** and determine the root cause(s) of the defects.
   - **Improve** the process by eliminating defects.
   - **Control** future process performance.
2. The DMADV methodology also has five phases and is for the creation of new processes:
   - **Define** the project goals and customer (internal and external) deliverables.
   - **Measure** and determine customer needs and specifications.
   - **Analyze** the process options to meet customer needs.

- **Design** (detailed) the process to meet customer needs.
- **Verify** the design performance and ability to meet customer needs.

The Six Sigma methodology also has roles and certifications that go by names such as Green Belt, Black Belt, Master Black Belt, and Champion.

8.10 IT'S NOT JUST REGULATORY COMPLIANCE

While this chapter provides a taste of the world of IT compliance, as required by various pieces of legislation, there are other compliance activities outside of enacted statutes.

Electronic Discovery

Frequently, IT departments are involved in many of the lawsuits that are brought against an organization. It's becoming more and more common for lawsuits to require a search for e-mail, documents, and system logs.

- Class action lawsuits against a company (perhaps by investors or customers)
- Disgruntled employees (often claiming wrongful termination) may bring action against an organization
- Allegations by current employees of discrimination or harassment
- Invasion of privacy concerns (e.g., one employee claiming that another has had unauthorized access to the first employee's documents and e-mails)
- Lawsuits brought by partners, suppliers, customers, vendors, etc.

IT has found itself working with increasing frequency with the company's Legal department to provide information about IT operations (e.g., e-mail archiving policy, availability of backup tapes, responses to subpoenas). As such, it's becoming increasingly common for IT to review policies and procedures with in-house lawyers before considering them approved.

Information and Records Retention

Usually, the Legal department defines how long different type of business records must be retained. It is important to remember that is up to the user and business owners of those files and records to hold on to them, and then delete them when appropriate. While IT is essentially the custodian of those files and can assist with implementing procedures to comply with retention requirements, it is not up to IT to determine when files can be deleted. However, IT (with input from legal and the business departments) can set policies on the retention of backup tapes, which should not be used as an archival mechanism. Remember, backups are just copies of the files.

Working with Auditors

It's usually not sufficient for IT to simply establish their own procedures to meet regulatory compliance. Very often, they need to prove their compliance to external auditors as well as internal auditors. The discussion earlier in the chapter about maintaining evidence (section **"Hidden Benefits of Maintaining Evidence"** on **page 238**) goes a long way to help you prove that you're doing what you're claiming.

While these audits can take a toll on IT resources, they do serve to help ensure that defined procedures are followed. Also, if something is overlooked, it's better to find them during an audit than as a result of an interruption of service or loss of data.

Disaster Recovery and Business Continuity

While disaster recovery and business continuity may also be the subject of some regulatory compliance, most organizations are concerned about it more for their own interests. Both of these subjects are covered in **Chapter 9, Disaster Recovery** on **page 247.**

Definition of Policies and Procedures

The compliance legislation discussed previously is sufficient reason for establishing policies and procedures. However, even without being compelled by law, it's always wise to define and document policies and procedures for the IT department, as well as the user community.

For example, there may be an informal policy that has determined when personal printers (as opposed to shared network printers) are permitted. However, if this policy is documented and posted, it helps ensure that all employees (both IT and users) are aware of it and that it can be applied consistently. Other examples of policies that can be defined include:

- Password requirements (length, frequency of changes, etc.)
- Limits on the size of e-mail messages and mailboxes
- Retention period for files and messages
- Resources and rules in place for spam and virus defense (e.g., the blocking of certain attachment types)
- Rules and approvals needed for nonstandard equipment requests (laptops, over-sized monitors, equipment at home)
- Requirements for password-protected screen savers
- Process for dealing with nonstandard software requests
- Policies for disabling/deleting unused accounts
- Policies pertaining to IDs and access for nonemployees (temps, consultants, partners, suppliers, etc.)
- Provisions for requesting a restore of files
- Approval required for accessing the files of a former or unreachable employee
- Employee reimbursement for special services (cell phones, broadband connections at home)
- Proper use of IT resources (e.g., no personal use of computer equipment, handhelds)
- Guidelines for use of social networking sites during working hours and/or on company equipment.
- Limitations of support for company equipment at home

Of course, many of these policies should include comment and approval beyond IT before being considered official. In some cases (e.g., file and message retention), Legal should be involved. In other cases (e.g., company equipment at home), it would be wise to involve HR and Finance. Involving other departments not only helps IT establish partnerships with these groups, but it ensures that IT isn't determining policies in a vacuum.

Outsourcing

Over the past few years, outsourcing and offshoring have become very attractive solutions. However, it's important to remember that when you outsource certain business activities, your organization is still responsible for ethical and compliance activities. While outsourcing is adding value to your organization's services, products, and bottom line, you want to make sure that you're not risking the company's reputation or compliance responsibilities as a result. Any agreement for the use of third parties should take compliance, security, privacy, etc. into consideration; and detail the responsibilities and expectations of the outsourcer.

For a much more detailed discussion on outsourcing, see **Chapter 6, Managing the Money,** on **page 161.**

8.11 Further References

Websites

bugtraq-subscribe@securityfocus.com (Bugtrac mailing list).

www.accenture.com/SiteCollectionDocuments/PDF/global_millennial_generation_research.pdf (report on Millennials use of technology).

www.aicpa.org/InterestAreas/InformationTechnology/Resources/Privacy/PrivacyOutsourcing/DownloadableDocuments/9127383_Privacy4.pdf (privacy and outsourcing).

www.cert.org (federally funded Computer Emergency Response Team at Carnegie Mellon).

www.checkpoint.com (security solutions vendor).

www.cisco.com (security solutions vendor).

news.cnet.com/Tesco-to-track-milk-deliveries-by-RFID/2100-1033_3-6079022.html?tag=lia;rcol.

www.cnn.com/2011/TECH/web/06/26/tech.lulzsec.hackers.

www.credant.com (mobile data encryption vendor).

www.discover6sigma.org (information about Six Sigma).

www.elcomsoft.com/survey/survey2009.pdf (survey about password security).

www.isaca.org (trade association for IT governance professionals).

www.isc2.org (industry organization leader in educating and certifying information security professionals).

www.isixsigma.com (information about Six Sigma).

www.iso.org (information about the International Organization for Standards and ISO 9000).

www.itgi.org (trade association for IT governance professionals).

www.itil-officialsite.com/home/home.asp (information about ITIL).

www.juniper.net (security solutions vendor).

www.mcafee.com/us (security software vendor).

www.microsoft.com/technet/security/default.mspx (Microsoft's security website).

technet.microsoft.com/en-us/library/dd206732.aspx (Microsoft's IT Compliance Management Guide).

onguardonline.gov (a U.S. government site about computer security).

csrc.nist.gov/index.html (National Institute of Standards and Technology's website about computer security).

www.organicconsumers.org/clothes/nike041505.cfm (article about Nike's offshore practices).

www.ponemon.org/blog/post/cost-of-a-data-breach-climbs-higher (report on the cost of data breaches).

www.privacyrights.org/ar/ChronDataBreaches.htm#CP (list of data breach/loss incidents).

www.sec.gov/news/studies/2009/sox-404_study.pdf (report on impact of Sarbanes–Oxley).

www.securityguidance.com (Microsoft security assessment tool).

www.security-risk-analysis.com/introduction.htm (introduction to risk analysis).

www.sei.cmu.edu/cmmi (information about CMMI).
www.slashdot.org.
www.snpx.com (security website for IT professionals).
www.symantec.com (security software vendor).
www.trendmicro.com (security software vendor).
pr.webroot.com/threat-research/cons/protect-your-computer-from-hackers-101210.html.

Books and Articles

Alexander, P., 2008. Information Security: A Manager's Guide to Thwarting Data Thieves and Hackers. Praeger.
Bacik, S., 2008. Building an Effective Information Security Policy Architecture. CRC.
Biegelman, M.T., Biegelman, D.R., 2008. Building a World-Class Compliance Program: Best Practices and Strategies for Success. Wiley.
Chickowski, E., 2009. Is Your Information Really Safe? Baseline Magazine April.
Chorafas, D.N., 2008. IT Auditing and Sarbanes–Oxley Compliance: Key Strategies for Business Improvement. Auerbach Publications.
DeLuccia, I.V., James, J., 2008. IT Compliance and Controls: Best Practices for Implementation. Wiley.
Foresti, S., 2010. Preserving Privacy in Data Outsourcing. Springer.
Greengard, S., 2011. Managing a Multigenerational Workforce. CIO Insight Magazine May/June.
Keefe, M., 2009. A Short History of Hacks, Worms, and Cyberterror. Computerworld April, 27.
Matwyshyn, A., 2009. Harboring Data: Information Security, Law, and the Corporation. Stanford Law Books.
McClure, S., Scambray, J., Kurtz, G., 2009. Hacking Exposed: Network Security Secrets and Solutions. McGraw-Hill Osborne.
Mitnick, K., 2011. Ghosts in the Wires. Little, Browne and Company.
Perkins, B., 2011. Data Breaches' Costly Fallout. Computerworld June 6.
Rashid, F., 2011. Cloud Security Services Can Reduce Malware. eWeek July 18.
Rashid, F., 2011. Hackers Shift from Vandalism to Data Theft. eWeek August 15.
Saporito, B., 2011. Hack Attack. Time July 4.
Selig, G.J., Wilkinson, J., 2008. Implementing IT Governance: A Practical Guide to Global Best Practices in IT Management. Van Haren Publishing.
Senft, S., Gallegos, F., 2008. Information Technology Control and Audit, third ed. Auerbach Publications.
Sengupta, S., 2011. Guardians of Internet Security Are Targets. New York Times August 4.
Steele, B.K., 2009. Due Diligence. Baseline Magazine March.
Tipton, H.F., Krause, M., 2009. Information Security Management Handbook. Auerback Publications.
Vijayan, J., 2009. Internet Warfare: Are We Focusing on the Wrong Things? Computerworld April, 27.
Wallace, M., Weber, L., 2008. IT Governance 2009: Policies & Procedures. Aspen Publishing.
Whitman, M.E., Mattord, H.J., 2011. Principles of Information Security. Course Technology.
Wright, C.S., 2008. The IT Regulatory and Standards Compliance Handbook: How to Survive Information Systems Audit and Assessments. Syngress.

SOX

www.aicpa.org/Advocacy/Issues/Pages/Section404bofSOX.aspxnews.findlaw.com/hdocs/docs/gwbush/sarbanesoxley072302.pdf.

HIPAA

www.hhs.gov/ocr/hipaa.
www.hhs.gov/ocr/privacy/hipaa/administrative/enforcementrule/hitechenforcementifr.html.
www.hipaa.com/.

Basel II
www.bis.org/bcbs/index.htm.
www.federalreserve.gov/generalinfo/basel2/default.htm.

SB-1386
info.sen.ca.gov/pub/01-02/bill/sen/sb_1351-1400/sb_1386_bill_20020926_chaptered.html.
www.giac.org/paper/gsec/3647/californiasnotice-security-breachs-about-means/105901.

FACTA
www.epic.org/privacy/fcra.
www.ftc.gov/os/statutes/fcrajump.shtm.

Gramm–Leach–Bliley
www.epic.org/privacy/glba.
www.ftc.gov/privacy/privacyinitiatives/glbact.html.

U.S. Securities
rules.nyse.com/nyse/www.sec.gov/rules/final/34-44992a.htm.
www.sec.gov/rules/final.shtml.

Patriot Act
thomas.loc.gov/cgi-bin/bdquery/z?d107:h.r.03162.
www.epic.org/privacy/terrorism/hr3162.html.

OFAC
www.asic.gov.au/asic/asic.nsf/byheadline/CLERP+9?openDocument.
www.treas.gov/offices/enforcement/ofac.
www.treasury.gov.au/contentitem.asp?NavId=013&ContentID=403.
www.treasury.gov/resource-center/sanctions/OFAC-Enforcement/Pages/enforcement.aspxCLERP-9.

PIPEDA
www.pipedainfo.com.
www.priv.gc.ca/leg_c/leg_c_p_e.cfm.

Privacy and Electronic Communications Directive
eur-lex.europa.eu/LexUriServ/LexUriServ.do?uri=CELEX:32002L0058:EN:NOT.
europa.eu/legislation_summares/information_society/legislative_framework/l24120_en.htm.

Data Protection Directive
ec.europa.eu/justice_home/fsj/privacy/index_en.htm.
www.spamlaws.com/eu.shtml.

Disaster Recovery

Organizing is what you do before you do something, so that when you do it, it is not all mixed up.

A. A. Milne

CHAPTER TABLE OF CONTENTS

9.1 Defining the Scope 248
9.2 Creating a Disaster Recovery Plan...253
9.3 A Word about Incident Response, Business Continuity, and Disaster Recovery 260
9.4 The Hidden Benefits of Good Disaster Recovery Planning..261
9.5 Further References 262

It's no secret that the daily routine of everyday life has become highly dependent on information technology. And incidents like September 11, 2001; hurricanes Katrina and Rita in 2005; the blackout of the Northeast in August of 2003; and many other crises serve as regular reminders that we have to be prepared for the worst. This is where disaster recovery comes in.

Disaster recovery is like buying insurance; you're planning for the worst, but the entire time you're hoping that you'll never need it. IT disasters come in all shapes and sizes, from hardware failures and computer viruses to blizzards, floods, chemical spills, fires, and terrorist attacks. As individuals, we routinely do things to be ready for the unexpected emergency. We keep Band-Aids in the medicine cabinet, a spare tire in the car, and a fire extinguisher in the house.

IT environments are replete with all kinds of solutions to deal with various outages and failures: clustered servers, transaction logs, backups, RAID disk drives, and so on. The problem with these kinds of solutions is that each can only handle the failure of a *specific component*. This leaves IT Managers with the issue of what to do if the *entire* environment fails, or becomes unavailable.

As shown in this chapter, the key to good disaster recovery planning is the involvement of as many areas of the organization as possible. IT can be the leader or motivator (although even that isn't required, but it's a common situation), but *all facets of a company must be involved* in disaster recovery planning. The reason is simple: disasters of every size (from brief power outages to city-wide blackouts) affect every department and affect every employee—possibly your customers and suppliers, too. Everyone should be ready. Murphy's Law that "anything that can go wrong will" would be just as apt a quote for the beginning of this chapter as the one that appears.

9.1 DEFINING THE SCOPE

The extent to which you as an IT Manager have to, or can, plan for a disaster is directly related to how much your organization is dependent on IT for its core business operation and how much money your organization is willing to invest to protect it. Today it is the rare organization that is not *highly* dependent on their IT operations.

When you start to think about disaster recovery and the infinite combination of things that could go wrong and what you might have to plan for, you can easily find yourself losing a lot of sleep, thinking there is simply no way you have it all covered. However, as stated in **Chapter 8, Security and Compliance,** on **page 205,** you need to take comfort in the very fact that you're taking the right steps to best protect your environment. Remember, disaster recovery planning is an ongoing and iterative process; you can never say, "Okay, now it's done."

Key Questions

One of the most important steps in disaster recovery planning is trying to define the scope. While it is not possible to think of every scenario, you can help put things in perspective with questions such as the following:

- Which exactly are my *critical* applications and services?
- How quickly do I have to recover those critical applications and services (seconds, minutes, hours, days)?
- What are the different scenarios to plan for?
  - No access to the building (e.g., snow storm)
  - Loss of data center (e.g., flood, fire)
  - Loss of building (e.g., fire, hurricane, collapse)
  - Loss of some public services (e.g., mass transit, access to Internet, electricity)
  - Geographic impact (e.g., a blackout that affects just a few blocks in your city or one that affects 50 million people across several states, such as the blackout in the northeast United States in August of 2003)
- How long of an interruption should be planned for (days, weeks, indefinite)?
- How quickly do I need access to my data and systems? Can I wait a few days, or do I need to be up and running in 24 hours?
- Is last week's backup good enough or do we need to be able to restore more current data?

Notice the range of disasters you need to think about. One- to three-day events such as snow storms all the way up to events such as terrorist attacks have permanently changed the way we think about disasters.

Obviously, these are questions you can't answer alone, and they can be the subject of endless discussion. The answers will vary greatly depending on the size of your organization, the industry you're in, and, probably most critically, the cost of the required resources.

Once the scope is agreed to by the key departments (HR, IT, Facilities, Legal, etc.), it's critical that it have the support of company executives. At a minimum, this would probably include the CIO and CFO. But there are others that should be considered. For example, the Legal department and the departments that deal with regulatory compliance may need to weigh in with their concerns. It is not unheard of for the scope to be presented to the CEO and Board of Directors or perhaps one of the board's committees.

During the process of defining the scope, you can expect to be educating others about your IT environment. Some of the people you're working with may assume that since they hear the word "server" so often, they think that the company has just 1, not 100. They may think of the computer room as that rack they saw in a closet five years ago and have no idea that it's now a 2500-square-foot facility with dedicated environmental services. In short, you'll be explaining to them what is a mountain and what is a mole hill. See the section **"Getting Approval and Defending Your Budget"** on **page 165** in **Chapter 6, Managing the Money,** about how to present technical information to a non-technical audience. If you are addressing a Board of Directors or senior management, especially about a topic as important as disaster recovery, you want to make sure your message gets across as cleanly and professionally as possible.

Recovery Time and Recover Point Objectives

As part of the scope definition phase, you have to determine two key objectives:

1. **Recovery Time Objective (RTO):** The amount of time between the disaster and when services are restored. The RTO parameter essentially quantifies how long you can/will be down for. Factors here include the availability of space (such as a data center and office space), availability of equipment (such as workstations, servers, storage), availability of connectivity (both local and wide area networks), and other resources (including staff and vendors) to help you restore the environment.
2. **Recovery Point Objective (RPO):** The age, or "freshness," of data available to be restored. The RPO could be a factor of how often you do backups or how often the tapes are sent off site. In fact, the exercise of determining your RPO may lead you to re-evaluate your processes and schedules for backups and sending tapes off-site. Technologies such as data duplication to remote facilities or the ability to replay transaction logs can be very useful in mitigating the RPO. See the section **"Value of Your Data"** later in this chapter.

RPO and RTO are sometimes best illustrated graphically (see Figure 9.1).

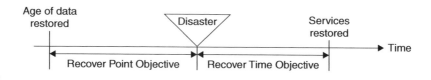

FIGURE 9.1

RPO and RTO.

Disaster Recovery Committee

To get the answers to the questions posed earlier, you'll need to work closely with others in the organization. Although it relies heavily on IT, disaster recovery planning isn't a function of IT alone. It requires the involvement of a number of other departments, including:

- Finance
- Human Resources

- Legal
- Key user departments (Manufacturing, Customer Service, etc.)
- Building Facilities

A committee like this can also help determine what the priorities are in the event of a disaster. What about customer service? Financial stability? Regulatory compliance? Health and safety? These answers can vary greatly depending on the organization's industry. A Web-based retailer may consider continued customer service as its key priority as a way of protecting its financial stability. A publicly traded financial services company may place a high priority on investor relations, regulatory compliance, and financial stability. A hospital may be willing to sacrifice all those things because it's focusing on the health and safety of its patients.

There are no standard answers to these questions and issues. Each organization must consider them and come to a decision about their own priorities. And the answers won't come easily or quickly. It could easily take months just to determine the answers, and all this must happen before you can begin to formulate the actual disaster recovery plans. Because of questions like these, and many more, it's important that the planning not be limited to IT alone.

The committee can serve not only to develop the plan, but also, in the event of a disaster, serve as a decision-making body—one that provides leadership and guidance to the rest of the organization for the duration of the disaster recovery effort.

Application Assessment

To start determining where your technology priorities are, you'll need an inventory of your applications. The items to track for each application in the inventory include:

- User community (departments, number of users)
- Vendor
- Database environment
- Operating system environment
- Interfaces to other applications, systems, and vendors/partners
- Whether the application is considered "critical"
- Which server(s) the application runs on
- Which teams support the application
- Periods of peak/critical usage (days of week, ends of months/quarters, season cycles)
- Executive usage
- Who needs to be notified when scheduling downtime or when there is an unexpected outage
- Where the application installation media and instructions are stored

This inventory will be a critical tool for disaster recovery planning, and essentially helps you develop a business impact analysis. A business impact analysis identifies the areas that may be the most vulnerable and that would cause the greatest loss to the organization. With this information, you can begin to assess, along with other departments, the criticality of your business's applications. See the section **"What Do We Have Here"** in **Chapter 7, Getting Started with the Technical Environment** on **page 189,** for more information about inventories

Compiling all of this information is a lot of work, of course, but you should have done most of this work for other reasons: you need these data to complete the inventory of your technical environment.

This topic is discussed in the last section of this chapter entitled **"The Hidden Benefits of Good Disaster Recovery Planning" (page 261)**.

You'll want to set up some guidelines for the assessment, probably along the framework of your organization's priorities. For example, if continued customer service is a key priority, you'll have to identify those applications associated with customer service.

In all likelihood, you'll probably end up with several priorities of applications. An example of those priorities, as shown in Figure 9.2, might be:

- Priority 1: Those applications that need to be returned to service within 6 business hours.
- Priority 2: Those applications that need to be returned to service within 24 to 48 hours.
- Priority 3: Those applications that need to be returned to service within 3 to 7 days.
- Priority 4: Those applications that need to be returned to service within 1 to 2 weeks.
- Priority 5: Those applications that can wait more than 2 weeks to be returned to service.

You may choose to define a Priority Zero for your applications, which would include the core services. This could include items such as a network environment, remote connectivity, Internet access, and DNS and DHCP services. For many organizations, e-mail might be considered a Priority Zero application, along with telephone services.

To help you judge the priorities of your different applications, consider different questions:

- Are there risks to the *safety* of employees, customers, or the general public with an outage of different applications?
- Are there any *regulatory costs* associated with an outage to this application? What happens if a requirement isn't met? Is there a financial penalty? Would you be allowed to conduct business if not compliant?

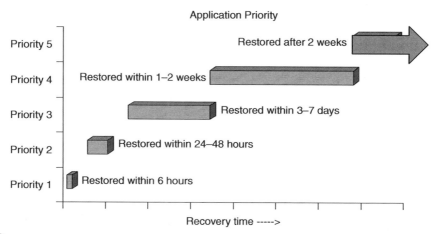

FIGURE 9.2

Sample application recovery priorities.

- What is the *loss to the business* if this system is unavailable? In addition to lost revenue, would there be penalties from partners for missed obligations? Would it impact the company's financial and credit ratings?
- How big is the concern about *loss of the organization's image or customer/public trust* that may result from an outage?
- What is the *likelihood of an outage of this application* as a result of different types of disasters?
- Are there *redundancies* already in place to help mitigate the impact of a disaster? These redundancies could include items such as clustered servers, RAID technology for data storage, and backup generators.

These types of questions force you to consider how big an impact each application, system, or resource has on the organization, as well as the risk probability of different types of disaster. As shown in Figure 9.3, the higher the risk and the higher the impact to the business, the higher the priority should be.

Again, the specifics of the application prioritization, as well as the number of priorities, will vary tremendously from organization to organization. And, these may even change depending on the time of year.

The Value of Your Data

At the same time you're considering application priorities, you have to consider how much *data loss* you can tolerate. For example, in a payroll system, it may not be that much of a problem if the last two days of changes have to be reentered (because the last backup available was taken 48 hours prior to the disaster, and not many changes occur on a daily basis). In a brokerage house trading system, however, the tolerance for data loss might be zero, necessitating real-time replication of all data. The volume of data change in these two scenarios is very different.

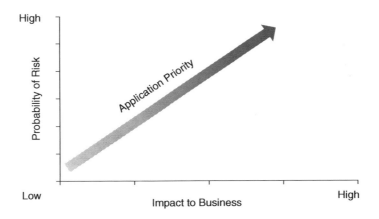

FIGURE 9.3

Application priority for disaster recovery.

9.2 CREATING A DISASTER RECOVERY PLAN

Once you have the scope and identified the critical applications, you can begin to develop a plan. If you expect to have any hope for any level of success in the event of a disaster, several key items must be identified in order to develop that plan.

- **Communication plan:** A plan for contacting key personnel, customers, vendors, and employees.
- **Documentation:** Written material describing the existing environment, procedures for declaring a disaster, procedures for reestablishing services in a disaster recovery mode, etc.
- **Real estate and IT facilities:** Determine which location(s) people should meet up at if the facility is suddenly off-limits, inaccessible, or out of commission. Where can you set up servers and get Internet connectivity?
- **Off-site storage of data:** If your facility is destroyed, or inaccessible, make sure you have an up-to-date copy of your data at an off-site facility.
- **Hardware availability:** Make sure that you can get replacement hardware if yours is destroyed. This list could include workstations, servers, routers, switches, storage (disk and tape), etc.
- **Regular updating and testing:** Your environment changes regularly (technology, people, needs, organization, procedures, etc.). You need to test and update your disaster recovery plan regularly to make sure it retains its value.

Each of these items is discussed in the sections that follow.

Communication Plan

The hallmark of a good disaster recovery plan is good communications. Disasters don't necessarily happen when everyone is sitting at their desks. They can happen on weekends or in the middle of the night. People may be on vacation, at off-site meetings, or in transit.

To ensure that you can get word to people in an emergency, your organization should have a call list that includes information, such as:

- Home phone number(s)
- Cell phone number(s)
- Non-work e-mail address(es)

This list should also include the geographic location of each person's home, as well as cell phone carrier(s). This information could be useful to quickly identify those people that may (or may not) be impacted in an isolated disaster, such as a highway out of service due to a chemical spill or those using a carrier struggling with restoring service.

The list should include individuals from within the company and from outside the company:

- All members of IT
- Key executives, customers, and clients
- Individuals from key departments (Facilities, HR, etc.)
- Key partners and suppliers (vendors, financial institutions, telecomm carriers, off-site storage facility, etc.)
- Appropriate regulatory agencies

For some contacts (such as vendors and suppliers), you should also be sure that the list includes appropriate identifying information (such as account numbers) to help avoid delays and confusion. Remember, it is not IT's job alone to put together the contact information; each team and department has responsibility.

The list should exist in electronic form (such as on your phone or handheld device, your PC, or USB memory drive) as well as in paper form in multiple locations (home, office, car, predetermined off-site meeting locations). In a situation where a large number of individuals have to be contacted, a phone tree can be used. Alternatively (or in addition), you can use a third-party crisis communications service such as Send Word Now (www.sendwordnow.com) or Everbridge (www.everbridge.com), which can facilitate communications to very large groups of people quickly through multiple means (phone, e-mail, text messages). Similarly, a web site set up specifically for providing information in an emergency can be invaluable. A web site like this should be hosted external to your facility to ensure that it can be reached if your facility is off-line. Of course, such a web site has to be secured properly so that sensitive and critical information isn't available to unauthorized individuals, and hosted separately from your regular IT environment so that it stays up while the rest of the environment is down.

Documentation

Thorough and up-to-date disaster recovery documentation is the foundation of an effective disaster recovery plan. Although the document can be distributed electronically, as discussed in the previous section, it should also be distributed in hard copy as well. After all, in the event of a disaster, there is no certainty that you'll be able to access the electronic version. (We don't like to admit it, but sometimes that note you scribbled on the back of a restaurant receipt ends up being more accessible and more useful than that Outlook reminder you sent yourself last Thursday.)

Key individuals should have at least two copies—one copy in their office and one in their home—since there is no guarantee that a disaster will happen between 9 and 5 on a business day. Finally, keep a copy with your off-site backup tapes at locations that can be used during a disaster.

This documentation will become an indispensable resource. Memories fail, particularly in a crisis. In fact, aside from your backup tapes, your plan may be the only resource available to you during a disaster. As such, it's in your best interest to make it as useful as possible by including as much information as possible in this document. This should include documentation about the existing environment.

All documentation should be reviewed and updated at least once a year to reflect changes to the environment, operations, personnel, procedures, etc. These review opportunities can be a great time to keep key people current on the plans and to educate new employees—don't assume that everyone will read the plans on their own.

Real Estate and IT Facilities

One of the first questions that must be considered in regard to disaster recovery planning is "Where should we go now?" If you're unable to use your organization's facilities, where will everyone go when disaster strikes? If your organization is very small, you might be able get away with operating for a small time out of someone's residence. A slightly larger organization might be able to use a meeting or banquet room at a nearby hotel, assuming that the same disaster hasn't impacted those facilities.

Other alternatives might include a nearby branch office of your organization or perhaps the office of a sister, subsidiary, or parent company.

However, if your IT organization is more than a few people in size, you're probably going to need specialized facilities with sufficient space, air conditioning, electricity, telecommunications resources, and so on. This may be the case even if you're only supporting a portion of your normal operation, even for just an interim period. Many companies offer disaster recovery facilities. They can generally tailor their offerings to your needs, perhaps just providing space or, at the other extreme, providing specified computer hardware, telecommunications, and perhaps even some staffing.

Of course, the ultimate in disaster recovery facilities is for an organization to maintain its own standby site with redundant hardware. For the most critical environments, the standby site is always live, connected to the network, with a mirrored copy of the database and applications, and so on.

Disaster Recovery Facilities Considerations

When looking at companies that provide disaster recovery facilities, you have to consider several issues:

- **Proximity to your location:** You generally want a nearby location in order to get to it easily, but not so close that the facility is likely to be hit by the same disaster that affects yours. You may need to consider a facility that is reachable by mass transit if you're in a large metropolitan area where not everyone has their own car.
- **Costs:** The more services and facilities you want to be ready for your needs, the more it will cost. Contracts for disaster recovery usually last at least two years and are billed monthly. However, there are several aspects to disaster recovery fees:
  - Standby fees: The monthly fees you pay to have contracted facilities available for your use
  - Activation fee: A fee you pay when you decide that you have a disaster that warrants use of the facilities
  - Use fee: The rate (weekly, monthly) that you pay while you're using the facilities during a disaster
  - Test fee: A fee that is paid when you want to make use of the facilities to test your disaster recovery plans
- **Number of clients:** You want to be sure that the provider you're working with hasn't contracted with more clients than it can provide services for. If there is a regional disaster, and all the provider's customers suddenly need to use the facilities, will there be enough to go around? Disaster recovery providers can either provide you with dedicated space that will always be there for you, or non-dedicated space that is made available to their subscribers on a first-come–first-served basis. Of course, the dedicated space is far more expensive.
- **Other required services:** Space, hardware, staff, telecommunications, air conditioning, electricity. Don't forget basics such as furniture, phones, and so on.

In the event of a disaster, one of the critical decision points is when to fail-over to the recovery site. In the event of a catastrophe such as an earthquake that destroys your primary facility, the decision is pretty easy. However, in the case of a blackout, it is reasonable to think that the power will be back on soon enough, and the time, cost, and effort to bring up the disaster recovery facility (along with reverting back to the primary facility) does not outweigh the benefits of being down for a short period.

Because of this, many environments don't configure their hardware and software to automatically fail-over to the backup facilities if a problem is detected at the primary site. Often, the fail-over process is something that has to wait for a human decision to be specifically initiated.

Off-Site Storage of Data

Backup Tapes

If you need to activate a disaster recovery plan, make sure that you can get your company's systems and data up and available. Most likely, you'll have to do some sort of restore from your backup tapes. If your regular facility is destroyed or inaccessible, you'll have to retrieve the backup tapes from your off-site storage vendor.

To get those tapes, you'll need several items:

- Contact information for your off-site location
- A method of identifying which set of tapes you want retrieved
- A customer ID, account number, and possibly a password as a way of identifying yourself to the off-site location as someone authorized to request that the tapes be retrieved
- The address of, and probably directions to, the location of where the tapes should be delivered (you most likely won't want them delivered to your usual facility)

Getting the tapes is the first step. Then you have to begin the restore process. You'll need to have access to compatible hardware and software that can read those tapes, and have procedures for doing the restore. Also, if you normally encrypt your backup tapes, your recovery site has to have the appropriate technology and copies of the encryption keys to ensure that the backup tapes can be unencrypted. Some companies are moving to tapeless backup by copying their files to a remote facility over a network (see the next section, **"Data Replication" on page 256**). While this simplifies some of the issues of getting your tapes, you still have to make sure that your recovery site has connectivity to the backup data. For those organizations operating in the cloud (discussed further in **Chapter 5, Software, Operating Systems, and Enterprise Applications** on **page 135**), things are even simpler.

Data Replication

If you have an identified disaster recovery facility, with hardware, there are a number of options, in addition to backup tapes, that you can use for making data readily available in an emergency.

- A number of storage vendors (e.g., EMC, NetApps, IBM, Hewlett-Packard) have solutions for replicating data between sites. These utilities don't duplicate the entire data set, but merely the changes (usually referred to as the "*deltas*"), which results in the two copies being in synch. Similarly, third-party utilities can do the same thing (Double Take, LinkPro, Neverfail, etc.).
- Database vendors (e.g., Oracle, IBM, Microsoft) have features and utilities for keeping multiple copies of databases in synch. Similar to the data replication feature just discussed, this is strictly for databases.
- Transaction logs can be regularly replicated to your secondary site where they can be imported into the copy of the database.

Hardware Availability

If your regular computer hardware is unusable for any reason (e.g., a power outage or the destruction of your facilities), you'll have to quickly get your hands on some computer hardware before you can even begin rebuilding your environment.

Size of Your Environment

The smaller and more generic your environment is, the more options you'll have. For example, if your environment is based on Microsoft Windows and Intel PCs and servers, you may be able to rely on local retailers or your regular reseller. Alternatively, you can contract with your disaster recovery facility to keep a quantity of these units on hand for you.

With larger or more complex environments, it will be more difficult (and more expensive) to make sure the equipment will be available. You may want to purchase some of this equipment yourself to have in an emergency, or your disaster recovery facility provider may do this and pass the cost on to you. Your vendor may also have options and provisions available to allow you to receive emergency delivery of specified equipment in the event of a disaster.

For larger environments you may consider having a dedicated facility, either at your own site or from a disaster recovery provider, that is a running environment with all your necessary hardware.

Duplicating Your Entire Environment

In case of a disaster, you may not need to duplicate your entire environment. You probably just want to plan for bringing up the systems that are the most critical to the continued operation and survival of the organization (as discussed previously in this chapter in the section, **"Application Assessment"** on **page 250**). To make sure that your recovery operation is as smooth as possible, you'll want to ensure that you're using equipment as comparable as possible to your existing environment. The middle of a crisis isn't the time to find out that the emergency tape drive you have isn't compatible with the backup tapes you use, that you don't have the proper drivers for the network interface cards you're using, or that your application software has to be recompiled before it will run on the hardware you have.

Equipment at Home

If your plan includes people working from home, be sure they have what they need:

*   Workstations with appropriate software (either the applications they need and/or software for remote access to reach those applications and data). If it's a laptop you gave them strictly to be used in the event of a disaster, you'll want to check the laptop periodically to make sure it's still functioning, has up-to-date software, etc.
*   Familiarity with procedures for connecting remotely (especially for connecting to a recovery site).

Regular Updating and Testing

A disaster recovery plan needs to be reviewed and updated regularly. Just as important is testing the plan periodically.

Review and Update

At least once a year you should review your plan for the following:

- Is the emergency contact list current? Check it to verify that it doesn't contain individuals who have left the company or are no longer relevant to the plan, that new employees have been added, and that the contact information on the list is accurate.
- Are your own internal safety nets still working? You've probably installed a number of redundant resources to use in case of emergency. However, too often, when an emergency strikes, the backup facility fails because it isn't working either. Perhaps it hasn't been used for so long that it's fallen into disrepair or perhaps it hasn't been kept up to date with upgrades. Regular testing of your redundant resources is important. A spare tire is of no use if there's no air in it.
- Can the backup tapes be read by the equipment at the backup site?
- Do you have copies of the media and installation instructions for the requisite software (operating systems, applications, backup software, etc.) that may have to be installed before you can begin restoring your data from tape?
- Are all associated components factored in? If your check-printing application is considered critical, for example, you have to include the availability of a printer during an emergency in addition to bringing up the application to be adequately prepared.
- Do you have current critical passwords for applications, servers, websites, databases, etc?

Testing

Just like you check the pressure in your spare tire periodically to make sure it would be useful when you need it, you also need to test your disaster recovery plan periodically to make sure it will work for you when needed. This can be an enormous task, requiring a fair amount of planning of its own.

- You'll need a way to take your primary site off-line (or at least have it seem off-line). You may be able to power down your environment or disconnect its WAN connections. Regardless, your monitoring and management solution will start sending a number of alerts.
- Develop a test plan and script to run through to make a determination if things are working as expected.
- Coordinate with all parts of IT and user department representatives to prepare for and participate in the test.
- To get the most value from the test, you want to have a rigorous postmortem process to evaluate what aspects didn't work, why they didn't work, and what has to be changed so that they'll work the next time.

If there is simply no way to plan downtime to your production environment (perhaps because your organization runs 24/7), you **may** have to consider doing tests in phases, testing just a few systems or components at a time. In very large environments, it can take months to plan out a single test of a disaster recovery plan.

Don't be surprised if your testing isn't 100% successful. Developing and testing disaster recovery plans are iterative processes. Also, remind yourself that it is certainly better to identify problems during a test than during a real crisis.

After the Disaster

An often forgotten aspect of disaster recovery planning are the steps required once the disaster abates and things can return to normal. While in disaster-recovery mode, you've been running critical systems and applications out of your disaster recovery facility. When the disaster is over and you can return to your primary facility, you now need to have a plan to get data from the disaster recovery facility (which now has the most current data) back to your primary site.

The process will probably be somewhat similar to the one you used to get then-current data to your disaster recovery facility (duplication of transaction logs, tapes, data replication, etc.). Of course, this process has to be done after you've repaired any damage that may have occurred to the primary facility, or the systems it contains.

Regional and Catastrophic Disasters

Many disasters are often a result of the forces of nature (e.g., the Northeast blackout of 2003 and Hurricane Katrina in 2005). As such, if your organization suffers a disaster, it's likely that many other organizations in your geographic area will also suffer, and they may be scrambling for the same recovery resources that you're planning to rely on.

- The local computer retailer may be rushed by other organizations trying to get their hands on hardware.
- Hotel rooms may be sold out.
- Because telecommunications companies will be working around the clock to get regular services restored, your plans to install temporary lines may not pan out.
- The very vendors and service providers you had planned on may not be functioning because they are dealing with the same disaster you are.

A key issue to keep in mind in this regard when crafting your disaster recovery plan is to incorporate some non-local options for each category in the plan.

Finally, it's important to remember that in the event of a truly catastrophic disaster, employees' priorities will quickly shift from trying to aid their employer to trying to aid their families. For dealing with the human side of disasters, see the next section.

The ACT Model

Most of the chapter has focused on the mechanics and technologies of dealing with a crisis. However, it's also wise to plan for individuals (staff, employees, etc.) during a crisis.

Consider the guidelines of the ACT model:

A—Acknowledge and name the trauma. Have the courage to use names and the real words describing what happened, including the word "death" (if warranted, of course). It's important to validate the accuracy of information and share only what is known for sure. Know the facts and don't speculate. (New York City's Mayor Rudy Giuliani's refusal to speculate on the cost in human lives during the 9/11 disaster was an excellent example of the value of waiting until all the facts were in.

He was asked about the toll repeatedly for many days, but refused to give a number until he knew the facts.) Straying from the script can be very harmful. Personally acknowledge the incident in order to position company management as also being impacted by the event, thereby aligning leaders with the staff.

C—Communicate both competence and caring. Competence and caring aren't mutually exclusive! Demonstrate expertise in dealing with the issue and express compassion for the personal impact to those who are affected.

T—Transition. Communicate an expectation of recovery. Show sensitivity and flexibility as people return to life and return to work. Communicate clearly that leadership will take steps to help people transition back to health and productivity. Identify internal and external resources for additional information and support. Be especially visible and accessible to employees for support and information.

The ACT model focuses on direct and honest communications and demonstrating sensitivity.

9.3 A WORD ABOUT INCIDENT RESPONSE, BUSINESS CONTINUITY, AND DISASTER RECOVERY

Incident Response, Business Continuity Planning (BCP), and Disaster Recovery (DR) are often used as interchangeable terms. Although the three types of planning are similar, there are differences.

- **Incident Response**: This is the name for the immediate steps taken to ensure the protection of people. The focus is on employee safety and well-being. Incident response includes simple building evacuation procedures, communications, accounting for all employees to ensure that they are safe, and determining next steps like initiating business continuity and disaster recovery plans.
- **Business Continuity Planning:** BCP is a methodology used to create a plan for how an organization will resume partially or completely interrupted critical function(s) within a predetermined time after a disaster or disruption. BCP helps prioritize recovery activities for critical functions. BCP may be a part of a larger organizational effort to reduce operational risk, and thus has a number of overlaps with the practice of risk management.
- **Disaster Recovery**: DR is the ability to establish (or restart) an infrastructure for resuming critical functions after a disaster.

These areas do overlap and, to a certain degree, are interdependent. Most confusion rests with the terms "business continuity planning" and "disaster recovery." To help differentiate between the two, it's best to think of disaster recovery as those areas and issues related to the IT environment and infrastructure (data center, servers, access, data, applications, etc.). The remaining items, the business's day-to-day function, would generally fall into the area of business continuity planning.

Business continuity essentially picks up where disaster recovery leaves off. In a perfect world you have a parallel data center that is a mirror image of everything in your primary data center. When disaster hits, you can invoke your disaster recovery plans to bring the parallel data center online with all applications and no loss of data. Then business continuity comes into play as the user departments attempt to continue functioning. "Continuing their normal function" becomes quite challenging if there is no electricity and/or phones, travel is severely curtailed, people can't get to the office, etc.

For example, while disaster recovery planning would cover the following issues:

- Secondary data centers
- Off-site storage of backup tapes
- Redundancy/availability of technical resources
- Replication of data
- Procedures and resources for installing applications, related systems, and making them available
- UPS and generator solutions

BCP would cover issues such as:

- Communication plans
    - Lists of cell phone numbers
    - Plans for communicating to the employee population at large, as well as those critical in a disaster scenario (emergency phone numbers, websites)
- Where people will meet to continue to conduct business if the office is unavailable
- Locations of nearby hotels, restaurants, and other services if the need arises
- Plans for continuing key business operations and working with critical customers and partners (banks, suppliers, etc.) during a crisis
- Copies of vital files and information
- Availability of cash
- What would the sales department do? Could/should they continue to try to sell products? How would they reassure customers?
- How would the accounting department make sure that the company's suppliers are paid and that receivables are collected?
- How would customers, suppliers, partners, clients, investors, and employees be kept informed?
- Could payroll continue to pay employees during the disaster?

As a general rule, the IT department's greater priority is disaster recovery, while user departments are generally concerned about BCP.

9.4 THE HIDDEN BENEFITS OF GOOD DISASTER RECOVERY PLANNING

One seldom recognized value of good disaster recovery planning is that it often helps tremendously with regular, everyday corporate process execution. Good disaster recovery makes for good everyday business performance.

- You need to know exactly where every piece of hardware in your company is anyway: where is it, how old is it, what applications/services does it provide, who supports it, etc. But if you can't find the time to do this kind of inventory on a regular basis, you should find the time to do it for a formal disaster recovery plan.
- If you don't have current contact lists for people outside your direct reports, here is a chance to create one and keep it current.
- Naturally, you should have very complete data backup procedures. But if you haven't yet set up off-site backup, creating a disaster recovery plan can force you—or higher ups, once you put it in the context of disaster recovery—to get the time and money to make this basic need happen.

9.5 Further References

Websites

www.capscenters.com (computer alternative processing sites, CAPS).

www.doubletake.com (data replication software).

www.drj.com (Disaster Recovery Journal).

www.drs.net (Disaster Recovery Services, DRS).

www.everbridge.com (crisis communication tool).

www.hp.com/go/continuityandavailability (HP Business Continuity and Availability Services).

www.ibm.com/services/continuity (IBM Business Continuity and Recovery Services).

www.linkpro.com (data replication software).

www.neverfailgroup.com (data replication software).

www.recovery.sungard.com (SunGard Recovery Services).

www.rentsys.com (Rentsys Recovery Services).

www.sendwordnow.com (crisis communication tool).

Books and Articles

Blokdijk, G., 2008. Disaster Recovery 100 Success Secrets—IT Business Continuity, Disaster Recovery Planning and Services. Emereo.

Bowman, R.H., 2008. Business Continuity Planning for Data Centers and Systems: A Strategic Implementation Guide. Wiley.

Dolewski, R., 2008. Disaster Recovery Planning. McPress.

Hiles, A., 2010. The Definitive Handbook of Business Continuity Management. Wiley.

Hotchkiss, S., 2010. Business Continuity Management: In Practice. British Informatics Society Ltd.

Nash, K.S., 2011. When Disaster Hits Home. CIO Magazine July 1.

National Fire Prevention Association, NFPA 1600, Standard on Disaster/Emergency Management and Business Continuity Programs. www.nfpa.org/assets/files/PDF/NFPA1600.pdf.

Preimesberger, C., 2011. Why Disaster Recovery Isn't Optional Anymore. eWeek July 18.

Rothstein, P.J., 2008. Disaster Recovery Testing. Rothstein.

Schmidt, K., 2010. High Availability and Disaster Recovery: Concepts, Design, Implementation. Springer.

Thejendra, B.S., 2008. Disaster Recovery and Business Continuity. IT Governance.

Wallace, M., Webber, L., 2010. The Disaster Recovery Handbook: A Step-by-Step Plan to Ensure Business Continuity and Protect Vital Operations, Facilities, and Assets. AMACOM.

Watters, J.P., 2010. The Business Continuity Management Desk Reference. Leverage.

Working with Users

Pay attention to what users do, not what they say.

Jakob Nielsen

CHAPTER TABLE OF CONTENTS

10.1 Relationships with Users 263
10.2 The Consumerization of IT 271
10.3 When Your Users are Part of a Mobile Work Force.....................................274
10.4 The Help Desk..275
10.5 Service Level Agreements..283
10.6 Further References 284

The relationship you and your team have with the user community is one of the most important relationships you will have to maintain. In some regards, your reputation in the company can be measured by your relationship with the users. If you have a positive relationship, the user community (which for IT is essentially everyone in the organization) will be your ally for almost anything you want to do. However, if that relationship is less than positive, the user community will question and doubt all your plans—both the value of those plans and your ability to implement them successfully. Later in this chapter there is a discussion about **Help Desk services** on **page 275**, the most visible and most commonly thought of aspect of working with users. But first we discuss the overall relationship you and the IT department must maintain with the users.

10.1 RELATIONSHIPS WITH USERS

One of the most important things you can do as an IT manager is to establish and maintain a good relationship with your users. They should see you as available, reliable, dedicated to service, and having their best interest at heart. For the most part, they do not care about your other customers, your bosses, the vendors, the technology issues—they care about their own needs. Prior to becoming a manager, you had exposure to only a portion of your users, and only a portion of their IT needs. Now that you're managing the entire department, all the users, and all their IT needs, rest squarely on your shoulders.

One of the recurring themes in this book is the importance of understanding who your users are, what they need, and what are they doing that could impact or benefit you. While this chapter is dedicated to your role with the users, we also discuss related issues in detail in other parts of the book:

- In the section **"The First 100 Days"** on **page 20** in **Chapter 1, The Role of an IT Manager**, it is explained that you need to determine who your team members and who your customers are; and that there are different user areas that will require your attention, and different user areas whose attention you require.
- The section **"People to Meet and Know"** on **page 24** in **Chapter 1, The Role of an IT Manager**, discusses that there are many people you should establish relationships with, including your staff, your peers, and your boss, but it doesn't end there.
- As discussed in the section **"Communicate with Your Team"** on **page 32** in **Chapter 2, Managing Your IT Team**, communicate your vision for the department to your staff. They should understand both where you want the department to go and the plans you have for getting there.
- Users of different generations may have different priorities, styles, and preferred ways of dealing with others. The discussion in the section **"Generational Issues at Work"** in **Chapter 2, Managing Your IT Team** on **page 57** covers this in detail.

Who Are Your Users?

IT departments have all kinds of users that represent a cross-section of the company: executives, assistants, local users, remote users, finance, marketing, warehouse, human resources, facilities, users that love technology and users that hate technology.

It's important to note that some organizations don't like the term "user." Because IT is a service-focused organization, many organizations prefer "customer" or "client" instead. In an organization like a law firm, the term "client" could cause confusion, just as in other organizations the term "customer" might cause confusion.

Regardless of what they are called, users' needs are best addressed in a thorough and planned manner. Everyone knows what the results of knee-jerk reactions to problems are; the problem may get solved, but much more money and/or time is spent than should have been. Or the visible part of the problem goes away, while the underlying cause remains only to resurface at some point in the future. Spend some time in advance planning to address your users' needs.

Find Out Who Your Department Thinks Its Users Are

Don't quibble, keep focused: who are the people your department is trying to serve?

This can be a simple inquiry; ask your team while you are discussing other matters with them. Keep it informal. They may say that their users are a small subset of the company; they may reply that their users are mostly in Legal or "Tom S., who calls me all the time." While these are true, they are not the entire story. Your users may also include customers or business partners of the company; find out who they are, where they are, and how they function within their company, what their relationship is with your department, and what they want out of the relationship.

For a fuller discussion of this very important topic, see the sections **"Developing an IT Strategy"** on **page 10** and **"Determine Who Your Customers Are and What Their Needs Are"** in **Chapter 1, The Role of an IT Manager** on **page 12**. Your "customers" may or may not be who you think they are.

Find Out Who Your Boss Thinks Your Users Are

This is an important perspective for a few reasons. First, it gives you some insight into how he views the organization's world. Second, it will probably alert you to where some of the challenges are. Those challenges might include some political minefields, or perhaps information on areas that have been particularly critical of IT's services.

If your boss's perception of who your users are varies significantly from yours, you need to learn why the difference exists, and which one of you is right. (It's a safe bet you're both right, though.) If your boss always mentions the shipping department's needs and problems, ask why he never mentions the sales department.

Having spoken to your team and your boss, now canvass the rest of the organization. Contact the heads of the major departments of the company. Obviously, size matters. If you work for a 10-person start-up, talking to all the key players will not take long, nor will it be a major effort. You still need to prepare, but you can do it fairly quickly. On the other hand, if you work for a Fortune 500 corporation with divisions around the globe, canvassing your users is going to require some careful sampling.

Meet the Users

Once you've started to assemble a list of who your users are (either by name, or group, or function) you need to meet with them, establish a relationship, and ask them some questions about their needs.

These questions can help to get the discussion started:

- What services do you currently get from the IT department?
- How well does IT satisfy your needs?
- Have we fallen short in any areas? Or surpassed expectations in others?
- Which services do you need, or would you like, that you are not currently getting?
- How do you view the use of information technology in your department?
- Who else would be worth speaking to?
- What are your short-term and long-term goals and needs?
- Have you read, or heard, about any technology solutions, perhaps used by competitors, that you'd like to explore?

Ask these questions of the key department managers in your company. Tell them you are trying to align your department's functions with their needs. They may look at you funny—especially if they haven't seen this level of interest before from IT—but they will usually be happy to chat.

Use meetings like this to establish a continuing dialog and relationship with key users and departments. This might be an ongoing process, or it might be facilitated through periodic meetings, perhaps a few times a year.

And remember that these discussions should not be one way. You have as much information to share as your users do. See the section **"Sharing Information"** later in this chapter on **page 266**.

Although much of the discussion may be at a high level, you may also get one or two detail items (e.g., "This printer always jams with legal paper," or "Whenever I log in from home I always have to enter my password twice"). These are great opportunities to demonstrate for them what they can expect from you as the new IT Manager. You should investigate these problems and make sure that they are resolved. Then, just as important, follow up with that department head to tell him you looked into the problem(s) he reported and provide an explanation of what was found, and how it was addressed. Even though they are small problems, you'll be showing that you listened to what was said, cared about it, took action, and followed up. You'll never be faulted for demonstrating those traits.

What you are trying to do is establish and develop a relationship. Remember that in the beginning, the most important asset you may bring to these discussions will probably be a set of ears.

Being Available and Reachable

It is important to remember that IT is a service organization and is there to provide services to others, whether they are customers, partners, or end users. As such, one of the easiest ways to damage your reputation is by ignoring those you are supposed to be servicing. "Ignoring people" comes in all shapes and sizes; it can be not responding to phone calls and e-mails, skipping meetings you're invited to, or failure to follow up on commitments you make. Invert the last sentence and you can see how you *should be* operating with the users.

Of course, a prompt follow-up and response are only half the equation. The other half is being pro-active. A number of things can be done to show that you are always thinking about the user community:

- Call and/or meet periodically with various key users and department heads to review project status and to discuss new initiatives, pain points, etc.
- Send e-mails to users about new solutions that you think they might find valuable and offer your team's assistance to help investigate.
- Alert users to articles in your trade journals about what other organizations are doing and how others have addressed the same problems the business areas in your company are facing.
- Notify them if you hear about seminars, webinars, trade shows, conferences, user group meetings, websites, and so on that you think would be of value to them.
- Discuss with your users activities that are going on in the industry that relate to them. If your HRIS vendor merges with another or releases a new version of their software, your VP of HR will probably be very interested.
- Make training, FAQs, and tips and tricks available.
- Share IT plans and activities (see next section).

Sharing Information

Some individuals and teams seem to be reluctant to share information about what they are doing, and what's going on in their areas. However, one of the best ways to get others to share information with you is to start off by sharing information with them. In addition to some of the ideas mentioned in the previous section, there are other ways to share information with your user community:

- Share a high-level status of all of IT's projects, particularly those that will benefit the user community. The users may not care as much about purely technical activities (such as expanding the SAN), but they will be interested in those that benefit them directly, improve service levels and reliability, enhance functionality, generate revenues or cost-savings, etc.
- For key users and department heads, provide a deeper dive into the projects that are directly related to them. Of course, as discussed in **Chapter 4, Project Management (page 103)**, these stakeholders should be getting regular project status reports from the project managers. But there will be added emphasis if you personally review the status with the key individuals.

- Share the results of your own metrics, both good and bad. These metrics can include statistics about the Help Desk, user surveys, transaction processing, response time, system reliability, etc. You should include commentary explaining what led to the metrics changing (or why they haven't changed) and what steps you plan to address areas that haven't improved or have deteriorated.
- Don't be afraid to alert users to problems that IT is having. When there is a problem it is important to acknowledge it and to talk about your plans. For example, if one of your databases is suddenly responding very slowly, advise the users that IT is aware of it and is working on the problem. If nothing else, you may deflect some calls that were going to the Help Desk. Provide periodic updates until the problem is resolved.
- Make others aware of steps you're taking to reduce costs, as well as significant changes in IT's operations and strategies.
- Share how changes to the industry (either IT or your organization's), changes in key vendor plans, or changes in regulatory requirements will impact your team, and your plans to address them.
- Let your users know about the mission, values, strategies, and goals you've developed for IT.
- Consider doing a high-level presentation of IT's activities on a regular basis (quarterly, semiannually, annually).

Not only does this put your and your department in a positive light regarding transparency and information, it also helps convey a sense of what IT actually does. *You* know the IT department does a lot more than resetting passwords; now it is your job to show *them* that.

Just as important as what information you share is *how* you share it. As mentioned earlier, you're better off sharing proactively instead of just responding to request and inquiries. However, consider different mechanisms for sharing. In some cases, an e-mail is appropriate. In other cases, a more interactive mode, such as a phone call or in-person meeting, or even just walking around for the spontaneous chat, will help to greatly further the discussion and the relationship. Alternatively, you may want to meet formally with a group of key users to share some information. Also consider posting information like this on an internal website so they can always find the most up-to-date information. Doing this helps them see that everyone is getting the same information and also fosters greater discussion and Q&A. Finally, make sure you give credit where credit is due. Identify members of your team and those departments and user areas that helped you achieve successes. A little bit of credit sharing and modesty can go a long way.

Collecting Information

The flip side to sharing information is collecting it. Some information you'll already have within IT, such as Help Desk metrics, IT spending, system and resource statistics (response times, availability, etc.), project status reports, etc. But other types of information you'll have to go out and gather. Ideas for information you can collect are:

- **User satisfaction surveys.** Don't just rely on statistics from the Help Desk and your call tracking software. In addition, go out and ask users directly about the Help Desk. See how well this matches up with the other metrics. As is often said, perception can be more important than reality. User surveys can also ask users about new features, functionality, services, and so on they'd like to see from IT. See the section **"User Surveys"** later in this chapter on **page 280** for more information.

- **Post implementation project reviews.** When a project is completed, it is tempting to just move on to the next project. But you should first stop and take a moment to objectively assess how well it went. You can use a survey format or a focus group format to ask the key participants in the project how things went. For example: Were objectives met? Is the system functioning as expected and is it easy to use? How did IT's role in the project work? Were there sufficient communications? Was the project well planned? Were there good training and documentation? For specific advice on what to include in a Closeout Report (as reports at the end of projects are called), see the section **"Writing a Closeout Report" on page 121** in **Chapter 4, Project Management**.
- **Feedback about various IT services.** Ask for comments about all IT services, such as training (a class evaluation survey, for example), the company website, and any communications to users.

Other methods of getting information include:

- **Attend meetings with department heads.** When you meet with key users and department heads, listen for items that may identify an opportunity. These can include challenges they are trying to address, difficulties with existing systems and resources, changes they are expecting or trying to implement, etc.
- **Periodically follow up with individual users.** Perhaps you can pick some random trouble tickets that were opened at the Help Desk and follow up with those users. Won't they be impressed that the manager of IT called to find out if they were satisfied with the support they received?
- **Ask users for information and advice.** Ask others how you are doing or if they are getting what they need from you and your department.

It is important to remember that the more information you can collect, the more valuable it is likely to become. For example, hearing about plans from the Sales and the Customer Service department heads individually is good. But hearing about both means you may be able to spot integration and leveraging opportunities or see overall changes in trends and directions that may not be apparent just from one set of plans alone.

Not only should you collect and share information, but you should encourage your team to do the same.

Proactive Solutions

Through information sharing and collecting you'll find lots of opportunities for IT to deliver solutions. However, an important set of solutions for you to bring are often the ones the users didn't even know existed or that they needed. Frequently, these can be delivered at little or no cost because they are features that are hidden in existing solutions or inexpensive to activate/implement. These can also be enterprise-wide solutions that no individual department or user group thought to ask for. Some examples include:

- Conference calling services. Many PBX solutions can provide limited conference calling capabilities that may suffice instead of paying for an outside service.
- Proactive alerts about printer problems. Printer manufacturers have free utilities to monitor their printers. These can alert your team (sometimes interfacing directly to your call tracking software) about issues such as paper jams and low toner.
- Virus detection alerts. In addition to alerting users when their antivirus software detects malware, the software may also be configurable to alert IT to respond. Not only does this make IT look

proactive, but it also ensures that the user doesn't ignore the problem by simply closing the warning prompt.

- Conference room reservation systems. These can be inexpensive and integrate with your calendaring solution to eliminate overbooking of conference rooms. Large companies have systems devoted solely to this function but small companies often assign rooms an Outlook user name and then schedule them in the Calendar.
- Webcasts of important meetings and announcements. These can be used for demos, training, major initiatives, etc. They can also be easily recorded and archived for on-demand viewing.
- Implementation of toll-free numbers for mobile workers. These can be 800 numbers to your main phone line and to your voicemail system. Not only are these convenient, but they can be far less expensive than hotel dialing fees and cell phone roaming charges.
- Instant messaging and Web-conferencing solutions help facilitate communications with remote workers. The growth of telecommuters has generated a whole new set of tools to facilitate workers who work remotely and for the teams that have to support them. Being involved with remote and telecommuting workers is a great opportunity for you and IT.
- Department and companywide intranet solutions. (Examples are discussed in **Chapter 11, Connectivity: Social Media, Handhelds, and More**, on **page 287**). Look to automatically install the links as favorites for all users so that they don't have to hunt for the URL.
- Have systems send out automated reports and alerts of important events. Imagine the department head of Sales automatically getting an alert or e-mail when the sales system reports a particularly big sale.
- Upgrade of end-user tools. Look to do end-user upgrades (e.g., Microsoft Windows or Office, updates on handheld devices) that deliver clearly visible new features and functionality to the users. Also, make sure that there is communication about these as you do them. In addition, look beyond the basics of tools. For example, Microsoft Office has a large volume of free add-ins for its Office suite that can be distributed, and applications for handheld devices are growing at an incredible rate, and many of them are free. Look for those that really seem like they'd deliver value to a large portion of your user community and show the users how to use them. (Consider distributing a list of useful free apps for phone and tablet devices and simple instructions on how to acquire them.)
- Set the configurations for end users to make life easier for them. For example, are the defaults set so that user documents are saved automatically to the network (or do they default to the local PC where they aren't backed up and a disk crash could spell disaster)? Is your e-mail client set to do auto-archiving or to display message sizes so that users can easily identify those taking up the most space? Does your directory of printers contain enough information so that users can find the one they are looking for?

Don't expect all your solutions to be welcomed and universally valued by all users. Some may find new implementations to be of no use or even annoying or burdensome. That's okay. As long as they have the flexibility to ignore, disable, or tweak what you've done they'll be fine. Also, as you deliver these solutions you're giving people a sense of what IT can do, which will generate more visibility and understanding. If you implement an alert for big sales in the Sales system, the head of manufacturing may ask you about implementing an alert when his area exceeds a quota or, after implementing a conference room reservation system, the head of audio-visual may ask you about expanding that to reserve/track those portable projectors.

Being Flexible

Most organizations have adopted certain IT standards to drive efficiency of support, which can make a great deal of sense. Organizations will standardize on a certain vendor for their computers, oftentimes picking one product line, or even one model. They will standardize on desktop images, software versions, printer types, naming conventions, and so on.

Along these lines, organizations may also "lock down" the desktop environment so that users are limited in what they can do (e.g., users don't have permission to install software). Such restrictions can address security and licensing concerns and reduce calls to the Help Desk if a user runs into trouble.

However, it is important not to take standards so far that they end up getting in the way of what your users need to do or are the catalyst for an adversarial relationship. For example, if you do lock down the desktop environment, consider giving the users some flexibility to choose their own wallpaper, colors, screen savers, etc. Allowing users to have pictures of their kids, pets, or favorite sports team for their desktop background can go a long way.

Similarly, some flexibility of technical standards is called for. In some cases, the bigger concern about exceptions to technical standards is not the impact on IT's support, but the concern that other users will take note and want to "keep up with the Joneses" (sometimes referred to as "technology envy"). So when you have standards, make sure you are clear to yourself as to why you have them. After all, it causes little impact to IT if some users have different keyboards/mice, monitors, or even slightly different hardware specifications (such as memory, hard disk size, processor). In the end, many of these items are fairly meaningless in the scope of the bigger picture of what the IT role is. See more discussion on this topic in the section **"Standards"** in **Chapter 7, Getting Started with the Technical Environment** on **page 199**.

Nonetheless, having *some* standards is important. As data moves all over the place, and the questions become what the user's hardware is and what the company's hardware is, you can get into some awkward situations quickly. Never mind the complexities involved when an employee is fired from the company—let's just stick with the "simple" issues of what your department will support. Without some standards, things get sticky fast. See the section **"The Consumerization of IT"**, on **page 271** later in this chapter and **Chapter 11, Connectivity: Social Media, Handhelds, and More** on **page 287** for a fuller discussion of these issues.

User Training

There are many options available for user training, as well as training for your staff. The ones you choose to use depend on the size and budget of your organization, as well as the skills you need to develop in your users.

In-House Classes

If you're able to have your own training staff and facilities, you can tailor course content, schedule, and class size exactly to your needs. The costs are readily identifiable in terms of staff and equipment needed for the training room.

Third-Party Training Providers

These organizations can provide quality training in popular skill sets. Alternatively, you can usually arrange (at an additional charge) for these providers to deliver classes customized to your needs. Training providers usually have a staff of professional and highly experienced trainers, and the curricula for many classes usually adhere to outlines established by the appropriate vendor (e.g., Microsoft) to maintain their authorizations.

Web-Based Training

Web-based training has exploded in recent years; "e-learning" is now a standard—not unusual—offering for many training needs. Web training can be a recorded session or it can be conducted live and interactive so that attendees can ask questions. Similarly, many vendors offer short videos on specific application functions, features, and tasks. There are many different varieties of Web training that you can customize to your particular staffing and budget needs, and there are many companies that now either develop their own Web-based training (because the tools are so easy to use) or have a company develop courses just for their needs.

User Education and Awareness

In addition to formal training about new solutions, you'll also have to educate users about new policies, new features, changes in procedures, and so on. These can be accomplished through information communications like a newsletter or an in-house company portal. Keep in mind that when you are trying to change user behavior and habits, it will probably require repetition of the message. For example, since the user can be the weakest link for data security, it makes sense to have security become an ongoing theme as opposed to a one-time message.

10.2 THE CONSUMERIZATION OF IT

Traditionally, IT has defined the direction, path, and strategy of the solutions that are to be used and deployed. However, that has dramatically changed as users have started to tell (if not demand) IT which devices and applications that they want to use. While this shift may have started a while ago as computers became a common device to find in the home, it became an issue that could not be ignored as smart phones became popular, particularly with the release of Apple's first iPhone in 2007. Welcome to the consumerization of IT.

Consumerization of IT is a result of:

- The increase in availability and choices of new technology solutions for the consumer, along with
- The realization by these same consumers that these new products would not only be useful to them in their personal life, but in their corporate life as well.

On top of that, while most IT departments go through a lengthy process to evaluate and test technologies, invest in proper management and control, and analyze the ROI (return on investment), many consumers seem to be willing to be more flexible and to make technology purchases with a great less concern. As a result, it's not uncommon for corporate employees to say that they have a better PC at home than they do in the office. This is probably a result of the powers-that-be (very often Finance and IT) deciding that the useful life of a workstation is 3 to 4 years, while an individual consumer may be perfectly willing to invest $500 to $1000 when they feel it's time for a new PC at home.

As devices for the consumer became more and more functional, users began telling IT that they didn't want to wait weeks for bureaucratic red tape to get a device that wasn't nearly as useful as the device they could get today from the store down the street.

How to Deal with Consumerization

Unless you have a very rigid organization, with backing from the highest level of management, you're unlikely to successfully stem the tide of the consumerization of IT in your company. Failure to recognize the issue is likely to result in users seeing your department as out-of-touch and they will just go around your group to get what they want. And, since many requests for consumer devices may be coming from your senior executives, it's best to adopt a policy of flexibility. The following exchange may be apocryphal, but is probably familiar to some degree:

> **Help Desk Analyst:** Thank you for calling the Help Desk, how can I help you?
> **Executive Vice President:** I'm having difficulty setting up my iPhone to access company e-mail.
> **Help Desk Analyst:** We don't support the iPhone.
> **Executive Vice President:** You do now.

While there are plenty of areas where IT needs to stand firm in its selections and policies, there are also areas where there is little risk with showing a little flexibility. Consider some of these areas:

- **Desktop devices.** While IT may have selected a specific vendor and model, is there really an issue if a user requests a slightly bigger screen?
- **Laptop devices.** Similar to desktop, but be sure that you're offering a sufficient choice of models. While some users prefer a fully featured device, others may prefer a smaller, lighter model. If your vendor doesn't offer a sufficient range of choices, or you're not making them available to your users, you may want to rethink your position.
- **Software.** While IT plays a role in selecting, implementing, and supporting the large enterprise applications (messaging, finance, human resources, etc.) there are many individual users or departments that can benefit from small/inexpensive packages. Do you really mind if the sales reps use their own app to find the best deals on hotels when they travel?

Support Issues Associated with Consumerization and Handheld Devices

- **Accessories.** Sometimes a user will want a special keyboard (e.g., ergonomic, wireless), a trackball instead of a mouse, or a webcam. Even if you think the business justification is questionable, there is really little reason to turn down the request. As long as there is budget approval (devices like these are usually $100 or less), you have more to gain than to lose by taking care of requests like this.
- **Policies.** When it comes to formal corporate policies, they are often developed with very good intentions in mind and then never updated or reviewed. If you're are turning down requests simply because "that's what the policy says" then perhaps it may be time to take another look at those policies to see if they need to be updated to reflect the real world and how people actually work today.
- **Handheld devices (mobile phones and tablets).** Aside from the choice of devices you make available to your employees, it's important to consider that many (if not most) of your employees may already have their own devices and all they want to do is connect to the corporate network so that they can be more productive by doing company work on their own time after hours. See **Chapter 11, Connectivity: Social Media, Handhelds, and More** on **page 287** for more on the support issues for phones and tablets.

There are a number of issues associated with support as consumerization grows:

Depth and Breadth of Support

With so many choices of these devices from different carriers, different manufacturers, and running different operating systems, it would be impossible for an IT department to be able to develop sufficient proficiency with them to provide support. However, you may have to wonder if many users are actually expecting the IT team to be proficient with them. Nowadays, most users are fairly self-sufficient about these devices. They know what functionality their devices have, and how to try and locate those functions themselves without having to call the Help Desk. They also go to the Web, their colleagues, and the carrier or manufacturer support lines for help. Some of them even turn to their teenage children when they have a question. So, the number of questions that may come to your team could be fairly limited. Of course, there are users that also expect and demand a much higher degree of attention, support, and hand-holding.

Security

Of course security is a major concern, especially with mobile devices. Initially this was a challenge because the devices were targeted to individual consumers, and the devices had little (if any) capability for management by the enterprise. This has begun to change as additional features that allow for greater enterprise integration have been included. Instead of saying a particular device is or isn't secure, you can just define a set of requirements that devices must have to be allowed on your network. This might include features like the ability to remotely wipe the device, or for the device to have a password, among others.

Costs

The real expense of mobile devices is the recurring monthly plan costs. The upfront cost for the device is a pretty small portion of the total cost of ownership (TCO). (For a full discussion of TCO, see **Chapter 7, Getting Started with the Technical Environment** on **page 189**.) Therefore, when you look at a 12- or 24-month timeframe, the total cost differences between device X and device Y may not be that much. And if the employee wants to use their own device, there may not be any cost to the company.

Bring Your Own (BYO) Policies

Some companies have started to embrace a Bring Your Own (BYO) policy when it comes to certain technologies. With a BYO policy, employees bring their own technology products to work. This is most often done with mobile devices, but some organizations have also used the program for laptops. There are a number of variations of BYO. In some cases employees are reimbursed for a portion of the upfront costs, and/or the recurring fees. There are usually certain restrictions and provisions related to security, liability, company data, and so on. If you go down this path (and it seems like more and more companies are) there should be a number of departments engaged in setting up the policy, the guidelines, etc. These include IT, Human Resources, Finance and Risk Management, maybe even Legal. For more information about BYO, see section **"The Blurry Line between Company-Owned and Personally-Owned Equipment"** in **Chapter 11, Connectivity: Social Media, Handhelds, and More** on **page 288.**

10.3 WHEN YOUR USERS ARE PART OF A MOBILE WORK FORCE

Many users now spend some portion of their work day on a mobile device of some kind. That sounds commonplace, but it is actually a big shift in the way work gets done. It has large consequences for society as a whole, and for IT in particular.

As an IT Manager, here are some perceptions you will face:

- It is not that hard to deal with information technology issues anymore, because everything is on much smaller and easier-to-use machines. (Those guys back in the mainframe days had it really rough—their computers were huge!)
- How hard could it be to move stuff to where we can use it on our cell phone? All you have to do is cut and paste. Or download the app.
- Why doesn't the company help me with my broken phone? I bought it with my own money, but I read my company e-mail on it.
- Not only are there security and support issues, there are "workplace sociology" issues.

In the past, it was only the traveling sales reps who carried your company's valuable data outside your building—and you fought hard to prevent even that. Now everyone has a mobile phone and everyone carries all kinds of important data around.

Techniques for Supporting Your Mobile Users

Chapter 11, Connectivity: Social Media, Handhelds, and More on **page 287** is dedicated to the general issues of mobility. But there are a number of ways to facilitate support when your users are not in the office:

- Configure your e-mail client to allow users to read and write e-mail messages when not connected to the server.
- Use features of the operating system, or system utilities, to synchronize files so that files on network drives can be replicated to laptops for accessing when offline.
- Remote control capabilities (a feature of many desktop management suites) can ease the burden of trying to troubleshoot and solve a problem over the phone.
- If you automatically deploy software, configure your deployment tool to deploy to workstations only when they are locally connected (especially if you are pushing out very large updates). Otherwise, for a user on a wireless connection in a hotel room, it could take hours and prevent her from doing her work.
- When testing new tools, applications, features, and such, take into consideration how they will work for a user outside the office with limited or no connectivity. Consider first deploying these items to in-house users before deploying them to mobile users.
- Be flexible about communication methods. Depending on their location and circumstances at the moment, it can be more convenient for mobile users to contact you by text message, e-mail, telephone, IM, etc. This also means there could be extended periods when you don't hear back from the user. Be adaptable.
- Keep a ready supply of accessories for traveling users: power cords, USB flash drives, power adapters for different countries, etc. Be prepared for frantic calls for these items right before a user is about to leave the office, and don't expect the items to be returned to your inventory.

- Be sure to provide ample communications to your users about downtime, maintenance activities, upgrades, etc., and keep in mind that your mobile users may be in very different time zones. You may even want to have communications that are tailored to the mobile workforce.
- Mobile users often discover that small utilities or accessories can make their lives radically easier. Sometimes they hear about these while chatting at a conference, read about them in an airline magazine, or see the guy in the next seat using one. Be flexible in allowing them to use tools that are not on your approved standards list. See the section **"Being Flexible"** earlier in this chapter, as well as the section **"Standards"** in **Chapter 7, Getting Started with the Technical Environment** on **page 199.**
- Encourage your mobile users to report back to you on the things that work best and worst for them. Focus on addressing the items that work worst, and making sure that all users are aware of the things that work best.
- Look to your software vendors for your most used in-house applications and see if they have a version to run on handheld platforms.

10.4 **THE HELP DESK**

Whether it goes by the name of Help Desk, Support Center, User Services, or a variety of other names, your IT department needs some kind of support organization to provide assistance to your user population—employees, clients, customers, or business partners.

In general, IT Help Desks are designed to be one-stop shopping for all computer-related requests. For many users, your support organization is the only interaction they will have with IT. For these users, the IT department is only as good as their last call to the Help Desk. Managing a Help Desk well is a difficult task but a task with key specific rewards:

- **The company will be able to see a visible portion of IT's efforts.** Installing a new storage area network isn't a trivial task, but users are generally only aware of results they can see; they see a whole new range of applications and features but generally don't go and check out the shiny new hardware that you came in on the weekend to configure.
- **You get to help people.** IT departments in general, and Help Desks in particular, are service centers.
- **A well-run Help Desk can collect a multitude of data and metrics.** You will then be able to more clearly and concretely justify your need for manpower, budget, training, hardware, software—the types of resources you need—when budget time rolls around. You can quantify the Help Desk's performance and how, for example, you can use the fact that it took, on average, 15 minutes to answer incoming calls to justify the hiring of three new analysts. In some cases, that data can be shared with various department heads so that they can identify how systems are being used, where training is needed, etc.
- **You get insight into the entire company.** IT's support staff works with virtually every level of the company, from the loading dock to the CEO's office. If building key relationships is one of your goals (and as an IT manager, it should be), you can't ask for a better opportunity than running a Help Desk.

Typical Help Desk Activities

A Help Desk's responsibilities can include:

- Requests for new equipment
- Password resets
- Providing users with documentation and Web links
- Requests for new IDs and setting up new employees
- Coordinating the process and activities related to a new hire
- Managing computer supplies (toner, DVDs, flash drives)
- Installation and move requests
- Taking the appropriate steps when an employee leaves the organization—recovering equipment, disabling accounts, etc.
- Scheduling training
- Tracking each request to make sure that it doesn't fall into a black hole and that someone always has ownership
- Generating reports for management on the types and volume of calls
- Keeping current databases of users, inventory, etc.
- Routing and coordinating requests with other IT groups (application development, operations, networking, etc.)
- Maintaining a knowledge base of fixes and resolutions so that repeat problems can be addressed more quickly
- Providing application support
- Reporting and resolving hardware problems
- Helping remote users with connectivity issues

Procedures

Analysts at the Help Desk need clear procedures for handling different call types. They should know how to route different types of calls, how to escalate, when to follow up, and so on. These procedures should include detailed contact information of various internal and external resources. If your company offers 24/7 support, contact information should include times when personnel from other departments will be available. Call tracking software, intranets, and so on, can aid in ensuring that procedures are followed. These procedures should also be shared with other departments within the company.

Escalating a Call

Escalating calls that are beyond the skills or authority of your Help Desk personnel is an important part of the Help Desk's function and process.

Escalating a call occurs when an issue is too complex for first-level support. Many companies have several levels of support designed to have correctly skilled people taking the right calls. You don't want your very technical people answering simple calls about how to use Windows, nor do you want your first-level personnel addressing system architecture calls.

Typically, Help Desks have three levels of support: Tier 1, Tier 2, and Tier 3. Some have Tier 4. Each company defines the tiers to match their own processes, but the concept is the same: simple requests (password resets, etc.) are handled by Tier 1 and then the severity/complexity of the problem determines how far up the structure the problem is taken.

A call can also be escalated when the customer has an issue whose resolution requires more authority than the Help Desk person has. Approving a nonstandard request or addressing a security concern is an example of an issue a person further up the Help Desk ladder generally deals with. Similarly, a call may be escalated when the ticket has been open too long, as defined by the SLAs, or when the user is a VIP and should be getting extra attention.

In both types of situations, clear policies should be put in place so that personnel can know when and how to re-route the calls.

Access

The more a Help Desk analyst can do, the more effective she'll be and the more likely she'll be able to resolve a problem on that initial call. Consider giving your analysts various degrees of administrative access so that they can reset passwords, edit e-mail distribution lists, change access levels, see users' files or data, etc. Of course, this type of access has to be carefully considered first before it's granted. Analysts should be made aware of the capabilities they have and warned about the privileges they have—that it must not be abused. They also need to be aware that special access means they can cause problems as easily as they can solve problems.

Various tools from software vendors allow you to delegate specific administrative tasks to the support staff without giving them the "keys to the kingdom."

Self-Service

Today, every service-based organization is looking to allow its customer to perform some basic functions on their own (e.g., tracking their package at www.fedex.com) to avoid tying up support staff resources. The same expectations are true for Help Desk organizations.

IT has started to embrace and incorporate some self-service ideas to address Help Desk-type user needs. These self-service tools can be particularly helpful for those Help Desks that aren't staffed 24/7. Some common self-service techniques that have been put into place include:

- E-mailing requests to the Help Desk instead of talking to an analyst on the phone, or entering the request via an online portal
- Allowing users to see the status of their tickets
- Setting up knowledge bases for users to browse through on their own
- Setting up online forms for common requests (supplies, moves, etc.)
- Resetting their own password (although this is commonly implemented, there are security concerns that you should consider)
- Allowing users to see what messages have been identified as spam if they are trying to track down an e-mail that hasn't been delivered
- Online forms to request file restores; these are then passed on to the backup software and the files can be restored without human intervention if the tape library has the proper tapes

As in other aspects of our society, some people are more comfortable with self-service, as it allows them to feel that they have more control and involvement. Others demand as much personal interaction as they can get. Self-service options shouldn't be considered as a wholesale replacement for personal interaction or other existing methods. Instead, self-service should be thought of as one more tool in your toolbox.

Tools

Help Desk tools come in all shapes and sizes—www.helpdesk.com lists hundreds of different Help Desk software applications. Some common categories of tools include the following:

Call Tracking Software

Call tracking is a software category designed specifically for managing calls at call centers; this category includes more areas than just traditional corporate IT Help Desks. Prices range from free open source call tracking solutions to those that cost a few hundred thousand dollars. Because most offerings are licensed based on the number of concurrent users, however, the size of your staff may be the greatest factor in determining how much your implementation will cost.

In many companies, a user is required to go to a specific Web page to fill out an online form (usually referred to as a "trouble ticket") to request assistance. Initially users resisted this process—many companies require a ticket for every task, including mundane tasks such as new paper for the network printer—but as the breadth and size of IT functions have increased, so has its need to be more formalized about handling the workload. Precisely in the same way that you as a project manager for your department should avoid "scope creep" (for a discussion, see the section **"Clearly Define the Project's Objective and Scope to Avoid 'Scope Creep'"** on **page 106** in **Chapter 4, Project Management**), you need to carefully manage and track the Help Desk's activities and resources.

It is important that you educate users on the need to submit a ticket. Call centers and Help Desks can become overwhelmed quickly. One user's "simple" request ("I just need access to the high-speed color printer this one time") can balloon into work overload (four users in one afternoon each asking one tech for a different favor "just this once") or can distract from a more important function (the backup did not run correctly and needs to be rerun).

Trouble tickets also provide not only traceability but documentation. Once a user submits a ticket requesting a particular action, his request has been put in writing. Because the request can be tracked by both the user and the call center, any further issues can be documented ("I asked for a new laptop six weeks ago." "No, actually, you asked for it two weeks ago and the update on the ticket says it will be here Friday.") For a more complete discussion of this topic, see the section **"Measuring the Help Desk Workload"** on **page 281** later in this chapter.

Also, all that work that was performed invisibly now gets shown under the spotlight of automatic record keeping. Trouble-ticket software allows you to tell the company that not only did your department upgrade everyone's mobile phones and went to four client site problems, you also reset 37 passwords, replaced three stolen laptops, moved 15 users, handled 15 file-restore requests, etc.

Regardless of how a user contacts the Help Desk—phone, e-mail, or website—each contact is given a ticket number. All contacts are entered by Help Desk personnel into a tracking system that generates a ticket number for each item. The user is then given that number; both the caller and the Help Desk can then use it to reference the particular problem.

Because there are a surprisingly large number of offerings in this product area, a good resource to start narrowing your search is HDI, formerly known as the Help Desk Institute, (www.thinkhdi.com).

This organization, which you may want to consider joining to keep abreast of developments in the area of support services, can be a good resource to learn about call tracking software offerings and other aspects of Help Desk operations. There are a variety of factors to consider when evaluating this category of software:

- Ease of customization. Some packages can be customized using a point-and-click type interface, whereas others require scripting.
- Client, server, and database platforms supported.
- Auto-escalation (e-mail, cell phone, alerting management, etc.).
- Integration with your e-mail environment.
- Ad hoc queries and reports; the ability to define and generate customized reports.
- Integration with handheld devices to allow technicians to view/update tickets while away from their desks.
- Access from a web browser. This could be helpful for technicians who work from non-supported platforms (e.g., Macintosh or Linux) or allow technicians to access the database from any work-station without having to install the full client software package.
- Integration with third-party desktop management tools.
- Integration with third-party knowledge base packages.
- Ability to build an internal knowledge base of calls.
- Support for international use. If your organization will use the package in countries outside the United States, you may want to make sure that the package can be configured for multi-language support and that the vendor has a presence in the countries you will be operating in.
- How usable the package is out of the box. You may not have the resources available to dedicate for customizing the package to your exact needs.
- Extent of the implementation effort in terms of time, training, and need for consultants.

Selecting a Call Tracking package is a critical decision, as you will be using it for several years. In addition to the standard practices of checking references, investigating the vendor, and so on, you should also consider getting input from some (if not all) of the staff that will be using the package. You may want to solicit their assistance in narrowing down the field of candidates to a few finalists. Also, when you're down to deciding among the last two or three vendors, you should have some of the staff sit in on the vendor demos so that they can see how the packages operate and can ask questions.

Knowledge Base

Since no Help Desk analyst can be expected to know everything, a knowledge base of information can be a valuable resource. This might be something developed internally, or part of a call tracking system or an external resource. Most call tracking packages allow you to build a knowledge base for resolutions, but this requires that analysts at the Help Desk carefully enter comprehensive information and details about each call's resolution. Many vendors have a knowledge base function on their website, along with user forums. Both are great for finding solutions.

Remote Control

Very often an issue may go unresolved during the initial phone call because the user was unable to describe the problem accurately or couldn't follow directions provided by the Help Desk analyst. Using a remote control package (e.g., PC Anywhere from Symantec, SCCM from Microsoft, TeamViewer,

Remote Control from Dameware), a Help Desk analyst can see exactly what the user sees on their PC and even take control of the user's PC, all without ever leaving the Help Desk chair. (Of course, the support staff should always ask for the user's permission before accessing their workstation in this way.) This remote control access saves time, increases user satisfaction, and improves the effectiveness of the Help Desk tremendously.

Desktop Management

Many calls to the Help Desk result in a request for some type of installation (printer drivers, new software, upgrades, patches, etc.). By using various software tools, for example, remote control mentioned earlier, as well as solutions for the automatic deployment of software, the Help Desk can fulfill a request without having to dispatch a technician or walk a user through a complicated process. Desktop management tools can also automatically inventory users' hardware and software, note changes in configurations, and so on. Tools in the space include SCCM from Microsoft, Casper from JAMF (for Macs only), Altiris from Symantec, and LANdesk.

User Surveys

While reports from your Help Desk phone system and call tracking software can give you all kinds of statistics, they often don't tell you if your customers are satisfied. It can be very helpful to periodically survey a sample of users who have called your Help Desk and ask them a small handful of questions.

The survey can be done in person, over the phone, or via e-mail or the Web. Simple, free survey tools such as www.surveymonkey.com or www.zoomerang.com are great for this. A sample survey might include questions such as:

- How was your initial call to the Help Desk answered: by a person, by voicemail, or by e-mail?
- If your request was submitted by e-mail or by voicemail, how long was it before you received a response?
- How long did it take before your problem was completely resolved?
- Did it require multiple visits to your desk or multiple phone calls to resolve your problem?
- Did the analysts who worked to resolve your call act in a professional and courteous manner?
- Overall, how would you rate this specific call to the Help Desk (using a scale of 1 to 10, with 10 being perfect)?
- Please feel free to make any additional comments, complaints, or suggestions you may have regarding the Help Desk.

You may find that a survey yields very different numbers than the statistics you get from other tools. Your call tracking software may report that the average call is resolved in 3.2 hours. However, the user survey may indicate that the average is 4.5 hours. Even if the call tracking statistics are more accurate, as a manager it is often more important to deal with the *perception*. Regardless of the results, the act of taking the survey will help users believe that you're concerned about the quality of service being delivered. After each survey, statistics should be compiled and decisions made about what the results indicate, and what actions should be taken to improve service levels. Include your team in these discussions. When you do surveys periodically, you can then evaluate trends and patterns.

Measuring the Help Desk Workload

Tracking the performance of your Help Desk is important because, as discussed earlier, this department is often the only face of the IT department that the rest of the organization knows. Within most call tracking applications, tools exist to monitor typical Help Desk activities. You can track:

- Service ticket submissions
- Service ticket categorization
- Response and resolution times
- Activities by technician (volume of tickets, resolution time, etc.)
- Busy periods (by hour, day, month)
- Service tickets due and completed
- Volume of calls in different categories (e.g., password resets, hardware, software)
- Service ticket billing (if you chargeback for services)
- Reporting and performance charts
- Billable time/expense tracking
- E-mail ticket volume

Staffing

It's important to remember that a Help Desk is essentially a *complaint* desk—people only call when there is a problem. As such, callers to the Help Desk are likely to be frustrated and impatient.

Accordingly, one of the most vital prerequisites for Help Desk analysts is their interpersonal skills. The staff on the Help Desk has to be sensitive to callers' needs; remain calm, mature, polite, professional, and demonstrate confidence. The last item is of particular importance. If a caller to the Help Desk feels that the analyst isn't qualified or capable, the caller is likely to become more frustrated. On the other hand, if the caller believes (whether it's true or not) that the analyst is confident and capable of finding a resolution, the caller will immediately feel better. Confidence is contagious.

A user is likely to appreciate and value a quick, courteous, and helpful response to a basic support question more than they would appreciate major upgrades and investments to your infrastructure. A friendly voice helping a road warrior through a hotel connectivity issue (which helps only one person) will usually generate more goodwill than an operating system upgrade to a file and print server (which helps the whole company). Both are required for a successful organization, but the former may be more appreciated than the latter.

In addition to interpersonal skills, individuals at the Help Desk need to have skills in whichever technologies they're supporting. Since you're unlikely to find someone who knows everything, it's important that they're also resourceful enough to find solutions to problems they haven't seen before, and be able to think through problems and explore alternatives on their own.

Specific Considerations When Hiring for a Help Desk

Chapter 3, Staffing Your IT Team on **page 65**, covers staffing and recruiting in detail, but when hiring for a Help Desk, you should especially consider how they perform in a telephone screening. This call should give you some feel for the candidates' telephone personality.

Develop a set of representative questions that might come into the Help Desk, and see how the candidate handles them. The questions should be ones that don't draw on technical skills exclusively, but also allow you to get a glimpse as to how the candidate thinks through troubleshooting and how she reacts when the answers aren't clear-cut.

- Look for evidence that the candidate can learn on his own. Have all his technical skills been developed through formal training or self-taught?
- Is the candidate prepared for full shifts answering phones?
- If the candidate sees the Help Desk as a stepping stone to a higher level position in IT, you and she should agree on a minimum time commitment at the Help Desk before such a transfer is possible. Note that if such a goal is not realistic—some companies have no direct route from this job to any other, either for geographical or other reasons—make sure you mention that right away. It could be a deal breaker, for you or the candidate. And there is no sense in wasting anyone's time.

Size of Support Staff

How many people you need supporting your Help Desk depends on the number of calls that come in during a given period, your service level targets, average length of each call, and so on. A Help Desk that has multiple shifts will obviously need more analysts than one that runs just a single shift. You'll probably need to be flexible in your staffing: you'll want more analysts during peak periods and fewer during quiet periods. Statistics from your ACD and your call tracking software can help you evaluate call patterns.

Taking calls at the Help Desk for eight hours a day can be exhausting and may be a short path to quick burnout. Consider rotation of assignments with other positions or schedule shifts so that each analyst has some time away from the phone, perhaps to research questions that might normally have been escalated to some sort of second level. The section **"Avoid Burnout in Your Employees"** in **Chapter 2, Managing Your IT Team** on **page 35** addresses staff fatigue in more detail.

Staff Training

Ongoing training for your staff is critical to the success of your Help Desk. In addition to the obvious training of applications, there are a number of training ideas you may want to incorporate:

- Training on IT policies and procedures. When the staff is familiar with the policies, they're more likely to apply them consistently.
- Training from other IT teams (systems development, networking, etc.) on what those teams do and how they interact with each other, the Help Desk, and the users.
- Discussions with vendors: innovative ways to use their products, for example, or in-depth training on particular features.
- Training on trends in the industry; this could be a discussion you lead based on headlines in trade journals.
- Training on security issues; this discussion could be led by your internal networking team and could be a great way to inform your team about "social engineering," new vulnerabilities and viruses, and how to be on the lookout for them.
- Sharing knowledge with other Help Desk members; if one member encounters an unusual question or problem from a user, have the member share both the problem and its resolution with the team. This could be a great idea for regular team meetings.

Remember that training is an ongoing process. Periodic refresher courses are just as important as the initial training.

10.5 SERVICE LEVEL AGREEMENTS

When a user calls the Help Desk, they're hoping for immediate service and resolution. Of course, that may not be possible in all cases; a technician may have to be dispatched, it may be a problem that has to be researched or escalated to a specialist, and so on. If it's a hardware problem, a part may need to be ordered. When this happens, the user will usually ask, "How long will it take?" Service level agreements (SLAs) give you—and them—the answer to that question. SLAs are your targets for delivering service. There are many different types of SLAs:

- System uptime
- Hours of Help Desk operation
- How many rings before a phone is answered, or how long before a voice mail message is returned
- Time until call resolution
- Turnaround time for different types of tasks such as
  - Creating an ID
  - Restoring a file
  - A password reset
  - Break/fix repairs
  - Obtaining new hardware
  - Installations and/or moves

This list is just a short sample of SLAs specific to the Help Desk function. However, comparable SLAs can be set for all the systems and resources that IT provides.

Positive Values of SLAs

If you've never had SLAs, the process of just defining them may actually improve service—after all it's a lot easier for your staff to hit a target once they know there is a target. By defining and publishing your SLAs, you can help reduce anger and frustration—yours as well as the users. For example, if you tell users that it takes 24 hours to create an ID, you are likely to get users in the habit of requesting them in advance versus those emergency requests that come on Monday mornings because HR never informed IT about the new hires.

There will always be exceptions, emergencies, and special cases, but published service levels can be an enormous help in keeping a support organization from constantly operating in crisis mode. Of course, it's important that the service levels you set be ones that you can meet and that are reasonable for the user community. For example, don't tell users that e-mails will be responded to within one hour unless you have a very high degree of confidence that you can do so consistently. However, promising to respond to an e-mail within a week may be a target that you can meet, but one that your users are likely to find unacceptable.

Ask for Help from Your Staff

When setting service levels, solicit input from your support staff, as well as users, as to what is reasonable and what is feasible. Then, before publishing your service levels, have your staff work with them for a while to see how well they meet them. Once you're confident you have service levels that are both reasonable and feasible, let the users know. Post them on your intranet or send a company-wide e-mail. Afterward, monitor how well you're meeting them. They aren't carved in stone. It's okay to adjust them if they aren't working, and you may need to add to them as your support organization takes on additional responsibilities or types of services.

Writing Good SLAs

Good SLAs have several things in common:

- The levels of service should be specific and clearly defined (e.g., write "remote access to the database shall have 99.99 percent availability M–F, 8 AM–5 PM," not "the database will be available during normal business hours").
- SLAs should be written for the most requested tasks first.
- SLAs should be defined in such a way that measuring their performance is relatively easy, and, preferably, can be automated.
- SLAs should be written clearly so that they are understood by all. They should be focused on metrics that have meaning for the customer. Your customers may not be interested in a router's uptime, but they are interested in the reliability of Internet access.
- Consider SLAs for end-to-end tasks, as opposed to individual components. For example, consider the availability of the finance application to the end user, as opposed to individual SLAs for the network, the server, the database, the application, etc.

10.6 Further References

Websites

www.altiris.com (desktop management software).
www.bmc.com/remedy (Help Desk software vendor).
www.dameware.com (remote control software).
www.e11online.com (Help Desk software vendor).
www.helpdesk.com (Help Desk support).
www.helpdeskpro.net (Help Desk software vendor).
www.help-desk-world.com (Help Desk resources portal).
crm.ittoolbox.com (CRM site).
www.landesk.com (desktop management software).
www.microsoft.com/sccm (desktop management software).
www.numarasoftware.com (Help Desk software vendor).
www.pcanywhere.com (remote control software).
www.surveymonkey.com (survey tool).
www.teamviewer.com (remote control software).
www.thinkhdi.com (Help Desk Institute).
www.zoomerang.com (survey tool).

Books and Articles

Beisse, F., 2009. A Guide to Computer User Support for Help Desk and Support Specialists. Course Technology.
Blokdijk, G., 2008. Help Desk 100 Success Secrets—Help Desk Need to Know Topics Covering Help Desk Jobs, Help Desk Software, Computer Help Desk, Help Desk Support, Help Desk Jobs, IT Help Desk and Much More. Emereo Pty Ltd.

Gerbyshak, P., Brooks, J., 2009. Help Desk Manager's Crash Course. Booksurge.

Greengard, S., 2011. Managing a Multigenerational Workforce. CIO Insight Magazine May/June.

Jaffe, B.D., 1998. Taking the Measure of Customer Service. PC Week June 5.

Jaffe, B.D., 2000. Maturity Is a Help Desk Prerequisite. PC Week February 7.

Johnson, M., 2011. IT Service Desk: What You Need to Know for It Operations Management. Emereo Pty Ltd.

Knapp, D., 2009. A Guide to Service Desk Concepts: Service Desk and the IT Infrastructure Library. Course Technology.

Orand, B., 2010. Foundations of IT Service Management: The ITIL Foundations Course in a Book. CreateSpace.

Preston, R., 2011. Consumerization of IT Is No Fad. Information Week June 27.

Violino, B., 2011. Workers without Borders. Baseline Magazine July/August.

Connectivity: Social Media, Handhelds, and More

11

"One more thing . . . "
Steve Jobs

CHAPTER TABLE OF CONTENTS

11.1 Get in Front of the Curve 288
11.2 The Power of All These Connections...293
11.3 How Does This Affect You as IT Manager? 298
11.4 Further References 302

The workplace, and the entire world, for that matter, is more tightly integrated than it ever has been. You and your employees can be connected 24/7/365 to your customers, fellow employees, former colleagues, long-forgotten friends and relatives, and to your offices across the globe. You are connected to a lot of people almost all the time.

That is both good news and bad news. We'll examine both sides of the issues in this chapter as we discuss the various ways today's technologies allow unprecedented interaction among people—your users, suppliers, clients, customers, vendors, and you—often the facilitator for many of these electronic connections.

This chapter discusses new technologies and the significant impact they are having on users, your staff, your company, and the ways they live and work. It discusses the benefits and challenges of some technologies, but more to the point, it talks about how you should be dealing with them as an IT manager, and what your role is.

No organization, no matter how systematically they try to avoid this issue, can elude the giant wave of mobility. Nor should you try. In previous chapters, the guidance has been to provide careful, measured approaches. In this chapter you'll see that the guidance is toward more flexibility and adaptability, and not being afraid to fail.

Instead of pretending you have a choice in the matter, we are going to provide you with some ideas on how to deal with it.

- **Embrace it.** Like the old IT departments fighting the infiltration of PCs back in the 1980s, you are facing a losing battle. You know all about the inevitability of the march of technology—why are you still pretending like smart phones are not something that the IT department has to be concerned with? See the section **"Get in Front of the Curve"** on **page 288.**
- **See how other people are handling this issue.** For a long time, many IT managers knew exactly how many "computers" were in their environment. They had servers and laptops and a discrete number of software licenses to manage. Now all kinds of computational devices with all kinds of capabilities are being carried into the environment, sometimes through the "back door." And these "computers" are being used in ways no one would have guessed just a few years ago. Like any complex problem, your first step is to define the scope of issue: just exactly what exists and how they are being used. See the section **"The Power of All of These Connections"** on **page 293.**
- **Figure out exactly what (hardware and software) is being used and how and what you'll let into your system.** Like the other technologies you deal with daily, there are good ones, medium quality ones, and truly awful ones. Just because a user loves a new tablet's touch-and-feel doesn't mean you have to give them access to company shared drives on that device. But you'll have to do something about that issue. See the section **"How Does This Affect You as IT Manager?"** on **page 298.**
- **Don't just cry out "Security risk!" every time someone asks about a new device or app.** If you just whine about it, without addressing it, eventually they are going to ignore you and will look for someone who can figure out how to get it done, and not someone who only talks about why it can't be done. If you provide an approved list, if you test several devices and apps and send out recommendations, if you warn against certain solutions or approaches, you'll be listened to.

11.1 GET IN FRONT OF THE CURVE

The Blurry Line between Company-Owned and Personally-Owned Equipment (BYO Policies)

In a 2011 survey by *InformationWeek*, 54% of technical professionals said that their IT group either officially or unofficially supports personally-owned devices. The feeling is that "You can't beat 'em, so you might as well join 'em." While we hardly advocate such blatant submission for most IT issues, when it comes to holding back the tidal wave of personal devices into the workplace, we suggest you not try to resist but instead embrace, guide, and direct.

The line between what is a corporate tool and what is a personal piece of equipment has been blurred considerably as employees increase their use of personally-owned devices for their job, and the use of company-owned devices for personal use. It is in the best interests of both the company and the employee if that trend is recognized by the company and addressed directly. And one way to address the issue is for IT to implement a Bring Your Own (BYO) policy.

Due to their very nature and prevalence, there are many administrative issues associated with mobile devices. These include:

- Dealing with procurement (devices, accessories, service plans)
- Supporting users that have a myriad of different device types

- Updates to operating systems and applications
- Activities associated with lost, stolen, and broken devices and accessories
- Monitoring service plans and costs, etc.

In addition, companies are dealing with frequent requests from employees to change their devices just because something newer came out, to change carriers, and to transfer their number to another device when they leave the company. In addition, many employees already have their own devices and don't want to carry a second one for work.

With a BYO policy, employees use their own personal device for work needs. In some cases, the company may provide the employee with a stipend to help defray the initial purchase of the unit, and/or some sort of reimbursement for some of the monthly charges.

The biggest technical challenge associated with BYO has been with security concerns regarding the organization's network, data, and e-mail. While using a personally-owned device for this access may not increase the risk, there is a concern that the company may not have as much control over the device. To address this, some companies have granted personally-owned devices access only if the devices allow for some degree of organizational management, such as remote wipe, screen timeout, use of passwords, etc.

A BYO program can eliminate a lot of the headaches associated with the administration and management of mobile devices. With careful planning the program can adequately address the organization's security concerns, while giving employees a great deal of freedom in the type of device they use. BYO programs usually save the company money, but that is because a portion, if not all, of the expense is shifted to the employee.

The New Technologies of Connectedness

IT managers—and teachers, parents, and anyone in a supervisory role of any kind—are facing a crisis of attention. The ones being supervised (and you, of course) have a huge range of options from which to choose when looking for connections and/or distractions:

- Instant messages (IM)
- Social networks (Facebook, LinkedIn)
- Text messages
- Blogs
- Video sharing (YouTube)
- Microblogs (Twitter.com, Plurk.com, Yammer.com, Chatter.com)
- Podcasts
- Crowdsourcing (Kluster.com, IdeaScale.com, Crowdcast.com)
- Apps, gadgets, and widgets that can be installed on mobile devices
- Wikis
- Mashups
- RSS feeds

This list contains just *some* of the different connection types, and doesn't even cover the various devices that can be used with those connections. There will be another hot technology tomorrow.

We'd list it, but we don't know what it is yet. The particular technology is not as important as how you react to it, how you take advantage of it, and how you integrate it into your work (and your life). And all these tools and technologies can be accessed with machines ranging from smart phones to tablets, so that people can stay connected 24/7/365, from anywhere on the planet (even on a plane in flight) as long as they have a wireless connection.

Another point to remember is that many technologies are hot for a while and then totally disappear. The technologies and products in this industry are very dynamic. New tools can build slowly and then burst into mainstream use. In 2009 Twitter's use exploded when Oprah Winfrey joined. That same year CNN and Ashton Kutcher competed to see who would be the first with a million followers, only to see Lady Gaga leave that number in the dust when she hit 10 million followers in 2011. Today's "new thing" can be as dated as rotary telephones in short order. The same is true regarding the competition within each space. Friendster practically invented social networking, but is now just a historical reference. Check out this fun article on forgotten tech products (dot matrix printers and After Dark (remember the flying toasters?) are on the list): www.pcadvisor.co.uk/news/index.cfm?newsid=114088.

People instant message and check their Facebook page during meetings. They use their smart phones to find which restaurant has the best deal "right now." They download podcasts for audio tours when they go to a museum. They post negative reviews about neighborhood merchants as they are walking out of the store. They text while driving. And reports are that all this behavior is only going to get more common (extranet.neverfailgroup.com/get/?fileID=17ff8c&reg=0&ws=1).

You can't know if this kind of behavior is going to get better or worse, but it is going to be more common. Perhaps one of the great indicators of the popularity of these solutions and products on our culture is how they become part of the language. When products and technologies become verbs (to "google", "IM", "text", etc.), it is clear that they are having an enormous impact.

Like most of the topics discussed in this book, there are definite benefits and challenges with this level of connectivity (see Table 11.1).

Benefits and Challenges of Connectivity

Table 11.1 Benefits and Challenges of Connectivity

Benefits	Challenges
"Velocity matters," as Eric Schmidt, executive chairman of Google, is famously quoted as saying. In many corporate situations, speed is of the essence. Instead of measuring cycles in months and years, some trends are now being measured day by day, and hour by hour. Getting e-mail alerts when a particular price has dropped—say the airfare to Disney World for that vacation you have been talking about—is an example of a significantly shorter sales cycle. You'll "pull the trigger" on that sale the minute the price drops below a certain point; you might even have the purchase made automatically based on that event.	Some processes do not improve with more speed. People-centric events, for example, are typically not made better by increasing the velocity. A new employee, for example, needs some time to get acclimated to his new surroundings (see **Chapter 3, Staffing Your IT Team** on **page 65**). Although they should feel challenged and motivated, everybody is going to take a certain amount of time to get used to their new surroundings. Demanding that people adjust in minutes instead of days may not always improve the situation.

Continued

Table 11.1 Benefits and Challenges of Connectivity—Cont'd

Benefits	Challenges
Working online is the very essence of working "at the speed of thought" (as Bill Gates called his book). Most IT professionals have had the experience of thinking of an interesting and clever domain name—only to find out it was taken days ago.	It now takes—and will take in the future—an enormous amount of effort to find the proper balance to deal with the effects of all this connectivity. It has taken U.S. states a long time and a lot of energy and money to outlaw handheld cell phones and texting while driving; schools ban cell phones during classes; and employees are banned from bringing laptops to meetings.
Most business processes move better with faster information. If you order three laptops for new employees and only two machines are in stock with your vendor, you are better off finding that out when you're placing your order instead of when the partial shipment shows up.	Most people are not as good at multitasking as they think they are.
Offerings can be customized based on where you are. Using geo-location technology you can instantly see what restaurants and coupons are nearest you.	Too much information can be overwhelming. If you've ever researched a product online, such as a digital camera, the volume of information regarding features, specifications, reviews, models, resellers, and options can be numbing.
Get data about new technologies and new ideas fast. Who has not left a meeting, gone back to their computer, and Googled a key phrase they heard for the first time that morning? Not too long ago, that kind of information gathering took much more time and energy.	Many people are finding all these possibilities very hard to resist, and it can have negative impacts on their home and work lives. The word "addiction" is often used to describe some of these behaviors.
Find out what others are saying about a product. Online communities and reviews have feedback from others who are using the product and can report on the good and bad of it, as well as the vendor. Not only can you find out the lowest airfare, but you can also find out which seats on the plane are favored and/or hated. Many companies (e.g., Amazon, Dell) collect and share user feedback about their products with 1–5 star ratings.	Too much information can be as big a problem as too little information. Not only are many people uninterested in what their Facebook connections or Twitter followers had for breakfast, or that they were stuck in traffic going to work, but there are more and more stories about people getting in trouble as a result of what they shared.
Unprecedented levels of association—both professional and personal are available. The person who is looking at their Facebook page in a meeting may be reading a "post on his wall" from an old high school classmate. However, she might also be reading an e-mail from a colleague at another firm telling her about some bad experiences with a technology solution you're considering implementing, which means your implementation could avoid a major pitfall.	An innocuous posting can go viral and wreak havoc on a company's reputation. In 2009 musician David Carroll posted a song he wrote on YouTube on his 9-month experience trying to get reimbursed by United Airlines for a broken guitar. The story went viral, received over 10 million hits on You Tube, and was covered by national media outlets. Shortly after the video was posted, United reimbursed Carroll (which he donated to charity). Had their customer service team been more forgiving initially, United could've avoided untold amounts of negative publicity.

Continued

Table 11.1 Benefits and Challenges of Connectivity—Cont'd

Benefits	Challenges
Effective methods of staying in touch, particularly across geographic and time boundaries, are now common. (The Web has expedited a 24-hour "follow-the-sun" work cycle, for example: software code written in the United States is modified or enhanced overseas while U.S. programmers are sleeping. Then the process starts again the next day.)	IM-ing about innocent activities such as the planned department lunch is often the lead-in for extended, sidetracking "conversations." Whether it is at the water cooler or the computer, a little chit chat is harmless and often helps people enjoy their workday more, but too much can be too much.
A valuable way to develop and maintain contacts, find people with similar interests, and "stay in touch." (Social networking sites for professionals such as LinkedIn have become the Rotary Club breakfasts of the 21st century.)	The concept of downtime is rapidly disappearing. Leaving the laptop at home when leaving for vacation is no longer a method for "getting away," because the smart phone (with email) gets to go on the trip.
Easy to tap the knowledge base of your network by simply posting a question to the online community. (Google searches often return answers to tough questions that are posted on user forums.)	People spend more time building their network or Facebook page rather than actually maintaining their relationships. This action could impact interpersonal skills and leave people wondering about all your free time.
Multitasking at work is now common, and productivity (in some areas) has increased radically. You can check your e-mail while at lunch and download the latest sales figures while waiting for the elevator.	With all the noise, getting workers to focus on the tasks at hand is much harder. It requires skill to learn what is a critical phone call and what is a trivial IM or vice versa.
Enhanced career growth opportunities by being more connected, more informed, and more visible. Obscure positions in unheard of companies are now available for the dedicated job searcher.	With networking sites, you may be judged by the company you keep. Being "friended" on Facebook does not mean the same thing as being "connected" on LinkedIn. The two, though, are trying to crowd into each other's territory.
GoToMeeting, Webex, and videoconferencing tools have transformed the meeting experience radically. Attendees from around the globe can participate in large conferences or staff meetings at the click of a mouse and for minimal or no expense.	Risks of having your non-work activities being seen and judged by your boss and co-workers. Do you want your alcohol-induced karaoke contest entry on YouTube or family vacation pictures on Facebook seen by your work colleagues?

Dealing with a Lot More Empowered Users

Regardless of where they are on the food chain—be they the CEO or her less than computer-literate marketing advisor—everyone in the organization suddenly has a lot more computing power at their fingertips. That is, like many things in this book (and in life), both the good news and the bad news.

Smart phones have the power of computers built just a few years ago, handhelds have the power and mobility only dreamed of by laptop designers just a few product design cycles in the past.

Employees now want the freedom to access data, install applications, and to do whatever they feel will help them get their job done better and faster. Instead of looking at reports, employees may ask for the raw data so that they can analyze it themselves, and possibly (if not likely) find trends or present them in a manner that no one has seen before. More and more they want the tools so that they can do it themselves. And, they may not even want to use the tools you provide, because they read a review about, or a colleague mentioned, a tool that is "far better." But they then come back to you to figure out how to make that tool operate within your environment.

Wisdom of Crowds

An important point that should not be lost in this discussion is the "wisdom of crowds." James Surowiecki's bestselling book *The Wisdom of Crowds* is subtitled: "Why the Many Are Smarter Than the Few and How Collective Wisdom Shapes Business, Economies, Societies, and Nations." The concept is simple and counterintuitive: "groups are remarkably intelligent, and are often smarter than the smartest people in them." In fact, this concept, along with the capabilities of new technologies, has led to the coining of the term "crowdsourcing," which refers to taking advantage of the online community to solve problems. Trying to figure out the best way to integrate two applications? Instead of doing days or weeks of research, you may be able to get the best answer much faster by simply "asking the world." Want to find out if a product or technology really works as advertised? Before investing the time to set up your own trial, see what others think.

The rise of all these technologies is no less than the "trickling down" of that insight: groups are often (although not always) smarter than one person. This is one reason for the popularity of product reviews in online communities.

According to Facebook, over one billion pieces of content (Web links, news stories, blog posts, notes, photos, etc.) are shared on their site each week (www.facebook.com/press/info.php?statistics). As of December, 2011, Facebook had 800 million users with 75 of those outside the United States—these are not numbers that can be ignored.

11.2 THE POWER OF ALL THESE CONNECTIONS

There is a tremendous range of "real-world" (as opposed to IT-world only) applications for the new range of hyper-connected software and hardware. In this section we discuss:

- How companies use the Web
- How companies use intranets
- How companies use social media and mobile devices

How Companies Use the Web

The ways that the Web can benefit your company are probably only limited by your imagination. Some of the more successful efforts include the following.

- **Keep your "doors open" 24 hours a day:** Airline sites began using the Web for this reason, but now it is common for almost any enterprise to consider the 24/7/365 exposure of the Web to be critical to their success. Retail stores around the planet sell their goods to users online elsewhere on the Web. It seems obvious now, but even 20 years ago, that was unheard of. (Amazon was founded in 1995.)
- **Adjust to changing market conditions almost instantaneously with price adjustments, sales incentives, product placement, and so on.** Dell, for example, changes its product promotions every few days. Retailers use their websites to encourage retail store purchases, while their retail stores encourage visits to, and purchases from, the web site. Many retailers are adopting this model;

retail stores can increase the inventory they can claim to "have available" and online stores can promise quick delivery of products. In both cases, the brand name is strongly reinforced.

- **Provide product information (description, specifications, uses) or company data (financial, executive biographies, job postings, press releases) directly into the hands of consumers.**
- **Improve customer service.** Almost all companies provide e-mail options for feedback and questions. Most common (usually via a "Contact Us" link) is the ability to send e-mail feedback. In addition, many companies now are also employing an online chat option for customer service. You can IM, chat, e-mail—many companies offer several different contact options. Companies can receive more precise and immediate market research by tracking customer activity on the Web, as well as web-based surveys and direct marketing via e-mail. Customer service on the Web also includes posting product manuals and other documentation, having an FAQ section for common issues and questions, etc. Large companies are now monitoring what's being said about them on various social media, and taking action to address issues, respond to customer complaints, and change their image in the marketplace.

How Companies Use Intranets

Companies use intranet sites for many of the same reasons that they use an Internet site: for convenience, ease of use, speed, reduced errors, enhanced offerings, and to reduce costs. Common intranet uses include:

Function	Description
Posting of the company's policy manual	Putting the policy manual on the intranet eliminates the hassle of distributing periodic updates to the old three-ring binder. Plus, it ensures that everyone has immediate access to the latest version and dramatically reduces the inquiries to HR and other departments about policies.
Payroll information	Employees can use the intranet to view and update their tax information (e.g., W-4 forms) and view their pay stubs. These two functions alone can eliminate a great deal of paper and phone calls.
Time sheets	A convenient replacement for paper forms to track hours, sick days, vacation days, etc. An automatic feed to the payroll system can reduce a lot of paper movement and keying errors.
Benefit plan enrollment	In addition to viewing information about the differences in plans, employees can sign up, identify beneficiaries, and authorize payroll deductions.
Marketing material	Company branding information, common graphics, data sheets, sales presentations, and so on are kept on an intranet, making it easy to update and to give to people located around the country and around the globe.
Employee discounts	An intranet can provide information on getting employee discounts on the company's own products, as well as discount programs that may be available to employees from suppliers, customers, and partners.
T&E submissions	Employees can submit travel and expense information with a browser. Not only is the submission done online (including receipts, by scanning them to electronic files), but managers can approve the requests online, and accounting can review/audit them online and authorize reimbursement (which is often a direct deposit to the employee's bank account). Transactions from the company credit card can be posted automatically and reimbursed by electronic transfer to the card issuer.

Continued

Function	Description
Job postings	Many companies will post job openings on their intranet before they post them on the public Web site or job boards. By filling jobs with internal candidates (or referrals from employees), the company can save money on recruiting and advertising fees, and employees feel better about the potential for promotion and career growth.
Requesting supplies	Virtual catalogs from the supply room or approved vendors can be posted, and employees can submit their requests, which are delivered to their desks the next day.
Company announcements	The intranet (sometimes coupled with e-mail) can be used to make employees aware of everything from the year's holiday schedule to the plans for the company picnic, and from new hires and promotions to the cafeteria menu.
Department budgeting	Department managers can see their department's spending history and plan next year's budget. All budgets are then rolled up automatically to create a company-wide budget. It sure beats e-mailing spreadsheets around.
Request IT services and equipment	Tasks like requesting new equipment, conference room setups, submitting and tracking a problem, etc. can be done online. User guides and FAQs can also be posted. Tickets to the Help Desk can be submitted, and their current status can be viewed.
In-house catering	Ordering bagels for the morning meeting, lunch for the visiting speakers, everything but beer for the Friday bash—intranets often provide that quick-and-dirty method of getting the food brought in.
Conference room reservations	Avoid the hassles of having to call different people to see if a conference room is available when you need it; all usage and reservations are made online and available for all to see.
Training information	Both materials and the corporate training calendar can be posted, along with the ability to register for upcoming class. If you missed a class, you can view an archived recording of it online. You can also use it to post links to other training and information materials (such as vendor websites).

The possibilities for using an intranet are almost unlimited. Look at almost any manual and/or paper-based process and there's a good chance it would be more productive, more accurate, faster, and more efficient if it moved online. And, with many of these functions already online, companies are beginning to explore making them available with apps on handheld devices.

How Companies Use Social Media and Mobile Devices

Ways That Help the Company

- Staying in touch with professional colleagues
- Monitoring what's being said about company products and services, monitoring the competition
- Entering time sheets
- Tracking orders and shipments, and being notified instantly when a delivery is made
- Responding to customers' feedback
- Solving problems

- Seeking feedback and comment
- Accessing information from the field workforce (sales reps, police officers, health inspectors, delivery truck drivers, service technicians, etc.)
- Alerting customers to new products, features, services, and uses
- Identifying the core-base of customers and targeting campaigns to them
- Seeing how comparable companies are addressing issues and problems
- Evaluating feedback and suggestions from customer and suppliers
- Analyzing data
- Creating and showing presentations
- Entering customer info, and possibly orders, while meeting with customers
- Providing customer/supplier education
- Tracking expenses while traveling

Ways That Don't Really Help the Company
- Checking personal e-mail
- Staying in touch with friends and relatives
- Checking Facebook pages
- Doing job searches
- Online banking
- Checking sport scores

However, it is important to note that while these activities don't help the organization, they probably improve the employee's "work/life balance." The thinking is that it's better to allow some flexibility in what the employee does on company time, with company resources, as opposed to having the employee distracted that these issues need attention, and having to take time away from the company to deal with them. It is also a way for an employer to recognize that employees have a personal life. And, if employers are expecting employees to be available outside of work hours, it's only fair that employees get to use some work-time for personal matters.

Mobile Device Operating Systems, Apps, and Hardware

To say this market is "fluid" is like saying there have been "a few" patches to Windows. Things change in IT. (On the other hand, if we were scared of change, we never would have even bothered with a new edition of this book—and you would be working in some other industry right now.)

As this book was written, there are four main players in the smart phone operating system market:

- iOS (Apple)
- Windows Phone (Microsoft)
- Android (Google)
- BlackBerry (RIM)

Other names in this space have included Palm OS, Symbian, and WebOS. While you might prefer to choose only one for your company (and while that might happen, it is highly unlikely it will be the only one used at your company), OSes for handhelds often walk in your front door without your permission. See the section **"Consumerization of IT"** in **Chapter 10, Working with Users** on **page 271.**

Most likely, your corporate handheld OSes environment will consist of three:

- Android
- iOS
- BlackBerry

Note that we did *not* say the "largest number of handheld OSs around your office will be . . . " BlackBerry is often the preferred *corporate* choice, but Apple and Android are far more popular choices for operating systems on *personal* devices. The handheld market was virtually launched with RIM's Blackberry solution. And it is still considered the best at integration with corporate e-mail environments. But it has lost a lot of ground to the competitors and the limited supply of third-party apps. Android has gained tremendous popularity because it is available on a large number of different devices, from many carriers, and offers a healthy supply of third-party apps. There are concerns that Android is not a mature solution, and isn't as stable and secure as others—yet. Apple's iOS has a strong following due to the design of the devices and user interface, as well as the largest offering of third-party apps. However, this OS runs only on a limited number of Apple-manufactured devices, which are expensive compared to its competitors.

"Apps" (applications for the handhelds) are different from traditional applications running in your IT department for a couple of reasons:

- They are either free or often priced under $10.
- They are generally downloaded by the users themselves, not you or a member of your team. This is both good and bad news, of course; you don't have to worry about installing it, but you (probably) are still going to have to support it.

Handheld Hardware

Anything from a smart phone to a netbook and a tablet counts these days as a "handheld." But aside from being very portable, their claim to fame is that they can perform multiple functions and connect to the Internet. Handheld devices are available from vendors like Apple, Blackberry, Nokia, Samsung, Motorola, LG, and HTC to name a few. New models are released every few months with different form factors, capabilities, and features. In the United States, devices from one carrier will not work with another carrier. And while you may be able to find a user manual online somewhere (there definitely won't be one in the box), it seems that most users just feel that they can figure it on their own.

Of course, any handheld device that includes phone functionality requires carrier service to operate. However, netbooks and tablets may only be equipped with Wi-Fi capabilities and can connect to a mobile service as an option, or with an air-card. Every device has a large number of accessories available from ear-phones to cases of every color, design, and material.

Use of Mobile Devices

Because mobile devices are mobile, and may be entirely out of the control and visibility of the organization, it's a good idea to set some guidelines about their use:

- Report stolen or lost devices immediately
- Refrain from downloading for-fee services—ring tones or applications, music, video streaming, etc.
- Refrain from downloading large data files such as video
- Stay within the allotted minutes and feature sets of the service plan
- Notify IT ahead of any departure for international travel so that international roaming capabilities are enabled for the applicable travel dates and countries
- Limit use of directory assistance (411)

- Adhere to the same security guidelines and principles for general computer use (e.g., don't open files or links from unknown sources)
- Use a password
- Don't leave the device unattended

Many of these policies are related to managing costs for company-owned devices, but in many cases employees are using their own devices under a BYO policy, which was discussed earlier in this chapter in the section **"The Blurry Line between Company-Owned and Personally-Owned Equipment (BYO Policies)"** on **page 288.** Mobile device management (MDM) tools can also help with the security of mobile devices. Products from companies like Mobile Iron and Good Technology are popular in the MDM space and provide capabilities like device and app inventory, feature lockdown, device configuration, remote lock and wipe, encryption, and extensive logging.

11.3 HOW DOES THIS AFFECT YOU AS IT MANAGER?

> Success with Web 2.0 is coming at a cost. IT managers have to balance all the collaboration and innovation emanating from these tools against new security risks, as well as data access and management challenges. And they have to do it in many cases with products that lack security and data management features. This means that IT departments must find ways to get control over the use of these tools in the workplace.
> *www.internetevolution.com/document.asp?doc_id=172026*

The particular challenge with all these new social media and connectivity technologies (as with almost any new solution) is that it is a double-edged sword. While they can be strategic tools for business and improve employee productivity, they can also be factors contributing to employee distractions and performance problems.

Many companies are still trying to figure out how to best use these technologies, and the answers won't come from the IT department alone. As is always the case, many parts of the organization (such as Legal and HR) need to be involved.

Lead, Encourage, and Experiment

It may be appropriate to just let various groups experiment with these tools to see how well they work and what results they yield. Since the use of many of these tools is essentially viral, exercising too much control or trying too hard to influence its use and direction may simply lead to failure. Some companies have loved the idea of social networking, but instead of just making use of the tools that are already available, they have tried to build their own internal social networking sites. In many cases, their efforts have not been successful simply because the audience is too small to generate the necessary viral growth, companies are unable to build/buy something as functional as what already exists, or employees really don't have too much interest in maintaining their listing on a "company" site.

A compromise solution may be to make use of social media tools that are virtually private. For example, Yammer.com is very similar to Twitter.com, but is set up so that information is only shared among people of the same organization. Similarly, Google, which owns YouTube, has a video-sharing function for organizations through its Google Video for Business offering. This offering is completely hosted by Google, is similar to YouTube, but allows you to maintain strict control and ensures that videos are not available to the public at large. In the arena of crowdsourcing and collaboration, solutions such as Kluster.com allow you to harness the intelligence of your internal team (or any individuals that you designate).

For your organization's use, recruit people who are passionate about certain things and encourage their use of new solutions. If someone is passionate about all the different ways that your company's products can be used, encourage them to start a company-sponsored blog or Facebook page. If someone is very focused on what your company is doing to be green and save the environment, let them share those activities via Twitter.com. Work with the public relations team to create groups and networks on social networking sites to share announcements. Consider integrating some of these technologies into your corporate web site. Some ideas will flourish, whereas others may flounder; that's okay, it's an iterative process and there's minimal cost in seeing what happens. With social media and connectivity tools, speed and convenience are often the priorities over the quality of the specific tool, which may be antithetical to how IT and your company have traditionally operated—see the next section **"It's Not the Tools, But How They Are Used"** on **page 299.**

Social media and collaboration tools, whether used internally for employees, or externally for customer and partners, should not be considered an IT initiative. Like any other application or tool, they should be implemented for the benefit of the business, or the request of the business. Of course, IT should be involved in the selection and implementation of the tools, helping to monitor its usage, etc. But, this involvement needs to be with other business and department heads who are taking the lead on choosing to go down these paths. Working with these teams, you can help to move forward by discussing:

- What are we trying to accomplish?
- Who are the teams/employees that we think will be the most open to this, and get the most value from it?
- How do we evaluate progress and success?
- How do people communicate today? And with whom?
- What are the most effective communication paths and mechanisms currently in place and can those be leveraged to enhance further collaboration?
- How much control do we exert and how much monitoring do we do?
- Is it possible to effectively measure collaboration, teamwork, productivity, and effectiveness of communications? If so, have they been measured already, and how much improvement is necessary to say a change was justified and successful?

It's Not the Tools, But How They Are Used

Many organizations spend a great deal of time focusing on which tools to implement for their social networking and social media initiatives. However, as a general rule in life (and IT), it's not the tools, but how they are implemented and used.

- Make sure that whatever you do with social media that it fits your company's organization, values, and culture.
- Ideally the use of social media tools should not be separated from regular work-flow and processes; the more integrated the better.
- By definition, social media and collaboration tools are for two-way communications. If your organization only sees it for 'talking' (to employees and/or customers) and not for 'listening,' you're limiting the chances for success.

- Don't try to impose too much control on its use. Let the users play and experiment, find its best uses, and then encourage that sort of organic growth.
- Don't expect instant enterprise-wide adoption and success. Consider starting small, perhaps with one department, or one work-group that seems particularly well suited to collaborative and social media tools, perhaps because of the work they do, or how they work together already. Initially start with those who are more inclined to work collaboratively, without having to impose it on them. You're unlikely to ever get 100% participation, but that's fine.
- Different employees will use the tools in different way, and to different degrees. That's expected and normal. You may find the greatest differences among the various generations of employees. This topic is discussed more in the section **"Generational Issues at Work"** in **Chapter 2, Managing Your IT Team** on **page 57.**
- Don't be afraid of failure. If something isn't working, figure out why, and try something else. Similarly, if the tools are being used differently than originally expected, resist the urge to change those behaviors without first looking at the value and benefit in how employees are choosing to use it.
- Recognize failure. If you find that you have to develop marketing campaigns, remind employees to use the tools, or are forcing everyone to create their profiles, it's highly likely that your current plan isn't working.
- Be flexible, and reduce some of the traditional rigors associated with work in a large organization. Let employees choose their own profile photos, as opposed to having to use the formal (usually out of date) one on their company ID. Allow ground-rules and guidelines for use to evolve from the community itself, as opposed to having them defined by others. (See the next section on **page 300** for a discussion of some guidelines that shouldn't be ignored.)
- Consider implementing tools that monitor social media websites so that your company can actively know what's being said about your organization. There are many free tools you can use (like Google Alerts, Web search tools, and Social Mention) as well as a number of paid tools that are ideal for the enterprise like Attensity and Radian6.

As you can see, working on a social media or collaboration tool project is very different from traditional IT systems projects. These projects will require greater flexibility and adaptability, and less focus on rigorous project management techniques. The project may prove to have a learning curve for you as well as the users and the organization.

Set Guidelines

It may be effective and worthwhile to set some guidelines for the use of social media technologies, just as you have policies for the use of e-mail. For example:

- No posting of confidential or sensitive company information.
- Employees are responsible for the information they publish.
- Using their company e-mail addresses when posting information about themselves and their life outside of the office is not allowed.
- Reminding everyone that postings on the Web are available "for the world" to see and very often can't be removed.
- Reminding people of the importance of respecting intellectual property (the reason behind many lawsuits).

You don't want to define use so tightly that people feel constrained, just help them understand the boundaries. With all new tools and capabilities, some guidance and direction will help people get off to the right start and will help ensure that they don't make any severe mistakes. The media is full of stories of employees who have been disciplined or terminated because of what they posted on the Web.

Think of the Possibilities!

All the growth, enthusiasm, and excitement associated with these new tools and capabilities present wonderful opportunities for today's IT manager. They represent a whole new way of how people and companies will live and work. You have the opportunity to influence and guide your company's use of them. The last thing you want to do is be a naysayer and dismiss them, especially when your bosses are reading how other companies are using them. Be careful not to discourage use, or to exert too much control. Tech-savvy workers will find ways around whichever policies you implement. Also, your efforts at controlling too much may come back to haunt you via employee morale.

Some of this new behavior may be a break with how your company normally operates, but remember that connectivity has radically changed the way people live and work. If companies can't show the same sort of adaptability (not only to the technologies, but to their own personnel) they will be left behind by their competition.

Remember Your Goals

In **Chapter 1, The Role of an IT Manager,** there is a section called **"Develop an IT Strategy"** on **page 10.** That section discusses topics such as "What are your assets?" and "How do you plan to satisfy your customers' needs?" Overall, your goals are to leverage information technologies for the benefit of your organization. You and your department are enablers. It may be simpler and easier to just deny access to things, but it is important to remember that IT is not there to make things simpler and easier for itself—it's supposed to be doing that for the business and the users.

In the past, IT departments were slow to react to new trends, which pretty much left users to "forget about IT" and move ahead on their own. This happened in the 1980s when personal PCs first appeared and traditional mainframe-based IT dismissed them as toys. Similarly, IT was late to accept the Internet. In both cases, IT eventually woke up and embraced these technologies. But there is an important lesson here: Don't ignore your users, they might just be telling you about the next new thing.

What Is "Focused" and What Is "Distracted"?

First, a word on what these offerings are *not*: excuses for you to become the Attention Police. While there are all kinds of reasons why an employee should or should not be Twittering at work, your workplace may or may not be an organization that cares. If there are employees who seem to be spending far too much time online on activities unrelated to work, it is important to remember that this is primarily an HR issue, not an IT issue (although IT may be involved). These situations are similar to those where an employee is spending too much time on personal phone calls. Most workplaces today care about results, not style. There are CEOs that Twitter (twitter.com/zappos); Mark Cuban Twitters (and if billionaires Twitter, who are we to say it is not corporate?). As a Forbes.com article says, "[this] is no longer just for teenagers" (www.forbes.com/2009/03/11/social-networking-executives-leadership-managing-facebook.html).

These technologies are being embraced because they generally allow people to be more productive—do more, do it quicker, do it from anywhere, and do more than one thing at a time. They help the work–life balance by allowing working parents to stay in touch with their children and to know that they can be reached immediately if there is a problem. They enable employees to work at nontraditional hours and at nontraditional locations as they choose to, or need to.

However, these same technologies can distract people from the work they are supposed to be doing or using these technologies in less than honest ways (such as the employee who arranges for an e-mail to be sent to his boss at 1 AM so that it looks like the employee is working tirelessly).

Also, while your workers are using these tools for their work–life balance, corporations are embracing these tools for the benefit of their customers and clients. Companies are creating pages and groups on all the networking sites (such as Facebook.com and LinkedIn.com), as well as sending out news via Twitter.com. All of this helps with marketing and branding, keeps customers informed, creates a sense of community, and helps develop and maintain strong relationships. It is certainly a sign of the reach, power, and maturity of these technologies. Politicians have embraced them not only for campaigns, but also as worthwhile tools while serving in office. Even the White House has its own channel on YouTube.

USERS CHECK MOBILE E-MAIL FREQUENTLY

Our research found that 47% of mobile device users check their mobile e-mail more than 10 times per day while at work, while 10% check mobile e-mail more than 40 times each day when at work. After hours during the evening, 37% of mobile users check their mobile e-mail more than 10 times each day. Even on the weekend, 47% of mobile users check their mobile e-mail more than 10 times per day.

The Osterman Research, Inc.

Black Diamond, Washington

extranet.neverfailgroup.com/download/OR%20Executive%20Summary%20-%20Mobile%20Messaging%20Market%20Trends%202008-2011%20v2.pdf

---

And, remember this is not an IT-only issue. All the tools for social networking and mobility are just that—tools. IT shouldn't be the determining factor in what tools are used, how they are used, and what they are used for.

11.4 Further References

Websites

extranet.neverfailgroup.com/get/?fileID=17ff8c&reg=0&ws=1 (mobile messaging market trends).

www.attensity.com (social media monitoring tool).

www.ecommercetimes.com (e-commerce news).

www.facebook.com/press/info.php?statistics.

www.forbes.com/2009/03/11/social-networking-executives-leadership-managing-facebook.html (social networking at the executive levels).

www.good.com (mobile device management tool vendor).

www.google.com/apps/intl/en/business/video.html.

www.kluster.com (crowd-sourcing tool).

www.mobileiron.com (mobile device management tool vendor).

www.pcadvisor.co.uk/news/index.cfm?newsid=114088 (gone, but not forgotten technologies).

www.radian6.com (social media monitoring tool).

www.socialmention.com (social media monitoring tool).

www.yammer.com (micro-blogging tool for internal use).

Books and Articles

Bell, A., 2009. Exploring Web 2.0: Second Generation Interactive Tools—Blogs, Podcasts, Wikis, Networking, Virtual Words, and More. CreateSpace.

Blanchard, O., 2011. Social Media ROI: Managing and Measuring Social Media, Efforts in Your Organization. Que.

Carne, E.B., 2011. Connections for the Digital Age: Multimedia Communications for Mobile Nomadic and Fixed Devices. Wiley.

Custy, J., 2011. Unplanned Obsolescenc. Information Week August 15.

Faeth, F., Busateri, J., 2009. Web 2.0 Building Blocks. Baseline Magazine March.

Finneran, M., 2011. A New Approach for Mobile. Information Week August 15.

Fried, S., 2010. Mobile Device Security: A Comprehensive Guide to Securing Your Information in a Moving World. Auerbach Publications.

Healey, M., 2011. The OS Mess. Information Week July 11.

Janer, M., 2009. The Web 2.0 Balancing Act. Information Week February 16.

Johnson, M., 2011. Mobile Device Management: What you Need to Know For IT Operations Management. Emereo Pty Ltd.

Kang, S., 2011. Business Intelligence Moves to Mobile Devices. Baseline Magazine July/August.

Kerpen, D., 2011. Likeable Social Media: How to Delight Your Customers, Create an Irresistible Brand, and Be Generally Amazing on Facebook (& Other Social Networks). McGraw-Hill.

Klososky, S., 2011. Enterprise Social Technology: Helping Organizations Harness the Power of Social Media, Social Networking Social Relevance. Greenleaf Book Group Press.

Li, C., Bernoff, J., 2009. Groundswell: Winning in a World Transformed by Social Technologies. Harvard Business School.

Sankar, K., Bouchard, S.A., 2009. Enterprise Web 2.0 Fundamentals. Cisco Press.

Shah, R., 2011. Social Networking for Business: Choosing the Right Tools and Resources to Fit Your Needs. Pearson Prentice Hall.

Silver, D., 2009. The Social Network Business Plan: 18 Strategies That Will Create Great Wealth. Wiley.

Stackpole, B., 2011. Managing the Tablet Wave. Computerworld June 6.

Stackpole, B., 2011. The Mobile App Gold Rush. Computerworld August 22.

Surowiecki, J., 2005. The Wisdom of Crowds. Anchor.

Glossary

360 Reviews: a performance review in which employees receive feedback from not only their direct supervisor, but from other individuals as well, including peers and subordinates.

A

ACD (Automatic Call Distribution): a telephony solution that can route calls to technicians based on menu prompts and can provide detailed reports about activity.

Adware: software that installs itself on a workstation for the purpose of displaying ads to the user. Adware is generally unwanted and often installed without the knowledge of the user. It is considered to be malware.

AES: a data encryption standard.

Agile Development: a method of software development that stresses quick development cycles; it is seen as an alternative to the "waterfall" method.

Agile Meetings: daily meetings, often called "stand-ups" or "scrums." The idea is to radically increase communication but in much briefer formats; they are called "stand-ups" because people tend to ramble less when they have to stand up the entire meeting.

Annual Licensing: a software licensing model that requires the license to be renewed periodically, typically on an annual basis.

Asset management: processes and techniques employed to minimize TCO (total cost of ownership).

Automatic Call Distribution (ACD): a telephony solution that can route calls to technicians based on menu prompts and can provide detailed reports about activity.

B

B2B: Business-to-Business e-commerce marketing direction.

B2C: Business-to-Customer e-commerce marketing direction.

Backdoor Trojans: Trojan horse programs that allow a hacker to control your computer remotely.

Basel II: international agreement that sets out the details for adopting more risk-sensitive minimum capital requirements for banking organizations.

BCP (Business Continuity Planning): a methodology used to create a plan for how an organization will resume partially or completely interrupted critical function(s) within a predetermined time after a disaster or disruption. BCP differentiates from disaster recovery in that DR is associated primarily with resources and facilities, while BCP is associated primarily with processes.

Benevolent dictator: an individual with final say, who is not elected to their position, yet acts in a manner that benefits the group as a whole.

Black List: a list of e-mail originators (e-mail and IP addresses) whose messages should always be considered spam.

Black-hat hackers: hackers interested in discovering security flaws in order to take advantage and abuse them—usually for profit, but oftentimes just to see what trouble they can cause.

Bring Your Own (BYO) Policy: policy associated with mobile devices that allows employees to use their own devices for work.

Business Applications: software packages that allow the users and the business to do their job(s). Examples include the inventory system, the payroll application, or a simple application that allows administrative assistants to print mailing labels.

Business Continuity Planning (BCP): a methodology used to create a plan for how an organization will resume partially or completely interrupted critical function(s) within a predetermined time after a disaster or disruption. BCP differentiates from disaster recovery in that DR is primarily associated with resources and facilities, while BCP is associated primarily with processes.

BYO (Bring Your Own) Policy: policy associated with mobile devices that allows employees to use their own devices for work.

C

Call tracking: a software application designed specifically for managing large volumes of calls at call centers and help desks.

Capital expenditure: an expense category for an item that will have a useful life of several years, such as a piece of hardware.

Capital lease: an equipment lease where ownership of the equipment passes to the lessee at the end of the term.

CBT: Computer-Based Training; software-based (stand-alone or on the Web) education that trains the user in a particular product set.

CERT: research and development center at Carnegie Mellon University (funded U.S. Department of Defense and the Department of Homeland Security) that coordinates communication among security information experts.

Change Request (CR): change management notification for a change in current process/environment.

Chargeback: the process for charging individual departments for various IT resources (hardware, software, staffing, etc.).

Chief Security Officer (CSO): individual at a corporation in charge of defining and implementing security policies.

CIA: Confidentiality, Integrity, and Availability tenets of information security.

CISSP: Certified Information Systems Security Professional security certification.

CLERP-9: Australian legislation similar to U.S. version Sarbanes–Oxley.

Client/server: an application architecture that has two pieces of software associated with it—one that runs on the server and does the vast majority of the processing, and another piece that the user (or client) accesses that serves as the user interface.

Closeout Report: the report written at the end of a project summarizing the project's accomplishments, identifying areas that went well, discussion of problem areas, etc.

Cloud computing: using Internet-based resources (e.g., applications, servers, etc.) as opposed to buying and installing in-house.

CMMI: Capability Maturity Model Integration; a methodology for process improvement.

CNE: Novell certification for a Certified Netware Engineer.

COBIT: Control Objectives for Information and Related Technology; a set of documents developed by the Information Systems Audit and Control Association and the IT Governance Institute that provide guidance for computer security. Much of COBIT is available at no cost.

Collaboration: The style of management where all levels of the corporate organization are actively involved in the execution of business.

Command and Control: the style of management where there is a clear vertical chain of command: you direct your employees and your boss directs you.

Computer-Based Training (CBT): software-based (stand-alone or on the Web) education that trains the user in a particular product set.

Concurrent User Licensing: a software licensing model based on the number of users that will be accessing an application at the same time.

COSO (Committee of Sponsoring Organizations): a private sector organization dedicated to improving the quality of financial reporting through business ethics, effective internal controls, and corporate governance.

CR (Change Request): change management notification for change in current process/environment.

Critical path: the series of tasks or events that determine the project's total duration. Any delay in any of these tasks will cause the project's total duration to be delayed.

Crowdsourcing: the act of outsourcing a task to an undefined, generally large group of people or community, typically in the form of some sort of post on the Internet.

CSO (Chief Security Officer): individual at a corporation in charge of defining and implementing security policies.

D

DARPA (Defense Advanced Research Projects Agency): federal agency originally responsible for the "network of networks" that became the Internet.

Data Protection Directive (European Union): a component of the EU's human rights and privacy laws, and for the protection of individuals' personal data.

Database Management System (DBMS): sophisticated software system that controls the databases.

DBMS (Database Management System): sophisticated software system that controls the databases.

Defense Advanced Research Projects Agency (DARPA): the federal agency originally responsible for the "network of networks" that became the Internet.

Depreciation: the decrease in the value of an item over time.

DES: a data encryption standard.

Development tools: all elements of software used to create other software, such as compilers, linkers, debuggers, source code control systems, and languages.

Directory Services: a system application and database for tracking and administering resources (users, devices, etc.), that is used by all other applications. Frequently used for IDs and passwords in single sign on applications.

Disaster Recovery (DR): the ability of an infrastructure to resume operations after a disaster. Disaster Recovery differentiates from Business Continuity Planning in that Disaster Recovery is primarily associated with resources and facilities, while BCP is primarily associated with processes.

Disk Cloning: a tool to quickly copy large amounts of data in a fraction of the time it would take to use conventional methods.

Distributions: a package of Open Source Software that can include the code, utilities, documentation, and support. Distributions are usually packaged and sold for a fee by third parties.

Distros: a package of Open Source Software that can include the code, utilities, documentation, and support. Distros (distributions) are usually packaged and sold for a fee by third parties.

DMADV (Define, Measure, Analyze, Design, Verify): A Six Sigma methodology for the creation of new processes.

DMAIC (Define, Measure, Analyze , Improve, Control): A Six Sigma methodology for the refinement of existing processes.

DMZ (Demilitarized Zone): an area of a network that is used to host devices that are accessible via the Internet, but are still protected by the firewall.

Dodd–Frank Act: a bill that was passed in direct response to the massive financial collapse of 2008–2009; regulates the U.S. financial system with the goal of preventing another meltdown.

DR (Disaster Recovery): the ability of an infrastructure to resume operations after a disaster. Disaster Recovery differentiates from Business Continuity Planning in that Disaster Recovery is primarily associated with resources and facilities, while BCP is primarily associated with processes.

E

E-commerce: a term to describe the many activities involved in buying and selling over the Internet.

Electronic discovery: the legal discovery process (prior to a legal proceeding) associated with electronic data such as e-mail, spreadsheets, word processing, database files, and so on.

Enterprise applications: an application that is widely used throughout the organization and integrates the operations of many different departments and functions.

Enterprise Resource Planning (ERP): set of applications and systems that a company uses to manage its resources across the entire enterprise.

ERP: Enterprise Resource Planning; set of applications and systems that a company uses to manage its resources across the entire enterprise.

Expense item: a financial expenditure for something whose value is gone in a short period of time, typically less than a year. Also used for items that have a longer life, but are relatively inexpensive (below a threshold set by Accounting).

F

FACTA (Fair and Accurate Credit Transactions Act): a consumer rights bill that became fully effective June 1, 2005, and is an extension of the Fair Credit Reporting Act (FCRA). The rule says that in regard to consumer information (such as name, social security number, address, etc.) you must "take reasonable measures to protect against unauthorized access or use of the information."

FASB (Financial Accounting Standards Board): organization for establishing standards of financial accounting and reporting.

FCRA (Fair Credit Reporting Act): a consumer rights bill extended by FACTA.

Firewall: a device that is used to control access between two networks. Typically used when connecting a private network to the Internet as a way of protecting and securing the internal network from threats, hackers, and others. Also used when connecting two private networks (e.g., supplies, partners, etc.).

Fiscal year: twelve-month period used for budgeting. Frequently, the fiscal year that a budget tracks isn't the January–December calendar year. The year that the budget tracks can be any 12-month period, although it generally begins on January 1, April 1, July 1, or October 1.

Fixed asset: an asset, other than cash, that is used in the normal course of business. Examples include computers, machinery, buildings, and fixtures.

FTP (File Transfer Protocol): an application protocol that transfers files from the source where they were created to a server that makes them accessible to users on the Internet.

G

Gantt chart: a project planning/management tool that charts time on the horizontal axis, and tasks and activities on the vertical axis.

Generation X: people born between 1965 and 1980.

Generation Y ("Millennials"): people born between 1981 and 2000.

Governance: the function of ensuring that the enterprise's IT activities match and support the organization's strategies and objectives. Governance is very often associated with budgeting, project management, and compliance activities.

Gramm–Leach–Bliley Act: an act passed by Congress that has provisions to protect consumers' personal financial information held by financial institutions.

Grid computing: the use of multiple computing resources to leverage combined processing power. Usually associated with scientific applications.

H

HIPAA (Health Insurance Portability and Accountability Act): regulations passed by Congress promoting the privacy and security of medical records.

HRIS (Human Resources Information System): HR software.

I

IDS (Intrusion Detection Systems): security hardware/software that identifies suspicious traffic (i.e., potential security threats) based on patterns of activity.

IM: instant message.

Incident response: the response of an organization to a disaster or other significant event that may significantly affect the organization, its people, or its ability to function productively.

Infrastructure as a Service (IaaS): the use of typical infrastructure components (e.g., data centers, servers, network computers) from a third-party provider as opposed to purchasing for on-premise installation/use.

Internet Corporation for Assigned Names and Numbers (ICANN): an internationally organized, nonprofit corporation that has responsibility for IP address space allocation, domain name system management, and root server system management functions.

Interoperability: the ability for two (or more) components of technology to interface and work together.

Intranet: a private web site available only to those within a company or organization.

Intrusion Detection Systems (IDS): security software that identifies suspicious traffic (i.e., security threats) based on patterns of activity.

Intrusion Prevention System (IPS): security software that not only detects malicious activity (like an IDS), but also takes action to halt it.

IDS (Intrusion Detection Systems): security software that identifies suspicious traffic (i.e., security threats) based on patterns of activity.

IPS (Intrusion Prevention System): security software that not only detects malicious activity (like an IDS), but also takes action to halt it.

ISO 17799: an internationally recognized information security standard.

ISO 270001: international information security standard against which organizations can seek independent certification of their Information Security Management Systems.

ISO 9000: a standard framework for quality management throughout the processes of producing and delivering products and services.

ISP (Internet Service Provider): a company that provides connectivity to the Internet.

ITIL (IT Infrastructure Library): a set of guidelines for developing and managing IT operations and services.

K

Key loggers: small applications that reside on a computer to record key strokes, usually installed without the knowledge or consent of the user, and considered to be malware and spyware.

Kick-Off meeting: the meeting that launches a project. Activities may include team assignments, project charter, objectives review, among others.

L

LAN (Local Area Network): a network of computers that are physically connected within a single site (or campus) without the use of telecomm lines.

LDAP (Lightweight Direct Access Protocol): a subset of the X.500 and DAP standards for directory services.

Lease: an arrangement where a third party provides a piece of equipment for a defined period of time at an agreed upon rate.

Local Area Network (LAN): a network of computers that are physically connected within a single site (or campus) without the use of telecomm lines.

Locking down: configuring an operating system to limit the types of activities the user can do (e.g., configuration changes, software installations, etc.).

M

M&M security model: security model designed to make a system "hard on the outside and soft in the middle."

Malware: general term for software designed to damage a computer or computer system. Spyware, adware, and viruses are all considered forms of malware.

Mashups: two distinct functions or applications merged into a single one.

Microblogging: small text or multimedia messages sent to subscriber lists.

Middleware: software that connects other software.

Milestone: a point in a project that represents the completion of an important sequence of key tasks and activities.

Millennials: ("Generation Y") people born between 1981 and 2000.

Mission statement: explains the fundamental purpose of the company or organization.

Mobile device management (MDM): tools that provide capabilities like device and app inventory, feature lockdown, device configuration, remote lock and wipe, encryption, extensive logging.

Multiple Tier Licensing: a software licensing model that licenses the server portion of an application as well as the client portion.

Multiple Use Licensing: a software licensing model that allows an individual software license to be used on more than one device. Additional device(s) typically refers to a laptop computer or a home computer.

N

Network Access Control (NAC): solution for granting access to network resources based upon authentication of the user and the device.

Non-Perpetual Licensing (Subscription licenses, Annual licenses, Renewal licenses): a software licensing model that requires the license to be renewed periodically, typically on an annual basis.

O

Object-Oriented Programming (OOP): a methodology or a method that defines how you write a software program in a very specific way. Rather than have a series of commands that specify certain actions, objects interact with each other. C++ is an object-oriented programming language; C is not.

OCTAVE (Operationally Critical Threat, Asset, and Vulnerability Evaluation): a method of performing a risk analysis developed by CERT.

OFAC (Office of Foreign Assets Control): part of the U.S. Department of Treasury that administers and enforces economic sanctions programs primarily against countries and groups of individuals, such as terrorists and narcotics traffickers.

Off-shore Outsourcing: the process of a domestic company arranging with one or more overseas third parties to provide services that the first company could provide but chose not to.

OLTP: Online Transaction Processing.

On-demand computing: providing computing resources as they are needed, as opposed to the traditional full-time basis. Also sometimes referred to as "utility computing." Usually associated with cloud computing.

Open Source Software (OSS): software created by the worldwide user community. Open source software is generally free, can be modified by anyone, and usually doesn't have any single "owner."

Operating system: software that manages computer hardware and resources, and provides common services for applications to run. Examples include Mac OS, Linux, Windows, Android, iOS, etc.

Operating expense: a financial expenditure for something whose value is gone in a short period of time, typically less than a year. Also used for items that have a longer life, but are relatively inexpensive (below a threshold set by Accounting).

Operating lease: a lease for the rental of equipment for specified periods of time that are shorter than the total expected service lives of that equipment, and where ownership of the equipment is held by lessor during and after the lease.

OSS (Open Source Software): software created by the worldwide user community. Open source software is generally free, can be modified by anyone, and usually doesn't have any single "owner."

Outsourcing: the process of a company arranging with one or more third parties to provide services that the first company could provide but chose not to.

P

Page hijacker: a form of malware that changes a browser's default home settings, search settings, and such to point to other sites.

Patriot Act: U.S. legislation that has a number of requirements for financial institutions in regard to verifying customers' identities and determining whether the customer appears on any list of known or suspected terrorists or terrorist organizations.

PD (Position Description): detailed description of a specific role in the company.

PDCA (Plan, Do, Check, Act): continuous improvement cycle originally developed by Walter Shewhart in the 1930s.

Per seat licensing: a software licensing model that requires a license for any user connecting to an application.

Per server licensing: a software licensing model that requires a license for any server running an application.

Perpetual licenses: a licensing model where the licenses are purchased outright and don't have to be periodically renewed.

PERT chart: a type of chart used in project management, where tasks are represented as circles, and arrows between tasks are used to show the sequence and task dependencies.

PGP (Pretty Good Privacy): data encryption method.

Phishing: the process of trying to obtain confidential information (e.g., credit card numbers, passwords, social security numbers, bank account numbers, etc.) by sending e-mails that appear to be from legitimate organizations but are in fact fraudulent.

PII (Personal Identifying Information): term used frequently in a number of compliance regulations and legislations to refer to types of protected information.

PIPEDA (Personal Information Protection and Electronic Documents Act): a Canadian law that regulates the collection, use, and disclosure of personally identifiable information.

PKI (Public Key Infrastructure): enables users to securely exchange data through the use of a public and a private cryptographic key pair that is obtained and shared through a trusted authority.

Plan, Do, Check, Act (PDCA): a continuous improvement methodology.

Platform as a Service (PaaS): delivery of an application development platform (hardware and software) from a third party via the Internet without having to buy and manage these resources.

PMBOK (Project Management Book of Knowledge): globally recognized standard for Project Management, from the Project Management Institute (PMI), which provides practices, tools, and techniques that can be used in most projects.

PMO (Project Management Office): a function that oversees all projects within an organization. Responsibilities may also include setting standards (like for methodologies, document formats, etc.), defining best practices, etc.

PMP (Project Management Professional): a certification awarded by the Project Management Institute to individuals who have met the established minimum requirements in knowledge, education, experience, and service in the discipline of project management.

Podcasting: making digital media files available for download and playing.

Position Description (PD): a relatively detailed description of a specific job function.

Pretty Good Privacy (PGP): data encryption method.

Privacy and Electronic Communications Directive: the European Union's directive that covers many aspects of electronic communications such as security of data and networks and guaranteeing the privacy of communications.

Private cloud: the leveraging of very large IT environments to essentially offer on-demand/cloud-like offerings to their internal customers and subsidiaries, as a way to provide services in a more efficient, flexible, and scalable manner.

Productivity tools: common desktop applications such as word processing, spreadsheets, and presentation. Productivity tools are either sold in suites or as stand-alone components.

Project charter: a project management document that defines a project scope, objectives, benefits, assumptions, etc. May also identify team assignments, project sponsor, time and cost estimates and constraints, and areas that are out of scope.

Project Management Book of Knowledge (PMBOK): globally recognized standard for Project Management, from the Project Management Institute (PMI), which provides practices, tools, and techniques that can be used in most projects.

Project Management Institute (PMI): a professional association for project management professionals.

Project Management Office (PMO): a function that oversees all projects within an organization. Responsibilities may also include setting standards (like for methodologies, document formats, etc.), defining best practices, and so on.

Project Management Professional (PMP): a certification awarded by the Project Management Institute to individuals who have met the established minimum requirements in knowledge, education, experience, and service in the discipline of project management.

Project manager (PM): the person responsible for completing the project on time, within budget, and to an agreed scope.

Project milestones: significant events or the completion of a phase within a project.

Project plan: documentation of a project's projected activities including timing, resource assignments, assumptions, constraints, costs, etc.

Project sponsor: the individual whose support and approval is required for a project to start and continue. May also be the person who initially proposed the project.

Project stakeholder: any individual or organization who may be affected by a project and/or benefit from it.

Public cloud: cloud services that are available to any individual or organization to use, for a fee.

R

Recovery Point Objective (RPO): in disaster recovery planning, the age, or "freshness," of the data available to be restored in a disaster scenario.

Recovery Time Objective (RTO): in disaster recovery planning, the expected amount of time between the disaster, and when services are restored.

Renewal licensing: a software licensing model that requires the license to be renewed periodically, typically on an annual basis.

Request for Information (RFI): a document issued to potential suppliers and vendors to enable them to determine if they can meet the requirements of a project.

Request for Proposal (RFP): document issued to suppliers asking them to submit detailed proposals pricing and other information.

Request for Quotation (RFQ): document issued to suppliers asking them to submit detailed proposals pricing and other information.

Return on Investment (ROI): a calculation of the net benefits of a project against the total costs.

RFI (Request for Information): a document issued to potential suppliers and vendors to enable them to determine if they can meet the requirements of a project. The RFI helps narrow down the list of vendors that would get the RFP.

RFID (Radio Frequency Identification): technology used to identify and track items (e.g., inventory, consumer products) using very small components known as "tags".

RFP (Request for Proposal): document issued to suppliers asking them to submit detailed proposals pricing and other information.

RFQ (Request for Quotation): document issued to suppliers asking them to submit detailed proposals pricing and other information.

ROI (Return on Investment): Return on Investment.

Rootkits: a form of malware that is particularly difficult to detect because they are activated before the operating system.

RPO (Recovery Point Objective): in disaster recovery planning, the age, or "freshness," of the data available to be restored in a disaster scenario.

RTO (Recovery Time Objective): in disaster recovery planning, the expected amount of time between the disaster, and when services are restored.

Rule of Least Privilege: users should be granted only the least amount of access to the system, and for the least amount of time necessary, as is authorized and required for their job.

S

SaaS (Software as a Service): a software deployment model where a provider licenses an application to customers for use over the Internet, without requiring purchase and installation of the licenses.

Sarbanes–Oxley: law passed by the U.S. Congress to regulate the integrity of financial statements.

SB-1386: California state law requiring organizations that maintain personal information about individuals to inform those individuals if the security of their information is compromised.

SCAMPI (Standard CMMI Appraisal Method for Process Improvement): appraisal process for the CMMI process improvement methodology.

Scope Creep: adding features and functionality (project scope) without addressing the effects on time, costs, and resources, or without customer approval.

Search Engine Optimization (SEO): techniques to help ensure that a web site appears as close to the first position on a web search results page as possible.

Security Incident Response Team (SIRT): a formal group assembled within a company to respond to security breaches.

SEO (Search Engine Optimization): techniques to help ensure that a web site appears as close to the first position on a web search results page as possible.

Service Level Agreement (SLA): a statement to customers or the user community about the service the IT department will provide. It can refer to a variety of metrics, such as performance, up-time, resolution time, and so on.

Single Sign-On (SSO): a security solution that allows a user to authenticate once, and then have access to all systems and resources for which he has been granted permission. Eliminates the need to remember multiple IDs and passwords. Considered a convenience not only for users, but for system administrators as well.

SIRT (Security Incident Response Team): a formal group assembled within a company to respond to security breaches.

Six Sigma: process improvement methodology.

SLA (Service Level Agreement): a statement to customers or the user community about the service the IT department will provide. It can refer to a variety of metrics, such as performance, up-time, resolution time, etc.

Slack time: how much a noncritical-path task on a PERT chart can be delayed without impacting the project as a whole.

Social engineering: obtaining or attempting to obtain otherwise secure data with fraud and deceit by tricking an individual into revealing confidential information.

Social networking: the use of technologies to turn communication into an interactive dialogue, and to allow the creation and exchange of user-generated content.

Software as a Service (SaaS): a software deployment model where a provider licenses an application to customers for use over the Internet, without requiring purchase and installation of the licenses.

Spoofing: the process of forging an e-mail address or IP address. Usually used by hackers for illicit purposes like fraudulently entering a computer or computer network.

Spyware: software placed on a computer that monitors a user's activity. Usually installed without the knowledge or consent of the user, and considered to be malware.

SSO (Single Sign-On): a security solution that allows a user to authenticate once, and then have access to all systems and resources for which he has been granted permission. Eliminates the need to remember multiple IDs and passwords. Considered a convenience not only for users, but for system administrators as well.

Standard CMMI Appraisal Method for Process Improvement (SCAMPI): appraisal process for the CMMI process improvement methodology.

Subscription licensing: a software licensing model that requires the license to be renewed periodically, typically on an annual basis.

T

T&M Service (Time-and-Material): a hardware/software support model that requires the customer to pay for both the technician's time as well as any parts required.

TCO (Total Cost of Ownership): refers to the fact that there are many more items related to the cost of technology besides the initial price of the hardware and the software (e.g., training, support, etc.).

Teleworking: working from a location other than the company office, often using communications applications (like IM, WiFi, and cloud computing apps) to interact with coworkers.

Terms and Conditions (Ts and Cs): section of a contract with a vendor that deals with items such as service level guarantees and hardware and software specs.

Time-and-Material service (T&M service): a hardware/software support model that requires the customer to pay for both the technician's time as well as any parts required. Similar to a car repair bill.

Total Cost of Ownership (TCO): refers to the fact that there are many more items related to the cost of technology besides the initial price of the hardware and the software (e.g., training, support, etc.).

Trojan horse: software that appears to be an application but is, in fact, a destructive program.

Ts and Cs (Terms and Conditions): section of a contract with a vendor that deals with items such as service level guarantees and hardware and software specs.

U

Unified messaging: the term applied to integrating voice mail and e-mail systems.

USB (Universal Serial Bus): a standard used for connecting small devices (e.g., digital camera, flash memory, headset).

Utility tools: software to help optimize, manage, or configure the computer environment. Examples include backup, monitoring, management, and administration file compression, file conversion.

V

Value Added Reseller (VAR): a company that provides additional services (e.g., installation, upgrade) to products they sell.

VAR (Value Added Reseller): a company that provides additional services (e.g., installation, upgrade) to products they sell.

VDI (Virtual Desktop Infrastructure): an environment where desktop computers are virtualized, moved to the data center, and remotely accessed by end users, typically with thin-client devices.

Virtual Desktop Infrastructure (VDI): an environment where desktop computers are virtualized, moved to the data center, and remotely accessed by end users, typically with thin-client devices.

Virtual Machine (VM): software that allows you to take a single physical device (e.g., one PC) and run multiple instances of operating systems on it.

Virtual Private Cloud (VPC): a hybrid of the public and private clouds where the cloud provider logically segregates your resources from its other customers.

Vision statement: a company document that takes a mission statement to the next level by outlining what the organization wants to be; it focuses on the future and serves as a source of inspiration for employees.

VM (Virtual Machine): software that allows you to take a single physical device (e.g., one PC) and run multiple instances of operating systems on it.

Voice over IP (VOIP): a technology for using IP networking for phone calls.

VOIP (Voice over IP): a technology for using IP networking for phone calls.

VPC (Virtual Private Cloud): a hybrid of the public and private clouds where the cloud provider logically segregates your resources from its other customers.

VPN (Virtual Private Network): a method of establishing a secure connection between two devices over the public Internet.

W

WAN (Wide Area Network): a network that covers a large geographical area.

War room: a room provides team members a place to work on a project that is separate from their regular work area.

Web 2.0: a second generation of Internet-based tools and applications that facilitate communication, collaboration, connectivity, sharing, etc.

White hats: hackers are interested in security flaws as a way of identifying how security can be improved, and how systems can be better protected; sometimes called "ethical hackers."

White list: a list of e-mail originators (e-mail and IP addresses) whose messages should always be considered legitimate.

Wide Area Network (WAN): a network that covers a large geographical area.

Worm: a form of malware as a standalone program (opposed to viruses that attach themselves to other objects).

Z

Zero Day Attack: a malware attack that takes advantage of a software vulnerability for which the vendor has not released a patch.

Index

Note: Page numbers followed by *b* indicate boxes, *f* indicate figures and *t* indicate tables.

360 Reviews, 51, 51*t*

A

Accenture, 158
Access control, security technologies, 215
Access database, DBMS, 135
Access issues, Help Desk, 277
Accessories
    consumerization support issues, 272
    mobile user support, 274, 275
Access reviews
    ongoing maintenance, 221
    security solutions, 218
Accountability
    employee performance reviews, 46
    staffing and security, 223
Accounting Department
    BCP, 261
    budgeting process, 26, 165, 166
    capital expenditures, 167
    Closeout Report, 122
    cloud computing, 148–149
    company policies, 168
    customer needs, 12
    evaluation matrix, 177
    hiring help, 66
    IT manager decisions, 27
    IT manager duties, 2
    money gray issues, 168
    "people to know,", 24
    politics, 7
    project launch, 116
    project management, 109
    stakeholder identification, 108
    technology refresh cycle, 202
    vendor support, 174
Accounting and Finance users, project stakeholders, 108
Account provisioning, identity management, 220
Accounts Receivable and Payables, project stakeholders, 108
Account usage
    ongoing maintenance, 221
    security technologies, 216
ACD, *see* Automatic Call Distribution (ACD)
Active Directory, 143, 144
ACT model, disaster recovery plan, 259–260
Adelphia, 226

Adobe Connect, 91, 180
Advertising options, PD
    internal posting, 77
    job/recruiting fairs, 79
    networking, 77–79
    networking effectiveness, 78–79
    personal contacts, 78
    popular web sites, 77
    print, 79
    professional contacts, 78
    web posting issues, 77
Adware, 208, 224
AES encryption standard, 222
Agendas, project meetings, 128
Agile development, 34
Agile meetings, 34
Altiris, 143, 280
Amazon cloud computing, 148
Android, 296
Announcements
    intranet uses, 294–295
    webcast, 269
Annual Licensing, 131, 146
Application assessment
    disaster recovery scope, 250–252, 251*f*, 252*f*
    new job basics, 18–20
Application development, IT Department value, 9
Application inventory, technical environment, 193–194
Application software, IT issues, 201
Apps
    as connectedness technology, 289
    mobile devices and connectivity, 296–297
Asset management
    basic considerations, 198–199
    definition, 196–199
Attribute, directory structure, 156
Audits
    Information Systems Audit and Control Association, 239
    security audit, 209–210
    working with auditors, 242–243
Authentication
    challenge–response, 219
    identity management, 220
    methods, 220
    security solutions, 219–220
    SSO, 156, 219–220
    two-factor, 219

Authorization levels, security solutions, 218–219
Automated alerts, as proactive solution, 269
Automated reports, as proactive solution, 269
Automatic Call Distribution (ACD), 282
Availability, CIA model, 208
Awareness training, users, 271

B

Baby boomers, generation differences, 58*t*, 60*t*
Backdoor Trojans, 224
Background checks, 97, 223
Backup tapes, disaster recovery plan, 256
Basel Committee on Banking Supervision (BCBS), 229
Basel II, 229–230
BCBS, *see* Basel Committee on Banking Supervision (BCBS)
BCP, *see* Business Continuity Planning (BCP)
Benefit plan enrollment, intranet uses, 294–295
Benevolent dictator, 141
BestBuy, 225
Bidding, vendor management, 175
Bill 198 (Ontario, Canada), 228
Billing and invoicing, cloud computing, 151
BlackBerry (RIM), 296
Black-hat hackers, 208, 211–212
Black List, 154
Bliley, Thomas, 231
Blogs, as connectedness technology, 289
Bloomberg, Michael, 4
Body language, 33, 92
Boss relationship
    with IT Manager, 17–18
    view of users, 265
"Breaking the ice," 15
Brin, Sergey, 95, 209
Bring Your Own (BYO) Policy, 273, 288–289
Brute force method, 27
Budgeting factors
    department workload, 170
    hardware maintenance, 172–173
    key factors, 170–173
    software maintenance, 171
    staff, 171
    technological change, 171
Budgeting issues, *see also* Cost considerations; Money
    first 100 days, 26
    intranet uses, 294–295
    kick-off meeting, 116
    off-track projects, 125–126
    project funding, 131
Budgeting process
    approval, 165–166
    budget reviewers, 164–165

chargebacks, 164
    estimations, 165
    items, 162–163
    items to tracks, 162–163
    overview, 161–167
    revisions, 166–167
    tracking, 166–167
Burnout
    associated problems, 36
    avoiding/monitoring, 36–37
    employees, 36
Business Applications
    OS selection, 138
    as software type, 136
Business Continuity Planning (BCP)
    basic issues, 261
    and compliance, 243
    definition, 260
    disaster recovery, 260–261
Business-related degrees, candidate selection, 96
Business Software Alliance, 145
Buy *vs.* lease decision
    basic considerations, 168–170
    operating *vs.* capital lease, 169
    person deciding, 170
    pros and cons, 169, 169*t*
BYO, *see* Bring Your Own (BYO) Policy

C

Call centers, 183, 278
Call tracking
    Help Desk, 278–279, 282
    knowledge base, 279
    user satisfaction surveys, 280
Candidate selection
    ability to learn, 94
    background checks, 97
    business-related degrees, 96
    certification value, 94–95
    common mistakes, 98–99
    education, 95–97
    education's direct value, 96
    education's indirect value, 96
    hard sciences-related degree, 97
    high-volume response, 85
    interview guidelines, 86
    level of interview, 84
    list narrowing, 84–86
    multiple interviewers, 88–89
    multiple perspectives, 89*b*
    non-technical questions, 87–88
    off-limits questions, 88

overqualified candidates, 85–86
professional references, 97–98
profile/personality tests, 90*b*
project teams, 126
question preparation, 87–88
rank criteria, 93–94
reference checks, 97–98
remote interviews, 91–92
requirements flexibility, 93–94
résumé reviews, 83–84
salary range, 99–101
similar experience, 92–93
skill set, 92
soft sciences-related degrees, 97
technical courses, 97
technical interviews, 89–93
telephone screening, 84
30 qualified candidates, 85
CAP, *see* Certified Authorization Professional (CAP)
Capability Maturity Model Integration (CMMI), 240
Capital expenditure
company policies, 168
details, 167–168
gray areas, 168
vs. operating expense, 115, 167–168
Capital investment, vendor evaluation matrix, 177
Capital lease, 169
CareerBuilder.com, 77
Carrier connections, technical environment, 191–192
Casper (JAMF), 143, 280
Catastrophic disasters, DR plan, 259
CERT, 211
Certificates, security defenses, 222
Certification
checking value, 95
employee training, 41
job requirement flexibility, 94
position description, 74
project manager, 105
value, 94–95
Certified Authorization Professional (CAP), 223
Certified Information Systems Security Professional (CISSP), 41, 223
Certified Novell Engineer (CNE), 41, 94
Certified Secure Software Lifecycle Professional (CSSLP), 223
Chain letters, e-mail management, 153–154
Challenge–response authentication, 219
Change Request (CR), 212
Chargebacks, 164
Chatter.com, as connectedness technology, 289
Chemistry, Four C's of Hiring, 70
Chief Security Officer (CSO), 212

CIA, *see* Confidentiality, Integrity, Availability (CIA) model
Circumstance, Four C's of Hiring, 69
CISSP, *see* Certified Information Systems Security Professional (CISSP)
Clause 49 (India), 228
CLERP-9 (Australia), 228, 233
Client/server software type, 136
Clinton, Bill, 126–127
Closeout Report
additional accomplishments, 122
bad news, 122
follow-up activities, 122
as project plan guide, 112
writing, 121–122
Cloud computing
basic considerations, 150–152
benefits and challenges, 152*t*
non-perpetual licensing, 146
overview, 148–152
private *vs.* public, 149–150
pros and cons, 150*t*
types, 148–149
CMMI, *see* Capability Maturity Model Integration (CMMI)
CNE, *see* Certified Novell Engineer (CNE)
COBIT, *see* Control Objectives for Information and Related Technology (COBIT)
Code name, project management techniques, 127
Collaboration
connectivity tool issues, 298–299
employee performance reviews, 46
management style, 4
Command and Control management style, 4
Commitment, candidate selection, 95
Committee of Sponsoring Organizations (COSO), 226
Communication plan
disaster recovery, 253–254
mobile user support, 275
Communication skills, employee performance reviews, 45
Communication with team
Agile meetings, 34
focused employees, 32–34
goal achievement, 32–33
goals and objectives, 32
listening to employees, 33
meeting frequency, 33–34
project meetings, 34
staff questions, 33
Company objectives, project management, 107
Company-owned equipment, BYO policies, 288–289
Company values, team management, 34–35
Company-wide layoffs, alternatives, 57*b*
Complaint desk, *see* Help Desk

Compliance, *see also* Policies
   Basel II, 229–230
   disaster recovery and business continuity, 243
   Dodd–Frank Act, 233
   electronic discovery, 242
   employee performance reviews, 46
   Gramm–Leach–Bliley Act, 231–232
   information and records retention, 242
   Massachusetts Data Protection Law, 230–231
   non-compliance victims, 227
   Office of Foreign Assets Control, 233
   outsourcing, 244
   overview, 226–227
   personally identifiable information, 226–227
   PIPEDA, 233
   policies and procedures, 243
   Privacy and Electronic Communications Directive
      (European Union), 234
   rules, 227–234
   Sarbanes–Oxley, 227–228
   US securities, 232
   working with auditors, 242–243
Compliance benefits
   control mechanisms, 237
   documentation, 237
   employee education, 237–238
   evidence maintenance, 238
   overview, 237–238
Compliance processes
   CMMI, 240
   control mechanisms, 236
   COSO, 226
   employee education, 236
   evidence maintenance, 236
   ISO 9000, 240–241
   IT governance, 238–239
   IT Infrastructure Library, 240
   methodologies and frameworks, 238–239
   overview, 234–236
   policy documentation, 235
   Six Sigma, 241–242
Concurrent User Licensing, 146
Conference calling services, as proactive solution, 268
Conference calls, project meetings, 129
Conference room reservations
   intranet uses, 294–295
   as proactive solution, 269
Confidentiality, Integrity, Availability (CIA) model, 208
Connectivity
   basic considerations, 287
   benefits and challenges, 290–291, 290*t*
   benefits of Web, 293–294

BYO policies, 288–289
   effects on IT Manager, 298–302
   e-mail checking frequency, 302*b*
   empowered users, 292–293
   focus *vs.* distraction, 301–302
   goals, 301
   handheld hardware, 297–298
   handling new technologies, 287–288
   intranet uses, 294–295
   mobile device OSes/apps/hardware, 296–297
   mobile device uses, 295–296, 297–298
   new technologies, 289–290
   real-world applications, 293–298
   social media uses, 295–296
   tool implementation, 299–301
   tool use considerations, 298–299
   tool use guidelines, 300–301
   tool use opportunities, 301
   wisdom of crowds, 293
Constraints, project management, 109–110
Consultants
   cost considerations, 114
   vs. full-time employees, 70–74
   project planning, 113
   pros and cons, 72*t*
Consumerization of IT
   BYO policies, 273
   handling, 272
   overview, 271–273
   security issues, 273
   support depth and breadth, 273
   support issues, 272–273
Continuity, Four C's of Hiring, 70
Contracts
   vs. position descriptions, 75
   review with vendors, 175–176
Control mechanisms
   compliance benefits, 237
   identification, 236
Control Objectives for Information and Related Technology
      (COBIT), 239
Convenience, *vs.* security *vs.* privacy, 207
Conversation topics, one-on-one meetings, 16
Coordination with others, employee performance reviews, 46
Corporate Governance Code (Germany), 228
Corporate Law Economic Reform Program Act (2004),
      see CLERP-9 (Australia)
Corporate scandals, 227
COSO, *see* Committee of Sponsoring Organizations (COSO)
Cost considerations, *see also* Budgeting issues; Capital
      expenditure; Money; Operating expense
   consumerization of IT, 273

disaster recovery facilities, 255
employee training, 39, 42
ERP implementation, 158
Four C's of Hiring, 69
full-time *vs.* consultants, 71
information sharing with users, 267
off-track projects, 125–126
OSS, 142
project funding, 130–131, 132
project management, 109
project meetings, 129
recruiters, 82
tough economic times, 179–180
vendor evaluation matrix, 177–178
Courtesy interview, 68
CR, *see* Change Request (CR)
craigslist.org, 77
Crisis communication services, DR communication plan, 254
Critical path, project progress tracking, 118–119
Crowdcast.com, as connectedness technology, 289
Crowdsourcing
basic concept, 293
as connectedness technology, 289
connectivity tool issues, 298–299
CSO, *see* Chief Security Officer (CSO)
CSSLP, *see* Certified Secure Software Lifecycle Professional (CSSLP)
Customer needs
customer as user, 264
and employee training, 41
IT strategy development, 12
OS selection, 139
Customer service, benefits of Web, 294

D

Database Management System (DBMS), 135
Databases
DR data replication, 256
ERP, 157
first 100 days, 23
Data loss, DR scope, 252
Data protection, cloud computing, 151
Data Protection Directive (European Union), 234
Data recovery, cloud computing, 151
Data redundancy, cloud computing, 151
Data replication, disaster recovery plan, 256
Data retention, cloud computing, 151
Data storage
cloud computing, 151
disk/tape encryption, 222
off-site, 256
technical environment, 192

DB2 (IBM), DBMS, 135
DBMS, *see* Database Management System (DBMS)
Decision-making techniques
project management, 122–123
types, 122–123
Deloitte, 158
Demilitarized zone (DMZ), 190
Department objectives, project management, 107
Department of Defense (DoD), 215
De-perimeterization techniques, 215
Deployment, software management, 142–143
Depreciation
budget items, 163
company policies, 168
DES encryption standard, 222
Desktop devices
consumerization of IT, 272
software management, 144
Desktop management, Help Desk, 280
Development plan, performance reviews, 52–53
Development tools, software types, 136
Dice.com, 77
Digital certificates, 222
Direct funding sources, project stakeholders, 109
Directory entries, directory structure, 156
Directory Services, 156–157
Disaster Recovery (DR)
ACT model, 259–260
backup tapes, 256
basic considerations, 247
BCP, 260–261
communication plan, 253–254
and compliance, 243
data replication, 256
definition, 260
documentation, 254
facilities considerations, 255–256
good planning benefits, 261
hardware availability, 257
incident response, 260–261
IT facilities, 254–256
off-site data storage, 256
plan creation, 253–260
plan review/update, 258
post-disaster issues, 259
real estate, 254–256
regional/catastrophic disasters, 259
scope determination
application assessment, 250–252, 251*f*, 252*f*
basic considerations, 248–252
data value, 252
key questions, 248–249

Disaster Recovery (DR) (*Continued*)
    RPO, 249, 249*f*
    RTO, 249, 249*f*
    testing, 258
Disciplinary problems, employee performance,
    54–57
Disk Cloning, software management, 143
Disk image, software management, 143
Distraction issues, connectivity, 301–302
Distributions, 142
Distros, 142
DMADV, 241
DMAIC, 241
DMZ, *see* Demilitarized Zone (DMZ)
Documentation
    compliance benefits, 237
    compliance policies, 235
    disaster recovery plan, 254
    first 100 days, 23
    infrastructure, 189–190, 195–196
    server environment, 192
    trouble tickets as, 278
DoD, *see* Department of Defense (DoD)
Dodd–Frank Act, 233
"Downtime," connectivity issues, 290*t*
DR, *see* Disaster Recovery (DR)
DreamWorks Animation, 107

E

eBay, 225
Education
    candidate selection, 95–97
    compliance process, 236
    direct value to job, 96
    e-mail usage, 153
    hidden benefits, 237–238
    indirect value to job, 96
    job requirement flexibility, 93
    position description, 76
    user training, 271
Electronic discovery, 242
E-mail
    appropriate use, 155
    archiving, 155
    checking frequency, 302*b*
    electronic discovery, 242
    encryption, 222
    enterprise applications, 136, 152–153
    harassment, 154
    junk mail, 153–154
    management, 153–155
    mobile user support, 274
    self-service Help Desk, 277
    size limits and retention, 154–155
    threat types, 225
    usage statistics, 153
    user education, 153
    viruses, 154
Employee agreements, training costs, 42
Employee burnout
    avoiding/monitoring, 36–37
    employee burnout, 36
    team management, 36
Employee discounts, intranet uses, 294–295
Employee focus
    Agile Meetings, 34
    goal achievement, 32–33
    goals and objectives, 32
    listening to staff, 33
    meeting frequency, 33–34
    priorities, 32
    project meetings, 34
    staff input, 33
    team communication, 32–34
    team management, 32–38
Employee performance, *see also* Performance reviews
    disciplinary problems, 54–57
    evaluation areas, 44–47
    layoff alternatives, 57*b*
    layoffs, 55–57
    overview, 43–57
    project management, 133
    salary review, 53–54
    terminations, 54–57
Employee resources, project planning, 113–114
Employee training
    basic considerations, 39–43
    certification, 41
    compliance process, 236
    cost, 39
    departures after, 41–42
    hidden benefits, 237–238
    identifying employees, 40–41
    maximizing value, 42–43
    morale, 40
    needs, 39–40
    nontechnical training, 42
    scheduling demands, 40
    security impact, 214
Empowered users, connectivity issues, 292–293
Emulators, OS, 139
Encouragement, connectivity tool issues, 298–299
Encryption, security defenses, 222
End User Licence Agreement (EULA) [Microsoft], 144*b*

End-user upgrades, as proactive solution, 269
Enron, 226
Enterprise applications
    connectivity tool implementation, 300
    directory services, 156–157
    e-mail, 152–153
    overview, 152–157
    scalability issues, 178
    as software type, 136
    unified messaging, 155–156
Enterprise Resource Planning (ERP)
    as capital expense, 167
    client/server software, 136
    cost management, 180
    disadvantages, 159
    enterprise applications, 136
    implementation costs, 158
    implementation decisions, 158–159
    implementation issues, 157–158
    implementation requirements, 158
    overview, 157–159
    project management, 104
    TCO, 142
    value, 157
Ernst & Young, 158
ERP, *see* Enterprise Resource Planning (ERP)
Escalating calls, Help Desk procedures, 276–277
Ethics
    employee performance reviews, 46
    outsourcing, 244
EULA, *see* End User Licence Agreement (EULA) [Microsoft]
European Union
    Data Protection Directive, 234
    Privacy and Electronic Communications Directive, 234
Evaluation matrix (vendors)
    functionality, 177
    interoperability, 179
    performance, 178
    price, 177–178
    product market position, 179
    required training, 178
    scalability, 178
    services, 178
    support and service, 179
    typical components, 177–179
    viability, 178
Evidence maintenance
    compliance process, 236
    hidden benefits, 238
Exchange (Microsoft)
    client/server software, 136
    cloud computing, 148–149

ExecuNet.com, 77
Expense item
    company policies, 168
    gray areas, 168
Experienced workers
    job requirement flexibility, 93
    vs. "newbies," 61*t*
    position description, 76
    similar experience of candidates, 92–93
Experimentation, connectivity tool issues, 298–299
External employees, project planning, 113–114
External hires, *vs.* internal, 68–70
External referrals, as hiring starting point, 68
External use software licenses, 146

F
Facebook, 44, 290, 290*t*, 296, 299, 302
Face-to-face project meetings, 129
Facilities
    disaster recovery, 248, 254–256
    user identification, 264
Fair and Accurate Credit Transactions Act (FACTA), 231
Fair Credit Reporting Act (FCRA), 231
FASB, *see* Financial Accounting Standards Board (FASB)
Federal Deposit Insurance Corporation, 229
Federal Reserve System, 229
Federated identity, 220
Feedback
    IT service, 268
    leadership during tough economy, 181
FileMaker Pro, DBMS, 135
Finance Department
    budget approval, 165
    BYO policies, 273
    capital *vs.* operating expenses, 115, 167
    company money policies, 168
    consultant pros and cons, 72*t*
    consumerization of IT, 271, 272
    disaster recovery committee, 249
    employee education, 238
    full-time *vs.* consultants, 70
    internal resources costs, 115
    intranet software downloads, 143
    IT manager duties, 1, 6
    outsourcing, 186
    "people to know," 24
    policies and procedures, 243
    stakeholder identification, 108
    user identification, 264
    vendor management, 176
Financial Accounting Standards Board (FASB), 169
Financial Instruments and Exchange Law (Japan), 228

Financial Privacy Rule, GLB, 231
Financial scandals, 226, 237–238
Financial Security Law of France, 228
Firewall, 220
First-day issues
    new job basics, 14
    war stories, 19*b*
First 100 days
    advertising personal offerings
      asking questions, 22
      basic considerations, 21–22
      perspective, 21–22
      preliminary research, 21
    budgeting, 26
    developing relationships, 24
    HR issues, 25–26
    initial decisions, 26–27
    introductory meetings, 24–25
    organization dynamics, 20–21
    project inventory, 22–23
    status quo evaluation, 23
Fiscal year, budgeting process, 161
Fixed asset, expense gray areas, 168
Flexibility
    consumerization of IT, 272
    employee performance review, 45
    job requirements, 93–94
    unified messaging, 156
    user relationships, 270
"Flying Pig" award, 127*b*
Focus issues
    connectivity, 301–302
    management *vs.* leadership, 13
Follow-up, information collection, 268
Four C's of Hiring, 69*b*
Four directions of management, characteristics,
    7–8, 8*f*
Free software, GNU definition, 144*b*
Friendster, 290
Full-time employees
    vs. consultants, 70–74
    project planning, 113
    pros and cons, 73*t*
    resistance by companies, 74*b*
Funding, project management
    budget source, 131
    cost estimation, 130–131
    cost justification, 132
    overview, 130–132
    total cost, 131
Funding sources, project stakeholders, 109
Fusion (Oracle), enterprise applications, 136

G
Gadgets, as connectedness technology, 289
Gantt Chart
    example, 119*f*
    progress tracking, 117
    project milestones, 119
    project progress tracking, 118
Gates, Bill, 35, 95
Generational issues
    basic considerations, 57–62
    cross-generation management, 58–62
    differences, 58*t*, 60*t*
    experienced *vs.* "newbie" workers, 61*t*
    multigenerational workforce advantages, 59–62
Generation X, 58*t*, 60*t*
Generation Y ("Millenials")
    generation differences, 58*t*, 60*t*
    trends, 59
    user security training, 213
Geo-location technology, 290*t*
Giuliani, Rudy, 259
Glass–Steagall Act, 232
GLB, *see* Gramm–Leach–Bliley (GLB) Act
Global Crossing, 226, 227
GNU free software, 144*b*
Google Apps, 148
Google Docs, 148
Google Sites, 149
Google Talk, 91
GoToMeeting (Citrix), 180, 290*t*
Governance
    compliance processes, 238–239
    COSO, 239
Government agencies, project stakeholders, 109
Gramm, Phil, 231
Gramm–Leach–Bliley (GLB) Act, 231–232
Green indicators, project progress tracking, 121
Grid computing, 149
Grove, Andy, 4

H
Hackers
    black hats, white hats, 208, 211–212
    security assessment, 211
    SSO, 219–220
Handheld devices
    end-user upgrades, 269
    hardware, 297–298
    support issues, 272–273
Hands-off approach, dealing with mergers, 28
Harassment, e-mail management, 154

Hard costs, project funding, 130
Hard sciences-related degree, candidate selection, 97
Hardware
  budget items, 162
  disaster recovery plan
    basic considerations, 257
    environment duplication, 257
    environment size, 257
    home equipment, 257
  flexible approach to, 270
  handheld devices, 297–298
  job requirement flexibility, 94
  mobile devices and connectivity, 296–297
  project costs, 131
  vendor evaluation matrix, 178
Hardware configurations, IT issues, 200
Hardware maintenance
  basic considerations, 172–173
  T&M contracts, 172–173
  warranties, 173
HDI, *see* Help Desk Institute (HDI)
Health Information Technology for Economic and Clinical Health (HITECH) Act, 229
Health Insurance Portability and Accountability Act (HIPAA), 155, 210–211, 226, 228–229
HealthSouth, 226, 227
Help Desk
  access, 277
  call tracking software, 278–279
  desktop management, 280
  e-mail management, 154
  employee training, 41
  escalating calls, 276–277
  information sharing with users, 267
  knowledge base, 279
  outsourcing, 184
  overview, 275–282
  procedures, 276–277
  remote control, 279–280
  self-service, 277–278
  social engineering, 225–226
  staffing, 281–282
  tools, 278–280
  typical activities, 276
  user satisfaction surveys, 267, 280
  VM uses, 140
  workload measurement, 281
Help Desk Institute (HDI), 278–279
HIPAA, *see* Health Insurance Portability and Accountability Act (HIPAA)

Hiring
  basic considerations, 65–74
  candidate selection
    ability to learn, 94
    background checks, 97
    business-related degrees, 96
    certification value, 94–95
    common mistakes, 98–99
    education, 95–97
    education's direct value, 96
    education's indirect value, 96
    hard sciences-related degree, 97
    high-volume response, 85
    interview guidelines, 86
    level of interview, 84
    list narrowing, 84–86
    multiple interviewers, 88–89
    multiple perspectives, 89*b*
    non-technical questions, 87–88
    off-limits questions, 88
    overqualified candidates, 85–86
    professional references, 97–98
    profile/personality tests, 90*b*
    question preparation, 87–88
    rank criteria, 93–94
    reference checks, 97–98
    remote interviews, 91–92
    requirements flexibility, 93–94
    résumé reviews, 83–84
    salary range, 99–101
    similar experience, 92–93
    skill set, 92
    soft sciences-related degrees, 97
    technical courses, 97
    technical interviews, 89–93
    telephone screening, 84
    30 qualified candidates, 85
  consultant pros and cons, 72*t*
  Four C's, 69*b*
  full-time *vs.* consultants, 70–74
  full-time employee pros and cons, 73*t*
  full-time employees, reluctance, 74*b*
  help with, 66–67
  HR role, 66–67
  internal *vs.* external hires, 68–70
  internal and external referrals, 68
  internal hire pros and cons, 69*t*
  justification, 67–68, 68*b*
  position description
    advertising options, 77–79
    basic considerations, 74–79
    vs. contracts, 75

Hiring (*Continued*)
    example, 76*f*
    general requirements, 75–77
    recruiters
      basic considerations, 79–82
      current usefulness, 81*b*
      multiple recruiters, 82
      pros and cons, 80*t*
      selection, 81–82
      technical abilities, 82
    timing considerations, 71–74
HITECH, *see* Health Information Technology for Economic
    and Clinical Health (HITECH) Act
Home use licenses, 146
HR, *see* Human Resources (HR)
HRIS, *see* Human Resources Information Systems (HRIS)
Human Resources (HR)
    BYO policies, 273
    capital expenditures *vs.* operating expense, 167
    connectivity and attention issues, 301
    disciplinary problems, 54, 55
    e-mail archiving, 155
    employee performance reviews, 43–44
    first 100 day issues, 25–26
    full-time *vs.* consultants, 70
    high-volume applicant response, 85
    hiring role, 66–67
    multigenerational workforce issues, 61
    multiple interviewers, 88
    negative performance reviews, 50
    nontechnical employee training, 42
    policy documentation, 235
    professional reference checks, 98
    project stakeholders, 109
    recruiter pros and cons, 81
    recruiter selection, 81
    salary review, 53
    telework programs, 38
Human Resources Information Systems (HRIS), 148–149, 185

I

IaaS, *see* Infrastructure as a Service (IaaS)
IBM cloud computing, 148
IdeaScale.com, as connectedness technology, 289
Identity management, 220
IDS, *see* Intrusion Detection System (IDS)
IIHI, *see* Individually-Identifiable Health Information (IIHI)
IM, *see* Instant Messaging (IM)
Incident response
    definition, 260
    disaster recovery, 260–261
    security defenses, 223–224

Indeed.com, 77
Indirect funding sources, project stakeholders, 109
Individually-Identifiable Health Information (IIHI), 229
Industry experience, job requirement flexibility, 94
Information collection
    Help Desk, 275
    methods, 267–268
Information retention, compliance, 242
Information sharing
    methods, 267
    with users, 266–267
Information Systems Audit and Control Association, 239
Infrastructure as a Service (IaaS), 149, 151
Infrastructure documentation
    technical environment, 189–190
    value, 195–196
In-house catering, intranet uses, 294–295
In-house classes, user training, 270
Innovation, performance reviews, 45
Instant Messaging (IM)
    as connectedness technology, 289
    connectivity issues, 290*t*
    IT for business value, 180
    mobile user support, 274
    as proactive solution, 269
    remote interviews, 91
    telework programs, 38
Integrity, CIA model, 208
Interaction with others, employee performance reviews, 46
Interdependencies, project management, 109–110
Internal controls, security assessment, 210–211
Internal employees, project planning, 113–114
Internal hires
    vs. external, 68–70
    pros and cons, 69*t*
Internal posting, PD, 77
Internal referrals, as hiring starting point, 68
Internal resources, cost considerations, 115
Internal use software licenses, 146
International Convergence of Capital Measurement and Capital
    Standards, *see* Basel II
International Organization for Standards, 240–241
Internet
    application assessment, 251
    candidate interviews, 91–92
    capital expenditures, 167–168
    chargebacks, 164
    cloud computing, 148–149
    connection as capital expense, 167–168
    disaster recovery, 248, 253
    firewalls, 220
    handheld hardware, 297

IDS/IPS, 220–221
IT acceptance, 301
job searching, 84
LAN, 192*f*
phishing, 225
project management tools, 118
recruiter business model, 81
reference checks, 98
remote interviews, 91–92
security and compliance, 205
SLAs, 284
two-factor authentication, 219
VoIP, *see* Voice over IP (VOIP)
WAN, 190, 191*f*
Internet Service Provider (ISP), 113–114, 163
Interoperability, 177, 179
Interviews
    candidate selection, 84
    guidelines, 86
    multiple interviewers, 88–89
    non-technical questions, 87–88
    off-limits questions, 88
    question preparation, 87–88
    remote, 91–92
    technical, 89–93
Intranet
    as proactive solution, 269
    user-downloadable software, 143
    uses, 294–295
Introductory meetings, first 100 days, 24–25
Intrusion Detection System (IDS), 220–221
Intrusion Prevention System (IPS), 220–221
Invoicing, cloud computing, 151
iOS, 137, 138, 296
iPad, 137
iPhone, 10, 137, 271, 272
IPS, *see* Intrusion Prevention System (IPS)
ISO 9000, 240
ISO 17799, 223
ISO 270001, 223
ISP, *see* Internet Service Provider (ISP)
IT Department basics
    Application Development, 9
    BYO policies, 273
    central role, 12
    CEO role, 9*b*
    consumerization of IT, 271–273
    goals, 10
    merger issues, 27–28
    team members, 11
    Technical Operations, 9
    view of users, 264

IT facilities, disaster recovery, 254–256
IT Governance Institute, 239
IT Infrastructure Library (ITIL), 240
IT Manager role
    basic issues, 1
    connectivity issues, 298–302
    first 100 days, 20–27
    IT Department merger issues, 27–28
    IT Department strategic value, 8–10
    job benefits, 2
    job drawbacks, 2–3
    job pros/cons, 5
    leadership *vs.* management, 13, 13*t*
    management basics, 3–8
    manager's value, 10
    new job basics, 14–20
    responsibilities, 2–3
IT standards
    flexibility, 270
    technology products, 201
IT strategy development
    basic considerations, 10–12
    customer needs, 12
    IT Department's central role, 12
    team members, 11
    technology value, 11–12
iWork, productivity tools, 136

J

JBoss (Red Hat), enterprise applications, 136
Job criteria, candidate selection, 93–94
Job Description (JD), *see* Position Description (PD)
Job fairs, PD advertising, 79
Job postings, 294–295, *see also* Advertising options, PD
Job requirements, performance reviews, 45
Jobs, Steve, 35, 95, 287
Jobster.com, 77
Jokes, e-mail management, 153–154
Junk mail, management, 153–154

K

Katzenberg, Jeffrey, 107
Key loggers, 224
Keys, security defenses, 222
Kick-off meeting
    goals, 116–117
    with non-IT departments, 133
    project launch, 116–117
Kluster.com, 289, 298–299
Knowledge base, Help Desk, 279
KOffice, productivity tools, 136

L

L262/2005 (Italy), 228
Labor cost management, 180
LAN, *see* Local Area Network (LAN)
LANDesk, 143, 280
Language skills
 outsourcing agreements, 185
 performance reviews, 52
 web-based interviews, 92
Laptop devices, consumerization of IT, 272
Lawson, ERP, 157
Layoffs
 alternatives, 57*b*
 employee performance, 55–57
Leach, Jim, 231
Leadership
 behind-schedule projects, 125
 connectivity tool issues, 298–299
 vs. management, 13*t*
 tough economic times, 181
Lease *vs.* buy decision
 basic considerations, 168–170
 operating *vs.* capital lease, 169
 person deciding, 170
 pros and cons, 169, 169*t*
Legacy applications, VM uses, 140
Legal Department
 budget approval, 166
 BYO policies, 273
 connectivity technologies, 298
 consultants *vs.* employees, 71
 control mechanisms, 237
 disaster recovery, 248, 250
 disciplinary problems, 54, 55
 electronic discovery, 242
 e-mail archiving, 155
 e-mail harassment, 154
 evidence maintenance, 238
 full-time *vs.* consultants, 70–71
 information/records retention, 242
 interview questions, 88
 IT manager duties, 2
 negative reviews, 50
 ongoing security maintenance, 221
 outsourcing, 186
 "people to know," 24
 policies and procedures, 243
 policy documentation, 235
 security incident response, 223
 software licensing, 145, 147
 stakeholder identification, 109

 teleworkers, 38
 user identification, 264
 vendor contracts, 176
Legitimate purpose principle, Data Protection Directive, 234
Letterman, Rob, 107
Liability issues
 BYO policies, 273
 cloud computing, 151
 managing during tough times, 68
 vendor contracts, 175
Licensing, *see* Software licensing
Live Messenger, 91
LinkedIn, 302
Linux, 136, 138
Listening, team management, 33
Live Meeting, 180
Local Area Network (LAN)
 carrier connections, 191–192
 example schematic, 192*f*
 securing users, 213
 technical environment, 191
Locking down, desktop, 143, 144
Log files, 215, 221
Long-term focus, management *vs.* leadership, 13
Long-term project management, employee performance reviews, 47
Lotus Notes, client/server software, 136

M

Mac OS X, 136, 137
Macro viruses, 224
Madoff, Bernie, 226
Maintenance plans
 hardware budget, 172–173
 security defenses, 221–222
 software licensing, 147
Majority wins, decision-making techniques, 122
Malware
 computer security, 208
 prevention, 221
 types, 224
Management basics
 babysitting *vs.* managing, 7
 behind-schedule projects, 125
 choosing style, 5
 collaboration style, 4
 command and control style, 4
 job pros/cons, 5*t*
 management *vs.* leadership, 13*t*
 management styles, 3–5
 manager definition, 3
 managing in four directions, 7–8, 8*f*

non-tangible aspects, 6
overview, 3–8
politics, 7
resentment toward management, 7
Management buy-in, security management, 212
Manufacturing Department
disaster recovery committee, 250
ERP software, 157
"people to know," 24
proactive user solutions, 269
Mark Cuban Twitters, 301
Market conditions, benefits of Web, 293
Marketing Department, *see* Sales and Marketing Department
Marketing material, intranet uses, 294–295
Mashups, as connectedness technology, 289
Massachusetts Data Protection Law, 230–231
Meetings, *see also* Project meetings
first 100 days, 24–25
information collection, 268
key meeting determination, 19
one-on-one meetings, 15–16
team management, 33–34
webcast, 269
Mergers and acquisitions
dealing with, 27–28
security issues, 205
Metrics
employee performance reviews, 47–48
Help Desk, 275
sharing with users, 267
user satisfaction surveys, 267
vendor evaluation matrix, 177
Microblogging, as connectedness technology, 289
Microsoft cloud computing, 148
Microsoft EULA, 144*b*
Microsoft Office
end-user upgrades, 269
OS selection, 138
productivity tools, 136
support outsourcing, 184
user-downloadable software, 143
Microsoft Project, 117–118, 117*b*, 143
Middleware, as software type, 136
Milestone, 119–120
Millenials, *see* Generation Y ("Millenials")
Minutes, project meetings, 128–129
Miscellaneous, budget items, 163
Mission statement, 34–35, 267
Mitnick, Kevin, 225
M&M security model, 215
Mobile device management (MDM), 298
Mobile devices

connectivity uses, 295–296
mis-configuration/mal-configured, 211
operating systems, 296–297
uses, 297–298
widgets, 289
Mobile equipment, technical environment, 193
Mobile workforce, *see also* Remote workers; Telework programs
support techniques, 274–275
user issues, 274–275
Money, *see also* Budgeting issues; Cost considerations
capital *vs.* operating expenses, 115
consultants, 114
hidden costs, 114
internal resource costs, 115
multiple project management, 133
one-time costs, 114
ongoing costs, 114
as project component, 111, 111*f*, 114–115
Money management
budgeting factors, 170–173
budgeting process, 161–167
capital expenditures *vs.* operating expense, 167–168
lease *vs.* buy, 168–170
offshoring, 182–187
outsourcing, 182–187
tough economic times, 179–181
vendors, 173–179
Monitoring programs, 215–216
Monster.com, 77, 79
Morale, employee training, 40
MSN, 225
Multigenerational workforce, advantages, 59–62
Multiple bids, vendor management, 175
Multiple project management
basic considerations, 132–133
politics, 133
time/money prioritization, 133
Multiple Tier Licensing, 146
Multiple Use Licensing, 146
Multitasking, connectivity issues, 290*t*
MySQL, DBMS, 135

N

National Association of Securities Dealers (NASD), Rule 3010, 232
Network Access Control (NAC), 222
Networking
cloud computing, 151
effectiveness, 78–79
job postings, 77–79
outsourcing, 184

Network mapping tools, 216
"Newbie" workers, *vs.* experienced, 61*t*
New job basics
    boss/peer relationships, 17–18
    breaking the ice, 15
    first day, 14
    first-day war stories, 19*b*
    key meetings, 19
    key users/applications, 18–20
    meeting staff, 14–15
    one-on-one meetings, 15–16
    overview, 14–20
    problem fixing timetables, 19–20
    staff who wanted job, 16–17
    things not to do, 15
New technologies
    BYO policies, 288–289
    connectedness, 289–290
    handling new technologies, 287–288
New York Stock Exchange (NYSE)
    Rule 342, 232
    Rule 440, 232
Non-compliance victims, 227
Non-Perpetual Licensing (Subscription licenses, Annual
        licenses, Renewal licenses), 131, 146
Nontechnical training, employees, 42
NYSE, *see* New York Stock Exchange (NYSE)

O

Object class, directory structure, 157
Objectiveness, employee performance reviews, 48
Object-Oriented Programming (OOP), 89–90
Objects, directory structure, 156
OCTAVE, *see* Operationally Critical Threat, Asset, and
        Vulnerability Evaluation (OCTAVE)
OFAC, *see* Office of Foreign Assets Control (OFAC)
Office 365, 138
Office of the Comptroller of the Currency, 229
Office of Foreign Assets Control (OFAC), 233
Office of Thrift Supervision, 229
Off-shore outsourcing
    basic considerations, 182–187
    definitions, 182*t*
    overview, 182–183
    political considerations, 186
    pros and cons, 183*t*
Off-site data storage, disaster recovery plan, 256
Off-track projects
    basic considerations, 123–126
    behind schedule, 124–125
    cost issues, 125–126
    issues beyond control, 124

OLAP, *see* Online Analytical Processing (OLAP)
OLTP, *see* Online Transaction Processing (OLTP)
On-demand computing, 149
One-on-one meetings
    conversation topics, 16
    new job basics, 15–16
Online Analytical Processing (OLAP), 135
Online meeting services, project meetings, 130
Online Transaction Processing (OLTP), 135
OOP, *see* Object-Oriented Programming (OOP)
OpenID, 219
OpenOffice, productivity tools, 136
Open Source Software (OSS)
    cost issues, 142
    definition, 141
    Linux, 138
    overview, 141–142
    productivity tools, 136
    pros and cons, 141*t*
"Operate in the cloud," *see* Cloud computing
Operating expense
    vs. capital expense, 115, 167–168
    company policies, 168
    gray areas, 168
    vendor evaluation matrix, 177–178
Operating lease, 169
Operating systems
    applications in environment, 138–139
    customer needs, 139
    emulators, 139
    IT issues, 201
    Linux, 138
    Mac OS X, 137
    mobile devices, 296–297
    mobile user support, 274
    multiple OS environment, 139–140
    overview, 137–140
    selection, 138–139
    as software type, 136
    Unix variants, 138
    VDI, 140
    VMs, 139
    VM uses, 140
    Windows, 137
Operationally Critical Threat, Asset, and Vulnerability
        Evaluation (OCTAVE), 211
Operations tasks, cloud computing, 151
Oracle
    cloud computing, 148
    DBMS, 135
    enterprise applications, 136
    ERP, 157

Oracle Financials, software types, 136
Orange Book (DoD), 215
Organizational impact, cloud computing, 151
Organization unit, directory structure, 156
OSS, *see* Open Source Software (OSS)
"Out of scope," project objectives, 107
Outside services, budget items, 163
Outsourcing
    agreement evaluation, 184–186
    basic considerations, 182–187
    compliance, 244
    definitions, 182*t*
    determining factors, 184–187
    functions, 184
    hiring justification, 68
    overview, 182–183
    political considerations, 186
    pros and cons, 183*t*
Overhead, budget items, 163
Overqualified candidates, 85–86
Oxley, Michael G., 227

P

PaaS, *see* Platform as a Service (PaaS)
Page, Larry, 95, 209
Page hijacker, 224
Passwords
    authentication methods, 220
    backup tapes, 256
    BYO policies, 289
    challenge–response authentication, 219
    compliance, 243
    consumerization of IT, 273
    directory services, 156
    disaster recovery, 258
    Help Desk activities, 276–277, 281
    identity management, 220
    malware, 224
    mobile devices, 298
    NAC, 222
    phishing, 225
    risk mitigation, 212
    secure users, 213
    security incident response, 223
    security *vs.* privacy *vs.* convenience, 207
    security technologies, 217–218
    self-service help, 277
    SLAs, 283
    special privilege IDs, 218
    SSO, 219
    two-factor authentication, 219
    user training, 213

Patriot Act, 232
Pattern files updates, 222
PayPal, 225
Payroll Department
    cloud computing, 148–149
    disaster recovery, 261
    security authorization levels, 218–219
Payroll information, intranet uses, 294–295
PC Anywhere, 279–280
PD, *see* Position Description (PD)
PDCA, *see* Plan, Do, Check, Act (PDCA)
Performance measurement, IT governance, 239
Performance reviews
    360 reviews, 51, 51*t*
    accountability, 46
    basic considerations, 43–44
    communication skills, 45
    compliance, 46
    conduction discussion, 52
    creative problem solving, 45
    employee flexibility, 45
    ethics, 46
    evaluation statements, 47–48, 48*t*
    example, 50*b*
    guidelines, 48–49
    innovation, 45
    job requirements, 45
    learning new skills, 46–47
    metrics, 47–48
    negative reviews, 49–50
    objectiveness, 48
    plan/goals development, 52–53
    "plays well with others," 46
    privacy issues, 52
    quality of work, 44
    recording details, 48–49
    self-reviews, 50
    short-/long-term project management, 47
    team players, 47
    timely performance, 46
    tone, 52
Perks, project management techniques, 127
Per seat licensing, 146
Per server licensing, 146
Personal contacts, job postings, 78
Personal Information Protection and Electronic Documents
        Act (PIPEDA), 233
Personality tests, 90*b*
Personally identifiable information (PII), 226–227,
        230, 232
Personally-owned equipment, BYO policies, 288–289
Personnel, budget items, 162

PERT charts, *see* Program Evaluation and Review Technique (PERT) charts
PGP, *see* Pretty Good Privacy (PGP)
Phased integration, dealing with mergers, 28
PHI, *see* Protected Health Information (PHI)
Phishing, 153–154, 208, 225–226
Phone tree, DR communication plan, 254
Physical access, activity tracking, 216
Physical plant items
    budget process, 163
    as capital expense, 167
PII, *see* Personally identifiable information (PII)
PIPEDA, *see* Personal Information Protection and Electronic Documents Act (PIPEDA)
PKI, *see* Public Key Infrastructure (PKI)
Plan, Do, Check, Act (PDCA), 241
Platform as a Service (PaaS), 149, 151
PlayStation Network, 225
"Plays well with others," performance reviews, 46
Plurk.com, as connectedness technology, 289
PMBOK, *see* Project Management Book of Knowledge (PMBOK)
PMI, *see* Project Management Institute (PMI)
PMO, *see* Project Management Office (PMO)
PMP, *see* Project Management Professional (PMP)
Podcasting, 289, 290
Policies, *see also* Bring Your Own (BYO) Policy; Compliance; Procedures
    compliance, 243
    consumerization support issues, 272
    e-mail usage, 153, 154
    expense items, 168
    Help Desk training, 282
    securing users, 214
    T&M contracts, 172–173
Policy manuals, intranet uses, 294–295
Politics
    connectivity technologies, 302
    management basics, 7
    multiple project management, 133
    outsourcing, 186
Position Description (PD)
    advertising options, 77–79
    common hiring mistakes, 99
    vs. contracts, 75
    example, 76*f*
    general requirements, 75–77
    overview, 74–79
Pretexting, GLB, 231
Pretty Good Privacy (PGP), 222
Price adjustments, benefits of Web, 293
PricewaterhouseCoopers, 158

Print advertising, PDs, 79
Printer alerts, 268
Priorities, focused employees, 32
Priority Zero, 251
Privacy and Electronic Communications Directive (European Union), 234
Privacy issues
    electronic discovery, 242
    outsourcing, 244
    performance reviews, 52
    securing users, 214
    vs. security *vs.* convenience, 207
Privacy Rule, HIPAA, 229
Private *vs.* public cloud, 149–150
Proactive solutions
    employee training, 41
    user relationships, 268–269
Problem-solving skills
    behind-schedule projects, 125
    employee performance reviews, 45
Procedures, *see also* Policies
    compliance, 243
    Help Desk
        basic considerations, 276–277
        escalating calls, 276–277
        staff training, 282
Procurement Group, project stakeholders, 108
Product information
    benefits of Web, 294
    vendor evaluation matrix, 179
Productivity tools
    cloud computing, 148
    Microsoft Project, 117
    software types, 135, 136
Product placement, benefits of Web, 293
Professional contacts, job postings, 78
Professional courtesy
    consultant pros and cons, 72*t*
    e-mail user principles, 153
    outsourcing agreements, 185
Professionalism
    advertising personal offerings, 21
    candidate selection, 87, 88, 92, 98
    employee performance, 46, 47
    generational issues, 58
    meeting staff, 14
    negative performance reviews, 50
    one-to-one meetings, 16
    outsourcing agreements, 185
    towards staff who wanted job, 17
Professional references, candidate selection, 97–98
Profile tests, 90*b*

Program Evaluation and Review Technique (PERT)
    charts, 118–119, 120*f*
Project charter, 110, 121–122
Project frameworks, 127
Project management
    certified project manager, 105
    closeout report, 121–122
    cost management, 180
    decision-making techniques, 122–123
    employee performance reviews, 47
    formalized frameworks, 127
    funding
        budget source, 131
        cost estimation, 130–131
        cost justification, 132
        overview, 130–132
        total cost, 131
    key phases, 104–105
    "laws," 124*b*
    multiple projects
        basic considerations, 132–133
        politics, 133
        time/money prioritization, 133
    non-IT participation
        basic considerations, 133–134
        employee motivation, 133
        person in charge, 133–134
    off-track projects
        basic considerations, 123–126
        behind schedule, 124–125
        cost issues, 125–126
        issues beyond control, 124
    overview, 103
    PMI, 105–106, 105*b*
    PMO, 106
    progress tracking
        basic considerations, 117–121
        critical paths, 118–119
        Gantt Charts, 118, 119*f*
        management/team updates, 120–121
        Microsoft Project, 117–118
        milestones, 119–120
        PERT charts, 118–119, 120*f*
        red/yellow/green indicators, 121
        summary updates, 121
        time lines, 118
        tools, 118
    project launch
        kick-off meeting, 116–117
        options, 116
    project plan
        closeout report as guide, 112

        critical components, 111, 111*f*
        money, 114–115
        multiple projects, 115–116
        resources required, 113–114
        roles and responsibilities, 115
        time estimates, 112–113
    project teams, 126
    project types, 104
    scope
        basic considerations, 106–111
        constraints, interdependencies, risks, 109–110
        defined objectives, 106–107
        department *vs.* company objectives, 107
        historical perspective, 110–111
        project charter, 110
        sponsorship, 107–108
        stakeholders, 108–109
    value, 104
Project Management Book of Knowledge (PMBOK), 104–105
Project Management Institute (PMI), 105–106, 105*b*, 107
Project Management Office (PMO), 106
Project Management Professional (PMP), 41, 105
Project management techniques
    basic considerations, 126–130
    "Flying Pig" award, 127*b*
    manager participation, 127
    meeting agendas, 128
    meeting costs, 129
    meeting minutes, 128–129
    perk offerings, 127
    productive meetings, 128–130
    project code name, 127
    war room, 126–127
Project Manager (PM)
    certified, 105
    decision-making techniques, 123
    PMI, 105
    project cost estimation, 130–131
Project meetings
    agendas, 128
    basic considerations, 128–130
    hidden costs, 129
    minutes, 128–129
    non-IT participation, 133
    options, 129–130
    team management, 34
    useful techniques, 130
Project milestone, 119–120
Project objectives
    clear definition, 106–107
    department *vs.* company, 107
    mid-project change, 107*b*

Project plan
    closeout report as guide, 112
    critical components, 111, 111*f*
    money, 114–115
    multiple projects, 115–116
    resources required, 113–114
    roles and responsibilities, 115
    time estimates, 112–113
Project reviews, post-implementation, 268
Project sponsor, 107–108, 110
Project stakeholder
    behind-schedule projects, 124
    cost overruns, 125
    identification, 108–109
    information sharing, 266
    IT governance, 238
    leadership *vs.* management, 13*t*
    meeting costs, 129
    off-track projects, 123
    project charter, 110
    sponsorship, 108
    summary updates, 121
Project teams
    candidates, 126
    project management, 126
Proportionality principle, Data Protection Directive, 234
Protected Health Information (PHI), 229
Public cloud, *vs.* private, 149–150
Public Company Accounting Reform and Investor Protection
    Act (2002), *see* Sarbanes–Oxley (SOX)
Public Key Infrastructure (PKI), 222

Q

Qualitative risk analysis, security management, 210
Quality of work
    employee performance review, 44
    outsourcing agreements, 185
Quantitative risk analysis, security management, 210
Qwest Communications, 226

R

Rackspace, 148
Radio Frequency Identification (RFID), 207
Real estate, disaster recovery, 254–256
Records retention, compliance, 242
Recovery Point Objective (RPO), 249, 249*f*
Recovery Time Objective (RTO), 249, 249*f*
Recruiters
    basic considerations, 79–82
    current usefulness, 81*b*
    multiple recruiters, 82
    pros and cons, 80*t*
    selection, 81–82
    technical abilities, 82
Recruiting fairs, PD advertising, 79
Red indicators, project progress tracking, 121
Reference checks
    candidate selection, 97–98
    common hiring mistakes, 99
Referrals, as hiring starting point, 68
Regional disaster, DR plan, 259
Relationship issues
    with boss/peers, 17–18
    first 100 days, 24
    vendor management, 173–174
Remote control
    Help Desk, 279–280
    mobile user support, 274
Remote Control (Dameware), 279–280
Remote interviews, candidate selection, 91–92
Remote workers, 37–38, 37*b*, *see also* Mobile workforce;
    Telework programs
Renewal licensing, 146
Request for Information (RFI), 174
Request for Proposal (RFP), 174, 175
Request for Quotation (RFQ), 174
Resource management, 239
Resources, as project component, 111, 111*f*, 113–114
Résumé reviews, candidate selection, 83–84
Return on Investment (ROI)
    cloud computing, 151
    consumerization of IT, 271
    PMO, 106
    project cost justification, 132
    VDI, 140
RFI, *see* Request for Information (RFI)
RFID, *see* Radio Frequency Identification (RFID)
RFP, *see* Request for Proposal (RFP)
RFQ, *see* Request for Quotation (RFQ)
Risk analysis
    security management, 210
    tool options, 211
Risk management
    BYO policies, 273
    IT governance, 239
    project management, 109–110
    security management, 210, 211
    T&M contracts, 172
Risk mitigation, security management, 212–213
ROI, *see* Return on Investment (ROI)
Rootkits, 224
RPO, *see* Recovery Point Objective (RPO)
RSS feeds, as connectedness technology, 289
Rule 17a-3, Securities and Exchange Act (1934), 232

Rule 17a-4, Securities and Exchange Act (1934), 232
Rule 342, NYSE, 232
Rule 440, NYSE, 232
Rule 3010, NASD, 232
Rule of Least Privilege, 215

S

SaaS, *see* Software as a Service (SaaS)
Safeguards Rule, GLB, 231
Salary range
    candidate selection, 99–101
    making offer, 99
    non-monetary compensation, 100–101
    sharing with agencies, 99–100
Salary review, employee performance, 53–54
Salesforce.com, 148
Sales incentives, benefits of Web, 293
Sales and Marketing Department
    candidate selection, 96
    capital *vs.* operating expenses, 167
    customer identification, 12
    IT for business value, 181
    IT manager duties, 1, 2
    "people to know," 24
    user identification, 264
SAP
    enterprise applications, 136
    ERP, 157
    OS selection, 138
Sarbanes, Paul S., 227
Sarbanes–Oxley (SOX), 46, 155, 226, 227–228, 233
SB-1386, 230
Scalability, vendor evaluation matrix, 178
SCAMPI, *see* Standard CMMI Appraisal Method for
        Process Improvement (SCAMPI)
SCCM, 143, 279–280
Scheduling demands
    employee training, 40
    kick-off meeting, 116
    off-track projects, 124–125
    progress tracking, 117
Schmidt, Eric, 290*t*
Scope Creep
    call tracking software, 278
    Project Charter, 110
    project management, 106–107
Scope determination
    disaster recovery
        application assessment, 250–252, 251*f*, 252*f*
        basic considerations, 248–252
        data value, 252
        key questions, 248–249

RPO, 249, 249*f*
RTO, 249, 249*f*
project management
    basic considerations, 106–111
    constraints, interdependencies, risks, 109–110
    defined objectives, 106–107
    department *vs.* company objectives, 107
    historical perspective, 110–111
    project charter, 110
    sponsorship, 107–108
    stakeholders, 108–109
    technical environment, 190
Scrums, Agile Meetings, 34
Secure Sockets Layer (SSL), 222
Securities and Exchange Act (1934)
    Rule 17a-3, 232
    Rule 17a-4, 232
Security audit, basic considerations, 209–210
Security Breach Information Act (SB-1386), 230
Security defenses
    common solutions, 220–223
    encryption, keys, certificates, 222
    firewalls, 220
    IDS/IPS, 220–221
    incident response, 223–224
    malware prevention, 221
    network access control, 222
    ongoing maintenance, 221–222
    staffing issues, 223
Security Incident Response Team (SIRT), 223
Security issues
    assessing intentions, 208
    basic considerations, 205
    breach examples, 225*b*
    CIA, 208
    common themes, 207–209
    connectivity impact, 206–209
    consumerization of IT, 273
    importance of close examination, 208–209
    perspective, 206
    security *vs.* privacy *vs.* convenience, 207
    threat types, 224–226
Security management
    basic actions, 209–214
    care when web surfing, 214
    common weaknesses, 210*b*
    employee impact, 214
    needs, exposures, defenses, 209–212
    risk analysis, 210–211
    risk analysis tools, 211
    risk management, 210, 211
    securing users, 213–214

Security management (*Continued*)
    security audits, 209–210
    security as ongoing process, 214
    upper-level management buy-in, 212
    user training, 213
    white hats, 211–212
Security software, characteristics, 136
Security solutions
    authentication, 219–220
    authentication methods, 220
    authorization levels, 218–219
    challenge–response authentication, 219
    identity management, 220
    single sign-on, 219–220
    two-factor authentication, 219
Security technologies
    access reviews, 218
    account usage, 216
    control access, 215
    passwords, 217–218
    special privilege IDs, 218
    tracking activity, 214–219
Self-reviews, employee performance, 50
Self-service identity management, 220
Servers
    client/server software type, 136
    first 100 days, 23
    per server licensing, 146
    technical environment, 192
Service Level Agreement (SLA)
    basic considerations, 283–284
    first 100 days, 23
    good SLAs, 284
    outsourcing agreements, 185
    positive values, 283
    staff help, 283–284
    vendor contracts, 176
Service providers, project planning, 113–114
Service requests
    authorization levels, 218–219
    intranet uses, 294–295
    vendor evaluation matrix, 179
Shipping and Receiving, project stakeholders, 108
Short-term focus, management *vs.* leadership, 13
Short-term project management, employee performance
    reviews, 47
Single Sign-On (SSO), 156, 219–220
SIRT, *see* Security Incident Response Team (SIRT)
Six Sigma, 241–242
Skill building
    employee performance reviews, 46–47
    performance reviews, 52–53

Skill inflation, self-review of performance, 50
Skill set, candidate selection, 92
Skype, 180
SLA, *see* Service Level Agreement (SLA)
Slack time, 119
SMART, performance reviews, 53
Smart phones
    empowered users, 292
    iPhone, *see* iPhone
    securing users, 214
Social engineering
    computer security, 209
    Help Desk staff training, 282
    as threat type, 225–226
Social media
    connectivity uses, 295–296
    tool implementation, 299–300
    usage guidelines, 300
    virtually private tools, 298–299
Social networking
    as connectedness technology, 289
    connectivity issues, 290*t*
    team management, 33
    tool implementation, 299–300
Soft costs, project funding, 130
Soft sciences-related degrees, candidate selection, 97
Software
    budget items, 162–163
    call tracking, 278–279
    cloud computing, *see* Cloud computing
    consumerization of IT, 272
    end-user upgrades, 269
    enterprise applications, *see* Enterprise applications
    ERP, *see* Enterprise Resource Planning (ERP)
    IT issues, 201
    job requirement flexibility, 94
    maintenance budget, 171
    mobile user support, 274
    operating systems, *see* Operating systems
    OSS, 141–142, 141*t*
    project costs, 131
    technical environment, 193–194
    tracking tools, 194–195
    types, 135–136
Software as a Service (SaaS), 149, 151
Software and Information Industry Association, 145
Software licensing
    basic issues, 145–148
    cloud computing, 151
    consolidation on purchases, 147–148
    GNU free software, 144*b*
    maintenance/support plans, 147

Microsoft EULA, 144*b*
models and types, 146
negotiations, 147
types, 144–145
vendor evaluation matrix, 177
Software management
basic considerations, 142–148
deployment, 142–143
deployment tools, 143
desktop lockdown, 144
disk cloning, 143
e-mail, 153–155
standard disk image, 143
TCO, 142
techniques, 142–144
user-downloadable software, 143
Software patches, ongoing maintenance, 222
Software updates
deployment tools, 143
ongoing maintenance, 222
SOX, *see* Sarbanes–Oxley (SOX)
Spam, 153–154, 208
Special privilege IDs, security technologies, 218
Spoofing, 208, 225
Spyware, 208
SQL Server, DBMS, 135
SSA Global, ERP, 157
SSCP, *see* Systems Security Certified
        Practitioner (SSCP)
SSO, *see* Single Sign-On (SSO)
Staffing issues, *see also* Hiring
behind-schedule projects, 125
budgeting factors, 171
cost management, 180
encouraging questions, 33
Help Desk
overview, 281–282
specific considerations, 281–282
staff size, 282
training, 282
security defenses, 223
SLA help, 283–284
Standard CMMI Appraisal Method for Process Improvement
        (SCAMPI), 240
Standardization, 151, 201, 240–241
Standards, technical environment
basic considerations, 199–201
IT issues, 200–201
IT standards, 201
user issues, 199–200
Stand-ups, 34
Stoll, Clifford, 225

Storage
disk/tape encryption, 222
technical environment, 192
Strategic alignment, IT governance, 239
Subcommittees, decision-making techniques, 123
Subscription licenses, 146
Summary updates, project progress tracking, 121
Supply requests
budget items, 163
intranet uses, 294–295
Support Center, *see* Help Desk
Support issues
consumerization and handheld devices, 272–273
depth and breadth, 273
vs. maintenance issues, 171
mobile users, 274–275
vendor contracts, 176
vendor evaluation matrix, 179
Support plans, software licensing, 147
Surowiecki, James, 293
Surveymonkey.com, 280
System log files, tracking activity, 215
Systems Security Certified Practitioner (SSCP), 223

T
TCO, *see* Total Cost of Ownership (TCO)
Team management
Agile Meetings, 34
avoiding/monitoring burnout, 36–37
communication, 32–34
company values, 34–35
decision-making techniques, 123
employee burnout, 36
employee performance
disciplinary problems, 54–57
layoff alternatives, 57*b*
layoffs, 55–57
salary review, 53–54
terminations, 54–57
employee training
basic considerations, 39–43
certification, 41
cost, 39
departures after, 41–42
identifying employees, 40–41
maximizing value, 42–43
morale, 40
needs, 39–40
nontechnical training, 42
scheduling demands, 40
focused employees, 32–38
generational issues

Team management (*Continued*)
  basic considerations, 57–62
  cross-generation management, 58–62
  differences, 58*t*, 60*t*
  experienced *vs.* "newbie" workers, 61*t*
  multigenerational workforce advantages, 59–62
goal achievement, 32–33
goals and objectives, 32
listening importance, 33
meeting frequency, 33–34
mission statement, 34–35
overview, 31
performance reviews
  360 reviews, 51, 51*t*
  accountability, 46
  communication skills, 45
  compliance, 46
  conduction discussion, 52
  creative problem solving, 45
  ethics, 46
  evaluation areas, 44–47
  evaluation statements, 47–48, 48*t*
  flexibilty, 45
  guidelines, 48–49
  innovation, 45
  job requirements, 45
  learning new skills, 46–47
  metrics, 47–48
  negative reviews, 49–50, 50*b*
  objectiveness, 48
  overview, 43–57
  performance reviews, 43–44
  plan/goals development, 52–53
  "plays well with others," 46
  privacy issues, 52
  quality of work, 44
  recording details, 48–49
  self-reviews, 50
  short-/long-term project management, 47
  team players, 47
  timely performance, 46
  tone, 52
priorities, 32, 35
project meetings, 34
project progress updates, 120–121
remote workers, 37–38
staff input, 33
telework types, 37*b*
vision statement, 34–35
Team players, employee performance reviews, 47
TeamViewer, 279–280
Technical courses, candidate selection, 97

Technical environment
  application inventory, 193–194
  asset management, 196–199
  basic considerations, 189
  carrier connections, 191–192
  definition, 189–190
  disaster recovery, hardware availability, 257
  elements, 190–194
  infrastructure documentation, 195–196
  LAN, 191, 192*f*
  mobile equipment, 193
  OS selection, 138–139
  problem/risk areas, 196
  scope, 190
  security management, 209–212
  server/storage, 192
  software inventory, 193–194
  standards determination
    basic considerations, 199–201
    IT issues, 200–201
    IT standards, 201
    user issues, 199–200
  TCO, 196–199
  TCO calculation, 197–198
  team management, 31
  technology refresh cycles, 201–202
  tracking tools, 194–195
  user environment, 196
  vendors, 194
  WAN, 190, 191*f*
  workstations, 193
Technical interviews
  basic considerations, 89–93
  preliminary reading, 89
  technology explanation request, 89–90
  testing candidates, 90–91
Technical Operations, IT Department value, 9
Technical standards, flexibility, 270
"Technology envy," 199–200, 270
Technology refresh cycles, 171, 201–202
Technology value, IT strategy development, 11–12
Telecommunication services, budget items, 163
Telephone screening, candidate selection, 84
Telephone skills, Help Desk staffing, 281
Telework programs, *see also* Mobile workforce; Remote
    workers
  remote interviews, 91
  team management, 37–38
  types, 37*b*
Terminations, employee performance, 54–57
Term of agreement, cloud computing, 151
Terms and Conditions ("Ts and Cs"), 176

Testing
 disaster recovery plan, 258
 technical interviews, 90–91
Test-taking skills, candidate selection, 94–95
T&E submissions
 directory structure, 157
 intranet uses, 294–295
 IT for business value, 180–181
Text messages
 as connectedness technology, 289
 mobile user support, 274
TheLadders.com, 77
Third-party training providers, user training,
  270–271
Threat types
 basic considerations, 224–226
 malware, 224
 phishing, 225–226
 security breach examples, 225b
 social engineering, 225–226
Time-and-Material (T&M) contracts
 hardware maintenance, 172–173
 overview, 172–173
 risks, 172
 vendor policies, 172–173
Time estimates
 multiple project management, 133
 as project component, 111, 111f, 112–113
Time lines, project progress tracking, 118
Timely performance, employee reviews, 46
Time sheets, intranet uses, 294–295
Timing considerations, full-time vs. consultants, 71–74
T&M, see Time-and-Material
  (T&M) contracts
Toll-free numbers, mobile workers, 269
Tone, performance reviews, 52
Torvalds, Linus, 138, 141
Total Cost of Ownership (TCO)
 software management, 142
 technical environment
  vs. asset management, 198–199
  basic considerations, 189, 197–198
  calculation, 197–198
  definition, 196–199
 vendor evaluation matrix, 177–178
Tough economic times
 basic considerations, 179–181
 cost management, 179–180
 IT for business value, 180–181
 leadership, 181
 management ideas, 68b
 recruiters, 82

Tracking activities
 monitoring programs, 215–216
 network mapping tools, 216
 physical access, 216
 security technologies, 214–219
 system log files, 215
 technical environment, 194–195
Traditionalists, generation differences, 58t
Training, see also Employee training
 Help Desk staff, 282
 in-house classes, 270
 intranet uses, 294–295
 job requirement flexibility, 93
 position description, 76
 third-party training providers, 270–271
 user education and awareness, 271
 users, 270–271
 user security, 213
 vendor evaluation matrix components, 178
 web-based, 271
Transaction logs, DR data replication, 256
Transparency principle, Data Protection Directive, 234
Travel and Entertainment, budget items, 163
Trial evaluations, vendor management, 175
Trojan horse, 208, 224
Troubleshooting skills, Help Desk staffing, 281–282
Trouble tickets, 218–219, 278
"Ts and Cs," see Terms and Conditions ("Ts and Cs")
Turnover rates, staff budgeting factor, 171
24/7/365 exposure, benefits of Web, 293
Twitter.com, 44, 289, 298–299, 301, 302
Two-factor authentication, 219
Tyco, 226

U
Unified messaging, 155–156
Uniting and Strengthening America by Providing Appropriate
  Tools Required to Intercept and Obstruct Terrorism Act
  (2001), see Patriot Act
Unix, 136, 138
Upper-level management
 buy-in to security program, 212
 project management updates, 120–121
USB (Universal Serial Bus)
 data encryption, 222
 disaster recovery communication plan, 254
 Massachusetts Data Protection Law, 231
 mobile user support, 274
User environment
 new job basics, 18–20
 standards determination, 199–200
 understanding, 196

User issues
  basic considerations, 263–271
  boss's view of users, 265
  BYO policies, 273
  consumerization of IT, 271–273
  consumerization support issues, 272–273
  department's view of users, 264
  e-mail usage education, 153
  flexibility, 270
  handheld device support issues, 272–273
  handling consumerization, 272
  Help Desk
    access, 277
    activities, 276
    overview, 275–282
    procedures, 276–277
    self-service, 277–278
    staffing, 281–282
    tools, 278–280
    user surveys, 280
    workload measurement, 281
  information collection, 267–268
  information sharing, 266–267
  IT Manager availability/reachability, 266
  meeting users, 265–266
  mobile work force, 274–275
  proactive solutions, 268–269
  securing users, 213–214
  security training, 213
  SLAs, 283–284
  user training, 270–271
  user types, 264
User satisfaction surveys, 267, 280
User Services, *see* Help Desk
User terminations, security technologies, 217
U.S. securities, 232
Utility computing, *see* On-demand computing
Utility tools
  database integrity check, 27
  software types, 136
  TCO, 142

V

Value delivery, IT governance, 239
VDI, *see* Virtual Desktop Infrastructure (VDI)
Vendor management
  alternatives evaluation, 176
  basic considerations, 173–179
  contract review, 175–176
  evaluation matrix, 177–179
  multiple bids, 175
  relationships, 173–174

request for proposals, 174
  trial evaluations, 175
  from vendor POV, 174
Vendors
  certification value, 94
  cloud computing, 150*t*, 151
  data replication, 256
  feedback during tough economy, 181
  Help Desk staff training, 282
  information sharing with users, 267
  project costs, 131
  project planning, 113–114
  project stakeholders, 109
  software licensing plans, 147
  technical environment, 194
  technology refresh cycles, 202
  T&M policies, 172–173
Vernon, Conrad, 107
Veterans, generational differences, 60*t*
Videoconferencing tools
  connectivity issues, 290*t*
  IT for business value, 180
  project meetings, 129
  remote interviews, 91
  staff expenses, 180
  team management, 33
Video sharing
  as connectedness technology, 289
  connectivity tool issues, 298–299
Virtual Desktop Infrastructure (VDI), 140
Virtual Local Area Network (VLAN),
    149–150
Virtual Machine (VM)
  licensing models/types, 146
  multiple OSes, 139
  OS selection, 139
  technical environment, 192
  uses, 140
Virtual Private Cloud (VPC), 149–150
Virtual Private Network (VPN)
  data encryption, 222
  NAC, 222
  network access control, 222
  security software, 136
  security solutions, 222
  telework programs, 38
  WAN, 190, 191*f*
Viruses
  computer security, 208
  e-mail management, 154
  macro viruses, 224
  proactive detection, 268

Vision statement, team management, 34–35
VLAN, *see* Virtual Local Area Network (VLAN)
VM, *see* Virtual Machine (VM)
Voice over IP (VOIP), 156, 180, 191
VPC, *see* Virtual Private Cloud (VPC)
VPN, *see* Virtual Private Network (VPN)

W

W-2s, 70
WAN, *see* Wide Area Network (WAN)
Warranties, hardware maintenance, 173
War room, 126–127
The War Room, 126–127
Web 2.0, 298
Web-based training, 271
Web-cams, 33, 180
Webcasts, 269
Web-conferencing, 33, 180, 269
WebEx, 91, 180, 290*t*
Web sites
    benefits for companies, 293–294
    care when surfing, 214
    DR communication plan, 254
    PD advertising, 77
    spoofing, 225
WebSphere (IBM), 136
White hats, 208, 211–212
White list, 154
Wide Area Network (WAN)
    carrier connections, 191–192
    DR testing, 258
    example schematic, 191*f*
    technical environment, 190

Widgets, as connectedness technology, 289
Windows operating system
    firewalls, 220
    OS selection, 138
    as software type, 136
    versions, 137
Windows Phone (Microsoft), 296
Wisdom of crowds, connectivity issues, 293
The Wisdom of Crowds (Surowiecki), 293
WISP, *see* Written information security program (WISP)
WordPerfect Office (Corel), productivity tools, 136
Work-from-home staff, *see* Telework programs
Work/life balance, connectivity benefits, 296
Workload issues, Help Desk, 281
Workstations
    consumerization of IT, 271
    IT standards, 201
    remote control, 279–280
    technical environment, 193
WorldCom, 226
Worm, 221, 224
Written information security program (WISP), 230–231

Y

Yahoo, 91, 225
Yammer.com, 289, 298–299
Yellow indicators, project progress tracking, 121
YouTube, 289, 298–299, 302

Z

Zero Day Attack, 224
Zoomerang.com, 280
Zuckerberg, Mark, 4, 95

Made in the USA
Lexington, KY
26 April 2017